AMBUSH OF TEAM HECTOR

Staccato bursts of AK-47 assault rifle fire were directed at the team members as they were unpacking. The tempo of fire increased as well-positioned ambushers sprayed the center of the team's position from a break in the dense brush perimeter.

Running toward a nearby cleft, Vu Van Chi encountered four armed North Vietnamese and immediately opened fire . . . Now, the team was scattered around the landing zone, and contact was lost as each individual waited quietly for the North Vietnamese to make the next move . . .

Also in the Special Warfare Series from St. Martin's Paperbacks

NAKED WARRIORS by Cdr. Françis Douglas Fane, USNR (Ret.) and Don Moore
AIR COMMANDO by Philip D. Chinnery
MOBILE GUERRILLA FORCE by James C. Donahue

PROJECT ALPHA

WASHINGTON'S SECRET MILITARY OPERATIONS IN NORTH VIETNAM

SEDGWICK TOURISON

Published in hardcover as *Secret Army, Secret War*

St. Martin's Paperbacks

Published in hardcover as *Secret Army, Secret War*

Published by arrangement with Naval Institute Press

PROJECT ALPHA

Cover photograph by Corbis Bettman.

Library of Congress Catalog Card Number: 95-17380

ISBN: 0-312-96262-2

Printed in the United States of America

Naval Institute Press/hardcover edition published in 1995
St. Martin's Paperbacks edition/July 1997

St. Martin's Paperbacks are published by St. Martin's Press, 175 Fifth Avenue, New York, NY 10010.

10 9 8 7 6 5 4 3 2 1

To Le Van Ngung

CONTENTS

MAPS

ACKNOWLEDGMENTS

Over the past half dozen years, my various draft manuscripts have received constant scrutiny from Maj. Gen. John ("Jack") Morrison, USAF (Ret.), director of the Security Affairs Support Association. He offered sage advice as I was tempted to see conspiracy where the issue was one of human failure. We were both right.

Vice Adm. William Lawrence, a wartime prisoner and former superintendent of the United States Naval Academy, issued me a challenge to produce a serious writing that could withstand the test of time. This was echoed by Mark Gatlin, senior acquiring editor of the Naval Institute Press. I accepted the challenge. Maj. Gen. Joseph A. McChristian, USA (Ret.), my wartime commander and mentor, expected honesty, accuracy, and objectivity today no less than he demanded of me in Vietnam. That he has received.

Those familiar with the American side of the covert program that I describe offered advice and constant encouragement, including Brig. Gen. George Gaspard, South Carolina State Guard (Ret.); Col. Henry DuRant, South Carolina State Guard, my wartime commander in Laos; and Lt. Col. William McLean, USA (Ret.). Those I asked to provide criticism offered it honestly, including Owen Lock of Random House, Dan Cragg, Jim Davis, Russ Holmes, and someone known simply as JB. Cindy Tourison of Modified Concepts provided the graphic support, and David Tourison reproduced the photographs. Val Lynch provided much needed manuscript copies, Bob and Sheri Sheldon provided photocopy support, and former CIA officers William R. Johnson and Samuel Halpern offered the knowing advice of half a century of U.S. professional intelligence. "Miss Eleanor" Aldridge, "Miss Anna" Parker, and Rea and Reno Aldridge provided a resting place and the gallons of coffee consumed during five years of editing at Reno's Restaurant in Crofton, Maryland. Former professional colleagues over the past decade, including the late Robert Hyp and former intelligence officer colleagues Gary Sydow and Robert DeStatte, offered thoughtful insight.

Army historian Dale Andradé knew the long-hidden key official histories and brought them to the attention of the staff of the Senate Select Committee on POW/MIA Affairs. Senator John Kerry, Select Committee Chairman, and senior staff worked with the Joint Chiefs of Staff and other congressional liaison officials of the Bush administration to bring a major portion of the official American military history of this operation to the American public. Declassification efforts were accomplished by the Central Documentation Office at the Department of Defense.

It is my hope that our servicemen who made up that force known as MACSOG have the ability to speak of things long held within them and to speak the truth, not having to hide behind pseudonyms and writing fiction when the truth is made of sterner stuff. The declassification of their history will make that possible.

This is not the story of America's military covert operatives during the Vietnam War from the organization called Military Assistance Command Studies and Observations Group (MACSOG, or simply SOG). Instead, it is the story of the Vietnamese recruited by MACSOG and, as is the nature of war, sent into harm's way. Their story might otherwise be unheard, except by those who understand the Vietnamese language, for this is their story about their war, as much as ours, for which they paid a higher price than most.

Certain Vietnamese officers who trained these commandos or had direct knowledge of their operations have provided a portion of the South Vietnamese perspective. Their comments, like those of the CIA officers who worked with them, were for the record and for attribution.

I owe a special debt to Archimedes L. A. ("Al") Patti and Peggy Patti, both of whom instilled in me a perspective of half a century about Vietnam. They insisted I present facts that would stand on their own, stressing that it is in their interpretation that honest people can disagree. When Al Patti was invited to visit Vietnam in 1990, Vietnam's Ministry of

Interior described him as an aging American covert operative. Patti just smiled.

Lt. Col. Grace Johancen, USA (Ret.), gave friendship and counsel when I most needed it. For Ping, my wife of nearly thirty-two years, and our three sons, Kenny, Steve, and Sedgwick III, all of whom lived in Southeast Asia during the war, this writing represents ten years of time in preparation, also taken from their lives as much as my own.

Nearly three hundred former Vietnamese agents or the next of kin of those who died made contributions to this writing. More than half of these people currently reside in Vietnam. Their letters to me were of obvious interest to Vietnam's Ministry of Interior and its General Directorate of State Security. They and the Vietnam People's Army military intelligence service were directly or indirectly my adversaries during my own several decades of military and civilian intelligence service with the Department of Defense. Nevertheless, the mail came through.

I must therefore express my grudging appreciation to those of my opposite number in Hanoi and Ho Chi Minh City who did not unreasonably interfere with the flow of information needed to complete this work. It represents Vietnam's history as much as our own, and it is an unbiased recounting of what documents and hundreds of oral histories present as factual events. Next time, however, I urge my former adversaries to employ some other type of counterespionage operation than the one described in this book.

To our wartime allies, the former agents and the next of kin of those who perished, I express my profound appreciation for letting me tell your story. All of you have been quoted accurately and with respect for your sacrifices. It is time that others learn of them.

Finally, and as concrete evidence of the government-wide declassification program now underway, the CIA did not prohibit interviews of its former officials. The agency demanded the author follow established security review guidelines and the author adhered to them. The staff of the CIA's Publications Review Board, under its Chair, Molly Tasker, coordinated the security review and cleared for release, almost without exception, the material submitted by former CIA officials involved in the covert operations described in this work. The former officials' material is largely consistent with information from Department of Defense declassified documents, the oral histories of the former agents, and Vietnam's contemporary writings. This work acknowledges the contribution of those former CIA officers, who trusted their words would not be misrepresented. They were not. It is also an acknowledgment of the intelligence community's need to have some mechanism to learn from our past, lest we continue to be damned by our blindness to reality.

FOREWORD

"WHERE DO YOU get off saying it's the Americans' responsibility?'' my guest shouted into the telephone. ''Who do you think we were fighting for? Are you trying to say that we were only fighting for the Americans? . . . We were fighting for *our own people*! We believed in what we were doing! Sure, the Americans paid the bills, but that was because they had the money and we didn't, that's all. You're trying to argue that we were just mercenaries for the Americans and that is crap! Come on, we both know why we fought. It was *our* country, not theirs. We were fighting for *ourselves*, not them. Sure, we got screwed over in 1973 when no one fought to get us back, but whose fault is that? It's history now, you know that.''

I felt like a voyeur, listening to the conversation between my guest and his close friend half a country away. The emotions flowed back and forth over the long-distance telephone lines for what seemed like hours as the two spoke of people now gone and events long past, still so real in their minds that it all seemed like yesterday.

The two were not angry with each other. They simply had differing points of view, and each was arguing his own from the heart. It was the way of friends who had come close to death and had survived by helping one another. I felt the strength flowing between them that was a bonding—a brotherhood—I'd seldom seen and could barely comprehend.

I couldn't hear the other end of the conversation, but I could surmise its content. I'd often listened to others, like the former frogman at the other end of the line, and I knew what he had to be saying. Another commando, Mai Van Hoc, had once told me the way he felt about it all:

> You came to Vietnam.[1] You asked us to help you and we did. It was your money which paid for the boats, the guns, and our salaries. We got two pays a month,

one from our own people and one from yours. In the end it was all your money.

So we went on your missions and got captured and then we were abandoned in 1973 at Paris. You believed all that communist crap when they smiled at you. You had to get out of Southeast Asia so you got out. Us? We were expendable. Besides, your own policies of denial meant we never existed. Because the operations were covert, it was inevitable that our own people would have to be the ones to ask for us back. And—what could they do? You Americans were the ones who negotiated the Paris Peace Accords, not us. Your Mr. Kissinger worked out his secret deals with Le Duc Tho, and *our* government had *your* Paris Peace Accords shoved down *our* throat. It was a lousy agreement and full of holes. But you Americans didn't care about the holes. You just wanted out of Vietnam and you wanted out so badly you were willing to sacrifice anything to that end. You told everyone you'd withdrawn with honor. Sure you did. And *we* were the ones who got screwed in the end. So where was the honor? Tell me that—where was the honor? I think we're talking about a different definition of the word honor. And you Americans complain about the Vietnamese Communists playing word games.

There was nothing I could say in reply. His anger was not at me but reflected his belief that he had been betrayed. I wasn't angry at what he was saying. After all, he was the one who spent fifteen years in the prisons of northern Vietnam, not I.

The covert operations the Vietnamese former agents described did not happen in isolation. Instead, they had their origins in events of World War II but with a very bizarre twist.[2]

On 6 June 1944, Allied forces landed on the French coast in Normandy. The success of their landing was due in part to a masterful deception operation by the British and Americans.

In World War II, the Allies were determined to return to

the European continent. The deception operation supporting this objective was designed to deny to the Germans the ability to learn *when* and *where* that return would take place but not *if*.

Certain critical factors helped the Allies keep their plans and intentions from German intelligence.

First, the British, basically MI-5, had arrested nearly every German agent in England. Many were persuaded to operate their radio transmitters at London's behest. Through false information sent by these captured agents, the Germans were told what the Allies wanted them to hear.

Second, the Allies, basically MI-6, broke Germany's most top-secret codes and came to know as much about the Germans as they knew themselves. This helped the Allies to confirm the effectiveness of their deception operation and to plan accordingly.

Third, the Allies were able to neutralize an important number of German counterspies on the Continent. For example, dozens of Dutch agents were captured and used by the Germans in their own radio deception effort code-named North Pole. The German counterespionage operation began with the first agent who was apparently compromised to them weeks before he actually arrived. When the captured Dutch agents attempted to warn London that they were transmitting under German control, the British Special Operations Executive (SOE) seemed disinterested and sent in more agents and supplies. This encouraged the German counterspies to concentrate on what they believed to be valuable assets and expend their meager resources in a deception operation that SOE actually controlled, thus permitting other agents to accomplish their missions.

Each cog in the wheel of success was necessary to make the whole function as it should. The level of success of the Allied deception operation can be measured by the lives of those who survived the landings in June 1944. Many would not have lived if the German forces had been waiting, secure in the knowledge of when and where the Allies would land.

Fifteen years later, a near carbon copy of the Allied deception operation was played out halfway around the world but with different players and quite different objectives. This time, the North Vietnamese counterpart to North Pole was conducted in large part by the spy catchers of North Vietnam's Ministry of Public Security (MPS). Washington's wartime Office of Strategic Services (OSS) was supplanted by the Central Intelligence Agency (CIA). Now, the captured agents were teams of Vietnamese agents, recruited for the CIA and the Pentagon and parachuted into North Vietnam beginning in 1961 to establish behind-the-lines resistance bases. Some of the radio operators captured within hours of their landing were persuaded by Hanoi's Counter-Espionage Directorate to operate their radios for Hanoi and tell Saigon and Washington what Hanoi wanted them to hear.

The objective of the Allied return to the Continent in World War II had been to restore legal governments to their rightful power. In Vietnam, Hanoi's objective was to create conditions that would lead to an eventual unification of Vietnam under Hanoi's Communist leadership. Both operations ended as planned.

Hanoi's counterespionage service, however, apparently was able to do more. Evidently, the CIA was unable to confirm which teams were, and which were not, transmitting under Hanoi's control. With the CIA's operation barely under way, it was transferred to the Pentagon, apparently with the belief that certain critical teams behind the enemy's lines were carrying out their missions. This created an illusion that U.S.–directed paramilitary forces initially deployed and directed by CIA official William Colby could be employed effectively inside North Vietnam.

In 1963, Washington reached out to these agent teams and transferred them to the Pentagon. Defense Secretary Robert McNamara and the Pentagon's Pacific Commander portrayed them as capable of underwriting the objectives of William Colby's obsolete and ill-conceived operation dubbed Operations Plan 34A. Plan 34A became portrayed as a magic bullet to keep a war from happening when, from Hanoi's perspective, it would ensure that a war took place on Hanoi's terms. Apparently unknown to Washington, *all* paramilitary teams reporting to Saigon that the CIA had turned over to the Pentagon, teams whose very existence was crucial to the concepts in Plan 34A, were operating their radios under Hanoi's control.

In World War II, the Allies' grand deception operation

lasted approximately two years. In Vietnam, Hanoi's deception lasted at least ten years and would be played out again a decade after the end of the war.

During every war, the lives of some are at times sacrificed to save the lives of many others. In Vietnam, the life or death of the agents was of no consequence, as evidenced by even darker deeds you will now read about, deeds that have been kept hidden from public view for nearly thirty years.

In 1970, the key documents detailing part of the history of the secret army of Vietnamese agents went into locked safes. The classification of the documents, TOP SECRET TIGER, almost guaranteed that they would never see the light of day during the lives and in the memories of those who served in the Vietnam War. The documents were later forgotten, and many officials in Washington believed that everything about the operation had been destroyed.

Nearly all of the more than two dozen captured Dutch agents in the World War II operation perished. In Vietnam, nearly four hundred of the captured CIA- and Pentagon-controlled agents actually survived up to twenty-seven years in prison after they were convicted of espionage on behalf of the United States and the Republic of Vietnam. When the surviving agents began coming out of North Vietnam's prisons in the 1980s, they were largely shunned by the Americans and Vietnamese who had commanded them. These same American and Vietnamese officials also knew that they had led the agents' families to believe that the agents had all died, when they knew with a moral certainty that they had been captured and were still alive.

On 24 December 1992, Washington's wartime draft study by the Joint Chiefs of Staff about these covert operations was largely declassified in a joint decision by the Department of State, Department of Defense, and the Central Intelligence Agency. That study, and related documents, provided one part of the story. Patiently collected oral histories of the surviving agents, the CIA officers who directed them, and the South Vietnamese officers who commanded them contributed another missing piece of the puzzle. More documents were discovered, some detailing portions of Hanoi's own account of the grand deception. The fragmented pieces slowly fit together to define the shape of the whole.

This is the true account of America's wartime secret army. It was an army of more than five hundred agents captured while on Washington's most top secret covert operations against North Vietnam. The agents are part of the reason that the Vietnam War occurred, but they played no significant role in its later conduct. The secret army was written off and thrice denied in the headlong panic to withdraw from Vietnam with honor.

Many unanswered questions remain. Owing to the nature of this operation and the complex professional, legal, and moral issues it raises, there will never be answers to everything.

Hanoi's successes and our own failures can be measured by the war we know as the Vietnam War. For our South Vietnamese allies, the price paid was their country.

And this is how it all began. . . .

INTRODUCTION

SHORTLY AFTER MIDNIGHT on 27 May 1961, over mountainous Son La Province in far northwestern North Vietnam, the moon was hidden briefly by the shape of a lumbering World War II–vintage twin engine C-47. The plane came in low over Phu Yen, a speck of humanity in Moc Chau District due northeast of the neighboring Lao Communist capital at Sam Neua.

Four smaller shapes suddenly separated from the air transport. They blossomed instantly into parachutes, complying with the laws of nature to fall at a predictable rate of speed toward their intended landing zone in the tree-covered hills below. The members of Team CASTER were returning to the land of their birth.

The aging workhorse of an earlier war rose quickly as the pilot, a striking South Vietnamese Air Force officer named Nguyen Cao Ky, was glad to be relieved of his low-altitude mission. The C-47, gulping at the thin air, strained along its southern heading to seek an escape from enemy airspace over North Vietnam and the beckoning safety of nearby Laos. It was no longer visible when four green U.S. Army parachutes, rocking silently, disappeared softly into the gloom and brush reaching up to embrace them.

Within minutes of their landing, flickers of light reached out to greet the South Vietnamese commandos. The unmuffled crack of rifle and submachine-gun fire from invisible assailants quickly reached a crescendo and then, just as if on cue, subsided to a deathly quiet.

North Vietnamese regular army soldiers found one of the agents in a widening pool of blood. He was still alive. Nearby was his radio, undamaged.

A muffled call on the radio sent soldiers from the Northwest Military Region anticommando force scurrying, as they fanned out to locate the commandos who had somehow escaped their well-planned ambush. The soldiers had a wounded agent with his radio, but they desperately needed the team's codes.

Dinh Van Anh, a South Vietnamese Army sergeant and one of the fleeing survivors, was on the run for two days before he too was captured. With Dinh Van Anh were CASTER's codes, page after page of blocks of computer-generated random numbers.

The captors had everything—almost. The challenge now was to find agents who would cooperate.

Several days after he landed in the hail of gunfire, it was Anh's turn to face the inquisitor in that timeless posture of subjugation, arms tied sharply behind him, with the cords tightened harshly above his elbows so that his hands were nearly numb. His North Vietnamese tormentor had assumed the mandated setting: the captive sitting on the ground and the captor glaring down at him from his perch above. It was time to resume the ritual known as interrogation, that seemingly endless and untiring ballet of meticulous questions and answers.

Answers always came. Always.

"Tell me, where is Mister Chuong?"

The captive searched the recesses of his memory and found no answer.

To the interrogator, the captive's silence implied knowledge. The truth would have to be exposed as deftly as the careful peeling of the outer shell around a pomegranate to avoid bruising the fruit within. A cooperative and undamaged captive was always more valuable. It was too bad that some of the soldiers had opened fire too quickly.

"I'm going to ask you one more time. Where is Mister Chuong?"

"I . . . I don't know any Mister Chuong."

His response wasn't convincing. A positive answer was demanded. Always.

"You were supposed to contact Mister Chuong. *Who* is he and *where* is he?"

"I don't know. I don't know anyone named Mister Chuong."

Even without the pointed questions about a Mister Chuong he didn't know, Anh realized that everything possible had gone wrong. The team's maps, aerial photographs, and briefing back in Saigon had shown the agents would land in an unpopulated area. Instead of the anticipated speck of relative safety, they had landed smack in the center of a local militia training center along the edge of a small village. It was patently obvious that their arrival was expected, and it was equally clear that the North Vietnamese interrogators knew more about their operation than the four of them. Worst of all, their commander in Saigon had given them each the identical personal authenticator. This made it easy for Hanoi, almost too easy. What had gone wrong?

Team CASTER had been told that its mission was to create a resistance base and a network of agents deep behind the enemy's lines inside North Vietnam. More teams would follow, they were told. They believed what they were told, and that's why they had volunteered to join the crusade.

Not long after the team's landing, American radio intercept operators carefully transcribed the first radio message from Team CASTER. When decoded, the message said that the team had arrived on target and was prepared to carry out its mission. As the CIA had hoped, CASTER requested instructions.

The radio operator did not report the fact that he was tapping out his coded message at the point of a gun very carefully aimed at him by a North Vietnamese state security officer. He also could not report that there were indications that their captors had advance knowledge of CASTER's arrival and had been patiently waiting for two weeks before the team parachuted from the aging C-47.

Hanoi was even more ecstatic than the CIA, having been kept informed of the CIA's planned operations while waiting for CASTER to arrive. Hanoi was biding its time. It had other surprises in store for William Colby, the CIA's station chief in Saigon.

It didn't really begin with CASTER. It began twenty years earlier with a man named Patti.

ABBREVIATIONS

ARVN	Army of the Republic of Vietnam
ASD/FSA	Assistant Secretary of Defense for International Security Affairs
CAL	China Air Lines
CAT	China Air Transport
CIA	Central Intelligence Agency
CIDG	Civilian Irregular Defense Group
CI	counterintelligence
CINCPAC	Commander in Chief, Pacific
CIO	Central Intelligence Organization (South Vietnam)
CNO	Chief of Naval Operations
COMUSMACV	Commander, U.S. Military Assistance Command, Vietnam
COS	chief of station
CSD	Combined Studies Division
CSS	Coastal Security Service
DCI	Director of Central Intelligence
DCM	deputy chief of mission
DIA	Defense Intelligence Agency
DMZ	Demilitarized Zone
DOD	Department of Defense
DRV	Democratic Republic of Vietnam (North Vietnam)
GVN	Government of the Republic of Vietnam
INS	Immigration and Naturalization Service
JCRC	Joint Casualty Resolution Center

JCS	Joint Chiefs of Staff (U.S.)
JGS	Joint General Staff (South Vietnam)
JPRC	Joint Personnel Recovery Center
KMT	Kuo Min Tang (Nationalist Party, China)
MAAG	Military Assistance Advisory Group
MAP	Military Assistance Program
MACSOG	Military Assistance Command Studies and Observations Group
MACV	Military Assistance Command Vietnam
MIA	missing in action
MPS	Ministry of Public Security (North Vietnam)
NCO	noncommissioned officer
NSAM	National Security Action Memorandum
NSC	National Security Council (U.S.)
NSCID	National Security Council Intelligence Directive
OPLAN	Operations Plan
OSD	Office of the Secretary of Defense
OSS	Office of Strategic Services (U.S.)
PAPSF	People's Armed Public Security Force (North Vietnam)
POW	prisoner of war
PRC	People's Republic of China
PSS	Public Security Service (North Vietnam)
PSYOPS	psychological operations
PSYWAR	psychological warfare
RVN	Republic of Vietnam (South Vietnam)
SACSA	Special Assistant for Counterinsurgency and Special Activities
SAVA	Special Assistant for Vietnam Affairs
SEAL	Sea-Air-Land (Team) (generally referred to by acronym)
SMM	Saigon Military Mission

SOD	Special Operations Division
SOG	Special Operations Group; renamed Studies and Observations Group in 1964
SOP	standard operating procedure
SSPL	Sacred Sword Patriotic League (fictitious South Vietnamese resistance force)
STD	Strategic Technical Directorate (South Vietnam)
STS	Strategic Technical Service (South Vietnam)
VIAT	Vietnamese Air Transport
VNQDD	Viet Nam Quoc Dan Dang (Vietnamese political organization)

PROJECT ALPHA

GENESIS

1945–1963

Part 1

1

THE HANOI CONNECTION

TEAMS OF U.S. trained agents, such as CASTER, were a continuum of a concept of American covert intelligence operations in Vietnam that went back nearly two decades. The first major U.S. operation occurred in the spring of 1945 under Archimedes L. A. Patti, operations chief for northern Indochina with the Office of Strategic Services (OSS) group headquartered at Kunming in southern China. To Patti, who had been introduced to the region's background during 1943 while at OSS headquarters in Washington, the major local force within Indochina appeared to be the Communist-dominated Viet Minh.

The fact that the Viet Minh were predominately Communist was less important than their appearance of having a broad nationalist organization that offered the United States both an entrée into, and support throughout, Indochina. Further, the OSS in World War II was actively collaborating with various nationalist forces dominated by Communist groups extending from France to China. As Patti saw it, the arrangements he developed in Vietnam during 1945 were the result of, and consistent with, Washington's policies at that time and were not solely the by-product of Patti's personal preferences and views. Thus, the Viet Minh came to learn how the United States conducted its covert intelligence operations in Indochina, not by stealth, but from OSS officers who trained the Vietnamese in America's way of doing things.[1]

Patti's efforts began with meetings in China with the Viet Minh leader, Ho Chi Minh. Ho and other Vietnamese were soon recorded in Patti's files as America's collaborators. That July, Maj. Allison R. Thomas, in command of OSS Team DEER, parachuted into North Vietnam not far from the town of Tuyen Quang where he had his own meeting with Ho Chi Minh. Accompanying Thomas were two American sergeants, a French officer, and two Vietnamese.[2]

The tasks facing the OSS and its small teams in Indochina were enormous. They included the full range of U.S. tactical and strategic intelligence interests throughout Indochina: securing Japanese documents, psychological warfare, targeting Japanese forces, recovering downed U.S. air crews and U.S. prisoners of war (POWs), and information on Japanese war crimes.[3] Among the first tasks in which Ho Chi Minh played a role was directing Viet Minh cooperation in the collection and forwarding of information to the OSS in China about Japanese forces in Indochina.[4] As the summer progressed, Patti's trainers helped Vo Nguyen Giap's infant armed propaganda force create and train the first two units of Viet Minh special action forces.[5] Supporting the planning for OSS operations from Kunming were voluminous files on the personalities and organizations that the OSS had already encountered or could expect to encounter.[6]

Following his arrival at Kunming, Patti concluded that the two other major Vietnamese political organizations, the Dai Viet and Vietnamese Nationalist Party (Viet Nam Quoc Dan Dang, or VNQDD), were thoroughly untrustworthy. The Dai Viet, a pro-Japanese faction that originally had been part of the VNQDD, had already reached an accommodation with the Japanese military intelligence service in Vietnam prior to Patti's arrival. The VNQDD was a largely pro-Chinese force primarily active in northern Vietnam and patterned after Chiang Kai-shek's Nationalist Party in China, the Kuo Min Tang (KMT). The members of VNQDD with whom Patti had been dealing were found to be providing information about his operations to both the Chinese and the French. Patti judged that such activities precluded these groups, with policy interests directly opposite those of the United States, from association with the OSS at this juncture; otherwise, U.S. intelligence objectives could be compromised.[7]

Kunming was being deluged by OSS field operations personnel sent from Europe as Germany approached its final surrender. For Patti, the problem was convincing these aggressive young officers to read all the background material and be willing to learn before they charged off into battle as if they were still on the front lines in France.[8]

Late in August, Patti arrived at Gia Lam Airport in Hanoi to arrange for the surrender of the Japanese. Lucien Conein, a well-trained U.S. Army officer and a native French linguist newly assigned to the OSS force at Kunming, arrived later. Early in September at Ba Dinh Park, Hanoi, Ho Chi Minh read Vietnam's declaration of independence from the French and formally proclaimed the establishment of the Provisional Democratic Republic of Vietnam. Saigon, the pearl of the Orient in the South, was renamed Ho Chi Minh City by the Viet Minh, a name that would exist, albeit briefly, more on paper than in fact.

As Patti experienced, the death of President Franklin D. Roosevelt was followed in the fall of 1945 by an end to Washington's brief flirtation with Ho's notion of an independent Vietnam. President Ho's links to Moscow were presented in Washington as evidence of the extent of a Moscow-directed broad international Communist conspiracy now facing the United States. U.S. actions with its continental partners to rebuild a war-shattered Europe, including France, meant a temporary end to Washington's call for independence to Europe's overseas colonies. By late that October, Patti and the other OSS operatives had left Vietnam, and letters from President Ho to the Truman administration went unanswered. The following spring, French forces moved in to retake their former colonial possessions throughout Indochina.

In 1952, the French were heavily tied down in their war against the Viet Minh, the sparsely populated mountainous areas in most of northern Vietnam having been ceded to the Viet Minh's guerrilla forces. By then, most non-Communists had left the Viet Minh, when a young American officer, on his first overseas tour, arrived in Hanoi to carry out his agency's mandate in Vietnam. He recounts his impressions and experiences during 1952 while in northern Vietnam:

> The *official* point of view from those at the Department of State . . . was favoring the pro-French line; support

the French in fighting the war in Vietnam. The ambassador at that time was Donald Heath. Donald Heath was loyal to *that* line. So that there was war between his Deputy Chief of Mission (DCM) and the ambassador. Every time the ambassador took a trip upcountry or to one of the other countries to which he was accredited, Laos or Cambodia, ''Ed'' Gullian would fill the air with cables which were the opposite of the ambassador. How did he get away with that? Because he was sponsored by Dean Acheson.

The French achieved a pretty good understanding of what the Viet Minh was and of the united front tactics being used by the Viet Minh, which was a federation of various groups. As to the Dai Viet party, they were the people who were very enticed with the idea that the Japanese had offered them independence. The Dai Viet were loyal to the Japanese because the Japanese said as soon as World War II is over, you guys are going to become independent. So, they became the right wing party. By far the largest party, bigger than all the rest of them, including the Viet Minh, was a party called the VNQDD, the Vietnamese version of the KMT. They had tremendous numbers and clout.

The French and the Viet Minh had similar objectives vis-a-vis the VNQDD. The Viet Minh quite clearly were for eliminating, to the greatest extent possible, a majority of a large group of nationalists . . . and they were not about to seek the cooperation of the French. The French wanted to eliminate the VNQDD because the VNQDD had the greatest potential for appealing to the other western countries, including the United States, because they were bona fide nationalists. And the French were very interested in getting rid of them because they wanted to portray themselves in the European context as fighting against the Viet Minh as a bulwark against the Communist incursion. So, it is better to be fighting against the Viet Minh than it is to be fighting the VNQDD, which could be described as a bona fide nationalist organization. So, the two of them in effect cooperated while fighting to eliminate the VNQDD as a viable force.

> Before that had been achieved, there were several of us who were very much for setting up arrangements with the VNQDD and trying to influence the United States government to think, again, about giving unqualified support for the French and continue with the struggle against the Viet Minh but at the same time supporting bona fide nationalists. This view was shared by me and, in the Embassy, by Edmond Gullian. . . . Because of our views, we then established, first of all, a sort of a clandestine liaison and then we established penetrations of the VNQDD organization. And so we were pretty well understood by them and they pretty well understood us.
>
> This quarrel continued between Ed Gullian, supported by intelligence types like me, and the ambassador, and Washington, and to a degree, I think that this quarrel must have continued in Washington. But, the pressures were too great. . . . The decision was not to intervene. . . . The VNQDD had lost their cohesiveness, they still had an organization but they were not any longer a powerful group. So, the alternative was the Catholics.
>
> The Catholics were approached in the wrong way, I think. They were approached as a coherent Catholic disciplined movement in Vietnam. They may be in the eyes of the Vatican but not in terms of Vietnam. . . . The Catholics were essentially three. There was the bishop in Saigon, there was a bishop in Phat Diem, and there was a bishop in Bui Chu. These three guys were all different and they ran their bishoprics in a very different way. They were all barons and they owned their areas. They had enormous loyalty amongst the Catholics. There was a terrifically rich tradition and support for the type of things which would be effective against the then Viet Minh.[9]

The now retired officer recalled being approached in 1952 by his boss, who asked if he "could blow up one of the major bridges in the Viet Minh area."

> That seemed like a reasonable thing to me so I organized a team of saboteurs, most of them Chinese, and we organized it well. I imported C-3, mostly. I had a large stockpile of it and we divided it up. They were carrying it and they were caught by the French as they crossed the border into the Viet Minh area. There was hell to pay, a big furor. The French went nuts. . . .
>
> Now, two things happened. The French sent . . . the Chief of the French Service . . . to Washington and went to Bedell Smith to protest my action. . . . [10] Bedell Smith said, look, you stopped us from trying to do this operation. We were designing this operation to show you that it can be done and that you should be more aggressive about moving out into the Viet Minh area, and not just trying to protect your former colonial areas. . . . I later found a memorandum which was written by my boss to his boss and it said we would like to undertake this operation with the understanding that one of two things'll happen; either the young officer will be successful in blowing up that bridge or he will not be, which gives you an excellent opportunity to make the point and send a message to the French that they should be undertaking this kind of operation.

As to the question of the Viet Minh Communist intelligence service, the former officer chuckled: "Well, I ran into the French, not the Viet Minh."[11]

He was apparently unaware that at least one Viet Minh professional intelligence officer was keeping a close watch on the two individuals he had recruited. The Viet Minh officer was reportedly the chief of intelligence for the Viet Minh organization in Thai Binh Province. The in-place agent was able to ingratiate himself into the confidence of two Catholic bishops from Bui Chu and Phat Diem by posing as a devout Catholic; he later followed one of the bishops' flocks to South Vietnam where he monitored the activities of that bishop's self-defense forces.

As the American officer was meeting his agency's paramilitary objectives in the Red River Delta outside Hanoi, young Le Van Buoi, a deeply devoted Catholic in his twenties from northeastern North Vietnam, was joining the

French-led Vietnam National Army. After a year at officer's training school at Thu Duc in the South, he returned as a second lieutenant to duties with the intelligence staff under a Major Biker, the French commander of Quang Yen Sector, Buoi's native area. Buoi recounts the period:

> The French relied on we loyal Catholics to be their eyes and ears inside the Vietnamese community. When Dien Bien Phu fell, I was one of those selected for training in France. The object was to create a group of loyal Catholic Vietnamese who would remain behind as agents inside North Vietnam after the French withdrew in 1955. For various reasons, I never went to France.[12]

Lieutenant Buoi joined Vietnam National Army forces withdrawn to South Vietnam under the terms of the Geneva Accords of 1954. Agents, whom he never knew, remained behind in Quang Yen and other areas across the North.

The French surrender at Dien Bien Phu led directly to the signing of the Geneva Accords of 1954, which partitioned Vietnam at the 17th Parallel. It created what eventually became two states in Vietnam, the Democratic Republic of Vietnam (DRV) in the north and the Republic of Vietnam (RVN) in the south. A narrow band separated them at the 17th Parallel and was defined as the Demilitarized Zone (DMZ), the Ben Hai River running west to east across most of it. It was presented as a temporary division that would be resolved through general elections to unify the country in 1956.

One of the most frustrated individuals in 1954 was Chairman Ho Chi Minh. His thirty-year vision of a unified Vietnam under Vietnam's Communist party was delayed at Geneva. Pressure had been applied by his wartime Communist allies, Moscow and Beijing, both of whom persuaded Ho to accept the provisions of the Geneva Accords and not dally. Within a month of the signing of the Accords, and with the French scheduled to withdraw from the North within three hundred days, Chairman Ho singled out the United States as his next foreign opponent during a meeting of the Lao Dong Party Politburo: "The Americans are not just the enemy of the peoples of the world. The Americans have become the main and direct enemy of the Vietnamese, Cambodian and Lao peoples.''[13]

At the direction of Allen Dulles, director of the Central Intelligence Agency (CIA), U.S. Air Force Col. Edward Lansdale arrived in Vietnam after the signing of the Geneva Accords. His mission was to initiate paramilitary operations in the North on the eve of the Communist takeover. He later would go on to assist in the installation of a fellow Catholic as president of South Vietnam, Ngo Dinh Diem, who was to succeed Emperor Bao Dai.

Vietnamese agents were sent to the CIA's agent training base on Saipan Island. In 1955, the U.S. Navy helped such agents get ashore at the port of Hai Phong in North Vietnam, with the intention of their going underground until called to action. Their weapons, radios, and gold were carefully cached in areas where they believed the Vietnamese Communist intelligence services had not seen them.[14] With the Viet Minh preparing to take over the North under the terms of the Accords, the Catholic Church issued instructions to its faithful to relocate to the South.

Pham Xuan An, a youngish-looking Vietnamese, was in contact with Colonel Lansdale and his staff. Also joining Lansdale's force, dubbed the Saigon Military Mission (SMM), and intimately involved in the insertion of the Vietnamese paramilitary stay-behinds trained on Saipan was a seasoned combat veteran and covert operative, U.S. Army Maj. Lucien Conein. Unknown to Lansdale's team was the fact that Pham Xuan An was a decade-long Communist intelligence officer with an intense interest in Lansdale's operation.

Colonel Lansdale was a known quantity to the North's intelligence service; he had recently completed a string of highly publicized successes against Communist insurgents in the Philippines. Conein was equally well known from his service as a covert operative under Patti, and the North's intelligence services routinely monitored his flights between Saigon and Hanoi.

As the French withdrew from the North, they left behind an extensive network of agents, many from the ranks of Vietnamese Catholics. By one account, the files of the French stay-behind agents went to Paris and, as the French completed their withdrawal in 1955, certain of these files were turned over to Ngo Dinh Nhu, a brother of South Vietnam's new president, Ngo Dinh Diem.

The CIA's other agents from the Dai Viet and VNQDD parties were moved back into the North on the eve of the French withdrawal.

Lucien ("Lou") Conein described his stay-behind operation from his vantage point:

> I recall having about twenty paramilitary stay-behind agents from the North. We got them out of the North and we trained them in the Philippines. Most were from the Dai Viet Party, but there were a few from the VNQDD. After training, we shipped them to Okinawa. The CIA arranged for them to return back to the North by ship because we did not have a capability to send them into the North directly from the Philippines. What I was doing on the Philippines for Col. Ed Lansdale was totally separate from anything the CIA was doing on Saipan. . . .
>
> To support our agents once they returned, I set up cache sites with gold, radios, weapons, one time pads, and other material. The agents were scattered around, not all concentrated in one specific area. Their orders were to wait for further orders. I don't recall any of the agents trained in the Philippines ever being recalled to the South in 1956 to see if the North had captured any and might have been using them against us.
>
> I continued to send more agents into the North until as late as 1956. They were launched from Hue and . . . very few of them returned.
>
> Several stay-behind agents did transmit by radio from the North, but then, suddenly, everything went silent up North. It was as if the bottom had fallen out. That was in 1956. It became obvious that our agents had been captured, but I never figured out who talked.
>
> I now know the North's security service has written that they were watching my flights between Saigon and Hanoi but that doesn't explain what happened. That would not have led the North's counterespionage serv-

ice to our agents and our caches. No, it was more than that. They must have had someone on the inside to roll up the entire network the way they did, all at one time.[15]

Gilbert Layton, one of the CIA's former paramilitary experts, looks back on this period:

> When I arrived in Saigon early in 1960 from an assignment in Europe I inherited one or two safes which contained a lot of material from Ed Lansdale, including the cache reports from 1955 for the gold his men put into North Vietnam. I don't recall if there was anyone after Lansdale and before I arrived. The cache reports showed Lansdale's people had buried a lot of gold, some in house basements, and then had cemented some of it over with a foot or two of cement. Someone in Headquarters wanted us to send in a team to try and recover the gold. As I recall, it was worth about three quarters of a million dollars in 1960. They finally gave up the idea.
>
> Stay-behinds were trained at our base on Saipan. This was the same training site we used for the Chinese. I remember the last Vietnamese guy we had on Saipan. He was a little old man who we finally got back into the North where he operated a fireworks factory. Damn thing blew up one day and killed him so that ended his usefulness.[16]

As Lansdale carried out his assignment in Saigon during 1955 and 1956, President Diem consolidated his power in the Republic of Vietnam against a wide variety of opposition forces that included religious, criminal, and Communist stay-behind groups. The Communist Lao Dong party had been similarly active there. Policy directives that flowed from the Politburo seated in the North to Chairman Ho's designated representative in the South, Le Duan, crafted the direction for the Communist movement following the French withdrawal in 1955.[17]

The Lao Dong party decided that not everyone would be regrouped to the North in accordance with the Geneva Accords; some of the party's political faithful were ordered to stay behind and go underground. Many of the Viet Minh mass organizations that had rallied support for the Communist movement during the war years were disbanded on paper but reemerged to operate under the guise of anti-Diem opposition political groups. Weapons used against the French were cached for future armed combat against the Diem government, and a number of Viet Minh stay-behinds were formed into squad- or platoon-sized armed units. Many took to calling themselves battalions, though they had fewer than forty members, and adopted names usually associated with Diem's largely non-Communist adversaries, the Cao Dai, Binh Xuyen, and Hoa Hao.[18]

George Carver, a CIA officer in Saigon until 1960 and the CIA's senior intelligence analyst concerning Vietnamese affairs for the latter half of the Vietnam War, offered his own perspective on the challenges at this juncture:

> There were concerns about the domino effect and if the Vietnamese Communists took over all of Vietnam then the pressure on Laos and Cambodia would swiftly follow and the pressure on Thailand would be greater. This is regarded as laughable now by revisionist historians but it wasn't regarded as laughable at the time. And, the people who benefited from our doing it certainly don't regard it as laughable because I've heard people from Singapore and Thailand and elsewhere say that what's happened economically and politically in the rest of Southeast Asia could never have happened if we hadn't checked and checked the Vietnamese Communists.
>
> There was a great desire falling out from the post–Geneva Accord period not to allow Communist rule to be imposed on South Vietnam by the point of a gun. There was a provision in the Geneva Accords for elections except that the problem with the Geneva Accords was that Pierre Mendes-France, who was France's premier at the time, put himself under a totally impossible publicly announced deadline for settlement and so he made the division at the 17th Parallel, not at the 16th, which he should have. The North had about a two mil-

lion edge in population before the first ballot was counted and since they were going to deliver 99.9 percent of a majority of the votes and for that reason, Diem was unwilling to commit political suicide.[19]

As modern Vietnam now acknowledges, President Diem's early successes against the Communist stay-behinds were indeed telling, and members of the Lao Dong party's regional headquarters apparatus responsible for the southern half of South Vietnam, the Xu Uy Nam Bo, withdrew from the South in 1956 to a more secure base in Phnom Penh, Cambodia. From there, they could move back and forth easily and safely by air between Phnom Penh and Hanoi. Certain party officials in Central Vietnam began a similar long trek back to the North by crossing the Ben Hai River or returning by way of Laos. The senior leader of the southern branch of the party, Le Duan, was facing a protracted political struggle against Diem that was not working.[20]

U.S. support for Diem demanded an accurate understanding of the true level of the Communist threat faced by Diem. This called for timely and accurate intelligence in order to develop a comprehensive and cohesive plan of support for the South, including the military support being funded by Washington through the Mutual Assistance and Security Program. Differing views emerged concerning the nature and extent of the threat, not to mention the quality of Diem's leadership.

One body of intelligence information about forces in opposition to Diem came from Diem's covert intelligence organization operating out of the Presidential Palace. It was headed by a physician from the city of Hue, Tran Kim Tuyen, and relied on a largely Catholic force to carry out espionage for Diem. Another part of Diem's secret intelligence was a covert operations effort, also answering to Dr. Tuyen, known as the Liaison Service (So Lien-Lac), which was headed by Col. Le Quang Tung. Operating under the direct authority of President Diem, Dr. Tuyen's organization was able to call upon support from the Catholic faithful both inside and outside the government. Dr. Tuyen's effort carried out covert operations and also collected intelligence information. In addition, the organization located people with the background and skills that Dr. Tuyen needed for intelligence operations carried out by his force, throughout both South Vietnam and the neighboring countries where Dr. Tuyen stationed his staff. Allied with this organization was a newly formed covert political party, the Can Lao, also directed by President Diem.

One of Diem's brothers, Ngo Dinh Can, headed his own private intelligence organization and directed covert party and Catholic intelligence activities from Hue, where he served as Diem's adviser for Central Vietnam. Another brother, Ngo Dinh Nhu, acted similarly for the southern half of South Vietnam. Because of the physical separation of the two brothers, Dr. Tuyen reported to his president through Ngo Dinh Nhu. Nhu's physical closeness to Diem created a natural rivalry between him and Can and not unexpected competition for power and attention.

Can Lao membership and party member networking soon became the vehicle by which Diem's loyal supporters received lucrative government contracts and other direct financial benefits out of demonstrated loyalty to and support for Diem. By the end of the 1950s, this led to charges that U.S. foreign assistance to the Republic of Vietnam was largely ending up in the private coffers of those in the Can Lao.

The needs of the U.S. intelligence community were being met by the broad range of military and civilian intelligence officers collecting and processing information to produce the required intelligence. Former CIA Station Chief William Colby recalls the operating ground rules for his CIA officers working with the South Vietnamese:

> Ngo Dinh Can was running his own separate entity up at Hue. It was his business. So, what you did in that area you cleared with Mr. Can and what you did in the rest of Vietnam you cleared with Nhu. There was a natural rivalry between the staffs of the two and Diem was very positive about Can. Can had some very excellent ideas.
>
> For the CIA, the command line was Vietnamese through Tuyen, and later Le Quang Tung. We had advisers and we had some support that we provided but they were making the basic decisions and we would

> consult about where to look. But, that was one of my philosophies, always keep them as the commander. Don't try and take it over from them because that drove them crazy.
>
> I never met Ngo Dinh Can; he really never went to meetings. Theoretically I worked with him for years and so did a couple of our officers and they never saw him. I think I was the only one that liked Nhu. Colonel Tung was the most mild-mannered person I ever met.[21]

Within Dr. Tuyen's Liaison Service was Office 45 under Capt. Ngo The Linh, an army officer operating under the alias of Mr. Binh. Captain Linh was responsible for clandestine operations against North Vietnam and in neighboring Laos and Cambodia. When agents were needed, contacts were made with influential Catholic clergy to locate candidates, who were then introduced to Dr. Tuyen's officers. Those who appeared to qualify were recruited. For military manpower and skills, South Vietnamese Army personnel were secured by Colonel Tung. Capt. Le Quang Trieu, Colonel Tung's younger brother, directed the Liaison Service Administration Office under the guise of commanding a company in the Presidential Guard, to which prospective agents were often assigned to disguise their covert duties.

In 1956, the Liaison Service required wooden junks to take agents and supplies to and from North Vietnam. Late that year, a group of six young Vietnamese, mostly teenagers and all of them born in Quang Binh Province north of the DMZ, were recruited from the Catholic Church at the port of Nha Trang to join this new maritime force. Eventually, it became known as the Coastal Security Service, the covert maritime appendage of Ngo The Linh's northern operations. These young recruits made infrequent one- and two-day missions up the coast on junks resembling the same boats used by their northern compatriots, and they appeared to go unnoticed by the North's security services.[22]

CIA and Pentagon support for the Liaison Service's operations into the North came through the 1st Observation Group (Lien-Doi Quan-Sat So 1), an Army unit commanded by Colonel Tung. Established in 1956 with CIA assistance, it was intended to create a stay-behind force in the event that

South Vietnam was taken over by the Communists. Army personnel were assigned to the 1st Group for administrative purposes while performing intelligence activities controlled by the Liaison Service. Even as late as 1958, however, the unit was still caching weapons and its stay-behind effort was more a paper exercise than a serious covert operation.[23]

Another intelligence resource benefiting Washington monitored Hanoi's coded radio communications, a source of information whose reliability had often been judged among the highest. Intercepting the North's radio communications operations after 1955 came in part from a French signals intelligence detachment deployed in South Vietnam, with five field teams spread across Vietnam and Laos providing the "friendly" communications intelligence coverage during and after the Communist withdrawal to the North in 1955. With U.S. support, the French detachment remained behind when other French forces withdrew from South Vietnam in 1956. The French shared the results of their intercept operations with the Americans in exchange for U.S. locations for the Communist radio transmitters through American radio direction finding until the French team withdrew in mid-1957.[24]

The sum of the intelligence information available confirmed that Communist radio transmitters were still active in the South and in direct contact with Hanoi. This clearly demonstrated that Vietnamese Communist forces had not been withdrawn completely from the South and that a secret Communist underground continued to exist. For example, radio communications from Hanoi in 1958 confirmed two apparent headquarters in southern Vietnam, one west of Da Nang for Communist Inter-Zone 5 that was responsible for Central Vietnam and the other, which handled the southern delta, west of Saigon near the Cambodian border. The station west of Da Nang maintained contact with units reportedly infiltrating from the North into the South.[25] Notwithstanding Chairman Ho's commitment and support to the revolution in the South, the North's more pressing demands were consolidating its control and beginning the process of administering its newly won state. It was also a time, however, when the party's southern leadership, including Le Duan and his senior staffers, Nguyen Van Linh in charge of the southern delta and Vo Chi Cong in the sparsely populated coast of Central Vietnam, needed more than political rhetoric.

These three men, as well as Chairman Ho, were only too aware of the successes of President Diem because, by 1958, the Communist party organization in the South was a shambles. From a force of reportedly sixty thousand party members in the populous delta in 1954, it was down to approximately five thousand. To make matters worse, 70 percent of the grass-roots party organization up through district level had been decimated in Central Vietnam.[26] The crux of the problem was too many political leaders and too few followers.

With Le Duan stationed in the South, he and other southern leaders had been kept clear of northern-led politics for the first three years after the partitioning of the country. But, with the party organization in the South now in a shambles, a fundamental change was demanded in the level of support to the southern portion of the revolution if Hanoi's Politburo was to sustain broad credibility on the fundamental issue of one Vietnam under the party's leadership. What the party needed was a traditional solution similar to others that had mobilized the Vietnamese in the past: an identifiable foreign power whose physical presence in Vietnam could be defined as a foreign invasion.

By 1958, Le Duan was called to resume his rightful place in the Lao Dong Party Politburo's daily activities, and he now had the chance to outline the debacle in the South. While implementing the party's call for political struggle in an era of declining party organization in the South, he claimed he never received Hanoi's instructions in 1956 to resume the armed struggle.

President Ho and others had already singled out the United States as the main enemy. But, in the late 1950s, there were far too few Americans in the South to give credibility to any claim that the Americans had invaded Vietnam. Fortunately for Hanoi, this was the beginning of an era of wars of national liberation and Hanoi was ripe for external support. With Le Duan back, the Politburo was persuaded that it was time to issue a new call for renewed activity if the party's vision of a united Communist Vietnam was to take place.

At this juncture, the party was faced with a major limitation in efforts to jump start the stalled revolution in the South. It had a vision and manpower but lacked the weapons and materiel needed to create, expand, and sustain a conflict into something other than scattered pinpricks against the Diem government. The party also faced the reality that intense oppression in 1956 during the brutal land reform program instituted by Politburo member Truong Chinh, with the blessings of Chairman Ho, had seriously alienated many of its own people, whose interests were more their economic well-being than a return to open warfare.

In November 1958, nevertheless, a courier was reportedly dispatched from Hanoi with instructions that the war in the South was to "revert from political subversion to an armed struggle." These instructions acted as an advance copy of a resolution that the Politburo was preparing to vote on formally in January 1959 and that would be adopted nationwide at the party congress late in 1960.[27]

As the courier was being sent South, the North's intelligence service was preparing another traveler with an equally important secret mission in the South. This agent would become known in the annals of U.S. covert intelligence operations as ARES. ARES would arrive in the South at roughly the same time as Colby, then a CIA officer stationed in Rome and an OSS veteran of World War II. ARES and Colby, for quite opposite reasons, would each contribute a major rung to the ladder of escalation.

2

PINPRICKS

IN AUGUST 1958, President Diem once again requested U.S. assistance to conduct covert operations against the Vietnamese Communists. His discussions with CIA Station Saigon occurred as the U.S. Army attaché in Saigon was pushing for involvement by U.S. military intelligence specialists in joint operations with the Diem government. This came coincidentally with Diem's requests for cryptologic support from Washington. He would receive CIA station support, but the other areas were not acted on at that time.

U.S. thinking at the time was that, although such proposals for joint covert operations had surfaced earlier, the approach at this point might have application toward northern Vietnam. This led to a 1958 agreement in principle between the CIA and Diem's government to conduct joint agent operations against the North. The CIA station's effort became a formal relationship effective 1 January 1959, the month before Colby arrived in Saigon.

Colby clearly recalls the period:

> When I got there, we were still in the aftermath of the 1956 decision to go with President Diem, not to have the elections, and make South Vietnam into an independent country, and we were doing pretty well. The aid program was pumping along. Diem was no raving democrat by a long shot but he had pretty well suppressed the Communists in South Vietnam. They had removed their cadres and had taken them north for training and things were fairly quiet. They now confess

that the reason the 559th Transport Group, which established the Ho Chi Minh Trail, was called 559 was because it was started in May '59. That's when they decided to restart the war and they proceeded to do a few murders of village chiefs and things like that, following their idea that the first thing is to organize among the population, get your networks established and mobile, and at the right time they'd go for broke.

Our government's reaction was there seems to be an increase in violence and then we immediately split between the State Department and the military as to whether the conclusion should be let's build up the military, or the State Department's line, the government's got to be more democratic. This difference came about because they both had started from a different premise.

The Army quite sensibly said, if we're going to face a war we better build up the forces. The State Department people, however, had the feeling that you can't mobilize the support of a country unless you become more democratic, which I didn't think was necessarily a sequitur. But, nevertheless, that was their line. Of course, further on out it led to the overthrow of Diem. I think it was tragic, the biggest mistake we made.

But, in that period of '59, we were gradually getting oriented. The CIA was under pressure to develop some intelligence capabilities to tell us what the enemy was doing. We didn't have much independent capability and we were working with the Vietnamese Special Branch.

Diem's people spent most of the time in '59 trying to stir up trouble in Cambodia, that's what they were doing. And we spent a lot of our time trying to dissuade them from it.

As for keeping some of their operations separate from the Americans, I'd have no doubt of that because we were going through quite a roundelay, as I say, on Cambodia. They were dying to do something about Sihanouk [Cambodia's head of state], and we were well aware that Sihanouk knew all about it. . . . We'd go over and give them lectures and they wouldn't pay a damn bit of attention to us. They wanted to do it on their own and eventually they got caught.

The officers we had working with the Vietnamese were in uniform, under military cover. One of them is Gilbert Layton who was the head of my section working with the border security forces . . . and I had another officer, Russell Miller, direct our operations into the North.[1]

One of the questions came up very soon, why don't we do to them what they do to us, in North Vietnam. And we went back to our World War II experience of dropping people in by parachute and things like that which we had done out there too.

And, over the next year or so, we established a new thing called the Central Intelligence Organization, which was designed to bring the facts to a central place where we could access them. We also put under that, an interrogation capability for high-level interrogations, not the ordinary ones. We also tried to do some training of case officers and things like that, for how you run these kinds of operations, without enormous success.

We started training the Vietnamese Air Force to run these kinds of overflights and Col. Nguyen Cao Ky was the head of the transport command so he took that under his wing and we got some Chinese pilots from China Air Lines (CAL) down from Taipei to help train them. Then we set up a subsidiary in Vietnam called Vietnamese Air Transport (VIAT) as a cover for running it. It was a copy of China Air Transport (CAT), only this one was not under Air America, like CAT was. It was owned by the China Air Lines people.

Frankly, I wanted a little variety in the relationship with the Vietnamese instead of having only our CAS[2] people and Air America, which I thought was a misnamed organization. If you're going to have a private cover company, you don't call it Air America.

Then we trained some new maritime forces also. You know, you land on the beaches and go away from the beaches and that sort of thing, sabotage, and then came the idea of trying to get some people in with radios to be a connection and that sort of thing.

I've forgotten when we ran the first operation but it was probably in about early '61. Ky insisted on flying the first mission, although it was a violation of all principles for him to be in the aircraft. But he just wanted to go up and see Hanoi and he said, "I'm the commander, I'll fly the first mission."

The 1st Observation Group was their Special Forces and the first mission for our Special Forces was to train them. They came over for that. We in CIA didn't have anything to do with that. Then we picked up the relationship with the 1st Observation Group. . . .

We lost one of the aircraft in July 1961. It got shot down. We did get the check from them as they went over the coast and the North Vietnamese publicized the shootdown. We went through all the sterilization, but you go through it and say this really isn't ours but whose else would it be?

I don't think there was any terribly serious problem involved in it but we'd just been caught doing espionage in somebody else's country. I don't think there was any great policy problem because we had gone for policy approval with the joint Special Group, the 5412 Committee. We'd gotten approval from them, that was the initial thing we'd submitted, a proposal, which had operations into the North and operations into the South, both of them. That was in November '60. So, when we were carrying out the proposals, I don't think there was any problem with the policy aspect of it.[3]

According to Maj. Le Van Buoi at Hue in 1959–61, there was a resentment among some Vietnamese officers that the CIA's efforts coming out of the joint agreement were aimed at gaining access to all the agents in Dr. Tuyen's organization. Buoi saw it as less an issue of sharing and more an issue of control: "Was the CIA going to take over all of our agents and were we going to keep any? They kept wanting us to give them more and more of the stay-behinds that we got from the French. Did the French give us everything they set up? No, of course not. But, what we had we didn't necessarily want to share."[4]

William Colby wasn't surprised. "I can't cite you chapter and verse on it but that sounds about right."

As Colby was preparing to assume his new position as the CIA's deputy chief of station in Saigon, Politburo member Le Duan in Hanoi was laying out his own strategy to the senior political leadership of the Vietnam People's Army:

> "We will not use war to unify the country. But, if the United States and the puppets use war, then we too will have to use war and the war that the enemy will have created will provide us the perfect opportunity to unify the country."[5]

Le Duan had addressed the Central Military Party Committee immediately following the conclusion of the fifteenth session of the Lao Dong Party Politburo that January. That policy meeting was chaired by Ho Chi Minh and included representatives from the regional party organizations in the South. At the meeting, which occurred in the fifth year of the People's Army five-year plan, the party issued the call to liberate the South.[6] Le Duan's words argued the position that the only way the country could be unified was through an outright war. He implied it would be to Hanoi's advantage that the North not be branded the aggressor but that the North be perceived as merely reacting to what could be portrayed as a foreign invasion.

The January meeting presented the formal decision to escalate the Communist movement in the South and move the revolution forward, thus shifting it from a primarily political struggle to one of armed force by armed units in conjunction with political activities by the appropriate mass organizations. In that context, Chairman Ho made it clear that the struggle in the South would now aim at involving the forces of the entire country and be portrayed as part of an international Communist struggle against the capitalists. This became a political rallying cry directed by the party to all Vietnamese. Like all such formal decisions, it signaled an approval and approach that had already been put into motion many months earlier. However, Chairman Ho still lacked broad and substantive military support from the Communist bloc, whose greatly expanded military assistance would be crucial to the North's plans. That May, on orders of the Politburo, the People's Army established a special study group headed by Vo Bam, deputy director of the State Farm Directorate. Vo Bam had experience in the mountainous area of Central Vietnam. His task was to develop the supply lines needed to support the flow of supplies to the coming war in the South, which would have to rely on a pipeline from the North. On 19 May 1959, the 559th Military Transportation Group was established to carry out the Politburo's objectives through Vo Bam, thus creating the skeleton of what would later become known to history as the Ho Chi Minh Trail.[7]

That same month, the Ministry of Public Security dispatched five senior party members from the Ministry of Public Security to infiltrate into South Vietnam and augment the structure of security services already there. They brought the ministry's key current directives on the role of Communist intelligence and security services into the South. On 14 May 1959, a Morse code transmission over Radio Hanoi to the southern faithful reportedly signaled the implementation of the party's new plan to jump start the war in the South.

By the end of 1959, the 559th Group reportedly had moved 542 cadre into South Vietnam, 515 of these being assigned to develop its strategic base areas along Vietnam's western border with Laos. Weapons of Western manufacture were also moved down the infant supply line to reach guerrilla units in Central Vietnam. The 338th Division, one of two divisions of Viet Minh to go North in 1954–55, was placed on a combat alert, and southerners began to receive notices to return to their former unit, then located near Xuan Mai. That summer, the People's Army established a covert radio station near the strategic Hai Van Pass on Highway 1 in central South Vietnam. The station was to coordinate the first shipments of weapons by sea from a coastal storage base near Ben Thuy at the mouth of the Gianh River in Quang Binh Province. Strong seas and other weather problems prevented the first two shipments from arriving as planned.[8]

Throughout 1959, orders from Hanoi's Politburo to resume the armed struggle had produced an upsurge in small scattered incidents throughout the South.[9] That fall, Diem answered with a state decree aimed at crushing the reborn instability.

Although the U.S. community in Saigon was not yet seeing excessive cause for alarm, decisions were already being finalized in Washington and at the Pacific Command in Hawaii. Washington's sense of the escalating conflict in Vietnam and Laos prompted the National Security Council (NSC) to issue Directive 5809, which called for increased efforts to both support the Diem government and prevent the North from achieving an easy victory there. In Honolulu, the updated contingency planning for the region of Asia, Operation Plan 32-59, issued by the Pacific Command on 16 December 1959, incorporated the policy direction in NSC Directive 5809.

Plan 32-59, a four-phase regional contingency plan, covered phases from initial North Vietnamese external support to Communist guerrillas in the South to a scenario involving the presence of Chinese Communist combat forces in Vietnam. Within southern Vietnam, the U.S. Embassy Saigon Mid-1959 Country Plan echoed this heightened vigilance to Hanoi's maneuverings.

In 1960, the Pacific Command responded to increased North Vietnamese military operations into neighboring Laos with plans for the possible deployment there of an American expeditionary force. Through signs of such tactical maneuvering, Hanoi would have gleaned an important message: the United States was disposed to respond with an increased ground presence to defend its perceived interests in Southeast Asia.

The 1960 Country Study, produced by the U.S. Embassy in Saigon and endorsed by CIA station representative William Colby, argued that the philosophy of Diem's Can Lao party still represented a viable counterpoint to Communism. Implicit in Colby's position was a counterargument to criticism of the excesses of the Can Lao, whose officials were those most closely aligned with, and required to support, the CIA station's joint operations against the North. This linkage of Diem's brother to the CIA tied the United States to the heavy-handedness of Nhu's national police, at times seen as more the cause of the political problems in the South than the solution to them.

As Colby attempted to maintain his intelligence relationship with South Vietnam's leaders, Gilbert Layton arrived in

Saigon to join the CIA's efforts to prepare for an expansion in operations against Communist forces throughout the region. For the first several months, Layton had no real duties. Then Colby called him in for a new assignment. Layton recalls his mission order:

> Bill Colby called me in one day and said words to the effect, "Gil, there's something going on out there, find out what it is, and see what we can do about it."
>
> Over the next year we put together a force of roughly 36,000 local people, most of them the minorities, and had about three dozen U.S. Army Special Forces teams come in to do the training. We evidently trained some of the agent teams for Russ Miller but I wasn't aware of it at the time. This was before the agent training center was set up at Long Thanh. My Vietnamese counterpart was Col. Le Quang Tung, but I worked closely with Capt. Tran Van Minh.[10]

The U.S. Army advisers arriving in Saigon knew him as Col. Gilbert Layton from the Combined Studies Division (CSD), whatever that was. With a chuckle, Layton continues:

> When the U.S. military began arriving to train the people we recruited, our military needed to be assigned somewhere and it had to sound military like. So, we created a cover organization. That sounded neutral enough and the military was very happy. That division was not part of anything; it was just something which sounded official, that was all. The operations I directed came under what we called the ground studies group and the agent operations Russ Miller directed into North Vietnam were called the airborne studies group. Tucker Gougelmann was at Da Nang, as was Ed Regan, and Carl Jenkins was up in that area.[11]

It was, all in all, a modest investment.

Layton's presence and activities in Saigon served effectively to hide the CIA station's more secretive headquarters for Russell Miller's covert agent operations into northern

Vietnam. To visitors at Layton's office, Miller and his staff were just "guys in the back room."

Ed Regan, one of the station's officers working for Russell Miller and actively involved in launching the teams from Da Nang during the earliest period, described the early buildup from his perspective:

> It is a fair statement that none of us had any great hopes for the operation. I heard that [President Dwight D. Eisenhower's National Security Adviser] Gordon Grey came out from Washington on an inspection trip very early on and he assessed the operation during his visit. He concluded it wouldn't work, as I understand it.
>
> In the earliest period of our relationship with Colonel Tung's people, our involvement was primarily working with our South Vietnamese counterparts to cache material to prepare for the possibility that the Communists might take over the South. Then came the need to find out what was happening up in the North and we shifted to singleton agent operations. The objective was to get some people in and out so we knew what was happening up there. As I recall, we had about a dozen singles, singleton agents, going into and back out of the North (before the start of the agent teams).
>
> I cannot tell you everything our counterparts were doing because each of them was doing something and we had no way to know everything they did. For example, President Diem's brother at Hue was supposedly sending some of his own agents across the DMZ up into Quang Binh Province and we were not involved with them. Dr. Tuyen and Le Quang Tung also had their own operations which were separate from Ngo Dinh Can's.
>
> Our involvement with the South Vietnamese was for the purpose of helping them get information which would help us, the CIA, understand what was happening up North. We were paying for the operations, but we certainly did not have as much control as it might have seemed, and there were the inevitable competing

> groups both inside and outside President Diem's government.
>
> While Russ Miller had our very first meeting with Ngo Dinh Can in 1960, one of the other officers was able to work with Can a bit and I believe one of Can's agents was sent up North in the summer of 1961. We also had two fine U.S. Navy petty officers working for us at Da Nang who dealt primarily with the SEAL aspects of our boat operations into the North.[12]

As the North expanded its operations in the South and CIA Station Saigon expanded its operations into the North, Diem's spy catchers arrested a major northern Vietnamese–directed espionage net in the South, including an agent within the Army of the Republic of Vietnam (ARVN). He was a South Vietnamese Army communications officer in charge of the communications center of the Joint General Staff (JGS). The South Vietnamese cipher systems he watched were a holdover from the French and were probably already well known to Hanoi, but his arrest provided evidence of the North's high-level penetration objectives.[13]

One of Hanoi's penetrants, Pham Chuyen, was an agent from northeastern North Vietnam. One who saw his subsequent agent reports from North Vietnam recounts his recollections of Chuyen, soon to be known in Saigon and Washington as ARES:

> Agent ARES? Sure, I know him. I read his file. He had several names but his true name was Pham Chuyen. He came down South in 1959 and we recruited him. We sent him back into the North in February 1961. He was still in contact with us until at least 1969 and I was never really sure if he was working for us or for them. After the Communist takeover in 1975, I was interrogated by the North Vietnamese about Chuyen. They kept asking me over and over what I thought about him. You know, did we really trust him? I sensed from their questions they still had questions about him . . . was he really working for them or not. I don't think they trusted him completely.[14]

Another officer who had met Chuyen offers a similar view:

Chuyen? Yeah. . . . I was sent up to Hue and I was the interpreter during his polygraph. I recall he claimed he was Premier Pham Van Dong's nephew, that he'd held a high party position himself, and had become disaffected. I think he came down in 1959 and was recruited in about 1960. I do remember the results of his polygraph were inconclusive, though some of us in Tuyen's organization believed he was probably working for Hanoi and may have been sent down South. If he was really working for them all along, it wouldn't surprise me because that wouldn't be the first time something like that happened. Let me explain.

Early on, we captured one of Hanoi's senior intelligence cadre. We held him and attempted to indoctrinate him. Finally he agreed to work for us and he was sent back to them. . . . But, after 1975, he appeared as that cadre in charge of Vietnam's maritime products. That meant he was trusted and undoubtedly was a false defector, sent to check us out and learn how we were doing things. There was another situation which happened even earlier, right at the beginning, which shows that Hanoi knew who we were and what we were doing.

It happened at the beginning of 1959. There was a radio broadcast from Hanoi which the CIA's Foreign Broadcast Information Service monitored from Saigon. The broadcast contained a news report claiming that an infiltration boat had been captured in Ha Tinh Province, complete with crew and all the supplies on board. Radio Hanoi said it came from our organization under Dr. Tuyen and read a list of those in our organization responsible for these operations, plus its correct name, identifying Le Quang Tung, Tran Khac Kinh, Ngo The Linh, and others. Someone was getting them information very quickly and that didn't seem to sink into people's minds.

This broadcast was intended to be a warning to us, that was all. Hanoi was telling us that they knew who

> we were and what we were doing. You see, we had not lost a boat and that helped us define the purpose of the broadcast. It implied that we should stop what we were doing, or else. What did we do about it? We only changed our organization's name to the Topographic Exploitation Service, the So Khai-Thac Dia-Hinh.[15]

Le Van Buoi had a more compelling description of the agent sent by Colby's CIA station into North Vietnam in February 1961:

> In the spring of 1960, Ngo Dinh Can went to Vung Tau for a very high-level meeting involving all our intelligence service chiefs. Upon his return he informed us that he'd met with your vice president [Lyndon B. Johnson] and was informed that the United States was determined to undermine and eventually attack the North. This was the official authority for the conduct of joint operations involving our services and your CIA. After that meeting, Can decided to become part of the effort because American influence and support for our president was flowing from the CIA relationship with Tran Kim Tuyen and Ngo Dinh Nhu. Can felt left out because whatever Tuyen conducted, it was done independent of Can and this meant the CIA's support flowed to only one brother, Ngo Dinh Nhu.
>
> I met with Col. Le Quang Tung and outlined to him what Ngo Dinh Can had in mind. We wanted to start our own separate offensive intelligence operations against the North and were looking to Colonel Tung for support. Tung did not respond positively to our plan. He said he already had teams in the North and they were doing quite well. They'd lost a few men but believed they were being successful. It was obvious that Colonel Tung was not going to support us as we'd hoped. We also wanted to do some things into Laos as well but that proposal also didn't get much support from Colonel Tung.
>
> There were several types of operations then ongoing against the North. There were Colonel Tung's teams

of sergeants from the army who were assigned to the 1st Observation Group and by 1961 they were already going up North. We knew this because there was a certain amount of information sharing and coordination between Ngo Dinh Can and Ngo Dinh Nhu.

There were also stay-behind spy nets. These spy nets had been formed by the French before their withdrawal in 1955 and that's when the French turned over the agent dossiers and files to us. The French turned some over to a Vietnamese priest. The priest was assigned to the Vatican but had responsibilities which took him all over Asia. He frequently came to speak at the cathedral in Hue. We became aware that Ngo Dinh Nhu had been given access to these records by the French and by 1961 he had been making these stay-behind agents available to your CIA for the agent operations into North Vietnam with Tuyen's organization.

We communicated with these agents through the base at Dong Ha, just below the DMZ. The base was part of Tuyen's operation, not Can's personal thing, but Can could still transmit his own messages from that transmitting site. As I recall, your CIA was providing some support to this site at the time.

To get us involved in the operations, Ngo Dinh Can directed me to develop a proposal which was presented to Can's CIA adviser. I was to be the first one Ngo Dinh Can would send up North to show that we could do just as good a job as Ngo Dinh Nhu. The proposal was accepted and I attended a meeting with Ngo Dinh Can, Phan Quang Dong, the CIA adviser, and another Vietnamese.

The CIA officer briefed me that there was war coming and my job was to help everyone prepare for it. I had to identify targets for the airplanes to strike and the CIA officer told me that the air strikes would come in about two years. That meant the war would be out in the open sometime in 1963. Can later offered me all the money I might need. I knew it was all counterfeit. Your CIA had printed a lot of it. I didn't take any of it because I was worried I might be compromised if they found me with the bogus money and linked me to the CIA.

I was authorized to conduct sabotage without having to ask Hue for approval. I was shown photographs of each individual I was to contact from the first who would meet me just north of the Demilitarized Zone to those at my destination in Quang Yen. That way I knew what they looked like. I was also given an internal passport to be used if I was stopped before I made my first contact.

We all recognized that I might be stopped before I got very far. Regardless of when I was stopped, I would only admit to having just come from the South.

I was made aware by Phan Quang Dong, Can's Catholic intelligence service chief and my immediate superior, that Tran Kim Tuyen's organization had sent two agents into Quang Yen. The first one was a southerner. I don't know who he was, and I never heard anything more about him. The second was Pham Chuyen. I was next and there may have been someone after me but I'm not sure.

Chuyen was a mid-level Communist party cadre who'd come across the line into the South in 1959. He claimed he was disaffected and that was why he supposedly fled to South Vietnam. Dr. Tuyen's organization recruited him as an agent and sent him back into Quang Yen early in '61.

Ngo Dinh Can's desire to get me into the North was because there was a feeling that the successful insertion of Chuyen gave Tuyen's organization a boost in the eyes of the CIA. If Nhu and Tuyen could get Chuyen in there, I should be able to do the same. Besides, Chuyen was a known North Vietnamese Communist party member and there were real concerns that the Ministry of Public Security had sent him south with the mission of penetrating Tuyen's organization. So, Can told me to stay away from Chuyen but report whatever I learned about him.

We certainly wanted American support but there were limits. For example, Ngo Dinh Can was courting the Japanese because there was a lot of talk of Japanese investment in Vietnam and Can seemed disposed toward them.

As to the issue of an increased American presence in Vietnam, from everything I heard, President Diem wanted American aid but he did not want the American troops in the South and we discussed his views amongst ourselves. Diem's fear was that if American ground forces came in, then the Chinese would come into the North. If that happened, the Americans would eventually withdraw and let Hanoi's forces take over the South, using this to establish a relationship with the Beijing government. So, as long as the American ground troops were kept out, the Chinese would stay out and the North would be unable to secure broad support from the Communist bloc.[16]

Early in June 1961, Maj. Le Van Buoi crossed the Ben Hai River and entered North Vietnam. After passing from person to person, he reached the northeastern port of Hon Gai. Buoi continues:

There was a small stay-behind network still there. They'd been in routine contact with the South and had been resupplied with radio equipment and other supplies by Taiwanese fishing boats which were being used to keep the nets resupplied. I knew they were there because I'd gone up there once by boat in 1959 and met people who came out to our boat. Then, after I got up there in 1961, I went out with our people once and met the fishermen who made the periodic supply run. It was so easy at that point in time because everyone was fishing in the Gulf of Tonkin and they were not being interfered with.

Our agent net at Hon Gai used their radio to contact the South once a week and I would give my contact the information to be sent by radio message back to Ngo Dinh Can. We'd pass information back and forth at various locations in or around the city, places called dead drops sites where we could drop off or pick up documents without being seen. I didn't see the radio and don't know what kinds of codes they were using.

> Besides, I didn't need to know that. All I needed to know was that I could send and receive messages. I would get periodic messages from Ngo Dinh Can and I always knew they originated from him. Each message had a built in authenticator that meant it came personally from Can and the authenticator was always there.[17]

Then, after half a year of information collection and minor acts of sabotage, Buoi recalls that things started to change:

> There were coastal patrols in the area but nothing much seemed to be going on until at the start of 1962 when an infiltration boat from the South was captured near Hon Gai together with its crew. It wasn't supplying me and I knew that I couldn't have compromised it. So, I began to suspect Chuyen.
>
> One of my contacts pointed out Chuyen to me and said the network had concerns about him because he was dealing with the Ministry of Public Security people. The only question they had was whether he had been arrested and was being used by them or had been a double agent. Chuyen seemed to be well known and one of the local police officials once remarked that something was unusual about Chuyen's presence at Hon Gai. The Hon Gai police knew he'd gone to South Vietnam and had been away for a while but then, suddenly, he returned and carried on as if nothing had happened. The police official said that Chuyen must have been very highly regarded in the party to have done whatever he'd done and not have been arrested upon his return.
>
> In one of my messages to Can I reported our concerns about Chuyen. I got a message back from Can indicating that he and his CIA adviser were very pleased with the work I was doing. Then Chuyen left for Uong Bi and later went to Hanoi so I lost track of him.
>
> How could a possible double agent like Chuyen come from the North as a refugee and get all the way into Saigon without someone sounding a warning bell? Look, I don't have all the answers. There were so many

things going on and everything was compartmented. But, in Chuyen's case, I think he came through Quang Tri but I'm not sure. At the time he came through the refugee system, the system moved refugees to Quang Tri and then to Hue. If we processed someone who appeared to be bona fide, Ngo Dinh Can would pull that person out of the refugee flow at Hue and try to turn them around and send them back into the North to work for us. If we had the impression the person was a double agent, we'd send them to Saigon to be processed through the refugee center in Gia Dinh. If Chuyen's movements got him to Saigon, that tells me that those who processed Chuyen when he arrived had already concluded he was working for the North. So, if he was sent back up North, it isn't likely that this was done because they believed he was bona fide. It is more likely they recognized him for what he was and decided to see what Hanoi was up to, that's all. We all knew the rules. If Chuyen provided us good information, then we had good information. If he provided us bad information, we'd drop him.[18]

"So, what happened in Chuyen's case?" I asked Buoi.

"I don't know," he replied tiredly, his headaches returning. "I worked for Can and Chuyen worked for Tuyen. I had other missions to perform."

Ed Regan offered his view on the change in operations:

After Kennedy became president [following the November 1960 election], the pressure was on to increase the level of activity and switch from a low-level agent operation to the paramilitary teams. The pressure to get the paramilitary agent teams into the North didn't come from us at the Saigon Station; it came from Washington.[19]

President Diem and the Americans on station both seemed to agree that the Vietnamese Communist armed guerrilla forces in the South numbered perhaps no more than three thousand as of 1959. By late 1960, the "Viet Cong" forces had reportedly increased to seven thousand guerrillas as

Diem and certain Americans were sounding louder alarm bells.

Diem and his military commanders had been lobbying for increased U.S. support through the Military Assistance Program (MAP), and the new enemy strength increases seemed to be the impetus to get Washington to react. If Chairman Ho and Le Duan had been adept at massaging the Communist bloc and the Communists in responding, President Diem was equally talented at stroking Washington with no less skill than those in Washington who responded with their own vision of an expanded U.S. presence in Vietnam.

The North clearly understood that any expanding war in the South demanded as secure a rear base in the North as possible. To counter the South's agent operations, Hanoi's Ministry of Public Security issued Directive 20-VP/P4 on 8 January 1960 to seal the coastal and land borders of the North. The order implied an increase in the Ministry's own covert internal security operations in these areas. On 17 January, the Politburo issued Directive 186-CT/TW to refocus national attention on the two principal groups that it needed to eliminate politically and that it had identified as linked to foreign-directed ''counterrevolutionary'' activities: the Catholic hierarchy and mountain tribal minorities. In September, the Third Party Congress of the Lao Dong party specifically mentioned the psychological warfare (psywar), espionage, and paramilitary operations being launched against the North and it called for armed revolution in the South. This occurred as the party was preparing to initiate its first five-year state plan scheduled to start in 1961.

Writing about this period some three-plus decades later, Vietnam points to February 1960 as the time that its People's Armed Public Security Force (PAPSF) adopted Crypto System T90 to replace an older code system known as DB2. A variation of KTB4, a code system that would not be widely available to the Vietnam People's Army for another seven years, System T90 was viewed as twice as secure as the system provided to the People's Armed Public Security Force (PAPSF) in 1959. Today, Hanoi credits these improved codes and communications procedures as the key to its ability to counter the South's agents coming into North Vietnam.[20]

The change to a more secure code came as the result of a review on 17 February 1960 by Hanoi's Communist party leadership in the Politburo. This review examined the paramilitary agent operations being deployed against the North and updated plans to deal with them. PAPSF was given the mission to support the broad counterespionage operation being directed by the Ministry of Public Security. It was to assist in capturing the teams when they arrived and to help provide security around the area from which the team's recruited radio operators would be transmitting. To prepare for and monitor the South's arriving agents, PAPSF forces throughout Vietnam implemented a system of daily and weekly reporting on all suspicious activities along the entire border area of the North.

On 10 March, the PAPSF chief of staff authorized certain border posts and subregions along the border with Laos to begin direct radio reporting to the PAPSF Headquarters Command Committee on all suspected activities as soon as they were discovered. This was to make sure that the evidence of the arrival of suspected agent teams was brought to the immediate attention of the highest command level of the PAPSF forces.[21] Such evidence included, for example, sightings of suspected hostile aircraft and possible or actual airdrops of commandos. When this reporting began, instructions between the PAPSF command and border posts and stations could be relayed and received in Hanoi within two to three hours.

Owing to North Vietnam's simultaneous assessment that "enemy radio intercept activities were increasing," information to be sent by coded messages on PAPSF radio nets was limited to urgent matters. Radio messages were further disguised by jumbling their contents and using other deceptive practices designed to hinder the ability of any foreign communications intercept force attempting to decode the messages.

The counterespionage effort employed by the Ministry of Public Security, an effort referred to as "special operations," was viewed by the North as its "special method to be used by the security forces to attack the enemy." As the North has described its concept of operations, "first came an intense matching of wits with the enemy" when a team was captured and the radio operator began operating under Hanoi's control. Fundamental to each step in the operation was a demand for extreme security concerning the orders, directives, and information relating to the operation when such details had to be transmitted by coded message. One small bit of carelessness could make the enemy suspicious, and this silent warfare would end in defeat. Those cadre directly responsible for implementing the operation and the crypto cadre and specialists in direct support of such operations were the only persons permitted to know the secret contents of those operations.[22]

Through 1960, CIA Station Saigon continued its focus on relatively low-level espionage against the North. For the station officers in Saigon and those at Da Nang who were launching the agents, the success of this effort was measured by the fact that these agents had been able to get in and get out safely to return to the South with hard information on the state of affairs in the North. Then, late in 1960 and following the NSC Special Group's approval of the CIA proposal, CIA Station Saigon's operations prepared to shift to paramilitary teams of armed agents, not just spies.

By the start of 1961, Dr. Tuyen's organization was recruiting teams of paramilitary agents in response to Colby's effort to begin to inflict some level of discomfort on the North that paralleled the North's subversion in the South. Colby explained:

> Our strategy had been to just get the framework up there. Just get some kind of a framework up there upon which you can build resistance or sabotage, or whatever you need to do, psychological or whatever. Just try to get some people in place that you can communicate with, without being too refined about it.
>
> As I recall, and I'm sure my memory is dim on this, the locations for the teams were largely chosen on the basis of where somebody knew somebody. I mean, one of your team members came from a certain area and you were asking him to go back and make his contacts in that area. I think there was the idea that if you could live in the mountains you'd be safer than if you'd tried to live in a highly controlled structured society down

> in the lowlands so there was an inclination to get you out of the city centers. But, the idea was, I think, to build up a base, or bases, from which you could then penetrate the lowlands.[23]

As to the fact that the teams going into the North would soon be landing along Hanoi's rail lines, Colby said, "That could be an extra dividend. Plus the idea of eventually sabotaging them."[24]

As the CIA station chief, Colby also had to contend with Diem government officials who were necessary to implementation of the covert operation but were increasingly becoming the targets of domestic and foreign hostility over Diem's unwillingness to share power. Colby's support of Nhu and Dr. Tuyen was clearly tiring, and he joined the U.S. Embassy Saigon staff in urging their removal. Diem ignored their entreaties.

Agent ARES went into the North by boat in February 1961 and landed safely in northeastern Quang Ninh. He soon reported his safe arrival to Saigon. As Colby's new concept of paramilitary team activity was being implemented, another event took place half a world away that would have a long-range impact on the CIA's covert program, if not the Vietnam War itself. This was the abortive Bay of Pigs invasion of Cuba, 17–19 April 1961.

The impact on Vietnam came on 20 April, when President John F. Kennedy convened a special study group headed by Gen. Maxwell Taylor. Its task was to examine the Bay of Pigs disaster and make recommendations on how to strengthen similar future U.S. operations in an environment short of open combat.[25]

President Kennedy posited that "Communism" was engaged in a nibbling operation. He also conveyed a clear interest in paramilitary operations as opposed to a continually escalating arms race. His views implied that the Cuban "revolution" of 1959 and the disaster at the Bay of Pigs barely two years later were but harbingers of things to come. His message was that both South Vietnam and Laos were the next to go Communist unless something was done, and done quickly. The president's solution was to begin a process of transferring such paramilitary operations from the CIA to Defense Department control in Vietnam, insofar as they related to approved Joint Chiefs of Staff (JCS) war plans.

On 13 June, General Taylor's group presented its findings to President Kennedy. The study argued that the United States was in a "life and death struggle which we may be losing, and will lose unless we change our ways and [marshal] our resources with an intensity associated in the past only with times of war." The report called for a centralized coordination of the covert paramilitary effort in Vietnam, the major portions of which Kennedy approved on 28 June.[26]

As Kennedy was calling for an evaluation of the Bay of Pigs, four sergeants from the South Vietnamese Army's 22d Division were preparing to carry out the CIA's expanded program. They had been identified by the 22d Division's intelligence officer as potential candidates for Topographic Exploitation Service operations into the North. All were natives of Son La Province and had served in the Vietnam Army during the days of the French Union.

They were transferred to Saigon after agreeing to volunteer for a secret mission into the North. When the Office 45 staff informed them that they would be parachuted into Son La Province, they were not dissuaded from the mission. In May, the four became Team CASTER under the command of Ha Van Chap. They were parachuted into Son La, where the North's forces eagerly awaited them.[27] Not long after their capture, the team's radio operator was pressed into service by the Ministry of Public Security Counter-Espionage Directorate. He reported to Saigon that their team had arrived safely. CASTER continued on the air as an independent team until July 1963, when the CIA considered that it had lost contact with it. CASTER had been last reported in Laos.[28]

On 2 June, three men comprising Team ECHO parachuted into Lam Trach District in coastal Quang Binh Province. They were captured with three radio sets, which the Ministry of Public Security Counter-Espionage Directorate used to enlarge the burgeoning deception operation. The team's radio operator followed the instructions he received but secretly advised Saigon he was under hostile control. The CIA station then initiated what was termed "radio play," the silent cat-and-mouse game with an adversary over the air waves. This would continue until August 1962 when the CIA ended it.[29]

That same June, four more sergeants, also natives of northwestern North Vietnam, joined the growing paramilitary force. Formed into Team DIDO, they parachuted into northern Lai Chau Province not far from the provincial seat. One team member, describing their fate to another commando he met later in prison, said, "After we landed we ran out of food. I went home and got food for our team but I was captured before I got back to the team."

North Vietnamese security forces were led by their captive to DIDO's location, and the team's radio operator was persuaded to go on his radio under Hanoi's direction. He too followed proper procedure and alerted Saigon that he was transmitting under Hanoi's control, but two agents were parachuted in to reinforce the team. DIDO, like ECHO, became the object of "radio play" between the CIA and Hanoi until the CIA shut down DIDO's communications link. Even though Saigon was aware of its capture, DIDO reportedly was responsible for the later loss of Team REMUS.

Also in June 1961, CIA officer Samuel Halpern arrived in Saigon. As a desk officer at OSS Headquarters in Washington in 1945, he had monitored the actions of OSS operative Patti in Indochina. Halpern was in Saigon on a most unusual mission. He recounted his brief glimpse of Colby's operation:

> In June 1961, the Chief of the Far East Division, Desmond FitzGerald, sent me to Saigon on temporary assignment. I was there about four months concerning another of General [Edward] Lansdale's ideas. This one consisted of locating all the Viet Cong radio transmitters in South Vietnam and then dropping airborne troops at each location and capturing the radio operators with their equipment. I was the Saigon Station's representative on a joint U.S./GVN [South Vietnamese] group to carry out Lansdale's idea. It seemed so simple, but the idea never worked out.
>
> Lansdale was the deputy to Maj. Gen. Graves Erskine, who headed the Office of Special Operations, Office of the Secretary of Defense. Lansdale served as deputy from 1957 to 1963, and Erskine's office served as the focal point in Defense for military support the

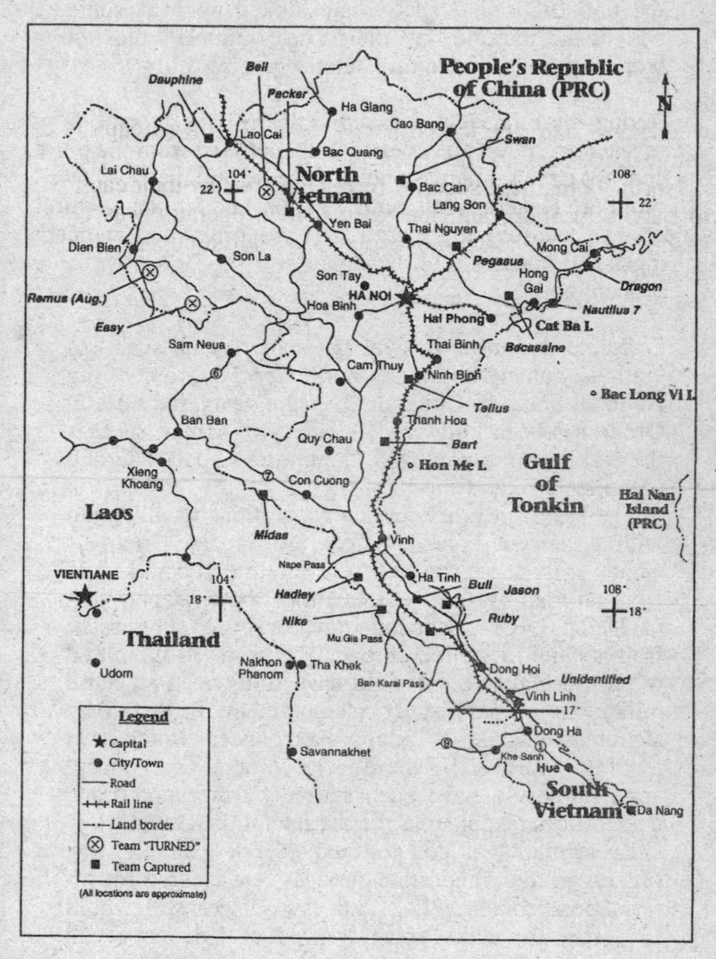

Figure 1. Agent teams landed and captured in 1961–1962. (*graphic by Cindy Tourison*)

> CIA might need or request. Lansdale had done a fine job with [President] Magsaysay in the Philippines in the mid-1950s and he became looked upon as some sort of a "miracle" worker. The "miracle" did not work in South Vietnam or later regarding Cuba.[30]

During my interview, I asked Halpern: "In general, how were such operations developed and approved from the point of concept development, concept approval by the NSC 5412 Committee, Headquarters authorization and station requirements, to coordinate operational proposals and concept changes and updates with headquarters?"

He continued:

> I assume the authority was the same for all such operations, namely approved by the Special Group of the National Security Council. Over the years, the Special Group has been known by a variety of names, such as the 5412 Committee, 303 Committee, Special Group (Augmented), and the like.
>
> The basic authority for such operations would begin with a concept approval from the Special Group or whatever its name was at any given time. It could come from an idea by the Department of State, Department of Defense, CIA Headquarters, or by a submission from a chief of station abroad. The proposal submitted to the Special Group would have followed a standard military-style staff study memorandum format. Any significant changes to an approved concept would have required approval by the Special Group. The concept approval would have been staffed by the appropriate desk officer responsible for the operational area.
>
> Everything was compartmented. For example, few officers in the clandestine service were cleared for information from the U-2 and even fewer still would have seen the actual imagery product. I do not recall Vietnam being that high a priority late in 1960 or early in 1961; not in terms of where our national priorities were concerned. Our priorities were the Soviet Union number one, China number two, and other things below that. Vietnam was simply not one of our top pri-

> orities. I represented my station at the early 1961 Chiefs of Station Conference in the Western Pacific and I do not recall anything particular about paramilitary operations being discussed then.[31]

"Were there pressures on the CIA station in Saigon?" I asked Halpern. He grinned and replied, "There may have been pressures at this time, since they definitely were present in other areas and at other times, such as MONGOOSE in Cuba in late 1961, in 1962, and later. For example, after the Bay of Pigs, the DCI [CIA director] sent a worldwide message to all field stations which said that the Agency would continue to move ahead. It was a troublesome period but we did move ahead. I do not think it had any impact on Saigon's own operations because Cuba was Cuba and Vietnam was Vietnam."[32]

When I asked Halpern what he saw of the Saigon station's operation while he was there, he continued:

> The Chief of Station (COS) was intimately involved in the paramilitary operations into the North. I learned about this aspect for the first time in late June 1961 when I went to see him in his office and found him and his deputy in the signal center on the top floor of the old embassy. The station had a team ready to launch but had not as yet received the go-ahead from Headquarters. The Chief of Station had sent an "immediate" cable sometime earlier and I was surprised he had not yet received an answer, particularly as the aircraft was waiting to go ahead with the drop. I suggested that a "flash" cable be sent, which was done. Within minutes, a "flash" reply to go ahead was received.
>
> At Saigon I learned little about the northern operations except that they were supposed to be for information collection. The idea was to try and get some people into the North, collect information, and report it back to Saigon. Their job was to go in on the ground, see what was there, find out who was who, and report on what was happening. It now appears that the teams were given other missions as well.[33]

Spending that night at the CIA station's signal center might have made Samuel Halpern a bystander to an international incident in the making.

In the early hours of 1 July, another of Col. Nguyen Cao Ky's C-47s was heading into the North to drop an agent team behind the enemy's lines. The aircraft crashed in Ninh Binh Province soon after crossing the coastline, reportedly after an antiaircraft unit known as Gun Crew 40 received authorization to open fire. One member of the agent team and two members of the crew survived the crash. They were captured on 2 July and lived to stand trial in Hanoi that November. Vietnam links this incident to the successful capture of CASTER while being silent about the true role of ARES.[34]

That December, the Vietnam People's Army published an account of the trial of the three captives from Ninh Binh, in which it argued that the agent operations against the North were conducted by the U.S. military. Statements from the C-47 pilot reiterated the orders that he described receiving from U.S. military operating from an office marked the "U.S. Advisory Team." As to any other Americans involved with the agent operations, they were portrayed by Hanoi as having been carried out by the Federal Bureau of Investigation. The CIA was not mentioned in the December 1961 public transcript of the trial.

The trial repeatedly singled out the 1st Observation Group and Ngo The Linh, the chief of Office 45, as being in charge of the agent teams operating largely under U.S. military direction. Given Hanoi's knowledge of the CIA's true sponsorship of the covert operations, its portrayal of the program as Pentagon inspired was another cog in its own careful orchestration aimed at convincing the North Vietnamese people of an expanding U.S. military threat.

Use of members of a uniformed military force was not sanctioned by National Security Council Intelligence Directive (NSCID) 5412/2. This caveat was seen by William Colby as not applicable in light of the November 1960 approval by the 5412 Committee which, he recalled, approved the CIA's concept for the northern operations and embodied the concept of the use of the South Vietnamese Air Force to deliver the agents.[35] Although Colby declined to call the C-47 downing an international incident, there was international press notice, including U.S. coverage, of the incident.

Samuel Halpern supports Colby's judgment: "I was in Saigon when that happened and never knew anything about it since I was not involved. There would be no conflict with 5412 which provided general guidelines. In Saigon's case, if it was uniformed personnel involved, then that meant that the Special Group approved their use in the particular operation. The prohibition was not so inflexible that it could not be modified by the 5412 Committee for good reason."[36]

There was one reason: the plausible denial provision in NSCID 5412/2 and the appearance that the operation was being conducted by the Republic of Vietnam.

Colby believed that an attempt had been made to remove U.S. identification from the aircraft, although the Hanoi trial produced bountiful evidence of U.S.–manufactured materiel recovered from the largely intact wreckage. Included in this was part of a 1954-vintage map produced by the U.S. Army Map Service with a penciled flight track that the C-47 was to follow and specific points where the aircraft was to change course headings. This, the pilot reportedly testified, was what he used to guide him on his route. His last course change in North Vietnam was to be over western Hoa Binh Province before he intended to fly to Udorn Air Base, Thailand, and then return to Saigon.

Regan recalls the shootdown of the C-47 and the loss of NAUTILUS 1 (N1), even after thirty-three years:

> I remember the shootdown of the C-47, but I don't recall how many men were in the team on board the aircraft. We got tracking reports about its flight path up until the time it crashed so we knew they had indeed shot it down. The same thing applied to the boat crew with the frogmen we lost at the end of June 1962. We were monitoring the North Vietnamese as they chased the infiltration boat, which was trying its best to reach the 17th Parallel because they'd be safe at that point. We were very frustrated just sitting there and following what was happening because we knew we couldn't run north of the DMZ to help them. Their boat finally sank north of the DMZ, and the crew was captured.
>
> The CIA has been blamed for a lot of things up

> North but not all of them were ours. For example, the air base at Da Nang was an emergency landing site for CIA–supported operations involving aircraft sent in over the People's Republic of China. I recall Hanoi reported downing one of our aircraft but we knew it wasn't ours. It turned out to be one of our aircraft which developed problems over China and crashed in the North trying to make it back to South Vietnam. I mention this as an example of an incident which Hanoi blamed on us which had nothing to do with the CIA station in Saigon.[37]

As the C-47 crash survivors were being interrogated that July, Maj. Le Van Buoi departed Hue on his own mission into Quang Ninh. In September, Ngo The Linh's boat crews took another agent to land in coastal Nghe An Province. Buoi reached the Hon Gai area, but the agent landing at Nghe An was captured soon after making landfall.

Ed Regan looks back on the happenings at Hue:

> While Russ Miller had our very first meeting with Ngo Dinh Can in 1960 [one of our officers] was able to work with Can a bit.
>
> I believe we probably did launch someone from Can's group in the summer of 1961, but our involvement there was limited to funding part of the effort in hopes of getting intelligence information from the agent once he got into the North. I don't remember what happened to that agent. There was another agent who got in, and we learned [the police] probably arrested him at a train stop.[38]

By year's end, at least three paramilitary teams had landed in the North, two of which were deemed to be under hostile control; a C-47 with a team on board was gone; and a third resource, the double agent known as ARES, was helping Hanoi prepare for its next victim, a crew known as NAUTILUS 1. (See Appendix 1 and Figure 1.)

3

MATCHING WITS

DURING THE NIGHT of 14 January 1962, a nondescript fishing boat rocked gently as it moved inside Vietnamese territorial waters in the far northern reaches of the Gulf of Tonkin.[1] To the casual observer, this was just one more group of local fishermen coming in late. Actually, the boat carried a CIA boat crew code-named NAUTILUS 1 (N1). Most of the crew were in their teens.

The crew had departed the South Vietnamese port of Da Nang at five o'clock in the morning on 12 January. With the exception of the captain, the crew were largely unaware of the planning at their immediate headquarters, the Coastal Security Service. None knew of the message from ARES that he needed more supplies, including radios. They perceived this to be just one more half-week trip. Several months earlier, N1 had transported an agent whom the crew knew only as Quang and put him ashore on the coast of Ha Tinh Province at a point of land known as Deo Ngang. This was a popular coastal landing site for agents, and boat crews routinely went ashore to mix with other fishermen at the town market and pick up the local gossip. The northern coast was still an easy place to get into and out of, with few coastal patrols in evidence.

The crew had spent two uneventful days quietly sailing north up the Gulf. Arriving near Hon Gai, they anchored along one of the hundreds of offshore karst islands dotting the coast and pretended to fish as they awaited dusk. Local fishermen came within hailing range and asked them what they were doing. Buying fish, came their answer, and after a while the locals moved on.

That night, NAUTILUS 1 got started late. The boat rounded a small island just north of the coastal port of Hon Gai and headed deliberately toward the shoreline. The boat's captain worked over in his mind precisely how he would unload the twenty-seven cases of supplies hidden below the well-worn decks. Saigon expected this equipment to be delivered to the agent known in Washington and Saigon as simply ARES.

To cut down the anticipated lengthy unloading time, the captain maneuvered the boat to a point just off the beach where they were almost grounded. The boat was in a potentially dangerous position, but there was no indication that they had been spotted. They lowered a dinghy to move supplies onto the shore, only meters away. Three crewmen climbed into it to load the supplies for the man known only as Thuy, an agent they had landed in 1961 in that general area.

The first cases of supplies were almost ready to be handed down to the dinghy when the boat was hailed by the crew of a North Vietnamese patrol boat that had moved in behind NAUTILUS 1 without being noticed. It blocked the only avenue of escape.

"Surrender or you're dead!"

The crew were unable to maneuver off the beach, and it was obvious to them that they could not resist the patrol boat. The three crewmen in the dinghy jumped into the water, but the North Vietnamese quickly hauled them into their boat.

The captain of N1 had all of the crew's Coastal Security Service identity cards with him, and their captors later grinned at such a discovery. It ended any question about the crew's identity and affiliation. As if to emphasize that there were few questions, one of their captors called to one of the boatmen by name, told him about his mother, and mentioned that other family members were all in good health.

"We've been waiting for you, you know," said one of the captors. "You all can't come up here without us knowing who is coming and what you're doing. We tracked you coming up the Gulf. . . ."

The N1 crew were quickly tied up, blindfolded, and then taken by truck to Hon Gai City, where they were locked, one to a cell, in the provincial temporary prison. Each crewman was photographed and then underwent six months of exhaustive interrogation. The questions covered the minutest details about their officers and the Americans who advised them, their boats, and each mission by N1 and the other boat crews at Da Nang.[2] That summer, they were tried by a military tribunal and sentenced to varying lengths of incarceration in Hanoi's maximum security hard-labor prison system operated by the Ministry of Public Security.[3]

Months later, the team's guide, fast approaching death, whispered to one of his fellow crewmen what he'd been afraid to speak about until then. His breath came in starts, but there was no misunderstanding what he was saying:

> It was Thuy, the one we landed in Quang Yen in '61. He came to see me in my cell at Hon Gai and he was wearing these black pajamas. He had on a fancy watch and stood there smoking while he talked. He told me he knew the prison commander and he'd been authorized to come and visit with me. We talked for a while and it was obvious what had happened. He's really working for them. He's a traitor and he's been one of theirs all along, a double agent.

The boatman died shortly after his revelation. The crewman to whom he passed on the information had no way to relay it to his officers at Da Nang.

Later that year, the Coastal Security Service commander, on orders of Ngo The Linh, reportedly ordered one of the NAUTILUS teams to head back to the area of Hon Gai. On board the boat were supposed to be the wife and two young children of the agent known as Thuy and his wife's younger brother. Some crewmen heard that Thuy had reported that he was operating safely not far from Hon Gai and had asked that his family be sent to join him. Saigon had readily obliged. The N1 crew were in prison when the boat arrived with the "instant" family, unloaded the quartet, and returned to South Vietnam without incident.

The capture of NAUTILUS 1 occurred as the North's border security forces were again changing their codes, replacing system T90 with code systems VQ1 through VQ5. They also developed a new format to report incidents of interest by radio to their headquarters. This format reduced the time needed to get the information into the proper hands. Although not indicating this, it also reduced the time a border security force radio station would be on the air, thus limiting the possibility that its messages might be intercepted.[4]

Such a code system was in effect when Team EUROPA took off for Hoa Binh Province on 20 February. The team was captured near its landing site on 22 February, and its radio operator agreed to join the growing stable of agent radio nets operating at Hanoi's behest.[5]

In March, Team ATLAS, under the command of former singleton agent Tran Huu Quang, flew in an air transport to Thailand. There, the team transferred to a waiting helicopter that took it to a landing site, south of EUROPA's landing zone, just inside Laos in Khammouan Province, close to its border with Nghe An Province in North Vietnam.[6] The four agents were spotted by a Lao hill tribe herder, who reported their arrival to a nearby border security post. The team was soon engaged by Vietnamese border security forces, and only two survived to stand trial after their capture on 5 April.[7]

While the ATLAS survivors were in Nghe An's provincial prison, Team REMUS, under the command of Dieu Chinh Ich, was parachuted into northwestern North Vietnam not far from the mountain town of Dien Bien Phu.[8] This team of ethnic Tai hill tribesmen, who had lived in that area before 1954, was launched on 16 April.[9]

By most accounts, REMUS was able to operate safely for nearly two months. It made contact with local relatives and arranged for resupply from Saigon. On its second resupply mission, the team moved with all its equipment to the preplanned supply drop point and found itself surrounded by a large North Vietnamese force. The team members scattered and abandoned all their equipment, including radios and the team's vital codes. The first one captured, on 23 June, was the commander. The team members' helpful relatives were arrested by local security forces and imprisoned at a permanent former French prison in neighboring Son La.

From members of DIDO, other captive agents learned of DIDO's capture and collaboration in 1961. One of the DIDO survivors later described to other prisoners DIDO's role in the loss of REMUS:

> In the spring of 1962, the team was ordered to move south to the area of Dien Bien Phu. Messages had gone to Saigon saying we'd run out of food and needed to be resupplied. The team moved down to southern Lai Chau Province and got its supplies at a site being used by resupply REMUS. This compromised REMUS.[10]

In July, singleton agent Nguyen Chau Thanh was brought in by boat to land in Ha Tinh Province. He was supposed to be taken in by NAUTILUS 3 but, at the last moment, was taken north by another crew. He too was captured not long after landing. Four members of Team EROS landed in Thanh Hoa on 20 May and were soon surrounded by border security forces, which seemed to be waiting for them. Their radio operator was recruited into the expanding net of co-opted radio operators now covering the length of most of North Vietnam's border with Laos.

As REMUS was landing in North Vietnam, the U.S. Navy's Pacific commander, Adm. Harry D. Felt, was describing the CIA's poor maritime performance as evidence that it could not perform the mission. Admiral Felt went even further and urged a response in kind against North Vietnam as retaliation for attacks in South Vietnam initiated by the Viet Cong. For example, he argued that an attack against some point in the southern Vietnamese railway system be answered by destroying the rail line between Hanoi and the Chinese border. He also suggested that commando teams be inserted by submarine into North Vietnam, as an indication of U.S. "technical superiority" against which North Vietnam had no "defensive capabilities."[11] Although such rhetoric might have helped move the transfer process forward, the navy was operating under tight budgetary constraints. It had few specialists in its ranks who could be committed to a covert maritime war without the funding necessary to support their training and reassignment.

In July 1962, Secretary of Defense Robert McNamara convened a meeting of State, Defense, and CIA officials to discuss transferring control of the paramilitary operations in

Vietnam from the CIA to the Department of Defense in a one-year program dubbed Operation Switchback.[12] Col. George C. Morton, chief of MACV (Military Assistance Command Vietnam) J-3 Special Warfare Branch, argued for more U.S. Special Forces involvement. Colonel Morton's background included stay-behind operations in Greece during the early 1950s, and he was viewed as "an expert on special warfare."[13]

That September, the National Security Council Special Group (5412) went on record as supporting Admiral Felt's earlier thinking by formally suggesting the use of motor torpedo boats and SEALs for covert operations against the North. There was no immediate effort, however, to secure either the boats or the SEALs.[14]

These events, in the context of the ever-widening covert operation against Hanoi, were based on National Security Council authority for the conduct of covert paramilitary operations, which was assigned to the CIA under NSCID 5412/2. This directive contained a philosophy that such operations would develop behind-the-lines agent teams that would constitute a viable paramilitary force to employ at the enemy's rear in time of open war and in support of the Pentagon's general war plans. This thinking embodied a notion that was a throwback to the European experiences of World War II OSS operatives who were now in the State Department, Pentagon, and CIA.

As such operations were applied during World War II, their success depended on a number of factors that were well known to officers directing the Vietnam paramilitary effort. Many were graduates of the OSS operations, upon which the CIA patterned its post–World War II programs; however, three fundamental dissimilarities suggested that the concept was not applicable in North Vietnam.

First, paramilitary teams required assistance from a population largely supportive of any Allied war effort. For example, in World War II, the OSS landed teams in France and other German-occupied countries but not in Germany itself. North Vietnam was certainly not France.

Second, neutralizing an enemy's counterespionage force that would be employed against such teams demanded an ability to know how and when these enemy forces would be applied. In World War II, the capture and control of German agents sent into England, as well as knowledge of the current and future plans of the enemy's counterespionage organization, helped to ensure a successful Allied return to the European continent. There is not yet conclusive evidence that this happened in North Vietnam.

Third, the ability to intercept and decode the enemy's codes was crucial to Allied successes against Germany. In Vietnam, the first significant U.S. military communications intelligence effort close to the North's low-power transmitters did not occur until spring 1961 when the U.S. Army's 3d Radio Research Unit reached Saigon. Several years later, a stroke of luck permitted U.S. intelligence to break Hanoi's most sensitive agent codes, but limited U.S. capabilities at this early juncture might have prevented interception and decoding of every North Vietnamese message.

Thus, the notion of a viable behind-the-lines force of Vietnamese agent teams existed only in the minds of those in the Pentagon who believed they were taking over a functional operation. Those in the CIA who realized the teams were failing and those in Hanoi who were controlling the teams and stimulating Washington to send in more were well aware that the concept was invalid.

Tran Van Minh, one of Gilbert Layton's South Vietnamese counterparts, suggested other reasons for the failures, even at that juncture:

> Most U.S. intelligence officers came to Vietnam wanting to show they could produce results quickly but without having to face the consequences of their actions. They wanted to impress their superiors so they would get high performance grades.
>
> As to the counterespionage effort, we had nothing to speak of ourselves at the time the first agent teams were going into the North. Office 25 was our counterespionage element, and they did very little. They were primarily concerned with background investigations of those being brought into the covert operations. Office 25 had too few people for the huge covert force we were fielding, each of whom they had to investigate. President Diem's Interior Ministry had nothing, and the

> Army intelligence staff had nothing of significance. As to the police, their principal job was maintaining public order, and we were having all these riots.[15]

Layton accepted the likelihood that enemy agents were within his border security forces. He recounted his own approach and the CIA station's experience with "turned" radio operations in adjacent Laos:

> In 1963, one of our teams was captured in the Attopeu area of extreme southeastern Laos. The team radio operator sent a message alerting us to the fact he was being forced to transmit under enemy control. His Pathet Lao and North Vietnamese adviser captors had the audacity to have the radio operator ask us to send in enough food for a battalion, ten times the amount of food the team would reasonably have needed. That helped confirm there was a battalion-size force which had captured our team. We had radio messages back and forth and we let the operator know we would get them out. We got several well-placed air strikes into the area to hit the enemy battalion and the team was able to escape and evade to the airfield at Attopeu. The Ambassador in Vientiane went nuts about our team having been discovered because we weren't supposed to be in Laos after the Harriman Line went into effect in the fall of 1962 after the signing of the Geneva Accords on Laos.
>
> In my shop, and most of the Agency shops, you assumed [your South Vietnamese counterparts] were penetrated. And you were probably right too, in most cases. When I started recruiting all these people, somebody said, aren't you afraid there might be some Viet Cong in there that you're hiring? I said, we figure on about ten percent but then we outnumber them nine to one. You deal with this possibility by making sure the teams know only what they need to know to accomplish their mission, but you make sure that they do have a mission if you're going to ask them to risk their lives for you.[16]

Layton acknowledged that the effectiveness of a paramilitary program would be insignificant if there were a lot more penetrants than anticipated. As to the availability of counterespionage specialists in the CIA station, Layton commented:

> Where would such people come from? We weren't getting that kind of support at that point in time, not from the few people we had out there. Besides, if you don't think that you've been penetrated then you ought to assume it anyhow and act like it. That's the only way you can do it. The enemy's just as smart as we are and in fact, several times, he's proved he's a hell of a lot smarter than we are.[17]

Ed Regan tells about this period of transition as seen from the operational level:

> We in the CIA station were both working with Diem's covert intelligence force while trying to monitor those trying to get rid of Diem. . . . In 1962 it was getting tense and Diem began to monitor our station officers and their contacts with those in opposition to Diem. . . . From President Diem's standpoint, he was fighting not only the Communists and the Buddhists, but he also had to contend with other political groups such as the Dai Viet and Viet Nam Quoc Dan Dang, the VNQDD.
>
> Lou Conein, for example, had contacts with groups such as the VNQDD and . . . learned from Vong A Sang, the former commander of the Nung forces up in northeastern North Vietnam, that Sang's old network there was apparently gone. Coming out of our contacts with the VNQDD and Dai Viet, we proposed to President Diem that we send some Dai Viet up North to assess what might still be active there. Captain Ngo The Linh, Colonel Tung's officer in charge of the northern operations, seemed to go along with everything and provided us several agents to go with our Dai Viet agents. We learned later from the radio operator that Linh had assigned an agent to the team primarily to keep track of what we in the CIA and Dai

Viet were up to. That team was never sent up North. . . .

It was once again Washington's push to expand the operation during Switchback and we responded to the direction we were given. For example, by late in 1962, Tucker Gougelmann was the base chief at Da Nang and Carl Jenkins was our paramilitary officer at the Hoang Hoa Tham training center.

Russ Miller left that spring in 1962, and he was replaced by "W. T. Cheney," who came from Europe. I understand he was a fine officer working in earlier assignments, but he was too Europe oriented and did not appear to grasp how to work with Asians. This was a time when Bill Colby was at headquarters, and he began to rotate officers through Southeast Asia to broaden their experience.

It now appears the paramilitary operations were penetrated a lot more than we ever knew. None of us in the clandestine service would have knowingly turned over a penetrated operation to the Pentagon if we had known it was penetrated. That would have been criminal.

The CIA station's need to track Diem opposition forces meant that by the spring of 1962 I was meeting with certain of these groups and that pulled me away from the paramilitary operations except for going up to launch the teams from Da Nang. Larry Jackson stayed on, but he was our demolitions instructor and went up to Long Thanh when it first opened that spring.[18]

Today, dealing with the reality that all the teams he launched were captured, some turned by the North Vietnamese, Regan asks the seemingly unanswerable:

It is reasonable to ask if this compromise was accidental or deliberate. Remember that the ethnic minorities represented a threat to Diem because the hill tribes were pushing for self-determination and we had all these young U.S. Army Special Forces men coming in to work with the hill tribes. So, to whose benefit would

> it have been if they were all captured? Diem, of course. It would be too speculative to say that they were deliberately compromised.[19]

If the CIA officers in Saigon were not looking for Hanoi's penetration, the question is why? One answer comes from William R. ("Bill") Johnson, former CIA chief of Far East counterintelligence, who served on the CI (counterintelligence) staff at CIA headquarters during this period. He offers the following observations:

> The Agency operations discussed here had no CI component and were not coordinated with any CI work going on elsewhere in the Agency or in any other elements of the government. . . . There was no CI or security effort included in the operations against the North, and none regarding security of the station or of penetration of the GVN [South Vietnamese government]. . . . [By 1965] when John Hart took over the station [in Saigon], he found, as he told me, that there was no counterintelligence discernible in Saigon—"no plumbing, only piles."[20]

Bill Johnson points to William Colby as the cause of the problem and describes its ramifications on the CIA's operation now being turned over to the Pentagon:

> It is generally true that our stations and officers in the Far East, and their desks in Washington, emphasized production in volume through collection by whatever means—including contacts and "agents" who were subsidized political action operators with political axes to grind—over clandestinely recruited and controlled penetrations of hostile targets. Operational security was mechanical—reliance on name checks of prospective agents through the operational approval process and reliance, even in the inappropriate cultures of Asia, on the polygraph.[21]

Former CIA counterintelligence officer Russell Holmes echoes similar views on this period:

> Vietnam was not viewed as a high priority counterintelligence threat at that time. Much of what we knew about Communist Vietnam came from the French, though we received relatively little of real CI interest. After all, Indochina was theirs.
>
> Were our operations penetrated during that period? Obviously they were. Why? Failure to give proper emphasis to the CI aspect of clandestine operations. The feud between the pro-CI and anti-CI forces had an adverse impact upon Agency operations in Vietnam. It is a safe bet that Far East Division officers had little incentive to apply CI tradecraft since division leaders had no interest in CI.
>
> Based upon the information coming from the Vietnamese paramilitary agents we sent into northern Vietnam in the early 1960s, it is clear [the Far East Division] operations [under William Colby] were thoroughly penetrated by the Communists from the start. By this I mean they had penetrated the South Vietnamese and because we were not even looking at them from a CI point of view, we inherited their penetration.[22]

The teams sent into North Vietnam in 1962 were largely ethnic minorities recruited in 1961 from within the South Vietnamese Army. They were augmented by others, such as border crossers from North Vietnam and former residents of North Vietnam now living in Laos. The number of potential recruits, however, was being exhausted because of a growing competition for people who would agree to undertake the northern operations as opposed to border security operations inside the South, not to mention the expanding cross-border operations into Laos.

One former agent looked back on this period:

> I don't think you can say that none of the teams were ever successful. There were teams which did get in and out, but I think that pertained more to the teams which went on very short-range missions just north of the DMZ. It was the teams with the long-range, long-term missions which failed. The same with the agent oper-

> ations. It makes sense, if you think about it. Those teams that represented the greatest threat were the ones which were always eliminated. Those which were not a significant threat were left alone.[23]

Tran Quoc Hung, a former singleton agent, offered his perspective on this same period. His initial training course dealt with general subjects, part of which taught the philosophy of the Can Lao party. He did not train exclusively for operations in northern Vietnam. One of his first assignments was to infiltrate the students in Saigon and collect information on anti–Diem government activities and attitudes. It was from this training and agent operations inside South Vietnam that Hung learned that Dr. Tuyen's organization dealt with internal political intelligence as much as foreign intelligence. Hung recounted his infiltration into the North:

> In 1962, I was taken up north on one of the infiltration boats. I left Da Nang and was put ashore in Ha Tinh Province, at the wrong landing spot and in the wrong province. And yet, I did get to Hanoi and I'll always believe that they knew I was coming. I had the distinct impression I detected surveillance from the time I reached Hanoi. I don't know how they got on to me, but something was compromised somewhere for them to spot me so quickly. They were on to me from the time I made my first contact at the church with the priests who had been working with the French before 1955.[24]

William Colby, CIA station chief at the time Hung was sent into the North, argues that the opposite was true and that CIA Station Saigon saw little real potential in such operations. Colby explained:

> I didn't know about the French turning them over but if they turned them over, I would think that some of the Vietnamese might still be a little suspicious of them because they were hyper, hyper about the French. They were convinced that the French were running some separate policy there at that time, particularly Ngo

> Dinh Nhu. He was always finding French manipulation in something. Diem, of course, had a lot of faith in the Catholics and the priests, that they were reliable. That was his test. And as a result of some of our paramilitary activities we did assist priests in organizing self-defense groups in their communities. It doesn't sound unlikely to me at all that Diem's people would get in touch with the Catholic priests up there because there was a great loyalty there. And the Catholics were still sort of dubiously viewed by the Communist regime in North Vietnam.[25]

When asked if there were still French assets that might be usable after 1955, Colby was emphatic:

> I think our impression was that everything that had been recruited up North disappeared. I don't recall we had any contacts there at all. I'm pretty sure we didn't. We may have had some ideas about who would be sympathetic if you got up there and talked to them. That would have come out of the refugee community and Diem's contact into the Catholic communities.[26]

Hung disagreed. In his experience, it was the Americans who provided him the clandestine intelligence training and with whom he worked out all the layers of cover stories he had to memorize and be prepared to use when he approached each of the Catholic priests he was to contact in Hanoi. The Americans instructed him one-on-one, whereas the Vietnamese merely interpreted. Hung continued his story:

> I got to know the area like the back of my hand. Someone had flown a reconnaissance mission, and the CIA training officers had the whole floor covered with aerial photographs which took me from my point of landing on north to Hanoi. It was incredible detail! Absolutely incredible! I don't how they got them but they were current and so detailed I could almost count the people on the boats.
>
> It seemed as if our agents were compromised before they were inserted. Most of the time there was some-

> one waiting for them on the ground. If someone did get in and get out, a question might be asked whether they had to let some teams get in and out to avoid tipping their hand that they knew everything that was going on.[27]

Had their voices been audible, many Catholics swelling Hanoi's prison system in 1962 would have cautioned against such contacts with the so-called Catholic faithful. One former prison inmate described both the atmosphere of the time and his own role in helping create it. He sat hunched over, looking off to one side, and cleared his throat:

> You're right of course. I was indeed there at the time. It was a nightmare. You had to have been there to have experienced it. [His voice drifted away as he sat there on the edge of the bed, his arms wrapped around himself.]
>
> My name was already on their list. I'd been arrested in 1955 when I tried to get out across the Ben Hai River. They knew my background. Not only had I showed my lack of solidarity with the State by trying to flee but I was also a novice priest. That made me automatically an enemy of the party. The State Security cadre from the Hanoi Public Security Office came to me in 1960. I was back in Hanoi after three years reeducation for trying to escape. They knew I was involved in Catholic religious affairs in Hanoi. They could have locked me up at any time. Instead, they made me an offer. They said that they just wanted to find out who the troublemakers were. They explained that "certain foreign forces" were trying to cause trouble. There were "certain criminal elements" trying to take advantage of the instability. They had lots of reasons. They just wanted me to keep track of what was going on. So, I went to work for them.
>
> Every month I'd have a meeting with a State Security cadre from the Hanoi Municipality state security section, which specialized in operations against the Catholic Church. We met in the small hotel across from the east side entrance to the main train station in

> Hanoi. Our meetings were usually brief. I'd tell him where I'd gone, with whom I'd met, what the priests were doing, what the parishioners were doing and saying.
>
> It continued until 1962. By then, the Hanoi Public Security Office had already arrested most of the priests and novices under the authority of the Concentration Decree. Those who were not arrested were under continual surveillance. I told the officer I was reporting to that I just couldn't work any more. He just smiled and said that he hoped I'd change my mind. Several weeks later they came before daybreak and knocked on my door. There were several uniformed police and a local ward official. I was handcuffed and they dragged me out to the middle of this narrow alley where they read a statement out loud. It could be heard a block away. It said that I had been found to have been engaged in activities harmful to the public order and was to be remanded to the custody of the Hanoi Public Security Office for detention under the authority of the Concentration Decree.[28]
>
> I was furious! I'd cooperated with them for over two years! And then they arrested me too! I'd only helped them a little, you understand. Not all that much. I mean, my reporting didn't cause anyone to die.[29]

His voice trailed off into silence, his arms wrapped around himself, gently rocking back and forth, as if that would make the pain go away.

"My arrest order did not specify the term of confinement," he continued after a few moments. "Later I learned it would be for three years. It was a joke. I spent fifteen years in prison at hard labor, most of it at Phong Quang and Tuyen Quang. I got out of prison in 1977, when they started releasing some of the novice priests."[30]

"What do you remember of that fifteen years?" I asked him.

"Remember?" He paused. "Remember? The pain. . . ."

One month to the day that Team REMUS parachuted into the Laos–North Vietnam border area, Team TOURBILLON was being assembled in Saigon to prepare for its mission into Son La Province to the east of REMUS. Out of sight of other team members, Captain Triet carefully briefed Vang A Giong, TOURBILLON's radio operator, on his signal operating instructions and issued the team's codes to him.[31]

Giong found the codes to be the same type that his army had used for years, the "one-time pads." He was also given his own personal authenticator, a special five-digit group, and instructed to place it in the third group in his message. This would let Saigon know that he was actually sending the message.

"Don't write anything down! You have to memorize it!" Captain Triet commanded. That evening, Giong wrote his personal authenticator on the outer cover of his thick book of signal operating instructions.

Years later, Giong explained:

> You must understand. I was afraid I'd forget it. . . . If that happened, I knew that we'd never be resupplied because I couldn't prove that it was me on the radio. I didn't trust my own memory. So, I wrote it down and that's what compromised me, and kept the compromise going.
>
> I'd joined in 1960 and was assigned to the 1st Observation Group at Nha Trang. That's when Col. Tran Khac Kinh, Col. Tung's deputy, began sending teams into Laos, working there with the ethnic Hmong in Laos under Vang Pao. There were ten teams of us, fifteen men to a team. I was the radio operator in Team 9. By 1961 I'd gone on five operations across the border. . . .
>
> Then in 1962 I was transferred down to Saigon and joined Team TOURBILLON as its radio operator. I got a one-month refresher training course, mostly about planting mines and tactics.
>
> Ngo The Linh brought us all together and said we were to go into Son La Province, in North Vietnam. He explained that they'd sent a team into Son La in 1961, a team called CASTER. CASTER had reported back to Saigon they'd arrived safely and over that first year they'd developed their base and had recruited a lot of

people to work for them. However, their team was too small to carry out their base development and training so they radioed Saigon that they needed more men to help train the force they developed. Our mission was to reinforce CASTER and act as their training cadre. We were also to conduct reconnaissance along Route 41, the road they later renumbered Route 6, running from Son La into Sam Neua Province, Laos, and were to destroy seventeen bridges along Route 6 after we got up there. I don't know how they expected us to carry out that part of the mission.

Linh told us there was nothing to worry about. CASTER was waiting for us and everything was secure. We got no briefing on any hostile forces in the area and no one told us what we should do in the event of capture. Linh and the team's operations officer, Pang, kept saying over and over that there was nothing to worry about, nothing. CASTER was there, CASTER was safe, and CASTER would take care of us.

Today, looking back on what happened thirty-two years ago and everything that has happened in between, it is clear that no one at our headquarters had any idea what we would be facing up North. I mean, we had no real intelligence about the area and we, like CASTER, were even having to rely on maps the French had used before 1954. By 1962, everything had changed. The greatest shortcoming was everyone underestimated the North Vietnamese counterespionage effort.

So, on 16 May 1962, we were flown up there on an American transport with a Taiwanese crew. We parachuted in at about midnight and we found people waiting for us on the ground. However, it wasn't CASTER that was waiting. It was the North Vietnamese.

The North Vietnamese had us surrounded when we landed, but some of us were able to evade for a few days. I thought of destroying my code book and signal instructions but I knew if I did that, I'd never be able to contact anyone. Then they captured me and found my documents. That's how they learned my personal authenticator.

Why did I cooperate with them? They kept hammering at me that it was all over. I now had to choose between cooperating with them and staying alive or being uncooperative and if I was uncooperative then that would be the end of me, my team, and Team CASTER. So, I cooperated and went on the radio. It was the only way we might survive, that was my thinking at the time. Eleven days after landing, I sent my first message to Saigon. Of course, it wasn't really *my* message; it was what Hanoi wanted Saigon to hear.

I was up there on the radio for two years before Team COOTS came in '64. I was pulled off the radio and Mao Van Thoi from COOTS became my replacement. That's when I was taken down to Thanh Tri Prison where they sent the teams who'd been captured and turned.

For the two years I was up in Son La, I was usually kept in the provincial prison. When it came time to send a message, I'd be taken out to a village in the hills where our team had told Saigon we were supposedly operating and I'd go on the radio, one hand free and the other hand handcuffed to something. I had been a pretty good radio operator when I first went up North, I used to send my messages very fast. But, my health deteriorated to the point I was sending everything so slow that I figured that Saigon would have to suspect that something was wrong. I guess they just never checked.

The counterespionage cadre from the Ministry of Public Security state security force were good. They only needed one person there to monitor me, listening to everything I was sending, and it was almost foolproof. Even if Saigon had been monitoring the North Vietnamese for some wisp of information that we'd been captured, they would never have heard anything. Let me explain.

Saigon would send a message but we never had to answer right away. After the radio schedule, I'd be taken back to a prison cell and the cadre in charge of me would go to Hanoi. There they'd decode the message and work out whatever they were going to do next. After I was captured, I never had access to my code books; they kept everything and I was just someone to be on the radio. When it came time to answer whatever Saigon had been requesting, the officer would come and get me out of the provincial prison and take me back to the village. I'd wait there until it was time to go on the radio and then I'd be given a coded message to send and when it was over, it was back to prison.

You know, if I'd had to send an immediate response it might have turned out different but everything was done so slow that the Ministry of Public Security counterespionage cadre had more than enough time to plan for how they were going to respond. Obviously, those guarding me didn't have the authority to make decisions on their own. They had to go back to Hanoi for that and they didn't need to use a radio; they'd just get in a truck and drive there. It went that way for two years and we were never resupplied during that entire time. As I look back on it, it was very poorly done. Think of it this way. If someone had just demanded that we do something immediately, have more messages going back and forth more frequently, this would have created problems for them. I don't know what Saigon was thinking and why they didn't think that Hanoi was really running us.

You know, even if we'd landed safely and had not been captured I suspect they would have found us, eventually. You see, we only used South Vietnamese Army radio procedure and if any North Vietnamese radio intercept operators were listening, they'd know it was an enemy radio transmitter. Besides, Ngo The Linh told me that when I transmitted, everyone would be picking it up because it was a frequency monitored by the U.S. Seventh Fleet, by the intelligence people in Japan, and from the Philippines. Hanoi had to have known that, if it was true.[32]

Late in 1962, TOURBILLON reported carrying out bridge sabotage on 24 September and again on 8 December, as Team ARES reported recruiting six agents. TOURBILLON's attacks never took place but were intended to give the impression that the team was actively carrying out its mission. ARES agents were another creation from Hanoi.[33]

On 28 June, boat crew NAUTILUS 2 had left Da Nang for a quick attack by frogmen against Swatow-class patrol boats anchored at the mouth of the Gianh River. Arriving on station, the frogmen got into the water and prepared to launch their attack. For unexplained reasons, one of their limpet devices detonated prematurely, killing one of the frogmen. The explosion alerted the local security forces. They set off in pursuit of N2's crew and sank their boat with gunfire before they could make it back across the 17th Parallel. CIA officers at Da Nang monitored these events but were unable to assist. Two of the frogmen survived into captivity, including their commander, Le Van Kinh.[34] The crew of N2, with one exception, was captured; one young crewman was recovered alive the next day in the open ocean by forces sent from Da Nang.

A seven-man team, known as Team LYRE, landed in Ha Tinh Province in December. The team had made two earlier attempts, but its Taiwanese air transport was repeatedly driven off by hostile ground fire. LYRE's mission was to conduct reconnaissance of a nuisance radar site at Deo Ngang and be prepared to destroy it, as well as local food storage depots.

In his first message to Saigon, Nguyen Quy, the team's radio chief, reported their safe arrival, but he warned that the area was unsafe and requested permission to move to their next base area. Saigon replied to remain in place and await further orders. Within days, the team was locked in combat with two local security companies that had it surrounded.[35]

Two members of LYRE, Tran Nghiem and Nguyen Ly, were killed in the heavy exchange of fire. The remaining team members were captured as they attempted to evade to the south in adjacent Quang Binh. The team's commander, Le Khoai, was executed after capture in retaliation for casualties suffered by the capturing forces.

The problem of teams landing a short distance away from their intended drop zones was not unexpected, at least according to Lt. Col. William McLean, USA (Ret.), who saw service in Laos during this period. He explained:

> The worst thing of all was the damn maps some of the people had to work with. They were the old French maps, and they created a problem all their own. You see, the French began their world grid system centered on Paris, not on London as the rest of us used. The French grids also were not as precise, and I found that in Laos and Vietnam, halfway around the world, that margin of error meant there was about a 3,000-meter difference between the coordinates we plotted from our maps and the same spot based on coordinates obtained from a French map. So, if you had a location plotted based on an American map but you were taking that location plot and trying to work with people who only had French maps to work with, which meant most of Southeast Asia, well then, you were going to have a problem unless you compared the two and made sure you were comparing apples to apples, not apples to oranges. I didn't have that kind of a problem in Laos because I had both sets of maps and could make sure that I took this into account.
>
> If some American was telling his team to go to such and such a coordinate and didn't realize that his teams might be relying on French maps, well then, the team would end up about three kilometers away from where they were supposed to be.
>
> Then came the 1962 Geneva Accords on Laos, and most of the paramilitary people were pulled out of Laos.[36]

As Team LYRE was moving toward completion of its training, Maj. Le Van Buoi received a message from Ngo Dinh Can through his local agent contact at Hon Gai. The message ordered Buoi back to South Vietnam. Buoi recounted his final days of freedom:

> I got down to Dong Hoi on 22 October and was waiting for the boatman to come and pick me up. I was directed to wait in a specific little coffee shop and someone would come with the recognition signal and I'd go back with them to Hue. I waited but no one came. On the twenty-third, I returned to the coffee shop

a second time. This had been worked out ahead of time in case there was a delay in the boatman's arrival. The details were all in the message from Can. I was just sitting there when several uniformed police walked in and came directly to where I was sitting.

"Are you Le Van Buoi?" they asked. They already knew the answer so there was no need to make a scene.

"Yes, I am."

"Please come with us," came their soft response.

They took me out of the coffee shop and over to the prison where I was put in isolation. They had a team of interrogators work me over for a few months, always in the middle of the night. I don't think the other prisoners at Dong Hoi knew I was even there.

Then I was brought out of my cell to meet some field grade officers. There was the director of the provincial security services, the officer in charge of the prison, and a man introduced to me as a lieutenant colonel from the Ministry of Public Security in Hanoi.

The lieutenant colonel brought with him a large sealed envelope. He opened it and took out a stack of photographs of people such as Ngo Dinh Can, Nhu, Tuyen . . . and a stack of codes and some messages.

"We know who you are. We know you came up here in the summer of 1961 and we know who you are working for. Here, read the message. . . ."

It had the text of the very message I'd received from Ngo Dinh Can a number of weeks earlier telling me to return to South Vietnam. However, I knew it wasn't the actual message because it lacked the personal authenticator of Ngo Dinh Can. That told me they knew what was in the message but it wasn't the actual message itself.

"We got this through our Liberation Front people and they've asked us to ask you some questions. . . ."

The lieutenant colonel paused, directing another visitor to join us. The visitor entered the room and stared intently at me. Then he spoke.

"I know you, Buoi, and you know me. Am I correct?"

I returned the gaze. I knew him all right. The man

had been at the National Police Headquarters in Saigon before I was transferred to Hue City. He had worn a uniform with the rank of captain, and there had been nothing to suggest that he was anything but someone assigned to work there.

I thought carefully before answering, "You can ask all you want but I will only admit to the fact that I just arrived from South Vietnam. You already know who I am. . . ."

The colonel was not persuaded.

"Who are your agents?" he asked.[37]

This was what Buoi had been waiting for. It had all been worked out ahead of time a year and a half earlier. Buoi continued:

I told them about General Giap. . . .

You must remember, we had been keeping track of General Giap's movements and we knew he was going to Moscow quite a bit but we were not sure what he was doing there. We also knew there were problems within the international Communist movement on the issue of international leadership. Tito had broken with the Soviets, and there had been the problems in the 1950s in East Germany and Poland. We were aware of the struggle between the Chinese and Soviets and there was debate in North Vietnam about who they should listen to. There was one group urging that Hanoi remain out of the infighting and be somewhat independent. This was the group called the Revisionists.

The CIA officer and Can, during my meeting with them before we left, went over the possible steps I might be able to take if I was arrested. Should that happen, particularly if the bombing started before my return, I could be useful by helping create a certain amount of confusion and discontent by labeling certain senior officials as members of the Revisionist group whose aims were contrary to those of the party.

So, I told them what I'd been instructed to say. I told them that Gen. Vo Nguyen Giap was working for the Americans. He'd been recruited while in Moscow

> and was the head of the Revisionists. That meant he wasn't willing to accept Moscow's leadership and was in favor of a Tito-style Communist North Vietnam which did not accept the leadership of either Moscow or Peking.[38]

Buoi had memorized a list of names to give the Ministry of Public Security, and the North Vietnamese officers scribbled furiously as he spoke. He named Tran Huu Duc in charge of agriculture in the Office of Prime Minister Tran Danh Tuyen, chairman of the Hanoi Municipality People's Committee; Trinh Nguyen, director of the coal mines outside Hon Gai; Nguyen Tho Tran, provincial chairman for Quang Yen; and a number of public security officials. Buoi continued:

> I recall sometime later hearing something about General Giap going to Peking. One of the prison officials said General Giap had gone there because he had been implicated as head of the group of Revisionists. The other names didn't appear in the newspapers any more except for that of Nguyen Tho Tran; he was said to have gone to Moscow as Hanoi's ambassador. I don't know that what I told the Ministry of Public Security had a direct impact on the arrest of the Revisionists, but I'm sure it played some small part in that wave of arrests. . . .
>
> I was at the prison at Vinh Linh at the start of the American bombing in August 1964. In 1965, three years after my arrest, I was sent before a military tribunal, convicted of espionage, and sentenced to twenty years at hard labor. After my conviction, I was moved to Central Prison Number 3 in Nghe An, and in about 1968 I was moved to Phong Quang Prison. I'll never forget the prison commander's question to me when I arrived there: "Well," said Hoang Thanh. "I know what you told the ministry earlier. Tell me, what would you like to tell me?" I didn't tell him anything, and that made him furious.
>
> While at Phong Quang Prison, I met Tran Quoc Hung and Luu Nghia Luong, two more agents the

North had captured. I also met Gen. Nguyen Cao Ky's brother there. He had remained in the North after the partition and had lived relatively unmolested until the Gulf of Tonkin incident. After that, he was arrested and he was being kept somewhat in isolation. I spoke with him briefly once and that caused all sorts of interrogation of me, trying to find something sinister in my talking to Ky's brother.

They kept us there until 1972, when we were told we'd been repatriated. After the pre-release indoctrination classes, they just laughed and said we'd be able to go home all right, after the liberation.[39]

By the end of 1962, Hanoi's files that recorded its successful counterespionage operations included "K26 (Moc Chau), K36 (Song Ma-Son La), K33 (Hoa Binh), K37 (Ha Bac), K34 (Quang Binh), K32 (Dien Bien), K35 (Yen Bai). . . .[40]

Vietnam reflected on its successes years later, following extensive interviews of former adversaries from South Vietnamese military and civilian intelligence services who surrendered on 30 April 1975, particularly those involved in communications intelligence operations against it:

> In particular and regarding the crypto organization support, the victory in each of these special operations demonstrates that the information related to the operation sent through encrypted means guaranteed total secrecy and correctly carried out the requirements of those above.[41]

Some of the agent radio operators alerted Saigon to their capture and use in Hanoi's radio deception operation, and some did not. In 1962, the CIA shut down those it deemed to be under hostile control. There began to emerge, however, a small number of teams that offered no hard evidence of their work for Hanoi as American paramilitary officers were being withdrawn from nearby Laos in accordance with the 1962 Geneva Accords on Laos.

For the new CIA station chief in Saigon, John ("Jocko") Richardson, the end of 1962 marked much more than the end of the first six months of his new duties in Vietnam. It coincided with the first steps in the transfer of some of his paramilitary operations to the U.S. military. Also, Richardson had to monitor political alternatives to President Diem, as Diem's forces kept watch on the CIA's officers and Ngo The Linh continued the flow of agents into the North.

For William Colby, with his attention diverted by coup rumblings in Saigon, Operation Switchback had become an issue for negotiations with the Defense Department. These negotiations resulted in a blind eye to Hanoi's fly in the ointment.

4

OPERATION SWITCHBACK

ON 1 JANUARY 1963, in accordance with the phased implementation plan for Operation Switchback, the U.S. military command in Saigon officially took over the border security function previously directed by the CIA's paramilitary forces under Gilbert Layton. Meanwhile, the CIA's northern operations from Saigon continued under "W. T. Cheney." Operation Switchback in southern Vietnam seemed to be headed toward a completion date of July 1963; however, the process lacked support from President Diem.

Gilbert Layton recalls the period:

> Col. George Morton had command of the Special Forces "C" Detachment now set up at Nha Trang. My southern paramilitary programs were turned over to him in a phased effort in accordance with Switchback. As soon as the military was ready to receive them, we turned them over. By the summer of 1963, as I recall, most of the turnover was completed and I stayed on as Morton's special assistant.
>
> From the outset, Colonel Morton understood that the southern programs relied on having U.S. Army Special Forces teams located with our civilian irregulars in the villages, not out in the middle of nowhere. This was central to the paramilitary concept; hire forces to protect their villages, keep the fish in the water around them.
>
> These village-level forces were our principal sources of information on enemy movement. They served as

our loyal eyes and ears in the villages from which they had been recruited and where they lived. They would fight to protect their villages because they had a lot at stake. Moving them to areas where there were no local people rendered them ineffective.

During Switchback, General [Richard G.] Stilwell decided to move the Special Forces detachments, plus the local irregular forces we transferred to Colonel Morton at Nha Trang, westward to the Lao border. General Stilwell's strategy was that the civilian irregular forces could spot and interdict the North Vietnamese as they came across the border, but this was completely opposite to our strategy prior to the transfer. Colonel Morton understood what I had been doing and I sat in on the meeting when Colonel Morton urged the teams remain in place, but General Stilwell insisted the teams be moved forward. It may have seemed a reasonable strategy, but it had the effect of taking the fish out of water. Our mobile strike forces placed up on the border soon lost interest because they didn't have the same dedication to operate in basically unpopulated areas where they had nothing at stake. There was a lot of pressure on General Stilwell and, in my judgment, it was all coming from Washington.[1]

As Switchback moved forward, the Diem government increased its watch over the CIA station officers having contact with outside political groups, such as the VNQDD. By the spring of 1963, Tucker Gougelmann was largely alone in handling the agent launches from Da Nang, except for assistance from Carl Jenkins, the CIA's paramilitary officer directing the training base at Hoang Hoa Tham. At the newly formed agent training base at Long Thanh, CIA paramilitary officer Larry ("Rock") Jackson worked with his Vietnamese counterparts to help train and ready the agent teams now being assembled there for the first time.

That April, Team PEGASUS was parachuted into Lang Son. Two weeks later, half of Team JASON went into Quang Binh, and the remainder went the following month. All members of both teams were captured.

The establishment of the Long Thanh training center in

April 1963 was another step in the CIA's preparation to transfer its northern paramilitary programs to the Pentagon. Other evidence of the transfer included internal reorganization within the agent teams and the use of team names that had a more military sound. The former chief of demolitions training at Long Thanh, Nguyen Hung, recalls the buildup:

> Larry Jackson was my principal CIA point of contact for the demolitions training, and he stayed with me until the U.S. military took over everything in the spring of '64. During the summer of '63, the U.S. Army Special Forces arrived at Long Thanh to conduct the training for the teams due to go up North. As teams went into the restricted area prior to launch, the CIA took over and it was their case officers who came to pick up the team to be parachuted in by the Taiwanese crews on the C-123s.
>
> With the setting up of the training center at Long Thanh, we ended up with two separate groups of agent teams. One group got to know the training center at Long Thanh. A second group, however, remained in the safe houses scattered around Saigon. Those at Long Thanh got to know one another but those still in the safe houses were completely compartmented. That was still considered to be the secret side of the operation.
>
> As to our demolition training, we provided it to both types of forces; those heading up North and those who would be operating in the South. My job was to make sure the teams could use demolitions in all these kinds of operations. I think we prepared them well for that.[2]

Professional disputes about the conduct of the war in the South were not confined to the Americans. They also occurred within the Vietnam People's Army B-2 Theater Headquarters in the South, known popularly as the Liberation Army Headquarters. For some years, cadre such as Gen. Tran Do, one of the Liberation Army's deputy commanders, had pushed for an extended guerrilla war, not an escalation. This view held sway until 1963 when Gen. Nguyen Chi Thanh arrived from Hanoi to take command of Hanoi's military forces in the South. With Thanh came Hanoi's firm decision to shift from guerrilla warfare to larger-scale operations. The views of Tran Do and others at the Liberation Army Headquarters in northern Tay Ninh Province were eclipsed as Hanoi dusted off its own contingency plans in preparation for sending its regular army infantry divisions into South Vietnam.[3]

As Switchback moved forward, a critical issue was either overlooked or not given sufficient visibility. This was the security status of teams then transmitting from North Vietnam, other than those the CIA knew were transmitting under hostile control and were shut down that summer.

Part of the problem came as a result of pressures from Washington to move the transfer forward. It was also apparent that there were relatively few paramilitary teams actually operating inside North Vietnam. This meant a major push to get the program up to Washington's expectation.

Another factor influencing a less than cautious approach came because of a fundamental difference in views between William Colby, in charge of the Far East Division, and the CIA's counterintelligence staff chief, James ("Jesus") Angleton. This was on top of a basic issue of the authority inherent in the decision-making process by the Agency's senior officer on station, the chief of station; chiefs of station are generally deferred to. In addition, as coup noises were overwhelming Saigon and Washington, the CIA was under pressure to turn over its largely incomplete paramilitary effort to the Pentagon.

During the spring of 1963, Buddhist anti-Diem sentiment was growing and Colby was embroiled in the arguments over whether to retain President Diem or to let him fall. Diem's Acting Defense Minister Thuan had given Gen. Maxwell Taylor a letter acceding to Washington's demand for a larger contingent of military advisers, while President Diem had remained steadfast against the very increases his acting minister had officially requested in the name of his president.

The U.S. military presence in Vietnam was now at over fifteen thousand, as Defense Secretary McNamara went in two directions simultaneously. On the one hand, for example, he directed the Pentagon plan to seriously cut military funding in Vietnam to zero within six years, to hold the line on any increases in U.S. military in Vietnam, and to plan for a reduction of one thousand men by the end of the year. On the other hand, he approved roughly a 10 percent increase in the current ceiling that made the numbers and funding manipulation out of date before the ink was dry.

The transfer of the northern operations to the military coincided with selected long-range teams of South Vietnamese civilians being trained as maritime assault teams, rather than airborne agents. At the same time, teams previously unable to get into the North by boat were sent to Saigon to undergo parachute training in preparation for insertion by air.

By June, rumors were rife among some teams that the effort to infiltrate paramilitary teams by boat from Da Nang was in serious trouble. No one realized this more than Nguyen Van Ngo, commander of a long-range team that had made repeated unsuccessful attempts to land by boat in the panhandle of North Vietnam. His force was one of those sent from Da Nang to Saigon to undergo parachute training.

Upon completion of its training, Ngo's force was divided into two teams: BART and TELLUS, with Ngo in command of TELLUS. TELLUS was to parachute into its target during a standard nighttime airdrop. In accordance with normal drop procedures, the team was supposed to be dropped approximately ten kilometers from any known residences.

The team's survivors later described having been dropped in populous Ninh Binh Province but at the wrong location. Worse yet, they came down over a large village and landed in front of the village cooperative office. The staff was working late at night and spotted them during their descent. The villagers captured the team before they could even draw weapons.

BART, under the command of Dinh Van Chuc, parachuted into nearby Thanh Hoa. The team was not dropped into a densely populated area, but alert local residents spotted the men and notified local security forces. They were quickly surrounded and captured.

On 4 June, Team BELL was parachuted into Van Ban District of Yen Bai Province northeast of Hanoi. It was captured almost immediately, and its radio operator, Lu The Toan, joined Hanoi's expanding deception operation. The agents later confirmed that the local hill tribe didn't speak their dialect, and any serious communication with them would have been extremely difficult. In September, BELL reported to Saigon that it had sabotaged the Hanoi-Lao Cai rail line on 31 August, but this incident, created by Hanoi, never took place.

Team DAUPHINE, accompanying BELL on the same parachute drop, dropped into Lao Cai shortly before BELL. The commander of Team DAUPHINE described his team's mission:

> Our team was formed in 1962. We were all ethnic Tay from the Lao Cai area and I was from Van Ban District. Between June 1962 and our final mission on 6 June 1963, we flew five missions over our intended operating area and selected our landing zone. The South Vietnamese Air Force flew us to Thailand, and a Taiwanese air crew flew the next part of the mission. We would take off from Thailand, overfly Vietnam, and come up the Gulf of Tonkin. We would fly up the Red River, go over Hai Phong, Ha Noi, Yen Bai, and then up to Lao Cai before heading back to Thailand.
>
> The first five missions seemed to be orientation flights for the Taiwanese crew. We used a light intensification scope to confirm ground locations that we matched with the maps the crew used. We always flew on moonlit nights at a fairly high altitude and the scopes made everything very clear.
>
> DAUPHINE's mission was to link up with our own ethnic Tay and develop a resistance base. Then we were to sabotage the Lao Cai–Ha Noi rail line. One of my team was called the "political officer" because he was a member of the Patriotic Sword Party that was supposed to be the political force behind our commando operations.
>
> There were two teams on our aircraft on my sixth mission. I knew Ly Van Choi was one of the members in the other team that I learned later was Team BELL. Our team jumped in first at a height of only about 300 meters. It was a little windy but we reached the ground in about twenty seconds.
>
> When we landed we soon found ourselves engaged by local militia. It became obvious we were not ex-

pected, but we had a ferocious engagement which lasted for some hours before we broke contact. I was shot up pretty bad but managed to evade for about seven days before they found me. They flew me by helicopter to a special Ministry of Public Security hospital in a small town called Pho Moi, and they interrogated me there. Since we fought to avoid capture, we were not very cooperative and later that year I was shipped to Quyet Tien Prison and I recall I met thirty-seven commandos already there. Two of my men didn't join me at Quyet Tien. We fought hard and would not cooperate with the Ministry of Public Security. My two men were executed for resisting capture.

Something went terribly wrong with my mission and to this day I do not know what happened. We were supposed to land in a small ethnic Tay village named Ban Lun. I knew the area and I'd picked it out on my earlier flights over the area. But, we were dropped twenty-five kilometers away on top of the Vo Lao Village Cooperative. The farmers were husking rice on the ground in front of the village office when we came down so they saw us right away. How could we have been dropped so far away from our intended target which the crew had flown over time after time? I've waited twenty-five years for some American to tell me what happened. Do you know why it was done that way?[4]

I had no answer.

Four days later, Team MIDAS went into Nghe An and came under Hanoi's control, as Team NIKE was being captured in Ha Tinh Province. Team EASY went into Son La, west of TOURBILLON, in August, and its radio operator expanded the list of recruited operators. Other teams were sent by the CIA into the North so quickly that the Pentagon's researchers were later unable to reconstruct precisely where and when every team landed.

In 1963, singleton agent Duong Chuc was landed at the much used Deo Ngang landing site in Ha Tinh Province. He was soon captured. The same fate befell singleton agent Nguyen Thuy.

More losses were closely linked to the double agent known as ARES. In November 1962, a group of six young men, who would become Team BECASSINE, began training in a safe house at house number 199 at the main Phu Nhuan intersection on the outskirts of Saigon.[5]

For eight months, the team trained under U.S. and Vietnamese instructors. A U.S. Army noncommissioned officer, known to them only as "Dick," provided instruction on demolitions. Vietnamese instructors taught intelligence collection methods and procedures, parachute training, and weapons familiarization. Weapons firing took place at the Thu Duc infantry officer training center. The team's radio operator received Morse code instruction at a private school in Saigon's Tan Dinh District.[6]

In June 1963, the team was assembled and briefed for its mission inside northeastern North Vietnam near the town of Hon Gai. It would make contact with local residents, establish a network of agents, and report information about military installations and other targets in the area. After landing, the team was to move to its first regrouping point, initiate radio communications with their headquarters, and establish a secure base of operations. At that time, headquarters would assign them other specific tasks and direct their subsequent movements to new base areas. The team's mission was to last three years, at which point the members would be exfiltrated.

The ability to launch such a team into northeastern North Vietnam was described to them as a great victory, and everyone was encouraged to have a positive attitude. Ngo The Linh, the senior operations officer at their headquarters, promised to take care of everything.

The area of the landing zone and the first regrouping point were carefully reviewed. Based on all of the map information shown to the team, its members were assured that the landing area was secure and uninhabited.

The team moved by closed truck to board an airplane at Tan Son Nhat Airport, Saigon. The flight crew consisted of Taiwanese pilots and "kickers," the crewmen who pushed

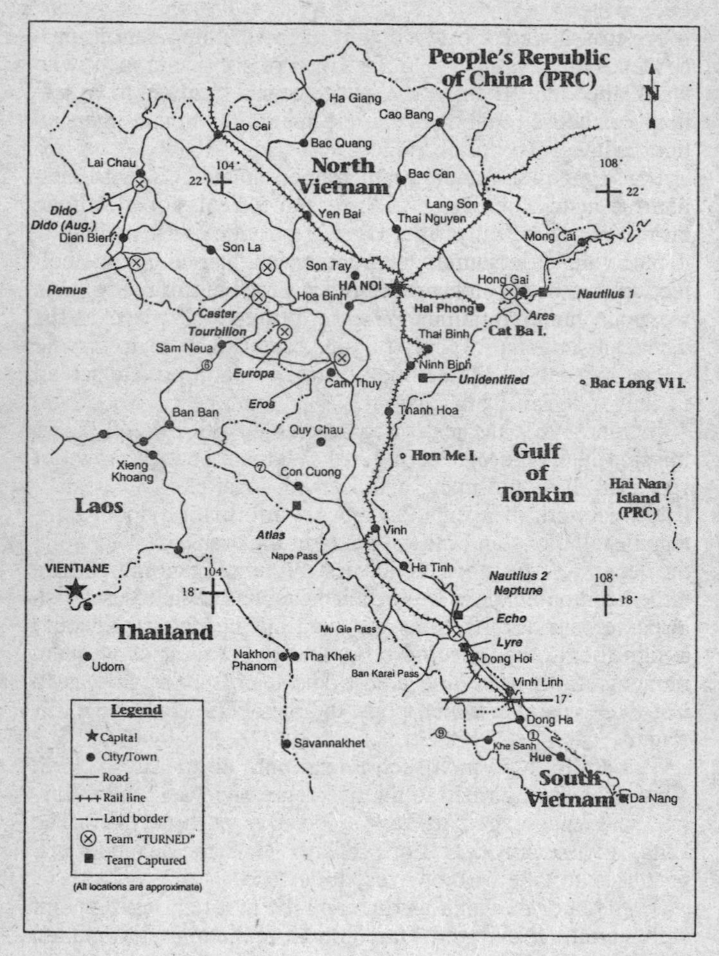

Figure 2. Agent teams landed and captured in 1963. (*graphic by Cindy Tourison*)

the cargo out during air drops. When the plane took off, it flew over the South China Sea and then headed north over open water. At times, it seemed to skim the tops of waves. After crossing the Gulf of Tonkin and Ha Long Bay, it proceeded toward the coastline, between the towns of Hon Gai and Cam Pha. As it approached the coast, the aircraft suddenly gained altitude and headed toward the team's planned midnight airdrop onto Yen Tu Mountain. Four large containers of supplies and equipment were dropped on the first pass. Then the plane circled, and the team exited at low altitude on its second pass over the target.

Once on the ground, team members homed in on their portable radios to locate the radio beacon dropped on the first pass and communicated with one another by using their small voice radios. Five of the six reached the beacon and began searching for the four containers of supplies and equipment and their missing team member, Cao Van Thong. At about five o'clock that morning, they located him. His parachute had not opened, and he had died when he fell onto some rocks. They located two of the containers and cached them in a cave for future use.

As the first rays of dawn lit the surrounding rocks, the team huddled to brew coffee and wait for more light to locate the other two containers. Their coffee soon finished, Nguyen Van Hiet and Bui Minh The were ordered to locate their missing supplies. With daylight, the team members found the entire area to be dotted with small state farms and other enterprises, none of which had been depicted on their maps. The area was anything but secure and uninhabited. Someone's planning certainly had been poor.[7]

Several hours later and a kilometer below the drop zone, Hiet and The found one missing canister on a grass-covered hill. Standing beside it were several local cattle herders and their animals.

They scrambled back up the mountain to report the loss of the container to Dinh Van Cuong, the team commander. This was an ominous piece of news because the cattle herders would report the container's discovery, and the commandos could expect an immediate and intensive search by local security forces. There was no time to set up their long-range radio to contact their headquarters, and it was obvious that the security situation would quickly deteriorate. They decided to split up; each man would try to evade separately.

They had given some thought to climbing down the mountain and getting to the nearby coast where they might be able to steal a boat and make for the open ocean. Unfortunately, the team's drop zone on the isolated rocky mountaintop made any downward movement extremely difficult, and it would be impossible to keep together. What at first had seemed such a secure landing site had now become a prison.

The supplies from the first two containers were abandoned. These containers held most of the team's medical supplies and other equipment. One reportedly contained money—lots of it—how much, no one knew precisely. Ngo The Linh had told them they were taking in four million dong in North Vietnamese currency to be used for certain unspecified tasks. He never mentioned where the money had come from and whether it was genuine or counterfeit. Also, a printing press for preparing leaflets was in one of the containers.

Throughout the day of 4 June, the team members were captured, one by one, by a mixed force of local village self-defense forces, members of the Public Security Service (PSS), and soldiers from the regular army. They were taken to Hon Gai City and locked in cells at the provincial temporary prison. The team was interrogated by members of the provincial PSS who asked about their training in the South and what they had done after arriving in the North. Strangely, there was no serious attempt to question them about any possible contacts with the local people where they were captured or about any other commando teams that they knew or suspected were in the area.

The interrogators admitted having recovered money from the team's containers but seemed only mildly interested in how much money they had with them. There were general questions about the team's signal operating instructions that had been destroyed by the radio operator before his capture. The interrogators seemed to know all about the commando organization and its activities. Curiously, one would later muse, they were never asked about the singleton agent known in Washington as ARES.

That December, the commando team was tried by a military tribunal of the People's Army of Vietnam area headquarters. The trial began at 10 o'clock in the morning; twelve hours later, the sentences were read. All team members were convicted of espionage and sentenced to prison. Because the unit had not opened fire, there were no death sentences pronounced.

Immediately after the trial, they were taken to Bat Bat Prison and locked in cells in the isolation detention area. Here, they found more than thirty captured commandos, agents from the airborne and maritime teams, including the two teams who had not been forced to operate under Hanoi's control. There was also one singleton agent, Nguyen Van Hong. No interrogation took place at Bat Bat, although several members of one boat crew were taken to Hoa Lo Prison for brief interrogation.

The team members passed the time quietly in their cells. Occasionally, they were sent out to cut grass and pick vegetables in the prison garden; other inmates were sent to an area near Son Tay to construct a new prison. The agents were surprised to see two or three very tanned Caucasians, one perhaps a Senegalese, who were working in the prison kitchen immediately outside the gate.[8] They learned that these men were French and spoke fluent northern Vietnamese. After a brief stay of about a month at Bat Bat, all of the commandos were moved to Yen Tho Prison in Phu Tho Province, where they observed the Lunar New Year of 1964.

That same July, a six-man maritime operations team of ethnic Nung commanded by Moc A Tai, a team now known as DRAGON, made its third attempt to land from NAUTILUS 7 for an indefinite mission into the area of Mong Cai, a stone's throw from the Chinese border.[9]

The DRAGON team members had received a general briefing at Hanoi by an American known only as "Robert" and a more detailed mission given by their own officers. Their mission was to attack an offshore North Vietnamese radar site and attempt to locate agents left in place during 1954 by Col. Vong A Sang when he withdrew his division of ethnic Nung to South Vietnam. The briefer emphasized that the Topographic Service had been in touch with Colonel Sang. Sang had identified his stay-behind agents but insisted that he had been out of contact with them since 1954. If DRAGON located Sang's agents, it was to use them in its own agent operations, which were to continue for an indefinite period. The team was cautioned to avoid the Chinese surveillance radar on Hai Nan Island that might spot them coming north into the Gulf.

A young boy saw evidence of their landing, and nearby fishermen alerted local security forces, which fanned out to capture the infiltrators. Trenh A Sam, the radio operator for DRAGON, refused to go on the radio for his captors.

While DRAGON had been preparing for its mission, a small reinforcement team was scheduled to be parachuted to Team EUROPA. Its C-123 and Taiwanese crew crashed into a mountain in Laos before the team reached its destination. A CIA paramilitary recovery team inspected the crash site and discovered that all on board had died in the crash.[10]

One month after the loss of DRAGON, NAUTILUS 7 followed that team into North Vietnamese prisons. One of the NAUTILUS 7 survivors recounted their final mission:

> Our maritime operations? Of course they worked! I'd been on eleven missions before I was finally captured.
>
> Our operations at Da Nang were under the Coastal Security Service. We did three things: conduct target reconnaissance along the North Vietnamese coast, insert agent teams, and conduct sabotage. The overall commander of the operation was Col. Le Quang Tung, the Special Forces commander, and Ngo The Linh was our senior operations officer. He had an American adviser named "Robert." Robert was based in Saigon and was described to us by Ngo The Linh as a lieutenant colonel working for the CIA and responsible for our operations. He was there in 1961 and may still have been there in 1963.
>
> I was always out drinking, raising hell, and running into our own military police. I had my story memorized. I'd just tell them I was from the Special Forces. I'd give them our unit postal number, KBC 4373, and that always took care of everything. On paper we were part of the Special Forces except for one thing: we had no military service number. It was all just a disguise.
>
> We had a small group of South Vietnamese Army

Special Forces officers at Da Nang, all regular military officers. The commander was Captain Dang. I think his deputy was Captain Phan. Captain Ly was the paymaster, and Mai Xuan De handled things like our fuel.

There was no question about who was directing our operations. We had two Americans there at the time; one was called John, and Captain Dang would interpret for him. The Americans would train us, assign us the mission, describe the characteristics of the target area, and lay out how we would enter it. The Americans had close-up photographs of the area they'd obtained from thirty miles out and they used them when giving our mission briefings.

We had seven fishing boat crews there, numbered one through seven. There were no markings on the boats, but we knew which was which. I got switched around quite a bit. I started with crew N2, then was switched to N4, and was on N7 when we were captured. We were more than just boat crew; we were also trained as frogmen.

I think we left on 13 August 1963. We reached Ha Long Bay on the fifteenth. I was in charge of the landing party, and I took five men with me in a rubber boat. When I checked out the landing site, everything looked all right at first. I knew it was an important mission because our commander told us we had cases of supplies, including one case reportedly containing four million dong in North Vietnamese currency and two cases of weapons and ammunition. The rest was supposedly regular supplies.

Our shore party had just finished checking the shore when our boat began receiving automatic weapons fire from a North Vietnamese Navy patrol boat, which came out of nowhere. Our boat was sitting about one hundred meters offshore, and it was getting hit. It had no choice but to move out to the open sea without unloading the supplies. This stranded some of us on shore. I heard later that our boat made it back to Da Nang on 17 August and reported the six of us had been killed and two of the crew were wounded. Cong, a Special Forces radio operator assigned on our boat, was one of the two wounded. Later, the North Vietnamese announced over the radio that we had been captured. That caused real confusion and anxiety for our families, who were told earlier we were all dead.

In my eleven missions before August 1963, I did not run into any problems. We did lose a crew from one of the shorter boats, N1, right at the end of 1961. I'd been on that boat originally and we'd gone in at least twice to the mouth of the Gianh River on mining operations. We blew up one North Vietnamese boat on one of the operations. The problem was the boat was just too small. On its last mission it went into Hon Gai and was lost without a trace.

N4 went into Hai Phong twice and returned. They were the crew on the boat which took in Thanh, the singleton agent who died later in prison. I had gone as far north as Mong Cai, up near the Chinese border, and into Deo Ngang, in Ha Tinh Province with N7. Then N2 was lost in about June 1962 while taking in a team of frogmen to plant mines on some boats. Those were our only losses. My crew, N7, was the last crew lost. After that I don't know what happened, but I heard from other commando prisoners there were some sabotage operations into Dong Hoi.

At the time we were stranded on shore, I couldn't figure out just how the North Vietnamese knew we were there. Then later, in prison, I heard others talking about a double agent and that he was the one we were supposedly going in to resupply near Hon Gai. He was probably the cause of what happened to us, but I'm not really sure.

I guess the North Vietnamese security forces didn't realize we'd been stranded. We set off in our rubber boat. We had no other choice. It was obvious we couldn't stay where we were. We rowed out into the open ocean and five days later reached the area of Kien An near Hai Phong City. We were really hungry by that point and figured if we made landfall we could get some food, water and might be able to somehow get back down south. We were captured outside Kien An on 20 August 1963. They took us first to Hai Phong

> and put us in Tran Phu Prison, where we were interrogated for five months. We were then placed on trial, convicted of espionage, and sentenced to twenty years at hard labor. We went to Bat Bat Prison for a short while and then to Yen Tho, where we were put in with other commandos. For the next nineteen years, it was just labor and reeducation. Nothing else.[11]

In May 1963, the Joint Chiefs of Staff directed Admiral Felt to develop his command's plan to support the "South Vietnamese" covert operations against the North.[12] In June, he forwarded Plan 34 to the Joint Chiefs of Staff. It was presented as based on an assumption that the increase in covert operations would somehow convince North Vietnam to de-escalate in the South.

Colby was still in the throes of Switchback and negotiating the turnover of covert operations to support Plan 34, as the People's Armed Public Security Force of North Vietnam faced the CIA's efforts to get the northern operations into higher gear.

PAPSF experienced the arrival of paramilitary commando teams in a veritable monsoon at clustered locations in separate regions of the country. Perhaps not surprisingly, in light of Washington's contingency preparations to strike the North, the teams of 1963 were dropped along lines of communication used to move supplies by road or rail from China across North Vietnam and into the panhandle. The following is paraphrased from one later North Vietnamese writing about this period:

> On the night of 4 June, three teams were dropped in three widely separated provinces: One five-man team landed in Lao Cai, one seven-man team dropped into Yen Bai, and one six-man team went in northwest of Uong Bi City. All were captured. On 7 June, one team was dropped into Thanh Hoa and another into Ninh Binh. Both were captured. On 9 June, one team entered Ha Tinh and another was deployed into Nghe An. They too were captured.[13]
>
> This veritable flood of agent teams led the PAPSF to be placed initially on a level 1 combat alert. This

was soon upgraded to a level 3 combat alert in the face of intensified agent team insertions.[14]

This flood was followed on 3 July by a team inserted into Ha Tinh, and another team was dropped over a wide area not far from Yen Bai. These teams were captured and their capture announced on Radio Hanoi. Interrogation of captured commandos revealed the teams had sabotage missions and were intent on monitoring the level of infiltration into Laos along Highways 217, 15, 7, and 8.[15]

On 12 August, a team of two men parachuted into Lai Chau to join REMUS in the far northwest. One of the survivors recounted their fate:

I volunteered to join the effort back in '61. I was an intermediate-level radio repairman in the army and I'd been transferred down to Saigon. A friend who'd been recruited, Lu The Toan, told me he'd joined the Topographic Service and it sounded exciting. I was twenty-two years old at the time. We were all young and ready to go tackle anything.

So, I applied and nothing happened. Then, in 1962, I was approached by one of the recruiters, Dao Vinh Loc, the one called Mau. They needed more people and I guess I had the skills they were looking for. Two of us, Be Ich Dam and I, were set up in a small apartment on Tran Hung Dao Street. They finally told us we were going to be trained to carry out demolition attacks, and we began a slow training program, first at Thu Duc and later at Long Thanh. Long Thanh was just being set up then, in 1963, and Major Hung had the training program there in the old ammunition depot they were converting over for us.

I knew a lot of guys who'd already gone up North, and no one had come back yet. The families were still getting paid, and I'd see them from time to time. It was only natural; I'm ethnically White Tai from Lai Chau and my uncle, Dieu Chinh Thach, had gone in as the radio operator with REMUS in 1962 so I was in touch with his family all the time.

One day our operations officer, Dao Vinh Loc, told us we were going on our mission, and Ngo The Linh personally briefed us on our mission. The two of us would parachute into Lai Chau to join REMUS. We were told we didn't need authenticators because REMUS had reported everything was fine but they needed demolitions people. REMUS had developed a resistance base and needed demolitions people to blow up bridges and roads so we were going to do that. They gave us some recognition phrases to use if we wanted to make sure the people we met were REMUS, but we were told that there was absolutely nothing to worry about.

We left on 12 August in a C-123 transport with a Taiwanese crew. We came in over the landing zone, and there was a light on the ground. The kicker pushed four huge cases out the rear, and then we jumped in at a little under one thousand feet. The cases had our explosives and food, at least that's what we were told in Saigon.

We landed at about two in the morning and stayed where we landed that night. At about 8:30 that morning, we were moving around when we were approached by someone wearing black pajamas, his rifle over his shoulder. My first thought was that this is one of the people REMUS has recruited, but I was wrong. When he got right up to me he unslung his rifle, pointed it in my face, and told me to raise my hands. It turned out he was a cell leader from the People's Armed Public Security Force leading some local militia to find us. I never did see where our four cases landed.

They kept us right there for three days and then escorted us under guard to a nearby camp. That's where I met Dieu Chinh Thach from REMUS. He was working there on the radio. We stayed there a week before being taken to Thanh Tri Prison outside Hanoi, and I stayed there until 1969 when we were shipped to Phong Quang.

I couldn't keep much from them, not really. I had two identical maps in my pocket that Ngo The Linh gave me, one of which I was supposed to turn over to Dieu Chinh Ich, the commander of REMUS. The maps covered an area from Dien Bien Phu off to the east along Route 41 to the road junction at Tuan Giao. He'd marked all the bridges along the road we were supposed to blow up in red pencil, and it was obvious what it meant. I wasn't willing to say anything at first, but they took me to Dieu Chinh Thach, my uncle, and the first thing he asked me was how his family was doing, were they still getting his pay every month. I told him they were fine and still getting paid on schedule.

After our capture, it became clear that the existence of our teams was being used by the North's security service to propagandize the people about the American presence in Vietnam. For example, we were teams of Vietnamese but the state security cadre always called us "American commandos" (biet kich My). That phrase was intended to link the Americans to our operations but not because it was the Americans who were directing us. Instead, the cadre were trying to emphasize the fact that Vietnam had been invaded by the United States and that the United States had invaded North Vietnam. Most of the rural people were uneducated, they believed what the cadre told them, and this helped them mobilize the people against us, even though we were all from the same ethnic minority stock.[16]

REMUS later reported its most recent grand success to Saigon. It reported mining a road on 18 November.

Team SWAN parachuted in on 4 September, Team BULL went into Ha Tinh on 7 October, and Team RUBY was captured following its landing in Ha Tinh at the end of December. RUBY tried to evade to the south but was captured in nearby Quang Binh Province.[17] The capture of most of the teams was announced by Hanoi and dutifully recorded by the CIA's Foreign Broadcast Information Service.

Throughout the fall, Plan 34 experienced delays in implementation. At CIA Headquarters, Colby would later describe the delay as the result of negotiations between the CIA and the Pentagon over the final transfer of the paramilitary effort and the follow-on Plan 34.[18] Colby was also embroiled in

Washington's inability to decide whether or not the United States should continue to support President Diem. The die was cast when Washington refused to intervene with Saigon's plotters, who launched their coup to topple Diem on 1 November.

By 3 November, both Diem and his brother, Ngo Dinh Nhu, were dead, as were Le Quang Tung and his brother, Le Quang Trieu. Within little more than two weeks of President Diem's assassination, Gen. Paul Harkins, the MACV commander, cabled Admiral Felt that, in his judgment, the "climate is right" for the military's covert operation to go into effect.[19]

By the end of 1963, planners at the National Security Council's Special Group, those on the staff of the Special Assistant for Counterinsurgency and Special Activities (SACSA) in the Office of the Secretary of Defense (OSD) at the Pentagon, and those at the CIA would have been well aware that the Vietnamese team concept was as singularly unproductive as General Lansdale's paramilitary teams were in Cuba during the summer of 1962. And still the Vietnamese teams went in, much to the delight of Hanoi. From Hanoi's perspective, the key remaining questions were timing and the conditions that would nudge Washington to launch bolder attacks against the North. For Washington, the answers would be found in Plan 34A, the bombing scenarios strongly urged by the Pacific Command in Phase II of Plan 34A, and the sustained bombing scenario supporting Plan 37 soon to be studied intently by Special Assistant to the President for National Security Affairs McGeorge Bundy.[20]

THE PRICE OF IGNORANCE

1964–1965

Part 2

5

MCNAMARA'S SOLUTION

THE EXECUTION OF the top leadership of Diem's covert effort directed by Tran Kim Tuyen removed a political liability that had long embarrassed some Washington officials. Compounding the leadership problems in the coup's aftermath were the inevitable instances of anti-Diem sentiment being used by certain Vietnamese to settle old scores, whether real or imagined. Repeatedly, individuals were singled out and charged with being secret agents for Diem. The managers of the northern and southern programs survived, many of whose agents had been actively involved in internal security operations for the Diem government, as the CIA finally seemed prepared to bequeath the covert operation to the Pentagon.

At Hue, Ngo Dinh Can and seven others, including Phan Quang Dong, were executed. The late Colonel Tung was replaced as Special Forces commander by a coup participant, Brig. Gen. Le Van Nghiem. Nghiem served only a matter of months before being replaced by Col. Lam Son. Both officers inspired little confidence in those they commanded and upon whom Plan 34A would ultimately rely for implementation. Tran Khac Kinh, Tung's longtime deputy, was also removed during the coup. The Vietnamese Army's Special Forces Headquarters continued as the command line over Ngo The Linh, who continued to direct the critical northern operations of Office 45 required to support Plan 34. Tran Van Minh, longtime head of the southern covert intelligence operations of Office 55, was still in command of that effort, but he faced evidence of shattered morale within the border security forces that the CIA had long supported and directed.[1] He would be imprisoned for a month before U.S. pressure secured his release.

For the paramilitary team agents still in the CIA's Saigon safe houses, the first visible indication of their transfer to Pentagon control occurred in mid-November 1963, when their operations officers began moving them, one team at a time, to Camp Yen The, also known as the Quyet Thang Training Center, east of Saigon near the town of Long Thanh. Their team Vietnamese operations officers explained that the move was necessary to confirm how many teams had existed under Dr. Tuyen's organization and to verify the identities of the agents in each team.

At Long Thanh, they found their new home to be the site of a conventional military training center. Other agent teams had been in training there since earlier that year. One former team deputy commander recounted how they were compromised at Long Thanh:

> We had been recruited to conduct a secret war against North Vietnam. Both the existence of the individual teams and the identity of individual members had to be kept from prying eyes, even the eyes of members of other teams. It was for everyone's protection. No one, except one's own team members and those operations and training officers responsible for us, had any need to know that we existed. We all knew we might be captured, and we knew that the less we knew the better it was for all of us.
>
> When you brought us to a central training center, regardless of the reasons why you felt you had to do it that way, you violated that fundamental rule of strict compartmentation inherent in the secrecy necessary to the type operations you hired us to conduct. For example, when I got to Long Thanh, I could see that there were a score plus other teams and I got to know the members of these teams. I heard their regional accents, and that meant I could deduce where they might be headed. I also found out that no team had ever completed its mission and returned from North Vietnam. This meant that I had learned too much.
>
> It was never supposed to have been done that way.

You compromised us by violating the most basic rules you told us were underlying our whole operation. Besides, you had supported President Diem and then stood by while he was murdered. If you did that to South Vietnam's president, we had no illusions that you could get rid of us just as quickly.

You cannot imagine what coming to Long Thanh did to our morale. The CIA had taken great pains to keep us totally ignorant, but your American military then put us all out in the open where everyone could see everything. We may not have liked the way the CIA did things, each team being hidden away in a separate location, but we accepted that arrangement as a necessary way this kind of operation had to be done.

Bringing us to Long Thanh told us you didn't care about the secrecy any more. You may not have meant to say that, but that's what it meant to us. And, if you didn't care about the secrecy anymore, that told us you didn't care about us either.

What happened? We began to have desertions. That was something which did not happen that much before the Diem coup. It didn't happen all at once, of course. But, by the start of 1964, it had begun and as time went on the desertions began to rise. Why should we have worked for you when it was obvious you didn't care about protecting us?[2]

This agent's observations are borne out by the former chief of the covert paramilitary operations in the South:

I'm sure they felt that way, and I don't disagree with his conclusions. After November 1963, we were in a period of turmoil and there were no responsible leaders. No one knew who would be in charge, and it was difficult to find someone to make a decision about anything. I had been scheduled to brief General Stilwell on 1 November about southern covert operations, but that meeting never took place because of the coup. It wasn't rescheduled for two months, until January 1964. It was just after the first of the year that General Stilwell came to me and I finally briefed him. He asked

> me to stay on, and I told him that the morale was gone in the CIDG [Civilian Irregular Defense Group] forces. Perhaps we made a mistake by keeping them so ignorant. We never told them what it was all about. We did this for their own protection. I guess we never prepared them for what might happen if they were captured.[3]

On 20 November, with turmoil in Saigon and two days prior to the assassination of President Kennedy, senior officials from Washington met with officials from Saigon and the Pacific Command in executive session at Honolulu. Their tasks included evaluating the situation coming out of the chaos that followed the demise of the Diem government and working out details for the final transfer of the intensified program of covert operations against North Vietnam.[4]

Attending the meeting with CIA Director John McCone, Colby was well aware that, in 1961, President Kennedy had directed that the CIA's paramilitary operations be prepared for turnover to the Pentagon and that the subsequent two years had evidenced a slow turnover of those operations.

Colby recalls that transfer process:

> The [1961] conclusion was that if it's a big paramilitary operation, it should be turned over to the military. And so that was the conclusion. When we were ordered to turn it over we turned it over, both the northern operations and the southern operations.[5]

By 1962, however, Colby had hard evidence of North Vietnam's capture of his teams and, in some cases, of its control of team radio operators' transmissions. This knowledge came from radio operators who dutifully followed instructions and alerted their controllers that they were being forced to transmit by their captors.

"That," Colby emphasized, "I remember vividly."[6]

Colby recalls that such messages coming from deep inside North Vietnam were not just saying the radio operators were controlled by the North Vietnamese. They sent Colby a larger message:

> The message sent to me was that the thing wouldn't work. So, stop doing it. But, it did take my deputy to come up and beat me over the ears with it. My deputy, Bob Myers, came to me with a summary of the lack of success in our operations in the Soviet Union, in Korea, and in China, to say look, they aren't being any more effective here so why don't you knock this damn thing off! That's when I took the position that let's close that down and do psychological warfare. That was just at the time of the turnover. The military did want to take them over, there's no question about it.[7]

Colby recounted the crucial November executive session in Hawaii when he brought his professional concerns to the attention of Defense Secretary Robert McNamara: "I stood up. I said, 'Mr. Secretary, it won't work.'"[8]

"What was McNamara's response?" I asked Colby. He answered without hesitation:

> He didn't answer. I don't think there's any doubt that McNamara thought he was doing the right thing. Shift it over to the military, get the military to put its power behind a program like this, and then it will have a strategic impact. You know his passion for numbers. If you do three thousand, you get more than if you do three hundred. It isn't necessarily true. He was thinking that the additional power that the Defense Department could put behind it would make it effective. I think that's genuinely what he thought. Tragic guy, McNamara. It fascinates you what influence does to people.
>
> You remember his talk with Des FitzGerald? A famous one, when Des says, "Mr. Secretary, it isn't going very well." He said, "Oh yes it is! Look at all the numbers here about what. We're adding this much and that much," and Des said: "Mr. Secretary, with all due respect, in the war there's something more important than numbers: it's spirit." And he said McNamara looked at him and didn't understand a word he was saying. Never talked to him again.[9]

CIA intelligence analyst George Carver offered his own perspective on the atmosphere at this juncture:

> When Diem was overthrown, his overthrow came as a surprise to the Communists. They realized there were a lot of problems, but they didn't realize precisely what was going to happen and they did not have a hand in his overthrow. In fact, they were very carefully kept out of it. [After Diem's death the North Vietnamese were] faced with a great opportunity and a great risk. The risk was that after the inevitable period of shake-up, they would get a post-Diem government that had Diem's strengths without his weaknesses and that to them spelled disaster. The opportunity was to strike while the iron was hot and before [the successor government] could get settled. They began in 1963 really escalating their level of military activity.[10]

On 26 November, four days after the death of President Kennedy and with Lyndon B. Johnson newly sworn in as president, the National Security Council issued National Security Action Memorandum (NSAM) 273 reaffirming a continuation of U.S. policies previously enunciated under Kennedy. Harkening to an earlier period of lower threat long overtaken by events, it reiterated support for an independent South Vietnam and the aim of withdrawing one thousand U.S. troops by the end of 1963. It also spoke of ending the insurgency in the three northern South Vietnamese Army corps areas by the end of 1964 and ending the insurgency in the Mekong Delta by the end of 1965. As to covert operations against North Vietnam, "plans were requested for clandestine operations . . . against the North and . . . up to 50 kilometers into Laos."[11]

Although NSAM 273 provided a formal mechanism to restate existing U.S. objectives following the change of chief executive, the National Security Council's assessment echoed a view that was antiquated, inconsistent with the times, and at serious odds with behind-the-scenes efforts to increase U.S. involvement, not decrease it.

What was Washington's national strategy at that point? Colby said:

> Just hold on by your teeth. In the first place, the entire strategic thinking was tied up until November 1 on the question of Diem or not Diem. That was the only subject in town for at least five months before. Thereafter, immediately, the question became what the hell do we do now? How do we put something together so that the whole thing doesn't disappear?[12]

Washington reached out to that corps of Vietnamese covert operational teams (whose efforts were still controlled by the Special Group through Colby at CIA), now in the final stages of official transfer from the CIA to the Pentagon, which each echelon in the military's chain of command argued on paper would be able to send a message to Hanoi. George Carver disagrees with the Pentagon's official view of any special value in the plan, set forth in its historical documents:

> Thirty-Four Alpha was an activity from which I didn't really expect very much. It was primarily a paramilitary activity devoted to sabotage and other things. Intelligence production was only secondary or tertiary on the priority scale. But, I thought that it was worth trying. The intelligence it produced? I can't recall any particular nuggets that came out of it that were of exceptional value. I think, again, it was an effort worth making, even though you had to realize that the effort was not likely to be very successful.[13]

By early December, the Pentagon's covert operations managers began to intensify their attention on the necessary procedures to take over the CIA's covert operations into southern Laos. As later to be experienced by MACSOG in Saigon, Washington withheld authorization for the transfer of the Laos operations to the Military Assistance Command Studies and Observations Group (MACSOG) and retained them under CIA control. Washington's messages to the military command in Saigon alluded to the 1962 Geneva Accords on Laos, and the prohibition on foreign forces there, as the crux of the problem, which was still under review.[14]

In the context of Kennedy's decision to transfer paramilitary operations to the Pentagon, the Special Group had no difficulty in approving the CIA's operations into Laos during 1962–63, following the 1962 Geneva Accords, while using U.S. Army Special Forces trainers and South Vietnamese Army Special Forces. Now, however, Washington balked at transferring the same paramilitary operation to the Pentagon.

Did the United States wait for a unified South Vietnamese national leadership before continuing with the covert operations? Did the historical picture of turmoil in Saigon effectively preclude Washington from moving ahead against North Vietnam independent of political consent from the government of the Republic of Vietnam? Did the loss of Col. Le Quang Tung and the absence of Dr. Tuyen so immobilize the Topographic Service that United States–directed covert operations could not be conducted absent approval from Saigon's national leadership?

Part of the answer to these questions can be found in the fact that, while the U.S. military and diplomatic chiefs were complaining about Saigon's musical chairs, South Vietnamese Special Forces and Ngo The Linh continued to respond to U.S. desires following the death of President Diem and before the formal implementation of Plan 34A. Thus, the United States moved forward on a firm course of action independent of Saigon political approval through private arrangements between U.S. military and CIA officers and those key South Vietnamese officers who had survived the coup and had the authority to order continued deployment of the covert maritime and airborne agent teams.

The first post-Diem operation took place on 5 December 1963, as Team RUBY parachuted into the spine of the Annamite mountains in Tuyen Hoa District adjacent to the Lao border. Its mission was to establish a behind-the-lines base and await further orders. Within hours, it was locked in combat with North Vietnamese border security forces and was captured on 6 December. The team's primary radio operator was later executed for having fought so hard to resist captivity.

There was always some lag time between the insertion of a paramilitary agent team and the possibility of a judgment regarding success or failure. With the covert maritime operations forces, the judgments were much more immediate.

One sense of the problems lurking on the horizon soon surfaced from the covert maritime portion of the forces to be committed to Plan 34A. As one former frogman described:

> In November 1963, the covert maritime operations force of newly trained Vietnamese frogmen from the Coastal Security were sent from their port base at Da Nang on their first practice mission. Their target was the South Vietnamese Navy base at Cua Viet, an estuary south of the Demilitarized Zone. Unfortunately, the winds were too strong and their boats were unable to land.
>
> The next mission, the first with a significant U.S. Navy presence, was against a target inside North Vietnam. It was launched in December 1963 against North Vietnamese boats at the mouth of the Gianh River in Quang Binh Province, the headquarters for North Vietnamese naval forces in the southern half of North Vietnam and within easy striking distance of the covert maritime operations base at Da Nang.
>
> The day before the December 1963 mission, the frogman team was restricted to base. Their U.S. advisers brought in aerial photographs of the North Vietnamese boats and covered all the details of their operational mission. The first mission was aborted because of bad weather in the target area, and the boats returned to Da Nang.[15]

The dismal prospects and an early lack of success notwithstanding, the November executive session in Honolulu reaffirmed support for the decision to escalate covert operations against North Vietnam as embodied within Plan 34-63, a concept fully endorsed by the Defense Department the previous August and with the obvious knowledge that key officials would issue the required orders. In this case, it came from Ngo The Linh, who was responsible for all northern operations, as well as those in neighboring Laos and Cambodia.

The November meeting had ended with the CIA and Defense Dcpartment agreeing to develop a joint plan for intensified covert effort against North Vietnam. Plan 34 and its successor, however, acknowledged that success required both full support from the South Vietnamese, something which did not exist, and an operating environment that had already changed so markedly as to make the plan obsolete.

On 15 December, the updated proposal, a joint plan known to the military in Saigon as OPLAN 34A-64 and by the CIA under the code name Plan TIGER, was forwarded to the Pacific Command in Hawaii. The Pacific Command, already aware of its substance and with a certain knowledge that the fundamental concept had been approved in Hawaii the previous month, rubber-stamped the plan, recommended approval of its twelve-month program, and forwarded it to the Joint Chiefs of Staff on 19 December.[16]

On that same date, as an indication of the Pentagon's level of preparedness to implement the covert plan still in the approval pipeline, the navy established a Mobile Support Team at Da Nang to augment the Navy SEALs, Marine Corps reconnaissance, and covert maritime operations staff already on station. The new team was formed from the American crews who had just delivered new motor torpedo boats (PTFs) to Da Nang. The crews formed a boat training team and a separate repair and maintenance team to train the South Vietnamese who would man the Norwegian-manufactured NASTY-type PTFs that were to be used in the maritime raids against North Vietnam. After arriving at Da Nang, the team members learned they would be serving as advisers, not boat operators; they were totally unprepared for an advisory function. Because of a navy-wide shortage of mobile training teams and SEALs, the teams arrived there for temporary duty only and would be replaced by others on expiration of their brief tours.[17]

On 21 December, Defense Secretary McNamara returned from a visit to Vietnam and formally informed President Johnson about Plan 34A-64. The available history of the period claims that the South Vietnamese national leaders had not been officially informed of the plan.

Effectively dismissing the need for South Vietnam's political commitment to Washington's covert program, McNamara felt confident enough that the South Vietnamese would follow orders to recommend formation of an interagency committee with representatives from the State Department, Defense Department, Joint Chiefs of Staff, and CIA. They were to examine Plan 34A and recommend appropriate actions to be taken.

Secretary McNamara then informed President Johnson that Plan 34A-64 was an "excellent" mechanism. Through increased covert attacks against the North, he argued that the North Vietnamese could be persuaded to rethink their infiltration of South Vietnam. As if to buttress his position, McNamara issued a gloomy prediction that something dramatic had to be done: "Current trends, unless reversed in the next two–three months, would lead to a neutralization at best and more likely to a Communist-controlled state."[18]

Such a statement effectively repudiated the forecast in NSAM 273 issued on 26 November, specifically the thinking that U.S. troops might be withdrawn and the conflict largely under control within a year and a half.

Although McNamara might have been overly optimistic at the outset about the potential for success of Plan 34A, his pronouncements were not shared by those such as George Carver:

> I know McNamara made that sort of glittering statement but I don't think people actually involved considered that these were very reliable conduits for sending messages and also, the very way they were structured as paramilitary operations, they were not channels for sending messages.
>
> Our policy was somewhat event driven out of Hanoi. It was to keep the Vietnamese Communists from being able to dictate South Vietnam's political future at gunpoint. Our messages were muted. What we wanted to do was to encourage [the North Vietnamese] to negotiate by stressing our implacable resolve but the problem is that you can't have one speech made by your negotiators in Paris and at the same time while you yourself are making a speech in Dubuque, Iowa, about how you're anxious to get out of Vietnam as quickly as you can, without having the text of both speeches land on the desks of the appropriate people in Hanoi at about the same time and without [the North Viet-

namese] realizing that your Dubuque speech is more important than your Paris speech.

The idea was to conduct paramilitary activities, harass, pinprick, go out and collect intelligence, but the idea that there was any deep political belief behind them certainly wasn't apparent to those who were involved in them at the time. Thirty-Four Alpha was at best an occasional painful pinprick but it was not a major strategic vehicle.

There was never a serious negotiating group [in North Vietnam]. This was one of the things that bedeviled us during the course of the war. We were interested in settlement; the [North] Vietnamese were interested in victory. There was an unbridgeable psychological gap there.[19]

In retrospect, Dr. Carver found Washington's problem-solving approach at this juncture, increasingly applied in the later stages of the war, to be fundamentally flawed:

We didn't realize that this was not [a typical] labor-management [problem]. Labor asked for two dollars an hour and management offered one dollar an hour. They both know they're going to settle somewhere around a buck fifty and the winner or loser experiments on whether it will be one forty-eight or one fifty-two. That analogy bore no relationship to the Vietnam situation whatsoever, and there was never a serious group wanting to achieve a "negotiated settlement." They wanted political control over the South and were determined to achieve it.[20]

Colby offered further views on the portrayal of the covert program he prepared and still indirectly controlled, which McNamara was now portraying as something that might send a message to the Hanoi regime. As Colby recalled, the phrase "send a message" was all the vogue in those days. As applied to the language of Plan 34A, it was meaningless. Colby explained:

> Those who used the phrase "send a message" didn't know what they were talking about. They didn't know what the message was. Except that America's determined.[21]

Did the United States have a strategy?
For Colby, the answer was:

> No! You know, we carried [the operations] on. I mean, CIA was going to cancel them by 1965. I had come to that conclusion. The record had been so devoid of success. There hadn't been anything really successful, and the military reaction to that was you CIA guys think too small. You know, we've got to think bigger. That's a respectable position, you know. I'm not going to quibble with that.[22]

Another CIA official shares Colby's and Carver's assessments, though in a much blunter vein:

> [CIA Director John] McCone found Lyndon Johnson colorless and crude in intelligence matters. . . . Increasingly, the president sought intelligence information almost exclusively from Secretary McNamara and the Defense Department. McCone's advice simply was no longer actively sought by the president. . . . Secretary McNamara . . . became more and more assertive. . . . The "tell it like it is" derived from photo intelligence that existed in the Kennedy administration was changed, with McNamara insisting that the Department of Defense, through the Defense Intelligence Agency, assume prime responsibility for intelligence reporting in support of military forces in the field. . . . McNamara and the Joint Chiefs began to control tightly the flow of information to the president. . . . One DIA briefer stated that the president "got very depressed and hard to handle when shown bad news."[23]

Thus, by the end of 1963, a program that Colby knew to have been a failure in 1962 and had so informed Secretary McNamara in November 1963, was miraculously transformed on paper from a CIA low-level espionage operation into a magic bullet ostensibly to send a message its designers had never intended, and most at the CIA were aware that it would never be effective against its target. New military commanders, however, were now assigned to carry out an impossible mission, soon to be dubbed Operations Plan (OPLAN) 34A.

6

PLAN 34 ALPHA

ON 2 JANUARY 1964, the interdepartmental committee reported its analysis of Plan 34A-64 and outlined the approved concept for the four types of forces to be employed by MACSOG (see Appendix 2).

The covert operations force under the authority of OPLAN 34A would carry out an increasing level of physical and psychological harassment, to include air strikes against appropriate targets inside North Vietnam. Plan 34A would be divided into three phases of four months per phase, and the level, mix, and scope of covert operations to be employed would increase by phase as approved in Washington. Officially, the objective was portrayed as designed to make clear to Hanoi that it would incur substantial costs if it did not reduce its infiltration into the South.[1] To ensure that each new step was carefully calculated to achieve specific results, a new operation was not supposed to take place until the previous operation had been analyzed.

On 16 January, the Defense Department directed that the responsibility for the covert operations against North Vietnam be assigned to General Harkins's command in Saigon and reiterated the tasks for the various covert operation components as contained in the 2 January recommendations of the interdepartmental committee.[2]

Three days later, on 19 January, Plan 34A-64 was formally implemented through a joint State Department–Defense Department–CIA message to the three corresponding U.S. mission components in Saigon.[3] This message emphasized that the actions approved were the most feasible and promised the greatest return for the least risk. Washington pointed out that certain covert operations would require the government of the Republic of Vietnam to accept responsibility for them should they become known. It was noted that no one had as yet coordinated this program with the new Saigon leadership.[4] On 21 January, the Joint Chiefs of Staff sent detailed procedures to the Military Assistance Command Vietnam that MACV was to follow when obtaining approval for the covert operations it would carry out under the authority of Plan 34A as approved in Washington. The message made it clear that Washington's operation required South Vietnamese approval, but it sidestepped the issue of continuing differences in policy and strategy and, if such differences existed, what alternate arrangements might be undertaken to resolve them.

As envisioned in Washington, there would be an approved list of targets for each phase. From this approved list, General Harkins would provide the Pentagon with a list of those operations that he intended to carry out during the following thirty-day period. Upon receipt of the general's proposal, the Assistant Secretary of Defense for International Security Affairs (ASD/ISA) would review the proposed operations and secure their approval from the White House and Department of State. Once the targets on the thirty-day list were approved, General Harkins would be required to request formal approval from Washington prior to actually carrying out each approved attack.

Also on 21 January, Ambassador Henry Cabot Lodge was finally able to brief Gen. Duong Van Minh in Saigon about Plan 34A. He advised Minh that the highest levels of the U.S. government had approved the plan and he hoped for an early review, agreement, and implementation by the Republic of Vietnam's national leadership.[5] There was no immediate response from General Minh. Such silence notwithstanding, Vietnamese counterparts of ''Cheney's'' Special Operations Group were already deploying their teams into the North.

Three days later, MACV officially established the military organization that would carry out Plan 34A's implementation by its forces in South Vietnam, the Special Operations Group (SOG) under the command of U.S. Army Col. Clyde R. Russell.[6] In its first official history, SOG recounted its initial mission and philosophical doctrine governing the covert operations to be conducted:

> SOG was organized on 24 January 1964 as the Special Operations Group under the direct supervision of the Chief of Staff, MACV. Its mission was to execute an intensified program of harassment, diversion, political pressure, capture of prisoners, physical destruction, acquisition of intelligence, generation of propaganda, and diversion of resources, against the Democratic Republic of Vietnam (DRV). Policy guidance for the conduct of special operations, as received from Washington in March, was based on the philosophy that such operations were desirable. The overall plan [at MACV] was designated MACV OPLAN 34A. The mission of the organization was directed by the [Joint Chiefs of Staff] to be an intensified program of action against North Vietnam. Initial manning was austere and operations depended largely on [temporary duty] augmentation.[7]

The covert operations to be conducted by SOG were divided among the four organizational groups it employed: covert airborne agent operations, air support, covert maritime operations, and psychological operations. The airborne group, by far the largest in terms of agents, was to conduct "small scale demolition operations, collection of intelligence, interdiction of lines of communication and limited psychological warfare operations."[8] To carry out these operations, SOG inherited from the CIA approximately 169 Vietnamese paramilitary agents now located at the covert operations training base at Long Thanh.[9] On the South Vietnamese side, Maj. Ngo The Linh provided the Vietnamese command line down to the actual agent teams, all under the South Vietnamese Army's Special Forces Headquarters headed by Col. Lam Son.[10]

The maritime operations group was to conduct raids against North Vietnamese coastal targets, including "facilities, Swatows . . . bombardment of shore installations and long-range probes."[11] The force to conduct these operations would be known outwardly as the Naval Advisory Detachment Da Nang and known within MACSOG by its classified title, Maritime Operations Group.[12]

Plan 34A was seemingly dealt a setback on 28 January when Gen. Nguyen Khanh, commander of South Vietnam's forces in the northern quadrant of South Vietnam known as I Corps, arrived in Saigon in civilian clothes and was joined by Gen. Tran Thien Khiem, commander of III Corps surrounding Saigon. They replaced General Minh and temporarily immobilized Saigon's government.[13] This meant that a new group of leaders had to be briefed and their approval secured for Plan 34A. Still without formal South Vietnamese government approval or interest, Washington moved inexorably forward on 1 February and advised General Harkins of the Defense Department's approval for implementation of Phase I of Operations Plan 34A with an approved list of thirty-three targets for action by the Special Operations Command (see Appendix 3).[14]

In February, SOG attempted to carry out the first six covert missions from the approved target list for Phase I. Five missions were intended to resupply agent teams inherited from the CIA. Four were unsuccessful, and the fifth air-dropped supplies to one team. The sixth mission was an unsuccessful attack in February against North Vietnamese boats anchored at the mouth of the Gianh River in coastal Quang Binh Province. Heavy seas overturned one of the boats, and nearly all the mines and weapons were lost.

In March, less than two months after assuming formal command of the paramilitary operations, Gen. William C. Westmoreland, future commander of U.S. forces in Vietnam, met with Secretary of Defense McNamara, General Taylor, and Ambassador Leonard Unger. At this time, they reached further agreement on carrying out Plan 34A and prepared to launch Vietnamese special forces into Laos under what would become known as ill-fated Operation Leaping Lena. Washington still had no indication of political approval for the covert operations from the South Vietnamese national leadership, and there were now indications that the earlier optimism of a Saigon-supported operation was being replaced by frustration.

SOG's official history continues:

> In the execution of approved actions under OPLAN 34A we should not press [the South Vietnamese] to put over-riding priority on resources they require for successful prosecution of the counter-insurgency effort. U.S. resources will be made available. Approved actions under OPLAN 34A constitute a desirable but not fundamental program from the Washington point of view. . . . After the visit . . . a report was made to the National Security Council. The report was considered and approved by the President at a meeting of the National Security Council on 17 March.[15]

A thirty-two–page message from the National Security Council, issued as a result of the 17 March decision in Washington, authorized MACSOG to proceed as a matter of national policy and under the guidance of the Department of State. A subsequent message from the Joint Chiefs of Staff to the Pacific Command and General Harkins stated that the Assistant Secretary of State for Far Eastern Affairs had been designated to coordinate the execution of the recommendations contained in the report.[16]

As SOG recorded in its official history, the defense secretary's early optimism in December 1963 was now replaced by a position that SOG would not be able to accomplish much. This implied, in part, that the notion of slowly escalating measures against Hanoi designed to reduce infiltration was no longer considered valid. Such admissions notwithstanding, there is no evidence of any attempt to reexamine the fundamental hypothesis underlying the operational plan now moving ahead as South Vietnam's covert operations managers moved forward, ostensibly still without Saigon's national political support.

SOG's command history evidences Washington's rethinking that resulted from the March 1964 National Security Council's decision:

> We are acting against the Democratic Republic of Vietnam (DRV) by a very modest [covert operation] which is so limited that it is unlikely to have any significant effect. (U.S. policy in Laos and [Cambodia] was touched on.)[17]

This further evidences that, by March, Washington had changed its views on the assumptions underlying Plan 34A-64, so boldly championed by McNamara the previous December; a change that occurred as CinCPac (Commander in Chief, Pacific) Plan 37 was being quickly moved through the planning phase. Plan 37, upon implementation, assumed that direct U.S. air strikes were taking place in North Vietnam, air strikes having been embodied in Plan 34A as one of the higher notches on the ladder of escalation.

Phase I of Plan 34A continued into March as eight missions were attempted. Six were unsuccessful, but the air support element reported one successful leaflet drop over North Vietnam and the maritime operations group reported one successful mission against a coastal target. The Vietnamese frogmen at Da Nang had a different view on the potential success of covert maritime missions and the true meaning of MACSOG's monthly numbers.

As one frogman recounted, his first mission that March had been to attack boats at the Cua Ron estuary in coastal Nghe An Province. When the frogmen arrived at Cua Ron, they found that the North Vietnamese boats had moved and there was insufficient time to complete the mission before they had to return to their PTFs. Vu Duc Guong, a survivor of the next raid, recounts what happened then:

> Our mission was on the morning of 12 March 1964. We were supposed to plant mines on North Vietnamese naval craft at two separate locations at the mouth of the Gianh River. There were four of us. When we arrived at both locations we found there were no boats! We were getting frustrated after nearly five months of unsuccessful missions, and I decided to go ahead and find a target of opportunity. We were in the brush off the beach when North Vietnamese boats suddenly appeared in the Gianh River.
>
> We knew we couldn't get off the beach and we could still hear our PTF's engine off the coast as the North Vietnamese were yelling from their boats, and we started moving out to the South along the coast. Then came the sound of weapons firing. Gioi and Ngu had moved out separately, and it must have been dur-

ing this initial firing that Gioi was killed and Ngu was captured. We'd almost reached the southern boundary of Quang Binh Province when the two of us were captured. There was evidently a large-scale sweep operating after us, and they had local self-defense militia forces, members of the police, and the regular army all around us. We were captured on 15 April 1964.[18]

Guong was aware that his own mission on 12 March was followed by another unsuccessful assault on 15 March when Nguyen Van Sac, a member of the coastal assault force, was apparently captured on the beach. Sac had served with French Union forces before 1954, and this had become a black mark against him. Guong continued:

I remember hearing the sound of Sac's mission on 15 March. There were sounds of 57-mm recoilless rifle fire from off the coast and the Public Security Service personnel told me that the sounds were coming from another maritime team attempting to rescue us. I think it was in May 1964 when I confirmed that Sac was in a cell adjacent to mine. He was sentenced to death in July 1964, taken out after the trial, and executed there at the prison by a firing squad.

I was tried in about June, together with Nguyen Van Le. He and another frogman named Gin had been part of a seven-man team sent in to check out the beach conditions in Quang Binh Province, but they were surprised by North Vietnamese forces. They were both ethnic Chinese and members of my frogman training course, but later on they had been reassigned to the coastal assault element. Gin was killed at the time Le was captured. Le was sentenced to death during my own trial and then taken out and shot by firing squad.

In September 1964, we were moved to Central Prison No. 3. By this point, the U.S. bombing was already taking place, and the inmates of prisons such as Central Prison No. 3 and Yen Tho were moved out of the permanent prisons into scattered rustic prison camps they called *trai so tan*, meaning a "dispersed prison." I didn't care a lot about these things at the time. I was a prisoner. That's what I was for the next fifteen years.[19]

The loss of the frogmen at the Gianh River base occurred as another mission was taking place to the north. An assault team attempted to destroy the Ky Anh Bridge in neighboring Ha Tinh Province. Voong A Cau and Chau Henh Xuong were left in the water off the target when their team was discovered before reaching its intended target. Three days later, they were in Public Security Service cells at Ha Tinh City.[20]

The results of the first operations by the covert maritime forces under MACSOG's management have been portrayed as discouraging to those outside SOG.[21] Such portrayals belie the fact that those making them were fully aware of the assumptions, thrust, and pitfalls of the obsolete plan known as 34A.

For example, Ambassador Lodge reported that the maritime operations were having no effect on Hanoi.[22] Later, Adm. U.S. Grant Sharp, CinCPac Fleet Commander, reported that the North Vietnamese "defensive posture in potential areas may be more extensive and effective than originally assessed" and viewed the "lack of adequate intelligence" as a factor in the failure of the maritime operations.[23] In South Vietnam, General Westmoreland began calling for more intelligence information on North Vietnamese coastal targets that could have an adverse impact on the 34A operations, but the Pacific Command responded that the sabotage targets were "more difficult to reach than was visualized at the time (Operations Plan 34A) was written."[24]

MACSOG found desertions increasing within its agent teams. In some cases, the original teams of six to ten men had been cut in half. In order to maintain some semblance of functionality, MACSOG's counterparts in the South Vietnamese Army recruited a small number of additional agents and instituted a program combining under-strength teams into new teams, whose size would match the missions listed in the approved targets under the Pentagon's Plan 34A-64.

In April, MACSOG launched six more missions, five of which it considered successful. On paper, it might have seemed that something had finally gone right.

7

"THEY" WANTED INSTANT RESULTS . . .

LESS THAN COMPLETE agreement on the state of the agent teams transmitting from North Vietnam existed between the Americans and their South Vietnamese counterparts. For Plan 34A to have any credibility, these airborne teams would have to be defined as "safe," not "dirty." "Safe" meant that the teams had reached North Vietnam safely, had set up their operations without being captured, and were now actually carrying out the actions reported to Saigon. If they were safe, the CIA's paramilitary concept and the philosophical underpinning of Plan 34A were valid. This also would imply that the CIA had turned over to the Pentagon a force capable of carrying out the Plan 34A mission planned for it by Washington.

"Dirty" meant that the teams had been captured and were operating under the control of the North Vietnamese. This would invalidate the potential for their success in carrying out Plan 34A. Colby had already advised Defense Secretary McNamara that the concept was not viable, but nothing suggests that he raised any concern that the CIA was transferring teams to the Pentagon that had been captured and "turned" by the North Vietnamese.[1]

If there was a possibility that the Pentagon was inheriting dirty teams, clarion calls of caution should have been heard. Such alarms could have been based on the CIA Plans Directorate's knowledge of nearly identical deception operations more than a decade earlier when CIA paramilitary team agents failed in Eastern Europe, particularly Poland. Although Colby acknowledges that his deputy reminded him of these very lessons before the crucial November 1963 executive session in Hawaii, it is evident that Colby failed to transmit adequately the import of the lessons learned by the CIA.

Washington's strategy underlying Plan 34A almost demanded that the teams transmitting from the North as of January 1964 be deemed safe. The pressures on the planners in Washington were no less intense than the pressures on those in the field. Thus, the very existence of six safe teams provided McNamara with the ammunition required to sustain the illusion that Plan 34A was viable.

Early in 1964, Col. Tran Van Ho took command of the Vietnamese counterpart of Colonel Russell's SOG, still named the Topographic Service. Colonel Ho went on record as questioning the usefulness of such teams and wanted to end the long-range team operations soon after assuming command. His entreaties were turned aside by Colonel Russell, and the operation continued. Some U.S. officials might have questioned the viability of Plan 34A and the fact that the operative assumptions already had been overtaken by events, but there is no statement on the record that anyone went so far as to say the teams transmitting from the North were dirty.

One individual who knew the risks in a parallel area was Gilbert Layton, the CIA's sage paramilitary operator from 1960 to February 1964. His CIDG program was now under the Pentagon's operational control, and his views already had made him less than popular with General Stilwell.

Layton knew that hostile forces might have penetrated his CIDG and cross-border teams, but he believed that he had a competitive edge of nine to one unless there were more hostile forces than he estimated. In the case of *his* teams and on the issue of capture and hostile control, Layton had the means to do something about such situations. But, distant North Vietnam was not Laos.[2]

The reality of total enemy control, under which the teams were transmitting from the North, was the very thing that Layton and others like him feared most. The import of this fact went beyond the exposure of Plan 34A as illusionary. It also meant that Hanoi was using precisely the same scenario against the Allies that had underwritten the Allies' success against the Germans on the eve of D day in June 1944. This should have been apparent to the military, as well as to those in the CIA who had adopted the World War II model for their operations into the North, but there is no evidence that it was.

Former CIA officer Samuel Halpern offers a more sobering assessment of the fundamental problem with the agent operations transferred by the CIA to the Pentagon: the lack of counterintelligence. He explains:

> There was none, to the best of my knowledge. There was a difference of view between Jim Angleton and Bill Colby. Angleton was in charge of the Counterintelligence Staff at Headquarters and Colby was the station chief in 1961. Colby just did not look at the South Vietnamese, and he did not want time and effort to be spent on it.
>
> The Saigon station did not have anyone seriously conducting the counterintelligence function until the late 1960s and later. Colby's views about Angleton and counterintelligence did not change after he left Saigon and became chief of the Far East Division. He differed with Angleton's view of things.
>
> Angleton had other ideas which people did not accept. For example, the Chinese-Soviet split of 1959 was said by Angleton not to be real. Although some officers agreed with Angleton, the general feeling was that the split had indeed taken place.
>
> Angleton could only encourage people to conduct the proper security checks, and he could not stop an operation on his own. In the case of Saigon's paramilitary operations, to the best of my knowledge, there was no attempt to examine the North Vietnamese penetration of the South Vietnamese and nothing was done to see what the South Vietnamese were doing to monitor the station.
>
> I do not think that anything was known in Saigon. The station did not really look at the penetration issue, whether from Hanoi or from Saigon, and that was a fundamental problem. Since Saigon was not looking at the penetration issue, it would only have been dealt

> with when it became a problem. The station obviously felt it was not a problem.
>
> If the teams were known to be under hostile control, the Pentagon should have been so advised. I do not believe the Saigon station knew they were under hostile control because, once again, no one was looking at this concern. I think it is a fair statement that if there were teams transmitting from the North and it was believed that they were *not* under hostile control, it would have been believed that everything was working as hoped for. I can only assume that if the teams were known to be under hostile control, it is reasonable to conjecture that further paramilitary operations would have had to be carefully reexamined. If CIA learned that the teams were under hostile control, CIA would have advised the Defense Department, but it rested with Defense to do something about it since it was a Defense Department operation after the CIA transferred it over.
>
> In general, the object of "radio play" would be to keep an agent alive. Officers in the field and at headquarters, if they were aware that an agent was under hostile control, would not disseminate the information from the agent but might be able to use what the agent was sending to assess how the agent was being used and what the other side wanted us to believe.[3]

Hanoi apparently wanted Saigon and Washington to believe that the paramilitary operations were possible, and the CIA did not confirm that all of the existing teams were under hostile control. This suggests that Hanoi knew what the CIA and its key counterparts knew.

Five agent teams were inherited by the Pentagon—ARES, BELL, REMUS, TOURBILLON, and EASY. (A sixth team, EUROPA, had been on its radio under hostile control, but it ceased transmitting the day after the official formation of SOG, which did not consider it a viable team.) Although the teams were under hostile control, their mere existence provided a vital underpinning to Plan 34A. Without them, it is questionable that the plan would have been accorded such a high degree of apparent confidence.

On paper, the five inherited teams had originally totaled thirty-two agents. Over the years, Hanoi had claimed the loss of four agents: one agent in TOURBILLON supposedly was killed during the airdrop into North Vietnam, and three members of BELL reportedly had died as the result of illness. Hanoi wanted Washington and Saigon to believe that the remaining twenty-eight agents were still considered "safe" when they were officially turned over to Colonel Russell in January 1964.[4] By year's end, Hanoi reported two more members of TOURBILLON had died in an ambush on 24 December. Hanoi's reports were all fiction.

Colonel Russell now prepared to carry out Washington's mandate. Thirteen more teams, with a total of eighty agents, were readied, a modest effort in light of Colby's impression that McNamara would do with quantity what the CIA had been unable to do with quality. But, the total was much less than the CIA had lost in the North during 1963. The facts, however, are that employment of these teams had little to do with the growing insurgency in South Vietnam and precious little to do with infiltration into the South.

Eight teams totaling forty-three agents, to reinforce four of the five teams previously under the CIA, were deployed in far northwestern North Vietnam. All were north of the 20th Parallel, and most concentrated along a rough line at the 21st Parallel.[5] This was the approximate southern edge of the area above which Chinese antiaircraft, engineer, and other support forces were based in northern Vietnam throughout the latter half of the 1960s.

Four more teams were to go into Nghe An Province that summer, all astride Highway 7 used by the Vietnam People's Army to funnel men and equipment into the Plaine des Jarres in the northern Lao province of Xieng Khouang. Statements from surviving agents and the verified location of their deployment document that their mission was to monitor the movement of North Vietnamese forces into North Laos. If successful, they would have functioned as part of an early warning net reporting on hostile forces that infiltrated into far northern Laos to face the CIA's paramilitary force of ethnic Hmong under General Vang Pao. Also, they could have met the Pacific Command's targeting needs as the Seventh Air Force and Seventh Fleet prepared to launch Yankee Team operations in this same area.

Deployment of these teams provides hard evidence that, at some point, the concept underlying Plan 34A's function of sending a message to Hanoi to reduce its infiltration into South Vietnam was no longer taken seriously. In addition, the actual landing sites and operation areas for all thirteen teams demonstrate that they had nothing to do with South Vietnam. Obviously, the Special Group, Department of State, CIA, and Pentagon covert operations staff knew this, and Plan 34A was modified. SOG's teams became the eyes and ears for CIA concerns about northern Laos, rather than a means of sending a message to Hanoi about infiltration into the South. Further, by the spring of 1964, Plan 34A was being treated as effectively unworkable. This is evidenced by obvious side arrangements developed at the National Security Council level to use the agent teams in support of U.S. operations in Laos, rather than in South Vietnam.

One team ended its training mission abruptly in South Vietnam on 28 December 1964. Twenty-eight members of Team CENTAUR died when their C-123 crashed shortly after takeoff during a severe rainstorm. The plane went down in heavy jungle on the side of the Son Tra Peninsula, an area of friendly control just outside the port city of Da Nang. The available records of the incident indicate that the team had been scheduled for a training mission, but MACSOG staff at Da Nang had not wanted the C-123 to take off because of the extremely poor weather; Saigon ordered it off the ground anyway. The remains of a U.S. Special Forces sergeant and the U.S. Air Force pilot were not located.[6]

The CIA retained an interest in Plan 34A by virtue of its retention of the psychological operations effort that was integrated into each paramilitary team mission. For example, MACSOG and the CIA still defined the teams as also being psychological operations (psyops) teams, and each one had an assigned psyops mission. In this way, the CIA had a direct say in how the teams were employed (see Appendix 4).

In another area, the CIA reviewed and approved, or disapproved, the monthly recommended target lists and kept track of the actual launch authorization. Although more aggressive operations were envisioned in the original fifty-five

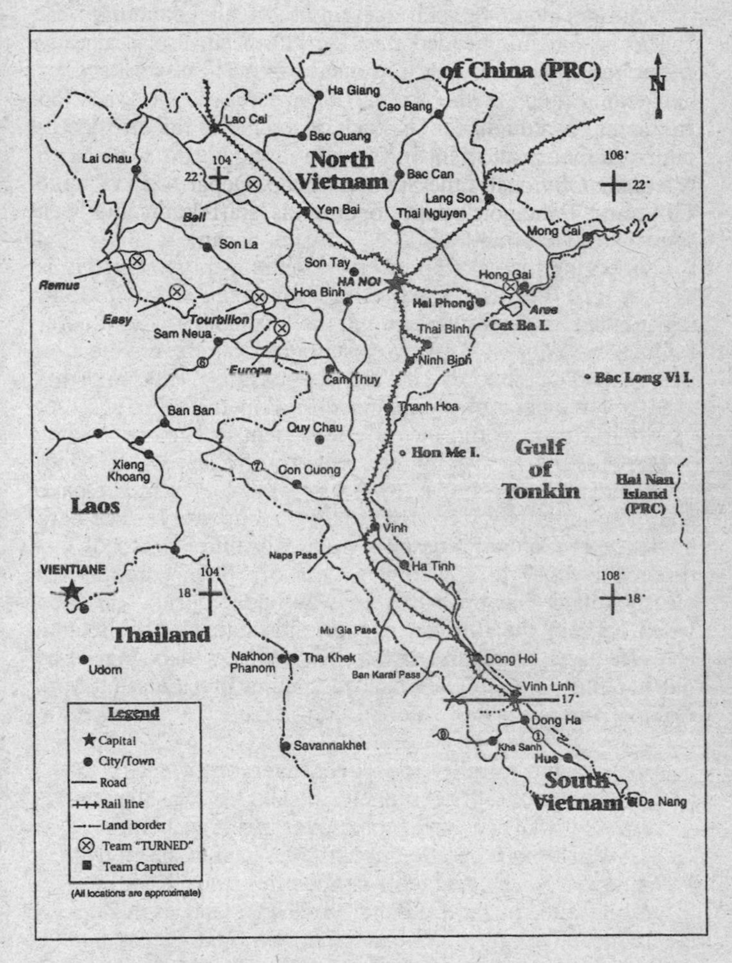

Figure 3. Agent teams reporting in January 1964. (*graphic by Cindy Tourison*)

targets approved under Phases I and II of Plan 34A, for example, landing Special Forces teams along Highway 7, the CIA did not approve such operations for final execution.

The new teams headed into the North and those already there were placed astride road and highway networks. Certain teams then on the air or to be deployed during 1964 would be placed adjacent to each of the major rail lines coming from China into North Vietnam (see Figures 1–3). Such a deployment could have provided information to the Pacific Command about events on the ground, if the teams had been safe. They were not.

Comparing the 1963 and 1964 team deployments, it is evident that the teams authorized for deployment in 1964 represented an actual decrease in the level and scope of paramilitary activity. This would support Colby's recollection that he had planned to end the operation by 1965 and that U.S. covert operations were winding down. By the summer of 1964, it also would have been evident in Hanoi.

MACSOG's first commander then took steps that effectively negated any impact that his agent teams might have had, assuming they were able to do the impossible. The hard evidence is Colonel Russell's pointedly bitter personal testimony in 1969 to the Joint Chiefs of Staff, words which clearly reflect the pressures he was under during 1964–65 when he sent the thirteen agent teams into North Vietnam and effectively sealed their fate. His remarks also suggest he did not fully appreciate what was taking place around him. Colonel Russell stated:

> Once . . . the military took over, everyone wanted immediate results. The biggest mistake . . . was the assumption that we would take over assets in being. . . . The Maritime Operation consisted of about six divers. None was ever capable of conducting a successful operation and, in fact, did not conduct a successful operation. The physical setup in Da Nang was not conducive to good maritime operations and the boats were all SWIFT-type boats which were limited in their capability, so our maritime operation assets consisted of very little. . . . [7]
>
> AirOps were being conducted by [the Chinese Na-

tionalists] who, when they transferred over, refused to work for the military. As a result, we never had a successful operation. . . .[8]

I think we could have done anything up and down the coast within the limitations of the weight of the ammunition and people you wanted. We could have had complete control of the coast up to a depth of three or four miles, in my opinion, and could have done any type of operation . . . [including] putting radios on the dining room tables or doing anything we wanted to, e.g., blowing up water systems. . . . When the boats went in, the North Vietnamese people were scared and their regional forces or national guard forces were no problem at all. . . .[9]

I don't think we'd have had a problem recruiting people had we been talking about a guerrilla operation up there where they could have gone up and recruited people and started tearing up the countryside. It's hazy where the restriction came that they could not recruit. . . . We could never get concurrence for this in-country . . . the ambassador was not strongly for it even though the military wanted to push it. . . . I do know at one time in one of the briefings that we were told to tell the team that they would not make contact with the populace in the north and at that time it became strictly a psychological operation as well as an intelligence collection operation. You don't collect much intelligence when you're hiding in the hills trying to protect your life. Really, they were running around the woods dropping a few hand-printed leaflets and it was a totally unacceptable operation. We should have real strong guidance on what we want these people to do. . . .[10]

When we took over, we found we had a number of so-called agents who were not qualified for anything. They had been on the payroll for a good number of years and they liked the pay, but when we got ready to commit them, they were not eager to go. We did commit most of these people without very high expectations at the time they were launched. We didn't expect them to come up on the air in some instances; we knew they would surrender immediately upon landing,

> and they did. This is one of the reasons for our lack of success in the first of the airborne operations. . . . The original assets we had in this effort were not capable of going anywhere and we had to get rid of them; at the same time, we couldn't turn them loose in South Vietnam because they'd been briefed and rebriefed on operations in North Vietnam. Our solution was to put them in the North; many of them were captured. . . . [11]
>
> I do feel that once you commit teams you must do everything you can to support them if you're going to have the effort succeed. You can't abandon people because invariably the word gets out and the rest of the teams will know. So, once you make up your mind you're going to quit supporting the people you have in an area, you better cancel the entire operation because its chances are real limited.[12]

By January 1964, when Russell inherited his pool of approximately 169 agents, the CIA and the Pentagon had already lost more than 200 agents in North Vietnam before and during Operation Switchback without any visible signs of success. And yet there were still recruits to be located, men all too willing to join up and quite willing to go into North Vietnam and fight the good fight.

The agent teams that Colonel Russell had inherited were largely operational teams of agents already in training for several years. Many had agreed to undertake missions into areas matching their language and knowledge. Switchback ended such careful planning, however, and agents heading north during and after 1963 were not necessarily from the areas where they were to operate. By the end of 1964, Russell had committed half his agents in thirteen teams out of the average number of fifteen teams available in 1964 (see Appendixes 1 and 5).

New agents were brought in to rebuild his teams. By January 1965, he had 197 agents, 115 of them in teams ready to be launched into the North. That spring, some agents were reassigned from long-range teams to build the cross-border teams then being formed for operations into Laos under Operations Plan 35A.

Thus, by the end of 1965, nearly all agents inherited in

January 1964 had indeed been sent into the North. This confirms that Russell did precisely as he described to the JCS: he did "get rid of them all." *All* of them. Few remained to be "turned loose."

Colonel Russell appears to have sincerely believed he had to commit the Vietnamese agents he inherited as the only alternative to releasing them. It has been suggested by some former U.S. officials that pressures from higher commanders may have led him to undertake such actions.

General Westmoreland insists that there was no pressure from him personally.[13] He viewed the operation as something born in and nurtured by Washington. He also acknowledged that, if there had been any pressure, it might have come from General Stilwell, his chief of staff, who was directly responsible for oversight of MACSOG; previously, Stilwell had been in charge of the CIA's covert paramilitary operations in the Far East.

Russell clearly believed that the teams largely surrendered. Even as late as 1969, he seemed unable to comprehend that he had sent his teams to their capture by hostile forces waiting for them on the ground. The evidence from survivors confirms that only Team BOONE did, in fact, surrender. Apparently, however, it did so at the point of a gun and under rather unusual circumstances.

The issue of whether the team members were so totally incompetent and cowardly that they had to be sent to their deaths or captivity can be addressed. They were, after all, the product of several years of Special Forces training by largely volunteer Green Berets who worked hard at what they did. If they and the agents failed, it was not for want of trying. Their failure can be attributed to a fundamental flaw in the concept and the lack of integrity on the part of those who continued to carry out an outmoded plan without due regard for the immediate and long-term consequences of their actions. It cannot be blamed on the efforts of those who died trying to turn black into white.

And still they went in: the men whom Colonel Russell found to be of so little use, the type of force that General Stilwell was intimately familiar with in another war but absent the CIA's in-depth lessons of hostile intelligence penetration learned during that war. The defense secretary had led the president to believe that the agents could take a message that most of those involved knew would be ignored by Hanoi, but the CIA remained silent about the potentially serious fly in the ointment.

8

THE SUMMER OF '64

PRESIDING AT A special political conference in Hanoi on 27–28 March 1964, Chairman Ho Chi Minh warned that in the event of a war, the Vietnamese would be united, Vietnam would gain support from all Socialist countries, and Washington would be turned against by both the American people and America's allies.[1] Ho made his predictions as Ministry of Public Security officers, operating through the captured agents, continued to mislead Saigon and Washington into believing that all was well behind the enemy's lines.

While Ho was issuing his warning, the Ministry of Public Security prepared to remove one minor annoyance to the Politburo with the summary arrest of the Revisionists. By April, the most senior Revisionists were imprisoned in a military security prison adjacent to Bat Bat Prison.

The Revisionists' link to the Soviets was explained in Hanoi as being the result of a Soviet espionage plot to recruit otherwise loyal Vietnamese to be spies for Moscow. Isolation of the Revisionists at Bat Bat Prison was apparently intended to mask their removal from Hanoi's political scene during the period in which Washington was attempting to send its undeliverable message to North Vietnam.

That Hanoi was following China's position of non-negotiation was evident to Secretary of State Dean Rusk at the time of the Gulf of Tonkin incident. He found Beijing to have little interest in helping to negotiate a settlement of the burgeoning conflict, whether unilaterally or through either the United Nations or Geneva process, a fact known to the State Department's intelligence analysts.[2] The Chinese were loathe to reverse their publicly stated position and thereby appear to be as much the appeasers as they had charged those inhabiting Moscow to be.

Hanoi's acquiescence to the Chinese position was a pragmatic acceptance of the need to follow Beijing's foreign policy, at least as a short-term strategy, its long antagonism toward China notwithstanding. For example, Hanoi required Chinese goodwill to permit rail transshipment across China of military equipment from the Soviet Union. China could shut down such shipments at its pleasure, or displeasure, as it did in the spring of 1964 when the Soviets attempted to ship high-performance aircraft across China to Vietnam. Hanoi required open supply lines, even if this meant temporary friendship with an old adversary.

The Politburo in Hanoi was also being tested. Its political credibility was at stake because of a three-decade claim that Vietnam's Communist party could guarantee the emergence of a unified Vietnam. Acceptance of an accommodation with the West would seriously alienate China and jeopardize Hanoi's goals in the South; thus, negotiation with Washington was not a serious option for the near term. This was not because negotiation was not an option per se, rather that negotiation in 1964 would have incurred political liabilities requiring Hanoi's preparation to conduct an approaching war without external support from the Communist bloc. This, Hanoi knew, was simply not possible.

During the planning stages of Phase II, Plan 34A, Admiral Felt, Pacific Commander, forwarded to the Joint Chiefs of Staff his recommendations on what the next phase should accomplish:

> Air strikes and aerial mining are the only physical destruction operations within the current GVN capability that provide sufficient impact to cause DRV [North Vietnam] to reevaluate their RVN [South Vietnam] and Laos activities. . . . I recommend that Phase II operations concentrate on intelligence collection, propaganda type psychological operations, the development of resistance movement cadre and intelligence nets, physical destruction by air attack and aerial mine laying.[3]

While the Revisionists were being imprisoned at Bat Bat that April and Admiral Felt was pushing for sterner operations against the North, MACSOG attempted six agent operations. Five were deemed successful, including a parachute drop on 23 April by a four-man team to reinforce Team REMUS. The next landing was scheduled for Nghe An on 25 April by Team ATILLA.

After the members of Team ATILLA had completed their basic airborne, weapons, jungle survival, and intelligence training, they had attended a special two-week class before departing on their mission into North Vietnam. The purpose of the class was to bring them up to date on all the changes that had taken place since the Communists took over in 1955. This information was necessary for them to survive behind the lines.[4] The team was driven to a refugee reception center at Binh Hoa on the outskirts of Saigon, where all new arrivals from the North were sent for debriefing and processing before resettlement in South Vietnam.

The orientation, given by a South Vietnamese Army officer accompanied by a Viet Cong defector, covered current North Vietnamese administrative organization from the national level down to the village. The various security forces, such as the self-defense militia and the Public Security Service's border defense forces, were explained in detail. The instructors described the contemporary life in the North: how people lived, how they traveled within the urban areas, and the types of documentation they needed to transact the myriad details of their daily lives. The course also covered the system of rationing, how people queued up to purchase goods, the types of coupons that were issued, and how much people were allocated for such purchases.

All of ATILLA's members were natives of the North. They knew the language, customs, and geography from personal experience, although some came from provinces with distinctive accents and slight variances in their customs. The team now learned that a whole new vocabulary, nonexistent ten years earlier, had come into being. Some words occasionally used a decade earlier were no longer in common usage, and other words frequently used in 1954 were seldom heard. This made it relatively easy to identify a resident who

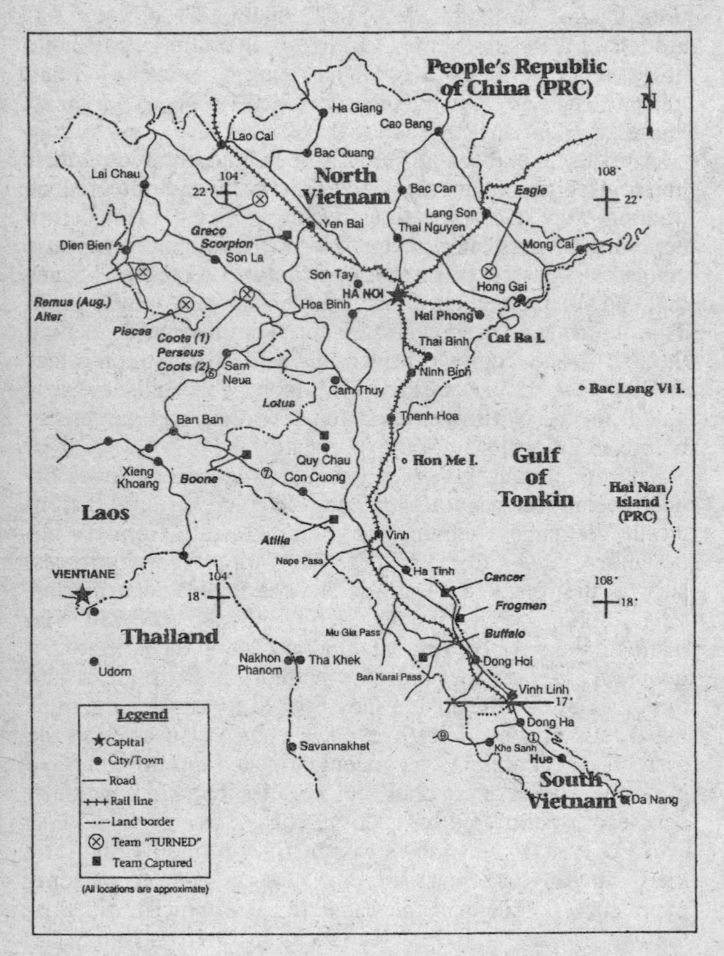

Figure 4. Agent teams landed and captured in 1964. (*graphic by Cindy Tourison*)

had lived there since 1955; anyone not familiar with the terms and their meanings stood out.[5]

After completing the course, the team left for its mission on a transport flown by a Taiwanese crew. Psychological warfare leaflets were dropped first, and the plane then flew on to drop the team at low altitude. Just prior to jumping, the team members saw people on the ground in the drop zone and refused to jump. The air crew became angry and returned them to Saigon, where they told officials the team would not jump.

Several weeks later, the team assembled again to receive another prelaunch briefing on its mission, designed to conduct reconnaissance on military and economic targets in the assigned area of operations. One specific target was the dam on the boundary of Thanh Chuong and Linh Cam districts. The dam was particularly important to the local economy because it controlled the flow of irrigation water for all of the farmers. The team was to be prepared to destroy it in the event of open armed conflict in the North. The team was also ordered to monitor all traffic on Highway 7 and attempt to determine the quantity and type of supplies being moved into neighboring Xieng Khouang Province, Laos. Obviously, air strikes would be necessary because the planned targets were clearly beyond the team's capability to attack and destroy. This implied that the conflict was heading toward a new level of escalation, with ATILLA being used to collect targeting information in support of future air strikes into the area of Highway 7.

The team had the capability to conduct sabotage in its assigned area, but it was not to initiate anything until receiving authorization from its headquarters. The briefer was most insistent that absolutely nothing could be done unless authorized.

Team ATILLA also had a mission to recruit agents, but it was not given any local points of contact. Team members would have to locate prospective agents and recruit them. At a later date, they were to receive information on whom to contact and where. The team was to carry out its mission in the North for a minimum of three months but not more than six.

As briefed, they would land in a mountainous area in

Thanh Chuong District, approximately seven kilometers inside North Vietnam from the border with Laos and north of Linh Cam District in adjacent Ha Tinh Province. The area of the immediate drop zone was unpopulated; the nearest local residents were at least a day's walk distant. The team was to move from its drop zone through the mountains for about three days to its first regrouping point. Once there and after determining that the area was secure, the team was to contact Saigon and receive specific operational instructions. The briefing officer produced what he termed "the most recent aerial photography," which showed no evidence of buildings in the area.

The briefer warned that ATILLA might encounter hostile North Vietnamese border defense security forces while it was moving. He identified by unit and location all battalion-sized North Vietnamese border defense public security forces that the team might encounter. The briefer emphasized that the only significant enemy forces in the area were of battalion size and there were no regular army division-sized units in the area where they would land. He also stated that battalion-sized forces did not represent an obstacle to the team's entry and that the border security forces were scattered in small platoon-sized teams, not concentrated as battalions. According to the briefer, there was no possibility that the North Vietnamese security forces could learn of the landing site, and the team's first encounter might come while en route to the regrouping site if a border defense patrol found evidence of its presence. The team members had to be particularly alert and guard against this possibility. They knew from earlier instruction what to do if they encountered such a force: If both sides spotted each other, the commandos would open fire first and attempt to wipe out the enemy force; if they saw the enemy force first and did not believe they were spotted, they were not to open fire.

Team ATILLA departed at 4 P.M. on 24 April from Tan Son Nhat Airport at Saigon and flew to Da Nang. The team was accompanied by its operations officer, Captain An, and an American wearing civilian clothes as far as Da Nang. After several hours on the ground there, the team members were loaded back into the C-123 transport. As they strapped into their seats, each man felt his own nervousness increase with the pitch of the aircraft's engines on takeoff. The pilot, co-pilot, jump master, and two kickers were all Taiwanese. Also on board were seven loads of equipment to be air-dropped with them.

At one o'clock in the morning, the aircraft made two passes over the drop zone. Six containers of supplies were dropped on the first pass; the seventh was the team's homing beacon. The six men parachuted from the plane on the second pass at a height of under one thousand feet. They landed relatively close together and used their small transistor radios to locate the beacon's beeping signal. This meant they were within five kilometers of the beacon, the beacon's range. Within thirty minutes, the entire team had assembled on the beacon, an absolutely essential device for airdrops where the commandos could not see each other after landing in difficult terrain.

They reached their regrouping point and searched the immediate area carefully for several days before establishing radio contact with their headquarters. Then they dug in to wait for the second radio contact and instructions. Two days after the first transmission, the men spotted several local residents approaching close to their temporary base. Confident they had not been seen, they remained in place.

One evening in early May, they heard sounds of people approaching. Dinh Van Lam, the team commander, dispatched two men to scout the visitors. They moved no more than several hundred meters before coming upon a patrol of approximately twenty well-armed soldiers setting up their bivouac along a stream. The hostile patrol was conducting a careful search and heading straight toward the team's location.

Lam decided to abandon their base immediately and head back west toward the drop zone. From there, they would evade into Laos and contact their headquarters by radio to arrange for extraction. The radio operator, Nguyen Van Hinh, sent off a hurried message reporting they were unable to continue their operation because of enemy activity and would withdraw in the preplanned direction.

The commander set off with two members of his team, and Nguyen Van Thi, his deputy, took the other two. As the North Vietnamese forces closed in on Lam's group, the team opened fire as they withdrew. The men were surprised when the encircling forces returned fire over their heads, obviously more interested in capturing than killing them.

After the initial skirmish and the start of their evasion, Thi's group agreed to split up and attempt to evade individually. They destroyed the radio and signal operating instructions and abandoned most of their equipment where it had been cached.

During their evasion, they saw indications that other teams had been in the area. While moving through the dense brush, a day's march due west of their base, they discovered the remains of risers from T-10 parachutes, the type used by the teams at that time. They also found 9-mm shell casings. This was the caliber used by the teams; the condition of the casings suggested that the shells had been fired perhaps six months earlier.

Nguyen Van Hinh recounted his capture:

> You know, [laughing] I must have seemed bizarre to the North Vietnamese soldier who found and captured me. I was exhausted and had fallen asleep several hours earlier. I had an automatic pistol stuck into my belt, and I was wearing a pair of American-made blue jeans my American trainer gave me at Long Thanh. Suddenly, I felt a booted foot jammed into my arm, which was reaching instinctively for my automatic. I opened my eyes, and the soldier just stood there with his AK assault rifle pointed at me. He just stared at me, and I stared back. Wearing those American jeans, I must really have looked strange. I'd been told not to take them with me, but there was no way I was going to leave them behind. One of the North Vietnamese soldiers later took them.[6]

The radio operator was captured early on the morning of 10 May. Most of the others were taken during the next several weeks; the last two were captured on 29 May when Lao Communist forces seized them in neighboring Laos and turned them over to North Vietnam. Throughout this entire period, the team members were kept tied up and under guard in the dense brush, while the border security forces recovered all of their weapons, equipment, and other supplies.

Thinking back on the circumstances of their capture, the commandos suspected that the border defense had located their landing zone by direct observation. It is quite easy to see clearly for two or three kilometers on a moonlit night. The border defense forces needed only to track the flight path of an aircraft flying along the high points of the mountains and then look for the deployment of parachutes, which would have been seen even at a distance.

The border defense forces, who were scattered throughout the mountains, listened for the sound of low-flying transport aircraft, tracked flight paths, and checked likely drop zones along them. If they were close enough, they could even pick up a team's beacon signal and home in on it to fix the drop location.

Nguyen Van Hinh explained:

> Don't forget, my own team was dropped into the North only once. But, there were many teams before mine and many teams after. These nighttime airdrops were almost always the same, and over a period of time the North Vietnamese border defense forces would have learned what to look for. One of the things, like with Team ATILLA, was an aircraft coming in at low altitude from the direction of the ocean, keeping to a flight line over mountain high points and then continuing into Laos before landing in Thailand.
>
> The aircraft which made our airdrop would have remained for a day in Thailand and then fly back to Saigon. There were no U.S. air strikes into North Vietnam until 5 August 1964, so it would be easy to identify which aircraft entering North Vietnamese air space were American. After tracking our operations for a year or so, they would have known what to look for.[7]

Hinh was interrogated immediately after capture. He was asked his name, date and place of birth, unit, position, and the team's planned mission. The interrogator was particularly interested in the size of the team and role of each member, the specific date his team had landed, the route it had taken after landing, the precise location of each place it stopped, and the identity of all other team members not yet captured.

Part of the interrogator's work was made easy because Hinh's 1:100,000-scale tactical map had been confiscated. It was a special type of map used by the commandos. Printed on thin, silky material, it was intended for stuffing into a pocket. The topographic information was highly accurate, and on it Hinh had marked their landing zone, the regrouping point, the route of travel between them, and the direction of withdrawal.

The radio operator was asked in detail about the prelaunch mission briefing but was never questioned about the aerial photographs that the team had been shown at Base 10. Later, other prisoners were asked about them in considerable detail.

Within three hours of his capture, Hinh was face to face with an experienced public security officer who had accompanied the pursuit force and was interested in only one thing. He wanted Hinh to operate his radio voluntarily "for Hanoi," but Hinh refused. The officer stayed with him but, after the first refusal, did not push the issue again. Hinh now understood why the pursuing force had merely fired over their heads.

By early June, Team ATILLA arrived at the provincial capital of Vinh, where each member was methodically questioned by provincial interrogators, except for information associated with the team's communications. Interrogations pertaining to communications equipment, signal operating instructions, and related matters were conducted by a special group of officers from Hanoi who said they were from "the Ministry" or "we're specialist interrogators who've come down from Hanoi."

Radio operators from other teams said later that these interrogators were already present at the time the commandos were first captured and it was they who made the first effort to recruit them. Attempts to induce the cooperation of these prisoners usually lasted no more than three hours from the time each was brought in. By that time, these specialists knew whether or not the prisoner was willing to cooperate.

The interrogators obviously knew the team's radio procedures. They knew that the first transmission had to include the safety signal, which had to be sent by the primary radio operator, and that the team commander had to be available at that time. If asked, the commander had to provide his personal safety signal, which only he knew, and other commandos could be asked for theirs if Saigon had any question about whether the team was safe or dirty. If anyone Saigon asked for was absent, the lack of a plausible explanation meant that the team was probably under hostile control.

On 15 July, the members of Team ATILLA were tried in public by a military tribunal at Vinh City. The trial lasted for three days, and the sentences were then handed down. All of them were convicted of espionage and soon moved to Central Prison No. 3, north of Con Cuong.

While Team ATILLA was still avoiding the North Vietnamese, the Joint Chiefs of Staff, with the concurrence of the Defense and State departments, authorized General Harkins on 5 May to begin joint planning with the South Vietnamese Joint General Staff for the June deployment of cross-border teams into Central Laos between Highway 9 and the town of Tchepone. On 12 May, Gen. Nguyen Khanh, chief of the Joint General Staff, approved the concept for the cross-border operations and the start of formal combined planning with the Joint General Staff.[8]

After General Taylor and Defense Secretary McNamara visited Saigon, U.S. aircraft from the force code-named YANKEE TEAM were flying over Laos. While in Saigon, Taylor and McNamara had heard General Harkins report that he could pacify South Vietnam in six months and would be able to reverse the situation if he was given command of the South Vietnamese military.[9]

Within MACSOG, details were being negotiated with the Joint General Staff to transfer ownership of the PTFs used in maritime operations from the United States to the South Vietnamese government. This was deemed necessary to permit denial by Washington that U.S.-registered boats were attacking North Vietnam. A cover story was prepared that would offer leases as evidence of the South Vietnamese using the craft for independent retaliatory strikes against the North. Documentation of the formal transfer, however, did not take place as anticipated.[10]

May, the last month of Phase I of Plan 34A, was drawing to a close. MACSOG reported two more successful paramilitary team insertions. On 19 May, a six-man team, designated Team LOTUS under the command of Tran Ngoc Binh, was dropped into mountainous Nghe An Province near the provincial boundary with Thanh Hoa.[11] Its mission ranged from attacking and destroying the Ham Rong Bridge in Thanh Hoa City to attacking the bridges from Thanh Hoa down to Highway 7, an overly ambitious plan for such a small team. LOTUS was captured just after landing, and its deputy commander, Nguyen Van Sinh, was executed. Arriving at the provincial temporary prison outside coastal Vinh City, the remaining members of LOTUS met the ATILLA captives.

Team COOTS parachuted in to reinforce Team TOURBILLON outside Lai Chau on 27 May. It was met by well-disguised members of the public security forces, who took the young agents into custody just off the landing zone.

The official record of Phase I, initially portrayed by Secretary McNamara as a vehicle to send a message to Hanoi, showed MACSOG had completed only eleven of the thirty-three missions approved by Washington for this phase.Twenty-two new missions were approved for Phase II, which began 1 June and was to run through 30 September, in addition to the twenty-two not completed in Phase I (see Appendix 3).

In June, Phase II started off with nine attempted operations. Eight were reported to have been successful—three maritime attacks, two air operations, and the insertion of three agent teams. The one unsuccessful mission was an aborted attempt to resupply one of the agent teams believed to be safe but was, in fact, just one more team that had been captured earlier and was under North Vietnam's control.

Also that month, the North's border defense forces were ordered to secure completely the border with Laos; prepare to defend against enemy attacks from the air; and secure the eastern coast of North Vietnam in Naval Patrol Areas 1 and 2, as well as along the DMZ. These measures coincided with a major North Vietnamese conference, held every five years, to discuss certain border defense activities, including border defense support of the program to capture and use the captured commando radio operators in the North's "playback."[12]

The agent team operations in the first month of Phase II

included Team BUFFALO parachuting into Quang Binh on 19 June. The team was quickly captured. The radio operators refused to cooperate and go on their radios for their captors. They were followed on 28 June by Team EAGLE, which parachuted into the area of a major rail line near Uong Bi, a major operating area of the double agent operating as Team ARES. As the members of EAGLE attempted to locate their local contact, they were attacked by local security forces and captured. Soon afterward, their radio began transmitting under the control of the Ministry of Public Security.

On the night of 17 June in the province of Yen Bai northwest of Hanoi, Team SCORPION prepared to jump into a new area on the south side of the Red River.[13] This was southeast of the location of Team BELL, which had been under North Vietnamese control since 1963. The Taiwanese pilot, copilot, and jump master were clearly tense when the SCORPION team members hooked up to jump. The rear ramp was down on the low-flying C-123 transport, and the men could see the lights from the town of Yen Bai as they flew south across the Red River.

Several minutes later, the jump master kicked out SCORPION's beacon and supply canisters. Then came a sudden bank and complete circle. On the second pass, the team jumped into the mountains from a height of less than a thousand feet. The planned drop zone was several dozen kilometers south of the town.

SCORPION's mission was to conduct sabotage along the railway line between Hanoi and Yen Bai, an action designed to reduce the flow of supplies coming into the North from China. The team had secondary missions of spreading antigovernment leaflets, collecting information, and recruiting local residents into agent nets. To help with its psywar mission, the team had leaflet bombs and a printing press in a separate canister, so that it could print leaflets once it was on the ground.[14]

As their parachutes rocked back and forth and they fast approached the ground, the men could see lights and people moving about below. Dang Cong Trinh's first thought was that the North Vietnamese knew of their drop. There seemed to be no other explanation for so many people in the drop zone. Some years later, the thought occurred that the low-flying transport might have given the team away. North Vietnam was not conducting low-altitude missions at night, and the team's C-123 must have drawn attention. Even with that possibility, there was no way of explaining why so many people were waiting for them on the ground.

Local militia, reinforced by public security forces and regular army, began closing in as the team landed. Dinh Qui Mui opened fire and was killed almost instantly by heavy return fire. Dang Cong Trinh and Nguyen Van Khai, landing close to one another, split up as they tried to make it out of the encirclement. Trinh was captured two days later. A few hours after that, Khai was the last team member captured. In a desperate attempt to break out of an encirclement, Khai killed several of his pursuers. For this, he was later executed.

Team SCORPION was taken to the provincial prison in Yen Bai City, where the men were isolated and interrogated for more than two months. Finally, before a large crowd of local residents at the city sports stadium, they were tried by a Viet Bac Military Region–level tribunal, found guilty of espionage, and sentenced to terms ranging up to life imprisonment. Afterward, they were loaded onto trucks and taken directly to Quyet Tien Prison, the home for those who would not cooperate with their captors.

The paramilitary agent teams arriving in the North that spring, teams such as ATILLA, were defined as psychological operations teams (see Appendixes 4 and 6). ATILLA, BUFFALO, SCORPION, and LOTUS had parachuted into the North with missions well beyond their capacity and at a time when morale in some teams had plummeted. Did someone, somewhere, have thoughts that these teams would be captured, their overblown missions an oblique message to Hanoi that Washington was prepared to escalate further?

To the notion of such a strategic psychological operations ploy, Colby offers his recollection about that period:

> You send a team in and you try to convince them they're going to do something pretty important. Otherwise, why the hell are they risking their lives? So, you give 'em a challenge like that but then you want to make sure you can control the damn thing. You

> can't just let 'em go and say, oh my God, six weeks later and try to stop them. They'd be out of control.[15]

If the psychological operations teams had been used as bait, would their psyops role be useful only if they were captured? Colby continued:

> I think the psyops idea was more the idea of building up a way of getting the words into North Vietnamese conversations that if you could get these teams to consciously say things in the local towns, that would go through the area. . . . That is what it was designed to do. Just get the word back there. Let the people hear it. . . . I don't think we had, at least I don't recall sending them up there with a very sensitive target to convince the enemy that it would somehow scare 'em to death. I think the idea of getting conversation running through North Vietnam about how futile this whole thing is, you know, the march South is such a disaster, lose so many kids and they disappear. They say goodbye and that's the last you ever hear of them, building up that dismay about the whole experience. I think that was the psychological thing we had in mind.[16]

Colby's recollection may be accurate. The team survivors, however, recall no such mission.

Ed Regan, one of the CIA officers who launched the teams from Da Nang and was back at headquarters as the Laos desk officer in the summer of 1964, sees it a bit differently:

> It is accurate to state that the teams which went into the North early in 1964 . . . were concentrated north of Highway 7 and in the mountains up to the northwest. We were involved in the coordination of their insertion. Why? Because there was pressure to keep sending in the teams. We knew the teams would not be able to survive in the populous lowlands so we sent them in somewhere where at least some of them might have had some chance of survival. We did not know at that time that the teams we were sending in were going to teams under hostile control. Once again, it was pres-

> sure to keep on sending them in and that pressure came from outside the agency, not from those of us on the inside in the [Plans Directorate].
>
> It now appears that our agency paramilitary operations were penetrated a lot more than we ever knew and that penetration was through our South Vietnamese counterparts. None of us in the clandestine service would have knowingly turned over a penetrated operation to the Pentagon if we had known it was penetrated. That would have been criminal.[17]

North Vietnam's preparation for the teams of 1964 began at the start of the year with the People's Armed Public Security Force disseminating Directive 57 that warned of an anticipated expansion in commando operations against the North. Thus, according to their accounts, the North Vietnamese were able to detect the maritime operations involving two frogmen at the Gianh River port on 23 February; a landing to attack and destroy the Khe Nuoc Bridge in Quang Binh Province on 16 March; and an attack against the bridge at Khe Luy, Ha Tinh Province, on 17 March.

During March, North Vietnam recorded a total of eight airborne agent team parachute drops into Yen Bai, Ha Bac, Quang Binh, Nghe An, and Son La provinces. In fact, there had been only three team landings. Nevertheless, the agent operations and a reported doubling in U-2 overflights were portrayed internally by North Vietnam as evidence that the war was escalating. By the end of June, Hanoi's Politburo alerted the border defense forces to be prepared for more enemy action involving increased maritime operations and air attacks. This was followed by the People's Army Joint General Staff directing a heightened alert status for the army. Given such alerts, it was almost anticlimactic when, on 30 June, frogmen attacked facilities at Nhat Le in coastal Quang Binh Province, followed by operations against North Vietnamese facilities at Ky Ninh in Ha Tinh Province and Cau Hang in Thanh Hoa. The North now instituted a national program of preventive detention at hard labor in maximum security prisons, plus increased surveillance, for eight categories of political dissidents, individuals who were potential threats and whom the commandos might try to contact.[18]

The Ministry of Public Security also expanded overt and covert intelligence operations against the civilian population in a broadly based grass-roots countercommando effort. This was designed to provide additional security through accurate and timely assessment of population attitudes, identification of potential weaknesses in the overall counterespionage operation, and attempts to prevent development of a potential fifth column. These were not new operations, merely updated efforts for operations that had been ongoing throughout the previous decade.

At the end of June, the U.S. Special Forces commander at Nha Trang sent five teams of eight men each across the border along Highway 9 in the plan dubbed Leaping Lena, a cross-border force drawn from the South Vietnamese 77th and 31st groups. Five survivors returned to South Vietnam. Col. Lam Son was subsequently dismissed from his position in command of Special Forces for the disastrous showing of these teams in an operation that McNamara had pushed two months earlier.

The first two months of Phase II were a time of transition. Gen. Maxwell Taylor arrived in July as the U.S. Ambassador to the Republic of Vietnam to replace Henry Cabot Lodge, who was returning to the United States to enter the Republican party primary.[19] General Harkins also departed, turning over command of the Military Assistance Command Vietnam to his deputy (since February), General Westmoreland. In Hawaii, Admiral Felt was replaced by his tough Pacific Fleet Commander, Admiral Sharp. These changes brought a new command group to the Pacific Theater within roughly one month of the Gulf of Tonkin incident.

The new ambassador, who had retired from the army during the Eisenhower administration after disagreements on the issue of massive nuclear retaliation, was in favor of a more conventional ground forces response. From Hanoi's perspective, this new American ambassador could be counted upon to respond with recommendations for a strong conventional response to Hanoi's provocations.

Taking over as field commander, Westmoreland saw MACSOG as a unit controlled by "intelligence types" in Washington that would provide little in the way of support to his immediate mission of trying to build up the South Vietnamese Army and confront hostile forces in South Vietnam proper.[20] This did not mean that he was unconcerned about the North's forces heading toward South Vietnam, but he believed that the Pacific Command had the responsibility for, and the capability to deal with, the North's encroachment on his command in South Vietnam.

The U.S. policy shift in Laos that summer was obviously watched with considerable interest in Hanoi as a barometer of Washington's intentions. For example, while U.S. military forces were prohibited from entering Laos on the ground, U.S. aircraft were now authorized to strike the source of hostile ground fire reaching U.S. reconnaissance aircraft overflying Laos. The leadership in Hanoi, now in line with Beijing's no-negotiation attitude, apparently welcomed this visible American involvement, which was more direct than the limited responses by paramilitary teams that had entered Laos overland. This increased American action meant that Hanoi could present further evidence of foreign involvement to rally its still largely ambivalent population and thereby give substance to the Politburo's claims that the United States was a foreign force invading Vietnam and attacking its Pathet Lao brethren, an effort which had to be defeated. MACSOG's maritime forces and the parallel DeSoto patrols, however, would push U.S. involvement more dramatically into the open.

9

THE SURRENDER OF TEAM BOONE

THE MOST SENIOR administration officials from Washington, the Pacific Command, and Saigon met in Honolulu to confer during June 1964. The tempo of covert operations increased in July, and an illusionary level of success now focused on numbers of missions, rather than substantive results tied to the stated goal of Plan 34A (see Appendix 7).

Eleven covert missions were attempted during July, nine of which MACSOG deemed successful. Eight of these are known: a safe standoff attack by the maritime force PTFs, one reconnaissance by the maritime cross-beach force, two maritime deception operations, the resupply of Team BELL in Yen Bai Province, and the landing of three new agent teams. The new teams consisted of six agents in Team PISCES, sent to reinforce Team EASY on 18 July; seven agents in Team PERSEUS, who parachuted in to reinforce Team TOURBILLON on 24 July; and nine agents in Team BOONE, who parachuted into Nghe An. PISCES, PERSEUS, and the supplies for BELL were met by the North Vietnamese. (The ninth mission probably was a psychological operations mission.)

Team BOONE was dropped in the North on 29 July.[1] Its area of assigned operations was north of Highway 7 outside the town of Con Cuong. From here, team members could easily monitor highway traffic flowing west toward Xieng Khouang Province in neighboring Laos.

Part of Team BOONE came from the residual agents of Team LANCE and part from original members of BOONE. Team BOONE had been assigned several missions into the North, but each time its mission had been unexpectedly canceled. Gradual attrition reduced the team to no more than four or five of the original members. For what would be its final mission, the team was brought to full strength by combining the members of BOONE and LANCE with members of a third under-strength team. The agents were loyal to their original team commanders, however, and the combined force lacked cohesion from the outset.

After their nighttime parachute drop, the team members used their small transistor radios to assemble on their landing beacon. They had landed approximately ten kilometers inside North Vietnam along Highway 7.

The first sign of disaster came when two men did not appear. A search located the primary radio operator, Hong Ton Khai. His parachute had failed to open fully, and he had fallen to his death. Unfortunately, Khai was the team's highly trained and experienced primary radio operator, and his loss meant the team would have to rely on the alternate radio operator, Nguyen Gia Thoa.

The only trace of the second missing agent was his parachute and weapon. Perhaps he had become disoriented and wandered away into Laos. Or, had he turned himself in to the North Vietnamese border guards? No one ever knew. In spite of their losses, most members of Team BOONE considered themselves fortunate to be in a secure drop zone.

The next day, they set out for their regrouping point some ten kilometers distant. Here, they set up their mountain base of operations in dense undergrowth. Visual reconnaissance confirmed that they were away from any inhabited areas. They should be safe. The team commander now learned that Thoa was incapable of operating the team's radio equipment. This meant that the team was effectively cut off from home and without any plan for rescue.

As they later related in prison, team members became increasingly depressed. Some opted to surrender, but others wanted to stay and attempt to carry out their mission. In the end, they formally voted to surrender. That surrender took place on 2 August, the day of the attack by three North Vietnamese torpedo boats against the USS *Maddox* in the Gulf of Tonkin.

Throughout their years in prison, members of BOONE spoke from time to time about their decision. Some said they sat outside Con Cuong for several weeks before deciding to surrender. Those listening to them detected inconsistencies in their stories; actually, BOONE surrendered five days after landing. No member of BOONE admitted who had made the decision to surrender, but most commandos knew such an order had to come from the team commander.

The team had already discarded their weapons and equipment when they marched out under a white flag and surrendered to local residents at the closest village cooperative, reportedly ten kilometers from their base. One team member armed with a 9-mm Schmeisser submachine gun remained at the base camp to secure the weapons and equipment. Some team members claimed that his possession of the only weapon not already discarded was instrumental in the surrender.

The men were taken to the temporary prison in Nghe An Province and joined ATILLA. They remained there for only a brief period before being taken to Hanoi, where they were reinterrogated and sentenced by a special military tribunal. Their trial was well publicized. Alternate radio operator Nguyen Gia Thoa was visited by an unidentified individual while preparing for his trial in Hanoi. Some claimed the relative came from the town of Ha Dong in the Hanoi suburbs. Thoa was released from prison at that point, reportedly accompanied by his mysterious "relative from Ha Dong," and was never seen again by the other team members.

As Team BOONE was surrendering near Con Cuong, an order was being flashed from the Vietnam People's Navy Command Headquarters to the forward transmitting site on Cat Ba Island for the 135th Torpedo Boat Squadron based at Van Hoa: Attack the enemy intruder!

The first lines of the final act were about to be played out in a body of water known as the Gulf of Tonkin.

10

THE INCIDENT

ON THE NIGHT of 1 August 1964, the USS *Maddox* approached the North Vietnamese coast to conduct observation and signals intelligence collection.[1] This was only hours after a MACSOG covert maritime raid, authorized under Phase II of OPLAN 34A, against a coastal target well within range of the American destroyer's electronic eavesdropping (see Appendix 7).

The following afternoon, the *Maddox*, reportedly twenty-five nautical miles from the coast of North Vietnam, was moving toward the southeast and away from the coast at a speed of twenty-seven knots.[2] She was being pursued at high speed by three North Vietnamese Navy motor torpedo boats that, according to U.S.-intercepted coded radio transmissions, had been ordered to "attack the enemy."[3] In the official naval history of the period, at least one of the motor torpedo boats was believed to have been sunk as a result of air attacks by F-8 Crusaders vectored against them from the USS *Ticonderoga* to assist the *Maddox*.[4]

Within hours of the attack, President Johnson met with senior administration officials. Although it did not respond militarily to the 2 August attack on the *Maddox*, the administration reportedly notified North Vietnam that the United States would continue to patrol in international waters and warned North Vietnam of "grave consequences . . . from any further unprovoked offensive military action against United States forces."[5]

The ability of U.S. naval forces to travel at will in international waters had been a recurring issue demanded by

Washington and an element in U.S. strategy at the time of the confrontation with the Soviet Union over the shipment of offensive missiles into Cuba. The Special Group and other national planners were fully aware that the offensive operations by the *Maddox* could well provoke military reaction by North Vietnam (see Appendix 3).

After the 2 August attack, the *Maddox* was ordered to complete its DeSoto patrol with certain course changes.[6] The *Maddox* was now ordered to approach no closer than twelve nautical miles from the North Vietnamese coastline. This, the State Department presented, would keep the *Maddox* outside the three-mile limit, which U.S. officials concluded had remained in place since the end of the French colonial period in 1954.

On the evening of 4 August, after an electronic intelligence mission to within sixteen nautical miles of the coast, the *Maddox* and her companion, the USS *Turner Joy*, were moving away from the coast of North Vietnam toward the center of the Gulf of Tonkin.[7] Seven hours earlier, another SOG covert maritime raid had taken place under Phase II and had once again hit the North Vietnamese coast within range of the destroyer's electronic ears (see Appendix 7).

The captain of the *Maddox* anticipated the possibility of North Vietnamese action. Earlier that afternoon, the North Vietnamese naval headquarters at Hai Phong reportedly had ordered its Swatow-class patrol boats T-142 and T-146 to prepare for operations that evening, and there had been communication with torpedo boat 333, which had engine problems. This, one U.S. Navy official history recounts, appears as the primary evidence that Vietnam People's Navy forces were preparing to attack again, an action which would not have surprised anyone with knowledge of Plan 34A and its potential consequences (see Appendix 3).[8]

At approximately 10:15 P.M., the *Maddox* and *Turner Joy*, at least halfway across the Gulf of Tonkin, were closer to the People's Republic of China (PRC) than to North Vietnam. They were deep within international waters and heading initially southeast away from North Vietnam. Such a track could be perceived as either heading outward or in the direction of southwestern Hai Nan Island, China. The U.S. destroyers believed that they picked up three or four contacts on radar at some distance behind them, together with a separate contact off to the east toward Hai Nan Island. Although the U.S. Navy's official history is mute on the nationality and origin of these vessels, the seemingly hostile patrol boats, then nearly fifty miles from the *Maddox*, were not coming from the direction of North Vietnam. They were approaching the *Maddox* from the relative direction of Hai Nan Island, to the east and northeast of the destroyers' position.[9]

During the next four hours, the *Maddox* and *Turner Joy* reported various contacts and suspected torpedo firings from patrol boats that appeared to make runs on them while U.S. aircraft flew combat air patrols overhead. The U.S. Navy's official history recounts a belief that several hostile patrol boats were sunk over a four-hour period. Some U.S. officials believed the sonar images were not accurate, however, and others at the time even questioned whether an attack had really taken place.[10]

There was a tense atmosphere in Washington when senior policymakers met to decide on a response to the reported attack. As the Joint Chiefs were recommending a military response, State Department officials met with Senator William Fulbright, chairman of the Senate Foreign Relations Committee, to develop President Johnson's public statement to the nation that would advise the American people of Washington's response to strike North Vietnam.

A telephone discussion between Secretary McNamara and the president addressed the issue of a need for hard evidence of the purported attack. Both the president and the defense secretary were well aware of the full scope of the 34A operations; the president had approved them at McNamara's urging the previous December. While Washington waited for more details and radio intercepts, reportedly picked up by the *Maddox*, to be decoded and analyzed back in the United States, a study group met to review air strike target options against North Vietnam.

Assistant to the President for National Security Affairs McGeorge Bundy, point man for the State Department on foreign policy aspects of Plan 34A, was reportedly evaluating the intercepts and was in contact with the State Department. He then met with Senator Fulbright. Alluding to MACSOG's earlier strike by the PTFs under Plan 34A, Fulbright reportedly asked Bundy if the covert maritime operations attacks were related to the activities of the two destroyers. According to the senator, Bundy replied that they were not ''operationally connected.'' This reportedly seemed to assuage Senator Fulbright, a staunch supporter of President Johnson's then ongoing bid for reelection, and to indicate that there seemed to be a rational need for some administration response. Fulbright then worked with Bundy to craft an administration message to be delivered by President Johnson on national television. Senator Fulbright would later assert that he had been misled about what happened at the time.[11]

If Senator Fulbright had been told about the U.S. Navy's officially acknowledged tandem relationship between the 34A maritime operations and the destroyers, perhaps he and other congressional and administration officials might have adopted a more cautious response. There is no indication, however, that he asked about or was given information on the broader operations of Plan 34A, which included the constantly escalating paramilitary agent team operations and the related U.S. overflights going back to the start of the decade (see Appendixes 2, 3, and 7).

Within five hours of the reported incident involving the *Maddox* and the *Turner Joy*, an electrical message emanated from the Joint Chiefs of Staff that directed Seventh Fleet air strikes against an oil storage facility and four coastal complexes in North Vietnam. The strikes were to be reprisals for the purported attack by North Vietnam against the two destroyers on 4 August.[12]

Did Saigon's headquarters play a role in the decision-making process? General Westmoreland was emphatic that he did not: ''I had nothing to do with it. The decision had already been made in Washington by the time I learned of it.''[13]

On 5 August, U.S. aircraft struck at Hon Gai in the northeast and in Thanh Hoa Province. The strikes also hit complexes at Vinh and the anchorage at the mouth of the Giang River, the target of the CIA's covert force of motorized junks and the newly arrived motor torpedo boats from SOG's covert navy.

* * *

On 5 August, President Johnson announced on national television that air strikes were already under way in response to what was being portrayed to Congress and the American people as an unprovoked attack on U.S. ships in international waters of the Gulf of Tonkin. Actually, Johnson's speech took place before the air strikes occurred. The apparent cause of the snafu was faulty estimation of the time difference between Washington and Vietnam, an error of one hour, which meant that the president, in effect, informed the North of attacks that would come in an hour.

On 7 August, Congress approved the president's Gulf of Tonkin Resolution authorizing the use of U.S. forces to support any member state of the Southeast Asia Collective Defense Treaty. One of the member states was the Republic of Vietnam. The resolution became portrayed as the legal basis for U.S. combat in Southeast Asia. The retaliatory strikes were ordered to come not closer than fifty miles from the People's Republic of China. Within five days, Ambassador Taylor was calling for implementation of the sustained bombing scenario.[14]

Also on 7 August, the Joint Chiefs of Staff approved CinCPac Operations Plan 37-65 to "stabilize the situation in RVN and/or Laos." This plan incorporated earlier CinCPac Operation Plans 33 and 37-64. It also incorporated Operations Plan 34A as a continuing covert operation. Plan 37-64 included operations into the Vietnam/Laos border area against infiltrating North Vietnamese forces and various scenarios for air operations against North Vietnamese military and economic targets.[15]

The Joint Chiefs were clearly satisfied that President Johnson had listened to, and followed, their recommendations of a tough response against North Vietnam. Johnson's popularity rose dramatically from 42 percent to 72 percent; the majority of Americans perceived that the president had made an appropriate and measured response to what was portrayed as an unprovoked attack in international waters. Coming three months before the November 1964 general elections, it provided the American people with an example of a firm leader whose response was clearly limited and therefore more acceptable than the portrayal of his Republican challenger,

Barry Goldwater, as a president who would take America to war.[16]

The subsequent congressional inquiry into the Gulf of Tonkin incident revealed that the United States was able to intercept and decrypt the messages from North Vietnam's naval high command, which ordered the attack against the *Maddox* on 2 August. They were high-grade coded messages to the 135th Torpedo Boat Group, which led the attack, and to the southern naval region headquarters controlling the Swatows, which the North's navy used to help vector the attacking motor torpedo boats.

These facts argue that if United States communications intelligence resources were able to intercept *these* messages, Washington also would have known that Hanoi had placed all its forces on a total war footing. Intercepted messages would have revealed how closely Hanoi was monitoring the raids undertaken by MACSOG's forces. Further, Washington would have known that Hanoi was closely watching the obvious high correlation between other Seventh Fleet electronic and communications intelligence activities in support of Plan 34A and the full range of covert maritime, airborne agent, and psychological operations being conducted by MACSOG and the CIA (see Appendix 2).[17] Information about these actions, in spite of increased questions about the widening war, was closely guarded by a select few in the executive branch who had a need to know.

Throughout this entire period, the nationality of the attacking boats was never mentioned. One U.S. Navy official history implies that they were North Vietnamese but stops short of saying so. The Vietnam People's Navy official history acknowledges ordering the attack by its Division 3 on 2 August and then asserts that Washington used such attacks to justify air strikes on 5 August. It remains silent about the events of 4 August.

So, historically, there are still doubts about whether an attack had indeed taken place on 4 August 1964 and, if so, by whom. One answer came on 4 July 1966 on board the USS *Cavalier* anchored at Da Nang, South Vietnam. The very existence of this answer was covered up no less fervently than the existence of the covert operations conducted by the CIA and MACSOG.

"Why did you attack the two U.S. destroyers in August 1964?" I asked Sr. Capt. Tran Bao, the senior North Vietnamese PT boat officer recovered from one of two boats sunk by U.S. destroyers on 1 July 1966, while they were well within international waters of the Gulf of Tonkin.[18]

As Bao related, on 2 August 1964, he was the chief of staff of Squadron 135 and the senior squadron officer on board his Division 3 command boat 333 assigned to attack the USS *Maddox*. He claimed that the attack on 2 August was driven in part by Hanoi's desire to send a message about months of covert attacks by U.S.–directed covert maritime forces, which Hanoi concluded had been operating in conjunction with the electronic intelligence mission of the U.S. destroyer. Two of Bao's motor torpedo boats were sunk, one after being towed close to shore. Bao, on board the division's command boat, 333, limped back to coastal Thanh Hoa Province, where the boat was hidden during repairs to a damaged engine. Bao went on to describe the after-action report he had written about the incident on 2 August. He detailed the flow of pre-attack messages from Hai Phong to the forward headquarters on Cat Ba Island, then to Patrol Region 1 Headquarters at Van Hoa, and finally to his squadron.

As with the attack of 2 August, Bao's boats had returned to the Gulf of Tonkin in their attack on 1 July 1966, within two days of an attack by MACSOG's covert maritime forces against coastal targets in the northern Gulf and in specific response to an attack on a fuel storage complex.

Senior Captain Bao's answer was direct:

> We warned your country that summer, a month before the Gulf of Tonkin incident, that we had extended our territorial boundaries. We were hoping that this notice would keep your ships out to sea. You didn't. That's why we attacked . . . I commanded the attack on 2 August . . . that's when my command boat was shot up and I got it back to one of the rivers in Thanh Hoa Province and we hid out until I could get the boat repaired. . . . I was the author of our navy's after-action report about the 2 August attack. . . .[19]

"What about the attack of 4 August?" I asked.

Bao continued:

> There was none, not as far as I know. Furthermore, our forces in that area only operated to 106 degree 30 minutes. We couldn't go beyond that because of fuel problems. We had another problem. The on-board radar was only really effective within about ten nautical miles of the target and was only really useful in the last five thousand meters. This is why we used the Swatows to vector us in close to the target, so we could find it.
>
> We had another problem. The P-4 did not do well in choppy seas and our speed in such waters was limited. Besides, most of the time we stayed in port or operated close to the shoreline, not some distance out in the Gulf.
>
> Our divisions operated with three boats per division and we only had the P-4. The Chinese, on the other hand, had both the P-4 and a longer-range motor torpedo boat known as the P-6. The P-6 was referred to as a long-range motor torpedo boat and could operate well beyond the range of the P-4. . . . [20]

The official history of the Gulf of Tonkin incident recounts attacks on the *Maddox* and *Turner Joy* occurring at approximately 107 degrees 30 minutes. Such attacks by three or four boats occurred intermittently for at least six hours. The People's Republic of China had four boats per division, as do most other motor torpedo boat units in foreign navies. North Vietnam had only three boats in each division.

Official U.S. naval histories of the era are singularly silent on accounting for the movement of North Vietnamese naval forces westward into the Gulf on 4 August, in the middle of an era of intensive signals, communications, and imagery intelligence examination of North Vietnam. Such histories are similarly silent on any role played by the Chinese People's Navy, a curious phenomenon in light of the presence of Chinese patrol boats at Region 2 prior to the attack of 2 August and the fact that other U.S. destroyers had conducted missions similar to that of the *Maddox* against the PRC.

Grady Stewart, another Army interrogator, and I went through the inventory of PT boats in the 135th Squadron of the Vietnam People's Navy with Tran Bao. Bao accounted for each. He described the sinking of each boat and which boat had been raised from which location. We went through his navy's torpedo inventory of sixty torpedoes, including the three fired against the *Maddox* on 2 August, leaving, by his account, the Vietnam People's Navy with fifty-seven torpedoes when Division 3 set forth on its ill-fated attack of 1 July 1966.

Bao said:

> There's an easy way to check, if you could do it. Look at our torpedo inventory at the storage site at Van Hoa. You'll find an accurate record of the status and location of every torpedo we have. I should know. I was the chief of staff and all supply reports came to me.[21]

On 6 July 1966, the first message with the results of our army team debriefing of the nineteen North Vietnamese crewmen was on its way. Two days earlier, the captain of the *Cavalier* had ordered us not to interrogate any of the prisoners until U.S. Marine Corps interrogators arrived on board the *Cavalier*, a terrible waste of precious time and potential lives. So for three days, while waiting for marine interrogators to arrive, we just "chatted." The captain of the *Cavalier* didn't object to that and obviously had a false notion about interrogation.

"Just no interrogation. Those are the orders from Seventh Fleet," the captain said.

"Can we at least talk with them? You know, just chat?" I asked.

"Yeah . . . sure, that's all right. But remember, don't interrogate them."

So, we just chatted.

A day or two after the Seventh Fleet Exploitation Team's formal activation on 6 July and its initial 120-page message on the way, we received an immediate message at the *Cavalier*. We sensed that it was a panic response to our initial knowledgeability report quoting Tran Bao and the other prisoners. The report had included the entire organization and deployment of the Vietnam People's Navy, its current location, and Tran Bao's statements about the nonevent of 4 August. The immediate response was relayed to our two-person team by Commander William R. Quisenberry, the Seventh Fleet officer directing the exploitation of the nineteen North Vietnamese Navy POWs.

The message read: "You will not, repeat not, debrief further concerning the Gulf of Tonkin incident. . . ."

Obviously, in July 1966, there were still questions about the attacks that were not to be covered.[22]

The U.S. Navy's official history of this period of the Vietnam War states that North Vietnam did not publicly claim a twelve-mile territorial limit until after the August attacks.[23] The U.S. Navy's history also finds it "ironic" that the August 1964 incidents precipitating open warfare came out of Operations Plan 34A. In fact, the authors of Plan 34A recognized this might well occur, and the authors of the U.S. Navy history possessed copies of both the MACSOG Documentation Study and the Seventh Fleet Exploitation Team's reporting (see Appendix 3).[24]

OPLAN 34A maritime operations began to escalate late in the fall of 1964, following a temporary cessation of the certain activities under the plan (see Appendix 4). In an apparent show of support for the effort, U.S. Army Chief of Staff Gen. Harold K. Johnson later offered his professional conclusion that the maritime operations of 34A were valuable. However, MACSOG's formal history of its operations that year (through December) showed precisely the opposite.[25]

Following the Gulf of Tonkin incident, General Westmoreland recommended that maritime operations be increased. Deputy Secretary of Defense Cyrus Vance approved these increases, with some modification. McGeorge Bundy also concurred, and, in January 1965, some earlier controls were relaxed.[26]

Ironically, the covert program, which had been a failure for four years, was suddenly being expanded. The plan originally proffered as sending a message to prevent a war was now helping to spur one onward, and the maritime operations, which had been largely ineffective, were now found to be laudatory.

As Hanoi launched new attacks in the South that fall and

into the spring of 1965, Washington prepared more ambitious actions against North Vietnam in line with the administration's approach of a tit-for-tat. It was in that context that MACSOG continued to drop more agent teams into the North, but it soon ran out of all the personnel inherited by Colonel Russell the previous January (see Appendixes 5 and 6).

COVER-UP

1965–1967

Part 3

11

"Romeo's BEEN CAPTURED . . ."

On 22 October 1964, four commandos comprising Team ALTER parachuted into Lai Chau to reinforce Team REMUS. The original team commander, Quach Rang, had been stranded at the southern mountain town of Banmethuot with the Montagnard uprising and did not accompany his team as planned. On 14 November, Rang was the near instant deputy commander of Team GRECO, which parachuted into Yen Bai Province to reinforce Team BELL.

As the year 1965 began, four more reinforcements were parachuted to Team REMUS. In May, the five agents known as Team HORSE, under the command of Quach Nhung, were air-dropped into Son La to reinforce Team TOURBILLON. All were met by the Ministry of Public Security.

American units in division size were now arriving in southern Vietnam. The escalation with sizable U.S. ground forces brought the American military presence—and combat—much more into the open. MACSOG's covert operations were being overtaken by a widening overt war. With the support of the Defense Intelligence Agency, MACSOG began to redirect its effort from agent operations to reconnaissance in support of an early warning net.[1]

That spring, MACSOG was alerted to take over the cross-border missions into southern Laos. The military training base at Long Thanh was filled with new recruits destined for operations against the burgeoning Ho Chi Minh Trail. Some trainees came from staff positions at the Strategic Technical Service's headquarters, but most had been recruited in 1962 and shared the history of their organization with the newer trainees.

During the fall of 1965, nine agents in Team DOG and three in Team GECKO parachuted into Son La to reinforce Team EASY. On 7 November, eight agents in Team VERSE were dropped into Son La to reinforce TOURBILLON. All were met by the People's Armed Public Security Force.

That same month, Team ROMEO was ready for launching.[2] The team's eleven members knew that other commando trainees had preceded them into the prelaunch restricted area during 1965, as replacements for teams they were led to believe were already operating deep inside North Vietnam. No one had ever returned from the North, but this was explained by the training staff as meaning that the agents were still doing their job up North. Morale was high, and the team members wanted to be off. Their Vietnamese and American Special Forces training staff was enthusiastic. There was no hint that anything was wrong.

Team ROMEO was issued a mission order to launch into the North, reach its regrouping point, await further orders, and be prepared to remain in place for two years. Beyond that, it received no instructions about what to do after arriving in North Vietnam. The team reviewed maps of the landing zone and the regrouping point. It all seemed clear and relatively uncomplicated: Go up north, wait there, and we'll tell you what to do next. This was the U.S. military's way of doing things.

The operational briefing in the restricted area stressed that this was an operation against the Communists and in defense of the Free World.[3] The team members all knew this. It was something they all believed in and were more than willing to fight for.

Afterward, members of Team ROMEO thought back to a remark made by one of the training officers near the end of their training:

> For every thousand men that we've already sent into the North, we've been lucky to have just one of them be able to operate successfully. I'm telling you this because I don't want you all to think that everyone we've sent in has been successful. It's a situation

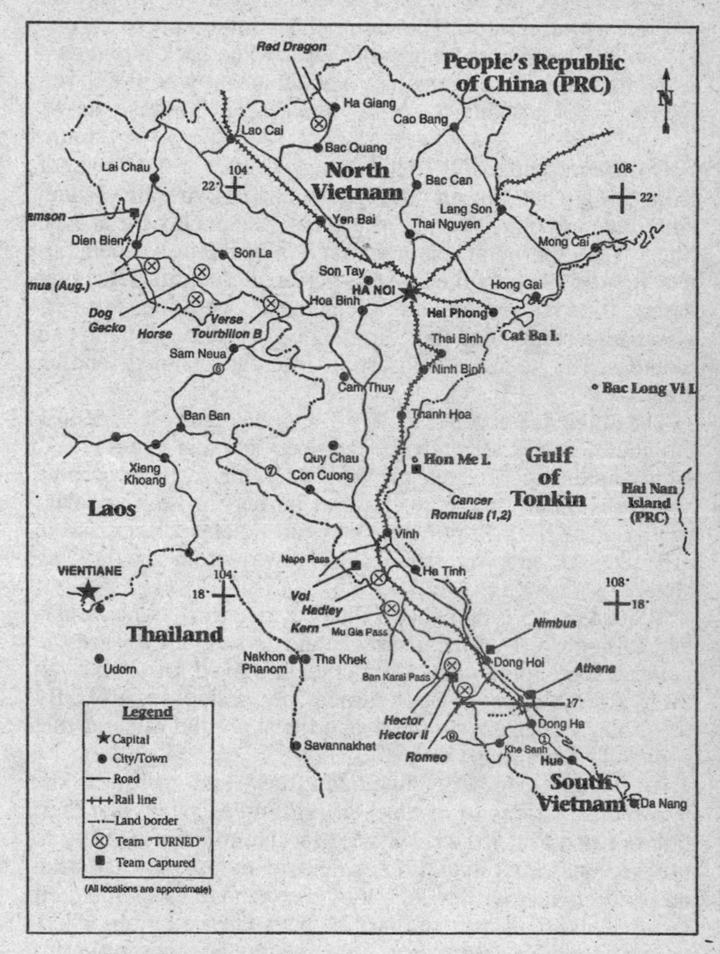

Figure 5. Agent teams landed and captured in 1965–1967 (*graphic by Cindy Tourison*)

where the more we have who are successful then it's so much the better. That's all. It really doesn't matter whether you are successful or not. You are all considered as successful. The thing most important to this whole operation is your willingness to go back into the North. That is what this is all about—that you're willing to go back into the North against the Communists.

On the morning of 19 November, Team ROMEO took off from Long Thanh in an American transport aircraft with an American crew and flew to the forward launch base at Khe Sanh. That afternoon, the commandos boarded two helicopters for the lift into their operating area. A third helicopter carried the American and Vietnamese operations officers who had accompanied the commandos from Long Thanh and would see to their safe insertion into the planned landing zone.

The three helicopters took off together and flew at low altitude through Lao airspace. Between four and five o'clock, they landed not far from the Ho Chi Minh Trail in an area known as Vitulu, close to the Lao border, in Le Thuy District, Quang Binh Province. The team quickly disembarked, offloaded its supplies, and moved away from the landing zone.

Team ROMEO established radio contact with its headquarters to confirm its safe insertion and movement toward the planned regrouping point. As the team moved forward, however, a ten-kilometer jaunt turned into a five-day trek. By this time, the terrain on the ground was not the same as that depicted on the map.

The team members concluded they had followed the proper instructions to reach their regrouping point, and their failure to be at that location was not due to their inability to use a compass and map. It became evident that they had been dropped in the wrong location! They had based all their movements on certain similarities between the terrain where they had landed and those depicted on the map, much of which looked the same. They were lost, totally and completely, with no idea where they were or even where they had landed.

A quick radio message to their headquarters brought the

reply confirming that, indeed, they had been dropped on the wrong landing zone. The solution, passed by their headquarters, was for their headquarters to attempt to locate the team and then direct it to its correct regrouping point.

The days stretched by as food rations began to run out. Then, after six weeks of tramping through unfamiliar jungle, with only the Strategic Technical Directorate completely aware of where they were and where they were headed, disaster struck. It occurred when, at long last, their headquarters reported locating them and told them to be prepared for aerial resupply.

The team members cleared a landing zone and spread a T-shaped panel on the ground to mark the location for the drop from an aircraft that they could clearly see approaching in the distance. They then watched in horror as the aircraft dropped their supplies four or five kilometers away, easily a forced march of several days under the best conditions.

While they pondered the idiots in the sky, they heard sounds of strange voices, laughter, and splashing water from a nearby stream. A careful search revealed the presence of five North Vietnamese soldiers. They watched as the troops frolicked, set up their kitchen, cooked, ate their evening meal, and finally strung hammocks as they prepared to settle in for the evening, unaware they were under close and continuous observation by a well-armed commando team.

Team ROMEO went into a huddle and discussed its options.

It was too early for the next scheduled radio transmission, so the team members could not contact their headquarters or request an air strike. Also, the loss of their supplies meant an immediate need for resupply, but an airdrop would alert the enemy patrol. Reaching a consensus, they quickly surrounded the now resting enemy patrol and captured it with little effort.

The five men were members of the Quang Binh Province border defense forces. From them, ROMEO learned that the border defense forces had been scouring the area for the team, supposedly after receiving reports from mountaintop animal herders that a flight of helicopters had unloaded commandos in the area.

As the captives spoke, it was evident they were not bragging when they said they had the border under total surveillance and that nothing went across it without their highly effective border security network picking up some indication. Every village and hamlet was obviously tied into this reporting system, which ran to the provincial border defense headquarters.

Team ROMEO was now in a quandary. The training doctrine received at Long Thanh demanded that the five captives be killed immediately. That was the only way the commandos could ensure that the North Vietnamese forces would not learn their precise location; however, it was obvious the North Vietnamese already knew they were in the area and were searching for them.

Doctrine notwithstanding, it went against the very nature of the men just to shoot the five captives. The school solution was one thing, but, face to face with the enemy, they now hesitated. After three days of agonizing, the team commander ordered the prisoners released. The team moved out in an attempt to evade capture, without advising the Directorate by radio of what had happened.

One week later, on 14 January 1966, Team ROMEO found itself surrounded and taken under fire in a carefully prepared ambush by a combined force of the People's Army, border defense forces, and militia. The team members learned that their five prisoners had returned to their unit immediately after release and reported their capture by the team.

Following capture, the team members were tied up with telephone wire and searched. Their supplies were carefully inventoried. A brief questioning provided their captors with the identity of the team's two radio operators. Both had been captured with their radio equipment and signal operating instructions. The two were separated from other members of the team and taken away.

The rest of the men were marched under guard through the mountains for the better part of a week, until they arrived just west of the coastal provincial capital of Dong Hoi City. They were thrust into the confines of the provincial temporary prison, a collection of thatched huts replacing the permanent prison in Dong Hoi City that was now threatened by American air strikes. This was to be their home for the next six months.

* * *

"The Public Security Service senior lieutenant held a gun to my head," one of the radio operators from Team ROMEO said. It was now the fall of 1973. After seven and a half years, he had been reunited with other members of his team in Quyet Tien Prison in Ha Giang Province. One team member was still being kept elsewhere and would not rejoin the others until the end of 1979, when nearly all of the survivors would be reunited at Thanh Phong Prison in Thanh Hoa Province.

"I just knew he was going to shoot me but for some reason he didn't. I told them I would cooperate and work the radio but I told them clearly I would only agree to send messages asking for resupply. No replacements."

During a conversation years later, his former teammate asked him what happened. After fourteen years, a lot of the early anger had dissipated.

"Well," began the radio operator, "the Ministry of Public Security had this special unit from the State Security General Directorate and they . . ."

He described the special unit that managed the radio operators recruited by the state security officers to work under the control of the Counter-Espionage Directorate of the State Security General Directorate. They were totally compartmented from everyone else and had their own separate radio communications links. A senior lieutenant from the Ministry's special unit had been sent down to manage the Team ROMEO radio operators.

"You know," said the radio operator, "I had my own special radio operator's code I could use, a way I could send something in the message which could tell the Directorate what had happened. I figured they might send in supplies but if they knew we were transmitting under duress, they wouldn't dare send in replacements who might be killed."

After the message had been decrypted, the radio operator learned that the Directorate would be sending in more men as augmentation. He knew he had to do something and decided to risk everything by sending a message in the clear.

"I sent it twice before the senior lieutenant realized what I had done. I sent it out twice, very fast: ROMEO BI BAT ROMEO BI BAT. 'Romeo's been captured. Romeo's been captured.'[4]

"The senior lieutenant standing there, his pistol drawn, was monitoring my transmission. He realized what I'd done and he pulled me off the radio. He put the pistol right up on my head. I know, I just know he wanted to shoot me right on the spot but he didn't."

The radio operator was kept there for two more days, and then another message was received from Saigon. By this time, a new state security officer had arrived to monitor the message. The transmission said the message that Hanh, the radio operator, had sent the day before had been incorrect. Hanh was then pulled off the radio, beaten up, and taken to prison. That was all that happened to him.

The radio operator's teammate turned away. Was he telling the truth?

The two radio operators had been separated from the others at the outset and taken away, but no one knew where. Besides, recruited radio operators were believed to be liars who invented stories about what had happened after their capture. So why believe this story? It just didn't sound plausible.

Other prisoners said they'd heard that some of the radio operators had been transmitting right in Hanoi City, or they were at one location but sending back messages saying they were at another. Also, the radio operators who had been recruited were never involved in the encryption and decryption of any message traffic. There was no way for them to know what was in the messages they were sending. Their sole job was to send messages and to make sure that the Directorate was satisfied the radio operator hadn't been replaced. The state security officers performed the encryption and decryption. The teammate was sure the radio operator was lying about that part of his story.

Each operator had his own way of sending. The Directorate had a tape of each operator's transmitting characteristics to make sure that the North Vietnamese had not made a switch with one of their own people. Also, the Directorate had radio direction-finding equipment that helped to confirm the radio operators' locations. The State Security General Directorate could not have managed the captured operators for very long without their own headquarters getting a fix on the location of the transmitter. The Directorate must have known all along that the operators were being managed by the enemy and had decided to let the operation continue in order to learn what the North Vietnamese were up to.

As he thought about this and reflected on what people at his headquarters had done and whom they had sent into the North, it became obvious to the radio operator that they had never sent anyone on a mission who was terribly important. Was this proof that they had known all along that the operation had been compromised? Were they playing with the North Vietnamese by continuing to send in teams in hopes of discovering their plans and intentions?

There was at least one point of solace. All team members had signed contracts when they joined the covert program. Written provisions guaranteed that they would be taken care of if they were captured or declared missing. One of these days, they would get back and have something waiting for them, hopefully.

Team ROMEO's first weeks of imprisonment west of Dong Hoi City passed with interrogations continuing day after day. The interrogators came from the Quang Binh provincial public security service and the Ministry of Public Security at Hanoi. There were air strikes too, but no indication of who was doing the bombing and what was being attacked.

One day in March 1966, a new prisoner arrived. "Who are you?" whispered a commando.

"My name is Nguyen Quoc Dat," came the quiet reply.

"How were you captured?"

"I'm a pilot. We were just on an air strike and I was hit. I was shot down and they captured me and brought me here."

Dat, recently of the Republic of Vietnam Air Force, soon departed Quang Binh for Hoa Lo Prison at Hanoi, but he became someone the commandos talked about. His story passed from man to man. Dat was a prisoner of the North Vietnamese, but he had been in combat against them! That was what they had all wanted to do. In their own way, they applauded him and, perhaps, were somewhat jealous.

The commandos from Team ROMEO, like teams before and after, had indeed signed an employment contract with the Strategic Technical Directorate, as required by MACSOG's standard operating procedure (SOP) and civilian personnel regulations that covered agents and nonagents alike. This was done at the time each new inductee was recruited into the covert operation program.

MACSOG did not contract directly with the inductee because U.S. policy was to employ the South Vietnamese counterpart government organization as the contract agent on behalf of the United States for the actual conduct of covert operations against North Vietnam.[5] This was designed to afford the United States some degree of plausible denial and permit the U.S. government to claim that this was not an American-directed operation. Such contracts were also necessary to ensure there were still agents on the payroll as South Vietnam went through its periodic changes in national government leadership. As Col. Clyde Russell, the first MACSOG Commander, stated:

> [Colonel] Ho was a fairly weak man, militarily. . . . An ex-banker, he was politically acceptable and went through every coup. . . . I felt sorry for the guy when we'd get his government moving in our direction and a month later we had to do it again and start from scratch and then again get his government to move in our direction. We went through that some four or five times when I was over there. . . . Due to his weakness in character, and that may not be the right description of the man, I found that I could get him to do anything the United States desired they do. . . . There were times when he wanted to disband the airborne [agent] effort because he felt that we couldn't put those people in the North, but again, because he was weak and we could put the pressure on him he would agree and we'd . . . go back . . . with the airborne [agent] crews and get them back in shape.[6]

Decisions were made regarding the commandos from Team ROMEO, as well as others on agent missions into North Vietnam, that changed the spirit and intent of the contractual arrangements made with the agents at the time of their recruitment. Unfortunately, no one told the agents. This change applied to the agreements in contracts made by agents already in North Vietnam prisons, contracts made by those still in training in the South, and contracts used to induce new recruits into the covert program. Specific provisions were changed at the order of Col. Donald Blackburn, MACSOG commander. This was done without regard to any pre-employment agreement, and the change was never reflected in the language of a power of attorney executed by each agent several months before going into North Vietnam. In short, MACSOG kept promising certain things to its agents and their families while intending deliberate disregard of these commitments that asked the men to risk their lives on behalf of the foreign policy interests of the United States.

The change occurred in 1966, according to Col. John J. Windsor, USMC, MACSOG operations chief, who had arrived at MACSOG in June 1965 before Team ROMEO was launched. In 1969, he described this change in the agent contracts to the Joint Chiefs of Staff:

> My principal counterpart relationship was with Colonel Ho, the South Vietnamese counterpart of Colonel Blackburn. . . . We had actually no problems at all. There is one example I can give of that.
>
> As you know, we lost quite a few agents (Vietnamese people) in the North and it had been our policy to continue to pay them as though they were not dead. After being there six or eight months, we had quite a large number of relatives of these folks whom we were paying.[7] Colonel Blackburn and I discussed it. His desire was these relatives should be paid the death allowance and that the agents' monthly pay to their relatives back in Saigon should be discontinued. Of course, this was sort of a touchy subject and I went to Colonel Ho and explained it to him. First, I asked him how many agents were in this category. We knew the answer before we asked the question. Ho sent out and got advice from his staff. When I told him what we wanted to do, they cooperated to the fullest. We reduced the number of dead gradually by declaring so many of them dead each month until we had written them all off (paid them) and removed them from the monthly payroll. We did this to reduce the possible criticism as to where

> this money might be going. Colonel Ho's first reaction was that he didn't want the Vietnamese agents and their relatives to know that we had lost so many. That was the reason he hadn't done it himself. He nevertheless agreed to our proposal. . . .
>
> I heard a lot of criticism of Colonel Ho and Major Bhin [sic][8] and other Vietnamese; however, they had a different outlook on life. They frequently pointed out, "You folks are here for one year and then you're gone to the U.S.A., but we have been fighting this war for 15 years and we don't know how much longer we are going to be fighting it after you leave here following your one year tour." They just have a different outlook and I don't feel they are incompetent necessarily or incapable of performing their duties. What I am saying is that they are not as actively ambitious and energetic as Americans, but I felt that, in general, they were capable.[9]

Colonel Windsor must have been aware that the majority of agents had been captured. Their capture was often well publicized in North Vietnam and well known to the JCS, CIA, and MACSOG. Why he would assert that the agents were dead when his own records indicated they were last known alive is unclear.

In many cases, the agent radio operators had been sending routine messages back to Saigon; these were monitored at an intercept site in the Philippines. Such information was also reportedly in the individual team files documenting Hanoi's Vietnamese- and English-language radio broadcasts that reported the capture of those teams unwilling to cooperate with North Vietnam. The broadcasts were intercepted by the CIA's Foreign Broadcast Information Service.

This knowledge notwithstanding, the Strategic Technical Directorate (STD), the South Vietnamese counterpart of MACSOG, followed the wishes of Colonel Blackburn and issued notices directly or indirectly to next of kin that their loved ones had become missing while on operations inside South Vietnam. The families were not told the truth—that they actually had been captured.[10] The knowledge they had been captured was clearly too damaging to be repeated in

South Vietnam, for the same reason that Hanoi's original public announcement of their capture was deliberately withheld from their next of kin.

One of the officers in a senior command position in the South Vietnamese Special Forces providing the disguise for the agent employment with the 1st Observations Group, and later the Technical Directorate, explained what happened from his perspective:

> Most of those sent into the North at the outset were sergeants from units like the 22d Division. I know that each of them signed a power of attorney before they left and that such documents included provisions for payments to their wives after they left. They were even told that those payments would continue until they came back. It just didn't happen that way, not the way they were led to believe.
>
> The reality is that we did not have any funds to keep paying them indefinitely and we depended on the U.S. for this money. When you decided you wanted to stop payments, we had no funds of our own and eventually you stopped all payments to us too.
>
> There's another aspect. Even though the agents who came from our army were used on an American controlled operation into the North, we on the South Vietnamese side had to apply our own military regulations to them when they didn't come back. That meant that when they didn't come back, we declared them missing in action one year from that date. I know that agents were told that their families would be taken care of and their pay continued until they returned but that part of the agreement was ignored. Our thinking was that if and when they did return, we would deal with them as we dealt with our own servicemen who were taken prisoner on normal military operations. When and if they got back, they would get all their back pay from the date of last payment to their family until date of return. Unfortunately, no one ever thought that we would lose the war. Of course, we never said they were dead, just missing. . . .[11]

"But," I asked, "what about the agents who were working for our CIA and Defense Department? We had them sign contracts in which we agreed to compensate them until they got back. We even told them we'd escrow pay for them in the event they were captured. Is that correct and, if so, what happened there?"

The former colonel was silent for a moment before continuing:

> All I can tell you is the Strategic Technical Directorate would send me a notice that such and such an individual from my Special Forces 77th Group was declared missing and I then ensured that within one year of that date the family was notified they were formally declared missing in action and paid death benefits.
>
> I didn't question what I was told. Besides, it would not have affected our decision. We did it all the time, even in the case of those we knew had been taken prisoner. One year later they all became missing. As I said, we did not have the money to just keep paying someone indefinitely. If they got back then, they'd get paid. I am pretty sure they all knew that.[12]

"Well then," I asked, "what about the civilian agents?"

"Ahhh, that's a different matter. I had nothing to do with them. That was something you Americans worked out with Col. Tran Van Ho. You'll have to ask him what happened there."[13]

Information from surviving agents and next of kin suggests the monthly payments to next of kin ended long before an individual was declared missing and long before MACSOG stopped payments to the Strategic Technical Directorate. Like the covert operation itself, those who had custody of the money that never reached the families would prefer that the subject be left closed.

What were the responsibilities of the United States over the covert operation, and what factors influenced the carrying out of such responsibilities? The critical Joint Chiefs of Staff evaluation of the covert effort is clear and unambiguous:

A problem area significant to both operational effectiveness and functional administration of the MACSOG programs from their inception was the pay, allowance and bonus system devised to recruit and support Vietnamese volunteer personnel. The basic procedure was introduced by CAS during the period prior to 1964. The precedent of bonus pay incentives has been frequently challenged but represented inducements that could not be withdrawn without the expectancy of desertion by trained on-board personnel, as well as political repercussions from RVN Government Joint General Staff (JGS) representatives supporting the program. The desirability of patriotic vice mercenary motivation was consistently expressed by MACSOG assigned U.S. personnel, but such philosophy was not effective in producing volunteer recruits or operators.

. . . Vietnamese volunteer recruits were initially signed to personal contracts with the Commander, Strategic Technical Directorate (STD) or the designated representative, e.g., Commander, Coastal Security Service (CSS), as the RVN contractor. Basic pay, gratuities, bonuses and periodic increases were included in the contract. . . . Complexity in the pay system was manifested in the MACSOG finance Standard Operating Procedures (SOPs) regulating salary scales, bonus inducements, disability/death gratuities, etc. . . . All payment vouchers were approved by the VN STD Commander, then submitted to the MACSOG finance officer for audit prior to transfer of funds to the STD finance officer. . . . Requests for payment of mission bonuses were directed to and required the approval of Chief, MACSOG. They were then reviewed and signed by an appropriate MACSOG officer and the STD Commander prior to transfer of funds to the STD finance officer for payment. All transfers were included in the financial returns of both the STD and the MACSOG operational units and were audited by the MACSOG comptroller.[14]

MACSOG, the Pacific Command, and the Defense Department developed the missions and forces needed to carry out those missions, but absent any assigned comptroller within MACSOG to provide the fiscal controls over such expenditures. Such planning inadequacies had been present since the plan's inception, as evident in a later look at the earliest period by the JCS:

> Logistical support for COMUSMACV [Commander, U.S. Military Command, Vietnam] OPLAN 34A, as initially conceived in November 1963, was to have been basically derived from in-country resources with the anticipated program limited to a 12-month period. Resources available in-country were estimated, in the initial plan, as adequate.[15]

As the covert operation moved forward in April 1964, the Assistant Secretary of Defense (Comptroller) attempted to work out how to pay for an organization and covert operations already in being under Phase I of Plan 34A. He reported:

> Prior to the reorganization of COMUSMACV/MAAG [Military Assistance Advisory Group]: COMUSMACV as a subordinated Unified Command Headquarters (under CINCPAC) had been financed by the Department of the Navy, using the Operation and Maintenance, Navy appropriation, Service Wide . . . by direct allotment from the Office of the Chief of Naval Operations and (2) MAAGV had been financed by the Department of the Navy, using MAP funds, by direct allotment, from the Department of the Navy to CINCPAC to MAAGV. . . . For the remainder of 1964 the financing . . . will remain unchanged except that COMUSMACV would assume the responsibilities and authorities for the use of MAP funds made available to MAAGV.[16]

Not until September 1964, however, did the Joint Chiefs of Staff record the details of the funding:

> The Chief of Naval Operations was tasked by the Joint Chiefs of Staff as the executive agent for providing

> MACSOG confidential funds. Funding procedures, satisfactory for security requirements and supporting non-attributability to the United States without prohibitive operating and procurement restrictions, were developed. DOD [Department of Defense] funding channels were through the Chief of Naval Operations (CNO), the designated DOD executive agent [CIA], and then to MACV. Annual budget requirements as estimated by MACSOG, were forwarded to the Joint Chief of Staff (SACSA) via MACV and CINCPAC. . . . Upon approval by the Joint Chiefs of Staff, CNO, as executive agent, programmed the funding and negotiated congressional approval on an appropriately classified disclosure basis. Funds were then passed quarterly by the CNO Comptroller (OP-345) sponsor. . . . [17]

U.S. Navy Capt. Bruce B. Dunning, staff officer and later division chief of the Defense Department's Special Operations Division (SOD) during 1966–67, described the Washington level actions, and inherent problems, in support of MACSOG's covert agent operations:

> . . . [T]here should be funding directly from the [Secretary of Defense], not funding by (the Services), out of a contingency fund of some sort that can be properly managed. . . . CIA has been doing it for years. The present conventional manner of authorizing a covert program and then directing a Service to assume budgetary and funding responsibility for that program is simply unsatisfactory. . . .
>
> Nobody at the Washington level scrubs out the SOG budget. Navy has the funding responsibility and, because of the manner in which SOG is set up, Navy puts on a "sponsored by SACSA" label. . . . they are not in a position, because of need-to-know, to judge the validity of the budget or the justification. Therefore it falls on us down at SACSA to go before the Congress every year and justify that budget—which we do. On the other hand, the Navy isn't looking at it from the standpoint of a comptroller. The Navy is saying, "Okay, here is the requirement, we will fill it." Then

> they put it into the Navy budget. We, in SOD, are not scrubbing out that budget once it comes in from CINCPAC because we don't have the capability. We don't have a comptroller capability. . . . We just don't have the time. As a result (incidently the House Appropriations Armed Forces Subcommittee staff members are aware of this because I was very frank to them on this point), the SOG budget presentation is not scrubbed out at any level higher than the CINCPAC. . . . We just take it the way it is submitted and hope we get the money.[18]

Unfortunately for the agents, Colonel Blackburn's decision to require that they be declared missing in action resulted in the creation of a force that would soon disappear from the financial ledgers of the United States. Before that, however, more teams would be sent into the North.

12

TEAM HECTOR

CAPT. NGUYEN HUU LUYEN, a Regular Army officer assigned to the Strategic Technical Directorate, was an experienced training officer dedicated professionally and personally to the defeat of the Communists. Luyen decided to do something to prove that the long-range team concept worked and worked well. His solution was to recruit his own team, one he could personally select, and bring in "volunteers," kids who had at least an eleventh-grade education, to form a large team named BAC BINH. He would personally supervise their training, insert them, and bring them back alive, and he predicted that they would eventually become core cadre to train the teams that would follow. As Captain Luyen explained it to his team members, the problem in locating the teams dropped into North Vietnam was that the teams were simply unable to locate and report their positions accurately.[1]

Team BAC BINH began training in November 1965. Luyen took personal command of the team's training. He tried to mold it into a large team that could be broken down into four smaller teams. By June 1966, the training had been completed and the teams were ready for launch; however, Captain Luyen's original group of more than forty was down to less than thirty, enough for only two teams.

The first team, BAC BINH 1, elected Bui Quang Cat as its commander. Captain Luyen, true to his convictions, informed the team that he would accompany it into North Vietnam as military adviser. The team moved into the restricted area that June and was redesignated HECTOR 1. On 22 June, it followed the same path as earlier teams, first to Thailand and then by helicopter into the karst formations of western Quang Binh Province. Safely on the ground, HECTOR 1 established its operational base and, for the first month, was able to operate without being captured.

Captain Luyen took the team commander and two other team members, Dinh Van Vuong and Nguyen Manh Hai, into a small mountain village to make contact with the local villagers. Other team members expressed some apprehension, but Captain Luyen assured them that it would be all right—they could get into the village and out again without any problem. Luyen had earlier espoused the doctrine that, when entering a village, one should not believe the first thing a villager said. He then ignored the very warning that he had so often passed on to his trainees. When the villagers asked him to wait, he waited while they informed local security services of his presence. The four men were captured.

The team members remaining at the operational base knew the correct procedures to follow. They were to wait for Captain Luyen and the others for no more than three hours before changing their base. Instead, they waited for five hours, so strong was their belief in the invincibility of Captain Luyen. Meanwhile, the North Vietnamese forced the team commander to lead them to the team's base and they captured the remainder of HECTOR 1. The team's two principal radio operators were added to the North Vietnamese list of agents now operating their radios under Hanoi's control.

MACSOG's steady transformation from covert agent operations to more overt reconnaissance missions coincided with General Westmoreland's efforts to move beyond the first phase of his campaign to deny Hanoi an early victory in the South. His first phase had employed U.S. forces to defend major population centers, which allowed the South Vietnamese Army to consolidate Vietnamese control in such areas. This shift from largely defensive operations in 1965 to Westmoreland's open-ended Phase II envisioned American forces pushing outward from South Vietnamese population centers into the Communist base areas.[2] Westmoreland believed that American attacks into the Communist base areas would disrupt the larger enemy units he faced and, through security

Reunion of the planners. William Colby, Chief, Far East Division, Plans Directorate, CIA Headquarters, and Col. Tran Khac Kinh, former Deputy Commander, 1st Observation Group, Army of the Republic of Vietnam, at Phuoc Hai, South Vietnam, 1965. (*Courtesy Gilbert Layton*)

Members of Team VOI and other commandos celebrate before VOI's final mission. VOI disappeared in Quang Binh Province in 1967. (*Courtesy a former commando*)

CIA maritime operations base at "China Beach," Da Nang, South Vietnam, circa 1962. *From left*: U.S. Navy maritime operations officer "Big John"; CIA officer Tucker Gougelmann; CIA officer Edward Regan; U.S. Navy maritime operations officer "Little John"; Major Tho, Da Nang-based chief, Liaison Service. (*Courtesy Edward Regan*)

Team BELL at Saigon safe house, South Vietnam, 1962. *From left*: Deo Van Hom, Ly Van Choi (commander), Lo Van Pieng, Lu The Toan (radio operator), Cam Van Cai (deputy commander), Lo Van Pieng. *(Courtesy a former commando)*

CIA preps the press, Dak Pek Special Forces Camp, Kontum Province, South Vietnam, 23 December 1962. *From left:* Pamela "Pam" Sanders, reporter, *Time/Life;* Col. "Hal" McCown, Senior Advisor, II Corps, Army of the Republic of Vietnam (ARVN); John "Jocko" Richardson, CIA Chief of Station, Saigon; 1st Lt. Bao, Commander, ARVN Special Forces Detachment, Dak Pek; Capt. George "Speedy" Gaspard. (*Courtesy George Gaspard*)

Planning for hasty agent extraction, Da Nang, South Vietnam, December 1969. *From left*: Capt. David Carr, Commander, Reconnaissance Company, Command and Control North, MACSOG; Brig. Gen. Donald "Don" Blackburn, Office of the Secretary of Defense; Lt. Col. Ernest "Pete" Hayes, MACSOG Liaison Officer to the Strategic Technical Directorate; Col. Clint Norman, General Blackburn's staff; Maj. George "Speedy" Gaspard, Operations Officer, STRATA program, MACSOG. (*Courtesy George Gaspard*)

Team EROS after completing parachute training jump at Cu Chi, South Vietnam, February 1962. *Top row, from left:* Ha Trong Thuong (commander, died in prison), Ha Cong Quan (radio operator), Pham Quang Tieu. *Bottom row, from left:* Pham Cong Thuong (radio operator), Thai, Pham Cong Dung (deputy commander). (*Courtesy Pham Cong Thuong and Pham Cong Ha*)

Tran Hieu Hoa, Team VOI, following practice parachute jump, 1967. (*Courtesy a former commando*)

Watching Switchback in progress, Dak Pek Special Forces Camp, Kontum Province, South Vietnam, 22 January 1963. *From left:* Col. James "Jim" Herbert, Military Assistance and Advisory Group Vietnam (MAAG Vietnam); Capt. George "Speedy" Gaspard; Col. Robert "Bob" Sweet, Senior Advisor, 22nd Infantry Division, Army of the Republic of Vietnam; Maj. Gen. Charles Timmes, Commanding General, MAAG Vietnam. (*Courtesy George Gaspard*)

STRATA 112 during training, South Vietnam, 1967. *From left:* "Major Crawford," Nguyen Van Tiem (supply specialist), Ngo Phong Hai (third from left), Nguyen Van Huan (looking to rear). (*Courtesy a former commando*)

Military special operations taking over, Dak Pek Special Forces Camp, Kontum Province, South Vietnam, 22 January 1963; Capt. Hoang, Commander, 2nd Battalion, 40th Regiment, 22nd Division; Capt. George "Speedy" Gaspard, Commander, Detachment A13; Lt. Col. Walter "The Shark Junior" Little, Commander, Detachment B210; Maj. Gen. William B. Rosson, Special Assistant for Counterinsurgency and Special Activities (SACSA), Office of the Secretary of Defense; Lt. Pete Skamser, Executive Officer, Detachment A13 (hidden behind General Rosson); Col. Gilbert "Gib" Strickler, CIA paramilitary officer, Combined Studies Division; Col. Gilbert "Gib" Strickler, CIA paramilitary officer, Combined Studies Division; Col. George S. Blanchard, Deputy Director, Special Warfare Directorate, SACSA (hidden behind Colonel Strickler); Col. George Morton, Commander, U.S. Army Special Forces Vietnam (Provisional); Lt. Col. "Butch" Kendrick, Operations Staff, Military Assistance Command Vietnam (MACV); Lt. Col. Eisler, Deputy Chief of Staff for Logistics, MACV (*Courtesy George Gaspard*)

during upcoming harvests, deny the enemy the ability to feed itself from foodstuffs grown inside South Vietnam.[3] Such ground operations were coordinated with Seventh Fleet efforts in the Gulf of Tonkin to shut down the maritime infiltration of supplies by the Vietnam People's Navy Group 125.[4]

The spring of 1966 saw continued public disturbances as the Buddhists demanded more reforms from the South Vietnamese government. Washington was advocating elections as the way to demonstrate the democratic process that the State Department had long felt was sorely needed to provide a fundamental foundation for the heirs of the late President Diem.

As HECTOR was preparing to go north, Vietnam People's Army forces struck directly across the DMZ, rather than make a roundabout march along its western edge through Laos. This coincided with increasing American air strikes down the Ho Chi Minh Trail, including the use of B-52 bombers inside Laos to the west of such border-crossing lanes as the Mu Gia Pass. The tens of thousands of local youths from the North's Assault Young Group, particularly teenage women, quickly repaired the roads and largely negated the temporary interdiction of the supply and personnel infiltration routes.

Brig. Gen. Joseph A. McChristian, Westmoreland's chief of intelligence (J-2), warned that North Vietnamese forces increasingly were relying on the Cambodian sanctuaries to sustain their growing ground attack.[5] This was supported by intelligence from all sources that provided hard evidence of Hanoi's 559th Group supply lines being enlarged and extended well into Cambodia. Defense Secretary McNamara, faced with growing pressure to strike into the Cambodian sanctuaries, was effectively prohibiting any statements from the senior commanders in the field about the growing role of these sanctuaries.[6] McNamara found support from CIA analysts who viewed General Westmoreland's command as "overstating the significance of Cambodia to the Communists fighting in South Vietnam."[7]

McNamara now let slip a new concept, called Project Jason, pushed on him by his advisers.[8] Publicized by McNamara in September and soon nicknamed "McNamara's

Line,'' this concept envisioned a line of sensors and interlocking defensive fortifications that threatened to tie down hundreds of thousands of American and South Vietnamese troops in static defensive positions. Although the massive defensive fortification aspect would never be implemented, the concept signaled the use of sensors in a concerted effort to bring electronics to the ground war. The agent teams still in training at Long Thanh were quietly prepared to play a small part in the early employment and test of the sensor concept on the ground inside North Vietnam.

On 13 September 1966, the remaining members of Team BAC BINH were designated Team HECTOR 2. They moved into the restricted area at Long Thanh to hear their mission briefing. A U.S. Army major, with Captain Dung[9] interpreting, outlined their mission: conduct reconnaissance on the Ho Chi Minh Trail. More precise mission orders would come by radio after they arrived in North Vietnam and had established contact with the Directorate. This operation would last two years, and they could expect monthly adjustments in their specific operating areas, depending on the mission and situation.

Captain Dung briefed separately that HECTOR 2's mission included searching for HECTOR 1 and reporting back on its location if found. After the Directorate lost contact with HECTOR 1, Captain Dung, flying over the area in an L-19, had personally searched for it. He even took aerial photographs of the area where the team was supposed to be, but they showed no sign of it. Captain Dung stressed the personal ties between the men in teams HECTOR 1 and 2.[10] He wanted HECTOR 2 to have a spirit of responsibility in fulfilling its role as an augmentation team by helping to locate HECTOR 1, just as HECTOR 1 had gone into North Vietnam to develop a ''safe and secure'' base of operations for itself and HECTOR 2. In short, HECTOR 1 was looking for HECTOR 2 to come to its rescue.

Dang Dinh Thuy, the military adviser for HECTOR 2, urged a launch as soon as possible, and his views were echoed by the team members, most of whom believed strongly in Captain Luyen and his ability to survive. They all accepted Captain Dung's explanation that HECTOR 1 somehow had become lost in the mountains.

Captain Dung reviewed each individual's position and duty in HECTOR 2. Mai Nhue Anh was team commander, and Vu Van Chi was deputy commander. When they landed in North Vietnam, Hoang Dinh Kha was to be the first off the helicopter. He would determine the security status of the area, while other team members assisted in off-loading the heavy boxes of equipment.

Aerial photography showed their landing zone as a tiny dot in an area of operations that would be approximately five thousand square kilometers. They would be dropped by helicopter some distance away from the Ho Chi Minh Trail and well away from any villages in an area of mountains and karst formations. Here, they would be safe and secure.

They were told that the helicopter they would use for the insertion was a modern, fast aircraft; forty of them had been sent to Southeast Asia exclusively for team insertions. The helicopter could also transport large amounts of supplies that would be off-loaded onto a landing zone, thus avoiding the problem of equipment lost during airdrops. Everything was being done to make sure that HECTOR 2 would succeed in its mission.

After the briefings, Team HECTOR 2 was airlifted by an American transport to Udorn Air Base in Thailand, where it transferred onto a new American helicopter for the relatively short flight to its landing site.

The flight in was uneventful. The team was soon inserted into an area that seemed more like a primitive park than a landing zone inside North Vietnam. Supposedly, it was the landing zone where HECTOR 1 had been inserted less than three months before.

The aerial photographs reviewed by the team at Long Thanh did not convey the quiet peace of the landing site, with a stream running through tall elephant grass. The area, measuring less than two hundred feet across, was surrounded by stark karst formations. The team members could imagine nighttime scenes of deer and other wild animals coming to feed there. As Captain Dung had said, it appeared far removed from any North Vietnamese forces, safely isolated, from which they could easily conduct reconnaissance against the Ho Chi Minh Trail. There seemed to be no more perfect a spot than this.

The helicopter came in slowly for its landing. The weight of the team and equipment unexpectedly caused the aircraft to become mired in the soft ground. Everyone, including Captain Dung and the American training officer who had come with them, joined in off-loading the equipment as quickly as possible. The helicopter's load was lightened sufficiently for it to take off, and there was a lot of joking, smiling, and waving good-bye as the helicopter lifted off for the flight back to Thailand.

Less than five minutes later, staccato bursts of AK-47 assault rifle fire were directed at the team members as they were unpacking crates. Everyone had the same thought instantly—they had walked into a trap!

Deputy Commander Vu Van Chi and one of his team members, Huan, returned fire, but the North Vietnamese ambushers appeared to fade away in the face of it. Huan began to move out in the direction of the enemy and was mortally wounded by a sudden burst of machine-gun fire within seconds. The tempo of fire increased as well-positioned ambushers sprayed the center of the team's position from a break in the dense brush perimeter.

During the opening fire, Hoang Dinh Kha also had been hit, possibly in the heart. His body lay covered in a massive amount of blood as the North Vietnamese opened up with a heavy volume of automatic weapons fire. Clearly, their objective was to kill the commandos, not merely keep them pinned down and capture them.

Running toward a nearby cleft in the karst, Vu Van Chi encountered four armed North Vietnamese and immediately opened fire. The lieutenant directing a three-man cell was hit in the arm, the bullet passing through it and hitting his trigger finger. One cell member was hit in the thigh, with the bullet lodging in his buttocks. The other two, lying close by, were killed almost immediately.

After an initial heavy exchange of fire, both sides ceased firing to consolidate their positions in the approaching dusk. By now, the team was scattered around the landing zone, and contact was lost as each individual waited quietly for the North Vietnamese to make their next move.

The next morning, a heavy rain started to fall. The team was now completely scattered. Several small, isolated groups prepared to attempt evasion. This "perfect" landing zone had now become a most perfect death trap.

Vu Van Chi, Nguyen Ngoc Nghia, and Tong Van Thai withdrew quickly into a nearby open cave, but they were prepared to move out at the first opportunity. As day broke in a downpour, the three found themselves surrounded by well-armed North Vietnamese, who approached with their automatic weapons pointing straight into the cave and called on the three to surrender. Chi told Nghia and Thai that he would go outside first and to open fire if he was shot. They were to fire until nearly out of ammunition and then commit suicide. They agreed, and Chi walked into the arms of the waiting North Vietnamese. He was quickly disarmed and tied tightly with telephone wire. Seeing that Chi had not been shot outright, his two comrades followed him out and surrendered. Nearly the entire team was captured that day, although the primary radio operator, Nguyen Van Dinh, managed to evade capture for eight days.

The sudden, fierce attack so soon after their landing meant that the team was unable to establish radio contact with the Directorate after its insertion. During their training at Long Thanh, Captain Dung had emphasized the need to establish communications with the Directorate within the first twenty-four hours of the mission. Their swift capture within that period could have resulted in their radio operators being recruited, but Nguyen Van Dinh's evasion prevented this. Nghia, who had been captured with Vu Van Chi, had the team's radio equipment but not the signal operating instructions and codes, which were with Dinh. By the time Dinh was captured, it was too late for the North Vietnamese to attempt radio contact with the Directorate because late contact would indicate that the team had been captured and was under hostile control.

As the individual commandos were captured and herded together, they learned that their captors were from a North Vietnamese border defense regiment permanently stationed along this part of the "strategic route," that broad system of roads and trails known as the Ho Chi Minh Trail. The troops bragged that they provided security for the North Vietnamese

Army units moving into Laos through Quang Binh Province as they made their way into South Vietnam. The captors were all so very young and spoke with the heavy accent of the natives of Quang Binh Province. To capture the commandos, they explained, they had been reinforced by local village militia as added insurance that the commandos would be unable to evade the ambush.

The next morning, the commandos saw the body of a dead North Vietnamese officer and learned that he was the unit medical technician. When they looked around, they saw other North Vietnamese wounded lying there, shivering.

The North Vietnamese quickly searched through the team's cases to find the medical supplies that should have been there, but at least half of the supplies, primarily those needed for field surgery, were missing. Someone at Long Thanh had stolen them. Also missing were ammunition and other supplies. Even if the team had not been captured, the wholesale theft of their supplies would have precluded a successful mission. From the few medical supplies available, the commandos administered morphine injections to the wounded and gave them APC tablets for pain. The members of Team HECTOR 2 did not know that its supplies had been packed and sealed by Americans.

The border defense unit started the march with its captives on 25 September. That first night, they rested in a small streamside village and started out again early the next morning. After a forced march through dense jungle, the prisoners arrived in another village at 10 P.M. on 26 September. Long abandoned by its former hill tribe residents, the village was now headquarters for the provincial border defense forces regiment that had captured the team.

At regimental headquarters, the team members waited for two or three days before the interrogators, who were coming from the coastal lowlands, could reach them. Then the questioning began in earnest, with two interrogators per prisoner. Each interrogation unit consisted of one interrogator from the Ministry of Public Security and one from the Quang Binh Province Public Security Office. The topics and methodology of each differed. For example, interrogators from the Ministry of Public Security asked the team members about their mission, the subjects of their training, and how they were to conduct their operations. The local men asked for the identity of the individual they would contact in the village they were to enter, and about the types of documents and information that the individual would provide them. In reality, the team had no plans to enter any specific village and did not have orders to make contact with anyone. Obviously, someone had misled the North Vietnamese into believing that Team HECTOR 2 had certain information that they clearly did not have. The two interrogators questioned one prisoner and then moved on to another. The questioning was almost cursory, as if HECTOR 2 had nothing to contribute. The North Vietnamese seemed to know everything about them they needed to know.

At the interrogation point, HECTOR 2 came face to face with what had happened to HECTOR 1. The latter's two primary radio operators, Tran Huu Tuan and Nguyen Van Thuy, who were kept separate under armed guard, were also at the headquarters. Their presence lent credibility to what a North Vietnamese officer told them after HECTOR 2's capture, "The part of your team sent in earlier was captured. After we captured your team, its radio operators were the ones who went on their radio and asked for reinforcements. That's why you all were sent in. The first half of your team has already been sent down to the coastal lowlands and you all will be sent there later. You know we've been waiting here for you for nearly two months?"

Shortly after mid-October, approximately three weeks following capture, HECTOR 2 was suddenly moved northeast in the direction of the coast. As the prisoners left the regimental headquarters, they were accompanied by Thuy, one of HECTOR 1's recruited radio operators. Tran Huu Tuan remained behind with the North Vietnamese border defense regiment to continue operation of his radio.

Moving along the Ho Chi Minh Trail, the team came within two minutes of being hit in an air strike as a flight of two American A-1 Skyraiders bombed the trail. The commandos and their escort guards saw the aircraft make their first bomb run and moved into the safety of rocks close to the road.

The commandos saw just how quickly and effectively the North Vietnamese were able to repair bomb damage, as dump trucks moved massive amounts of rock to fill in the bomb craters. The trucks had been kept hidden off the road in caves and sheltered locations close to massive piles of crushed rock. As soon as the American aircraft left the area, the trucks were loaded and large numbers of North Vietnamese children from the Assault Youth Group descended on the road from both sides to help fill in and level the craters. The children, who were permanently deployed along each road segment targeted by the bombers, remained up to a kilometer off the road during the raids to avoid being hit. Like an army of ants, they swarmed out to make the road completely usable within hours afterward.

The slow march northeast along the trail took nearly a week before the captives came out of the mountains and into the lowlands. This was obviously the northeastern terminus of the portion of the trail that ran into Laos through Quang Binh Province. By the end of October, they reached an area, within two kilometers of the coast, that local villagers said was still inside Quang Binh Province but close to its boundary with Nghe An Province.

While resting in a local village after lunch, the prisoners were shown the wreckage of an American aircraft, mangled remains of a jet sitting in a large, flat, grass-covered open area, perhaps a kilometer across. Only the skeleton of the aircraft and unidentifiable piles of wreckage remained; all the larger pieces of metal apparently had been salvaged by local residents. Villagers were only too happy to tell them how the aircraft had been shot down three months earlier. The two-man crew successfully bailed out and were reportedly taken prisoner.

Shortly after passing the crash site, the prisoners turned south toward Dong Hoi, the seat of Quang Binh Province, where they arrived the next evening. On the northern outskirts of coastal Dong Hoi City, almost on the beach in an area of dense pine forest, interrogations resumed for two weeks. The team members were housed in a temporary "dispersed" prison established in one of the four buildings comprising the office space of a long-abandoned village cooperative. Within several days, they were able to determine that Team HECTOR 1 was also there, in a separate building approximately one hundred meters away. The area was not fenced or walled, but there was never any thought of escape because the prisoners were shackled by their ankles to a heavy metal bar.

In approaching Dong Hoi, the prisoners had noticed that every tile-roofed building in the area was in shambles, obviously the result of air strikes. Strangely, their detention site was never hit, although the surrounding area was pounded. This led them to conclude that the Americans had determined it to be a prison and it was therefore off limits as a target.

After two weeks at Dong Hoi, the captives departed for Hanoi. Arriving a week later, they were jailed in Thanh Tri Prison. That fall, several prisoners, who spoke English with American accents, arrived at Thanh Tri and were quickly shunted into two cells in Area C. In the summer of 1967, Team HECTOR was transferred to Phong Quang Prison. The men had no way of knowing their cells were needed for a team known as HADLEY.

13

"WE KNEW YOU WERE COMING . . ."

THE SUMMER OF 1967 was long and hot in the coastal region of Ha Tinh Province. American bombers continued their attacks into the narrow panhandle against such targets as coastal Ha Tinh City and its suburbs. In the rural villages of Ha Tinh, life revolved around the August harvest more than the now all too frequent day and night air strikes.[1]

In one village near Ha Tinh City, militia and regular army guards sat drowsing outside prison huts. The prisoners inside were popularly known as "spy commandos." The Ministry of Public Security interrogators did not come around much now. Perhaps they had finished their interrogations, and the village could settle back to normalcy—until the next group of prisoners came through.

This late evening in July 1967 was like any other following a long day in the fields. It was the traditional time for farmers to get together to reflect on the course of the summer growing season and gossip about the recent heavy American bombing.

"It was unbelievable," came a voice out of the darkness, "the way those American jets hit the ammunition depot with the fire from their 20-mm cannons. They were so precise . . . that was the only thing they hit in the city . . . the depot just kept exploding, and exploding, and exploding."

"I know," came another voice hidden in the gloom of a small oil lamp, "but that still doesn't matter, you know. Don't forget, our soldiers aren't the only ones being hit. We've all lost family from the air strikes too. Remember when the villagers got that American, the one who parachuted down after his jet was hit and shot down by the antiaircraft fire? That one villager with the ox yoke . . . he just took it and beat the pilot to death before the army could get there."

"Right," came the quiet reply. "The troops just want to protect the pilots and keep the villagers from killing them. That's easy for them to do. They are the fighters. But how about us? We're losing family, too. So why does the army keep us from killing the Americans? If they can kill them, then we should be able to kill them too." There was a rumble of general agreement.

In the hut adjacent to the small circle of farmers, Le Van Ngung, commander of Team HADLEY, lay on his side with his arms still tied tightly behind him. The young girl from the village militia had not come tonight to loosen the telephone wires biting into his upper arms, but he had been too interested in listening to the two farmers to take note of his pain.

If he were not a prisoner, he would listen intently, trying to glean every scrap of information that he could from the conversation. This was the kind of information he would have reported back to the Directorate. But, now it was different. He was a prisoner, and his need was to live from day to day. He ignored the farmers. Sleep was the only thing on his mind.

Half a year earlier, the eleven members of training team T, redesignated Team HADLEY, had entered the restricted area at their training base outside Long Thanh. They had waited for that moment, trained for it, and now it was here. They had seen other teams enter this area and then leave on their own missions. None ever returned. But, that was understandable—it was still early. The teams would not be back for a couple of years.

The men of Team HADLEY clowned around, smiling, joking, and making brave faces at the camera held by their American adviser, Capt. Fred Caristo. In just a few more days they would leave. They were sure of it now.

Originally, the team had fifteen members. When they voted for Le Van Ngung to be their commander, four did not agree to accept his leadership. So, the four were split off to form a separate team, training team T2. Team T2 would stay behind and come later to reinforce Team HADLEY.

It was just days before the start of the Vietnamese Lunar New Year celebration. They knew that the closer they got to the Lunar New Year, the more lax things would become. People did not always pay attention to their work when they concentrated on planning the New Year festivities. If the team was going to be launched, the members wanted it done quickly, before someone forgot to do something and neglected to give the team all the attention it deserved.

Before departing the base, Captain Dung and Captain Caristo asked the team pointedly if they were afraid.

Afraid? No way!

Then the officers tried to test them. They told them that one year earlier another team had gone into the same area where they would land, had been declared missing, and never returned. The team members rationalized such statements as being something they were told to heighten their vigilance, a way to test the team's morale. Within hours, after a quick trip to the airport, they loaded onto their aircraft and took off. After they were in the air, Captain Caristo announced a sudden change in plans. They would not be dropping in by parachute after all. There was a storm with high winds and heavy rain in the area of the drop zone. This meant they would have to abort the mission.

The mission was aborted in part because Caristo and others at MACSOG believed they had a problem. Caristo was convinced that there had to be a North Vietnamese agent, a "mole," among the Vietnamese side of their force. They had been seeing it for months, teams dropped in and captured right after landing. Trying some changes, they withheld details of the operations from the South Vietnamese officers, did not tell them the true locations of landing zones, and gave them other false information. Although MACSOG tried to isolate the leak, the North Vietnamese were always waiting for the teams.

The abrupt change in HADLEY's plans was deliberate, designed to throw off whoever was informing the North Vietnamese about their agent team operation. The problem was, how would they know if and when it was working?

After returning to Long Thanh, Team HADLEY was rebriefed by Captain Caristo, Captain Dung, and the camp commander. One more week, the men were told, and then they would depart from the airfield at Long Thanh. Their mission was relatively simple: to conduct operations along Highway 4 inside North Vietnam. The team could operate there for up to two years. It would be pulled out at the end of that time, provided it was safe to exfiltrate them by helicopter. Few members of the team expected they would be able to operate for much more than six months.

The team was to plant a sensor south of Highway 4 in western Huong Son District of Ha Tinh Province, close to the border with Laos. The sensor was intended to detect trucks and other types of heavy vehicles; foot traffic would not activate it. The optimal location for the sensor was within five to ten meters of the roadway. The team also would conduct reconnaissance of the bridges along the highway that would be destroyed later by air strikes. Once the team had landed and established communication with the Directorate, it would receive further instructions and additional missions.

Reviewing the aerial photography of the landing area, Caristo pointed out the closest village, a small collection of houses approximately five kilometers south of their landing point. The team would move from there to its first base of operations, a point about five kilometers to the north of the landing zone. That would place it several kilometers southeast of Highway 4. Captain Dung warned the men of possible problems. Security in the area could not be guaranteed because the Directorate had lost another team in this same region a year earlier, but Dung did not mention any specific enemy forces in the area.

Captain Dung stressed that when the team reached the landing zone, Quy was to be the first person out of the helicopter. He was to reconnoiter to make sure the area was secure before the remainder of the team disembarked. Captain Dung went over each task with each of the team members. Le Van Ngung would have command once they were on the ground, but there was no question that Dung's instructions were to be followed.

The officers checked the items of equipment for each team member. Each would be armed with a Swedish K submachine gun, a Browning automatic pistol, and four grenades, and carry a pack containing rations for several days. The radio equipment was broken down and divided among the team's three radio operators. The men smiled. Obviously, they would be traveling light. Captain Dung stressed that the team was to contact the Directorate by radio on the evening of the landing or certainly not later than the next day, if at all possible.

On 25 January 1967, Team HADLEY boarded a truck for the quick ride to Tan Son Nhat Airport. Accompanied by Caristo and Dung, the team made the short flight to Thailand in a U.S. transport aircraft. In Thailand, the team transferred to a waiting dark-green helicopter piloted by Americans. The transfer took little more than an hour and was handled so smoothly that no one on the ground would have noticed their arrival and departure.

The helicopter flew at an altitude below five hundred feet to avoid being spotted. Shortly after crossing what the men were told was the border between Laos and North Vietnam, one of the officers leaned over and told them that the helicopter had just taken ground fire from Communist forces below. The men accepted this as something to be expected because the North Vietnamese Army was well entrenched in eastern Laos along the Ho Chi Minh Trail, over which they obviously had just flown.

Within minutes, at about 6:15 that evening, the helicopter dropped down and hovered. A second helicopter, circling the landing zone, stayed overhead to provide cover. By now, the ground fire was forgotten.

While their helicopter hovered a steady six to eight feet off the ground, Quy jumped out. Then, instead of waiting for the all clear and contrary to the mission order, the remainder of the team was told to jump off immediately. After jumping into tall elephant grass blown flat by the wash from the rotor, the men moved away from the landing point and watched the helicopter lift out of the area, circle once or twice, and head back toward Thailand. They were concerned about tigers, which frequently hid in such grass. The supposedly inclement weather that had delayed their initial launch was gone.

They moved away from the landing zone along the planned route of march to the first regrouping point some five kilometers distant. But, with the approaching darkness and slow progress because of a heavy equipment bag acquired in Thailand, the commander ordered them to stop after moving only two hundred meters. Ngung had concluded that the heavy brush would make any nighttime movement almost impossible.

The team set up a defensive perimeter and bivouacked for the night. Just before daybreak, the men assembled to set out again. A light rain had begun to fall, and they felt something strange in the air. Also, they had not expected more inclement weather.

Suddenly, from the direction of their landing zone came the sound of dogs barking, like German shepherds being used by people, not just dogs running wild. Then, the commandos heard men yelling in Vietnamese and bursts of fire, unmistakably sporadic fire from AK-47 assault rifles.

"Here they are . . . they're already here . . . here they are." The voices were faint but clearly audible in the early morning air. Obviously, the troops were searching for them. And, more disturbing, the troops must have been expecting them and knew the precise location of their landing zone.

The sound of barking dogs and automatic weapons fire continued for several minutes while the team froze. It was apparent that the North Vietnamese troops were firing at random, perhaps trying to spook the commandos into revealing their position. The sound of the dogs started to grow faint, and the weapons firing slacked off. It became evident that the troops were moving away in the opposite direction.

The team assembled its gear and started off. It moved for two days without incident but was able to cover only three kilometers. The route of march had been easy to see on the aerial photos, but, once on the ground, the commandos found themselves moving through unimaginably dense brush that was not visible in the photos. The drizzle now turned into heavy, driving rain that drenched everything and made any rapid movement impossible. Their heavy bag of equipment slowed them even more. The march was further impeded by Vu Van Hinh, one of the two team members Captain Dung had assigned as point man. Hinh was having difficulty using his compass and reading the map. He was unsure if they were even heading in the right direction. After a short distance, the commander relieved him and placed Hinh in the center of the column. Ngung took the point himself, as well as the portable voice radio.

Spaced well apart, the team moved in a staggered column to ensure that the entire team would not be ambushed from either the front or rear without some warning.

The unexpected arrival of the North Vietnamese troops had delayed establishing radio communications with the Directorate. Two team radio operators, Nguyen The Khoa and Pham Viet Phuc, refused to set up their radios to transmit the initial Morse code message to the Directorate. They were ordered to do so but still refused. They cited the length of time it would take to get the antenna up, put the components together, and get their equipment operating, all while trying to evade the pursuing North Vietnamese. The use of the voice radio was rejected because its radius was limited either to ground-to-air communications or to contact with another ground location within fifty kilometers, even though Captain Dung had said the radio could be used to contact the Directorate. Ngung did not push the point about getting on the air, which he would regret for years to come.

As team members looked back later, they realized that the North Vietnamese troops must have been following their forward movement and were just waiting for the right time to attack. They struck late on the afternoon of 27 January. Ngung, on point, was nearing the crest of a hill when he came under small-arms fire from the base of the reverse slope of the hill, while AK-47 fire slashed through the trees above him. Hitting the ground, each team member crawled a short distance from where he had been standing in the column of march and measured the volume of the fire and direction from which it was coming.

As the fire increased, it was evident that the team had been maneuvered to reach the hilltop. Using a quiet and clever trap, a North Vietnamese company-sized unit had surrounded Team HADLEY at the base of the hill. How had the North Vietnamese set up the ambush so quickly, without the commandos catching on? Had the North Vietnamese actually been there ahead of them, just waiting for them to arrive? Their encirclement meant one thing: the enemy had known their destination and deployed the ambushers to cut them off.

The enemy troops began moving slowly toward the

trapped men, who tossed grenades down the hill. Screams indicated that perhaps they wounded some of the North Vietnamese. The surrounding force was close enough for them to hear the tactical interrogation of one of their team when he was captured.

"Where are they? Where did the others go?" They could hear Vu Nhu Tung replying, "Over there, see, there they go over there . . . see them . . . see them?" Then came the sounds of the army troops moving off in the opposite direction.

The team commander and three others, Quy, Lao, and Khoa, found themselves in a depression of dense brush. They waited without moving, concerned that the ambushers were lurking nearby, and hoped they would give away their positions. After an hour, the four men crawled slowly down the hill and began to evade in the direction from which they had come. Two days later, they encountered Tinh and Ninh, who also had been evading to the west. At this point, they concluded that the absence of four team members probably meant the North Vietnamese had captured three of their team in addition to Vu Nhu Tung. Their capture spelled disaster for the team. Phuc and Luong Trong Thuong, two of the radio operators, had carried the key components for the communications equipment, including the hand-cranked power generator. This meant that the team could not warn the Directorate that the North Vietnamese had been waiting for them and they were now under attack. The short-range HT-1 voice radios were useless, and their principal voice radio had been carried by Vu Van Hinh, apparently also a prisoner.

The rain continued. The nights in the mountains were bitter cold, typical January weather for North Vietnam, but something they had never considered dealing with under their present circumstances. They had their weapons, but the packs with their field rations were gone, discarded in the initial firefight, as well as the heavy parachute pack of supplies. There was only one thing to do. They had to move west into Laos and try to reach Thailand. They had landed close to the border, near a major North Vietnamese infiltration network. Perhaps they could slip across it without being seen and reach Thailand safely.

One team member had a survival pack with fish hooks and

line. A little digging produced some small worms, a cut branch became a pole, and they were able to catch a dozen finger-sized minnows in a stream. Searching the dense vegetation, they discovered nothing to eat except a small red fruit. It was so bitter and acidic that it not only puckered the mouth but, within hours, caused the tongue to crack open. Several days later, they saw small green fruit high up in tall trees. It was out of reach, but they found a few that had fallen to the ground and cooked them in boiling rainwater. This was their first food in days.

The driving rain continued without letup as they moved west. On 1 February, they ran out of energy and could no longer move. It did not seem to matter now if they were discovered. They had found a small stream and an abandoned lean-to, little more than a useless artifact of some long-gone hill tribe hunter. Its roof was in tatters, but it represented a link to civilization. Huddling near the shack, even though it gave absolutely no shelter from the pouring rain, they discussed the situation. They decided to stay where they were and die together, if that was necessary. Their only activity was getting water from the stream and heating it before drinking.

Their situation deteriorated further on 3 February when three of them, Ngung, Khoa, and Khoan, came down with sudden high fevers followed by intense shivering. The next day, the rain suddenly stopped and the daytime temperature rose, as did their hopes.

At approximately nine o'clock that morning, the men heard an explosion. Several propeller-driven aircraft resembling Skyraiders appeared overhead and dived on a ground target perhaps five kilometers away. They quickly cleared an open area and gathered dead brush to light a fire in the hope that the smoke would attract one of the aircraft, which were obviously friendly, and the pilot might recognize them as "friendlies." One airplane flew in slow circles over their position as they jumped up and down and waved T-shirts. The aircraft didn't attack, just continued its lazy circling, and this gave them renewed hope. Certainly, the pilot would report what he had seen, and they all expected helicopters to come, almost immediately, to their rescue. They waited until long after the aircraft had departed, still expecting momentary rescue. They waited through noontime and into the late afternoon, but nothing came.

They heard sudden bursts of automatic weapons fire at about six o'clock that evening. Bullets whipped into the brush above them. North Vietnamese Army troops were still searching for them! Just as before, they fired high into the trees. Lao and Tinh returned the fire; Khoa and Le Van Ngung were still prone with fever. After fifteen minutes of sporadic shooting, the surrounding troops rushed the seven commandos and captured them without encountering any further resistance.

The North Vietnamese Army troops knew who the commandos were. As they tied them up with telephone wire, wrists and arms tied behind the back and above the elbow, the soldiers asked each one the same question: "Where is the team commander?"

Ngung replied that he was the commander. Their next question wasn't surprising. "Are you Ngung?"

Obviously, they had interrogated the first prisoners and had learned from them about the seven survivors. Ngung was still somewhat delirious from fever, and he replied that his name wasn't Ngung. The soldiers just laughed, smacked him, and yelled at him.

"Nonsense! You're the one named Ngung. You don't have any name other than that."

Almost immediately afterward, the North Vietnamese soldiers cooked rice gruel and fed it to their starving captives. They treated the captives gently, knowing of other uses for them that would require their complete cooperation.

As if to rub salt into an open wound, one of the soldiers looked at Ngung and laughed as he spoke, "You know, even before you landed we already knew of your planned arrival. We knew the precise time and we knew precisely where you would land. Because of this, we had already organized regular army forces, local units, and village militia to capture you after you landed."

The commandos didn't quite know what to make of the remark. Was it true? Did they really know, or were they just bluffing?

One North Vietnamese, obviously the officer in charge, went from prisoner to prisoner and asked only four questions:

name, age, position, and assigned duties. After that, the commandos were marched overland on foot to the west, evidently into Laos and perhaps close to Highway 4. At about ten o'clock that night, they finally came to a village of hill tribe Lao where they spent the night. The commandos were carefully watched by two armed guards at each house, one a member of the village militia and the other a uniformed member of the People's Army.

Early the next morning, a truck arrived before daybreak to take them to the start of their interrogation. They were now heading east.

"I promise you," said an interrogator in civilian clothes, his voice firm but friendly, "you will be rewarded if you cooperate. If you are honest and truthful, not only will the State reward you but your family in South Vietnam will be able to continue to receive your full pay and allowances."

Such remarks were unsettling and designed to entrap the unwary. The message was clear: If you cooperate and operate your radio for North Vietnam, the Directorate will never find out. The Directorate will think you are still alive and will continue paying your family.

The Public Security Service cadre knew that they had to have the safety signals of the team commander and the radio operators in order for their deception operation to work. They also knew that the safety signals employed were tricky and they could never be sure if they had the right one. If a wrong answer was given, the Directorate would be automatically alerted that the team was transmitting under duress. The interrogators pressed everyone for the responses that Captain Dung had given them prior to their departure. If any prisoner remained silent, the interrogations continued until he either provided an answer or refused to cooperate. Once Ngung and Thuong refused to provide their signals, the North Vietnamese interrogators did not accept as genuine any signals that were offered.

By the time the prisoners reached Trung Linh Village, the two radio operators, Khoa and Phuc, were no longer with them. The others had seen long wire antennas in the village. Is that where the radio operators were? Had they agreed to cooperate?

After one week at Trung Linh, the commandos were

moved east to the village of Cam Thach. They were now seven kilometers from the center of Ha Tinh City, the seat of Ha Tinh Province. Here, they saw groups of ten or twelve prisoners, in striped prison uniforms, on work details under armed guard. Apparently, they had arrived at the provincial prison that had been relocated temporarily to the countryside to escape the American bombing.

The interrogations continued at Cam Thach. Although the prisoners had been subconsciously prepared for the worst, they had no counterinterrogation training. This made it easier for the North Vietnamese interrogators to ply their craft.

Now came months of exhaustive interrogation. The younger of the two interrogators questioning one of the captives was a native of Ha Tinh. He came early in the morning and went nonstop until noon. After a two-hour break, the interrogations started again and continued uninterrupted until nightfall. This regimen went on for days. The older interrogator, a native of southern Vietnam, often just sat and listened. His job was not so much interrogation as breaking down the barriers of resistance when the prisoner wouldn't answer a question. There was no brutality here. They needed cooperative prisoners.

Every subject the team members had studied in training was covered, topic by topic. "Which teams were also undergoing training at the same time you were in training?" They wanted to know about every team, barracks by barracks, area by area, and they learned about training teams L, M, N, P, R, S, T, and U; the road-watch teams then being formed, name by name; the Lao team; the Hmong team. They also wanted to know which teams had already departed on missions, as well as the smaller augmentation teams, name by name; which teams would be dispatched in the future; who the instructors were; their names and ranks.

The interrogators asked about the Americans: Who were they? What did they do? What was their role? What were their names and ranks? They asked about the Taiwanese intelligence liaison officer at Long Thanh, and they went over every individual in the Strategic Technical Directorate and MACSOG, including physical descriptions of each, as well as every American and Vietnamese with whom they had contact.

The questions sometimes came in random sequence, but the probing came over and over for the same crucial facts: Which teams had already departed and which teams would be dispatched in the future? Clearly, they wanted to make sure that they knew about every team dispatched so far and every team that might be coming in the future.

The agents told their interrogators what they wanted to know. Except Le Van Ngung—he was not cooperative. The older interrogator came to "motivate" him and to begin the slow, inexorable process called "reeducation."

"The whole problem with all of you is that you have this religion you claim you believe in, this religion which is nothing more than superstition and witchcraft. All the religions like Buddhism and Christianity, they are all just witchcraft," the interrogator said, as he launched into another one of his sermons.

"Your religions can't help you if you're sick," he explained patiently. "When you're sick, you go to a doctor. You don't get rid of your illness through prayer. Your prayer can't cure you, only a doctor can. You all just pray to your gods, believing that your religion can make you well again."

Ngung knew the thrust of the interrogator's argument, a familiar one to all Vietnamese. He brought up the practices of many of the hill tribe people who believed in spirits and practiced witchcraft, people who made altars on which they placed various objects in an appeal to the spirits to cure their problems. The mountain people had an unshakable belief that the spirits could cure anything, including any form of sickness, and that the right prayer and ceremony would bring relief from pain.

The commando sat there, unmoved by the interrogator's logic.

"I will agree with you on one point," he conceded. "Those people who pray to the spirits are indeed practicing witchcraft. I would agree with you that those people are not going to get well by doing the things they do. But, I don't agree with your whole argument. After all, there are many doctors and other medical specialists who are also devout Catholics and Buddhists, people who are able to practice their religion and medical profession at the same time and without conflict. Do you understand just how many people there are in the Free World who are this way? There are countries in the Free World that have even produced spaceships. Do you think the people who did these things are not religious? There are Buddhists, Protestants, Catholics . . . do you think all these people practice witchcraft? How about the doctors? They dispense medicine, and yet they too are religious.''

"Damn liar! You are a stubborn liar, a troublemaker . . . I've been explaining everything to you and you continue to maintain this stubborn attitude.'' The interrogator stood up in a huff and then left the room.

That same kind of logic was repeated a year later at Thanh Tri Prison on the outskirts of Hanoi. Senior Captain Loc, the short, fifty-year-old prison commander, sat in the prison courtyard and read selections from the daily newspapers to the prisoners locked in their cells. From time to time, he would bring forth various arguments to explain the contradictions between the capitalists and the Communists, arguments he hoped would persuade his prisoners of the correctness of the Communist view of the world.

''The capitalists,'' Loc announced, ''would ask you to believe that they are rich, incredibly rich. In actuality, they are poor, very poor. Do you know why? Every one of these capitalists has two shirts. But *only* those two shirts! None of them has a third shirt, just two of them. Because of their poverty they had to invent nylon. It was a way to mask their poverty. It was a material which, when washed, could be hung out to dry and within fifteen or twenty minutes it would be completely dry. Some of you might mistakenly believe that nylon is a great advancement but you should understand that nylon came about because of the poverty of the capitalists.

''You all know the way we do things in Vietnam,'' he continued. ''We don't work straight through lunch the way the Americans do. We work in the morning and then rest for several hours at noon. Now, the capitalists in the South and other countries go home at noon, wash the shirt they wore in the morning, and hurry back to work with a clean shirt. This way, through the existence of nylon, they can wash their shirt, have it dry quickly, and not let others know they are so poor. You really must believe me. They only have two shirts. They are really poor. You can't imagine just how poor these capitalists are."

Captain Loc was always proud of his arguments. It was obvious to the prisoners that he really believed them. They always made sense to him.

WITHDRAWAL WITH HONOR

1967–1973

Part 4

14

BEGINNING OF THE END

BY 1966, THERE were already serious concerns that the long-range agent team effort had failed. CIA-directed teams of Lao irregulars had gone into Son La in 1965 to search for Team REMUS. The ethnic Hmong lost a team guide in confirming the presence of a 350-man North Vietnamese battalion-sized force at the precise coordinates where the agent team was supposed to be operating. A Lao team was sent from Luang Prabang, Laos, into the Song Ma area of Son La in 1967, and that team was also captured. The CIA dutifully reported its findings to MACSOG.

MACSOG's teams continued heading north.

On 5 October 1966, eight agents in Team SAMSON landed near Lai Chau. They were captured in early December. On 24 December, two more agents were sent into Lai Chau to reinforce Team TOURBILLON. Nong Van Long and Nguyen Van Thu were captured on 25 December by North Vietnamese disguised as commandos from TOURBILLON. They were the last team sent to TOURBILLON.

Two agents parachuted into the North on 21 August 1967, to reinforce Team REMUS. They became known as REMUS 23 and 24, the last in a line of nearly eighteen reinforcements sent to REMUS since 1963. These last two agents, Do Van Tam and Truong Tuan Hoang, had a unique mission for which they practiced during most of 1967. They were trained in the Skyhook System, which was, to them, a new method of extraction. This system would employ A-1 Skyraiders, to be flown by South Vietnamese pilots, with a tail hook that could pick up small parcels behind enemy lines. Poles would be erected and a line strung between them several meters off the ground. The Skyraider would swoop down, and its tail hook would snag the suspended line and pick up whatever was attached to the line. In the case of REMUS, the Skyraiders were to pick up tape recordings of wiretaps of North Vietnamese telephone lines that would be made by Tam and Hoang.

The agents practiced wiretaps that summer, first in the relatively cool air of Dalat, a southern mountain town, and later against an American field division, all with the approval of MACSOG. They listened to a practice tape, supposedly recovered by a behind-the-lines agent, but they heard little except the sound of a telephone cranking.

One of the agents was to remain in North Vietnam to replace the REMUS primary radio operator, who would be extracted by the skyhook technique in an effort to recover an agent from North Vietnam and test him for hostile control.

Truong Tuan Hoang related their fate:

> We landed at night, and the next morning they sent people to get us. They were wearing black pajamas and wore arm bands. They came up to us with the correct recognition phrase, and everything seemed perfect. Then they pointed their weapons at us, and we were taken prisoner. We got to the base camp from where REMUS was supposedly operating and it turned out to be a well-disguised camp run by the People's Armed Public Security Force disguised as commandos. That's where the REMUS radio operator was working.
>
> What happened then? They got all our equipment and there was little we could do. . . . Later, they sent me down to Thanh Tri Prison.[1]

The landing of the two men sent to REMUS occurred as MACSOG prepared to phase out the long-range teams. Those in the chain of command from Washington to Saigon, however, were demanding reliable information about the true state of the northern Vietnamese infiltration network known as the Ho Chi Minh Trail. A meandering network of roads and other facilities, it was often unnoticeable under a triple-canopy tree cover that could not be seen from above.

In the spring of 1967, MACSOG had developed the first four short-range reconnaissance teams, dubbed STRATA teams, whose mission would be to go into North Vietnam, often into areas nearly identical to those where the long-range teams had been inserted, and report what precisely was on the ground along the Ho Chi Minh Trail. Their anticipated operational range extended north from the DMZ to close to the Chinese border, although their missions were never approved north of Highway 7 in Nghe An Province. Within MACSOG, they became known as the forces of Plan 34B.

Formed at Long Thanh that summer, the initial teams landed in the southern narrow panhandle of North Vietnam. The first team landed approximately ten kilometers away from its preplanned landing site. Days later, it engaged North Vietnamese border forces and was captured. During the next year, however, the speedy entry and exit of such teams demonstrated that it was possible to get teams into extremely hostile areas and get them out after completion of their missions.

Maj. George Gaspard, operations officer for the effort beginning that December, knew the problems the teams would face:

> Get them in there and get them out safely. That's what we tried to do. The long-range agent operations didn't work out, but my STRATA teams did. So, the concept was successful in that sense.[2]

Unlike the long-range teams, the STRATA teams were indeed able to accomplish the impossible. They got in and got out, often before the border defense forces found them. During 1968, in dozens of missions, they lost all or part of five teams, an enviable accomplishment considering the seven-year failure of the long-range teams. Twenty-seven years later, a former member of one STRATA team put it this way:

> What did we accomplish? I can't say about the other teams but we went into the border area in the summer of '68 and accomplished one thing, at least. I was in command of STRATA Team 114, and before we left South Vietnam I was told to find that damn nest of

> North Vietnamese who were in control of one of our long-range agent team radios. Did we find them? Oh, yeah! We found them all right. But of course, they found us too. Got me and two of my men, but I'm sure the word got back that we'd found them.

Hoang Van Chuong, former commander of Team 114, spent nearly fifteen years at hard labor in order to get a message back with the surviving members of his team.

It was fortunate that MACSOG's long-range agent operations ended at this juncture. The growing list of long-range teams working for Hanoi was having an impact on more than just the diminishing pool of agents available to MACSOG.

By 1967, for example, MACSOG's private air force of Taiwanese- and American-crewed C-123 and C-130 transports, augmented by propeller aircraft and jets, was carrying an increasing tonnage of supplies and performing other missions related to the long-range teams inside North Vietnam. This meant that MACSOG's meager resources increasingly were being dissipated by Hanoi, which was now indirectly controlling more of MACSOG's resources directed against the North than its own commander, Col. John Singlaub.

Singlaub, who took over command of MACSOG in the summer of 1966, arrived in Vietnam in April of that year and quickly reached the conclusion that the agent teams in the North were probably all compromised. In his autobiography, he describes his in-depth study of the long-range agent team operations and the results of this survey reinforced his belief that these teams had probably surrendered.[3] Singlaub credits Lt. Col. Robert Kingston with beginning an intricate web of deception operations designed to foil the North Vietnamese, as Singlaub tried to establish the identity of the turncoats in the Vietnamese or United States side of the operation.[4]

The MACSOG Documentation Study confirms that these efforts were part of a much larger U.S. effort to tie up North Vietnamese security forces in the North's panhandle. Vietnam's military writings acknowledge concern about possible U.S. landings in the panhandle, a major thrust of the deception operation of which MACSOG was but one part, but the North devoted few resources to counter such a contingency.

This offers additional evidence that the North had a good grasp of the broad U.S. deception operation, not just such operations of its South Vietnamese counterparts.

In his autobiography, Singlaub describes an incident attributed to Capt. Fred Caristo, who reportedly discovered a North Vietnamese agent in the ranks of the Strategic Technical Directorate; Caristo then parachuted the agent back into North Vietnam.[5] This may equate to one of the North Vietnamese prisoners or defectors employed in another part of the deception program and not to one of the paramilitary long-range agent teams recruited in the South.

The MACSOG Documentation Study confirms that the diversionary operations began in the fall of 1967 when the last long-range agents were parachuted into the North. By this time, MACSOG was controlling and resupplying seventeen in-place agent teams (two singleton agents and fifteen agent teams, four of the teams and the singletons having been sent into the North during 1967). These agent teams received twenty-four aerial resupply missions during 1967.[6] All but one of the fifteen agent teams (Team VOI, which disappeared) were under Hanoi's control (see Figure 6). Not until the summer of 1968 were the long-range agent team operations finally brought to an end, and it took a joint CIA/MACV team to bring that about as Singlaub departed Vietnam for another assignment.

There is nothing in MACSOG documents supporting the account of the dispatch of an in-place enemy agent by Captain Caristo. Caristo's principal duties during 1966–67, as described by the commando survivors, were those of training officer for Team HADLEY, Team RED DRAGON, and the early STRATA teams based at Long Thanh in mid-1967. There is no evidence that Caristo actually established his own agent network in the North, and he had no operation against the North's intelligence service, which was among Caristo's accomplishments according to Singlaub.[7] Singlaub also credits Caristo with originating the STRATA concept, but this is questionable.[8] Documents in the author's possession indicate that the early STRATA program was failing until late in the year because of its initial lackluster performance; the first STRATA team sent into the North had been parachuted ten kilometers from its intended landing zone and captured after stumbling around the mountains for weeks. The STRATA program's efforts were improved dramatically with the assignment of its new operations officer, Maj. George Gaspard, in December 1967.

Coinciding with the end of the long-range agent teams, a new work project was assigned to the commando inmates in Area K at Quyet Tien Prison, the hard-labor prison in Ha Giang Province close to the border with the People's Republic of China.[9] Work began on the three-month project late in 1967, after orders came from prison headquarters to construct one additional barracks.

The prison staff did not explain why another building was needed, and it would have been inappropriate for the inmates to ask. They had learned years earlier to do only as they were told, without question.

Shortly after the February 1968 Tet Offensive in South Vietnam, new inmates arrived in the older part of Area K, but they were kept isolated from those already there. The only thing the existing commando inmates could determine was that the new arrivals were Vietnamese. Later in the year, two of the three new prisoners identified themselves as Pham Ngoc Khanh and Le Trung Tin, members of Team RED DRAGON. They were from the last long-range agent team sent into North Vietnam.

Khanh and Tin described to their fellow inmates how they had parachuted at night into Ha Giang Province. The drop turned into a disaster, with team members scattered down the spines of mountains. In the parlance of airborne soldiers, it was a "bad drop."

After landing, the commandos were captured, some by soldiers from People's Republic of China air defense units deployed in the area. Khanh and Tin knew that two other members of their team, Vu Su and Nguyen Huu Tan, were in adjacent cells. They had been held in isolation at the temporary detention camp of the Ha Giang Province Public Security Office until recently. Then, Khanh and Tin disclosed to the other inmates that the team's radio operators had turned traitor and operated their radio under the control of the Ministry of Public Security. They based their conclusion on the fact that the two radio operators were not with the rest of them.

Not long afterward, the voices of the other three missing members of Team RED DRAGON could be heard among other new arrivals in Area K. Notes were wrapped around rocks and thrown over the walls in hope of eliciting some type of response. There was none until Khanh and Tin addressed a note to the missing two radio operators from Team RED DRAGON. A reply confirmed that the remaining members of the team were in the new addition to Area K.

As time went on, other prisoners already at Quyet Tien were able to recognize new voices in Area K, and they slowly gleaned facts about who and what they were. All appeared to be radio operators from ethnic minorities native to the Son La and Lai Chau areas. Some prisoners, who had known of them, said they were from the original teams sent into North Vietnam during 1961–62. Thirty or more were eventually quartered in the new barracks in Area K.

The commandos at Quyet Tien were disheartened when they first learned that some of their operations had been compromised by team members who had voluntarily cooperated with the enemy. Talking among themselves, they realized that, as of 1967, none of the prisoners at Quyet Tien had been from teams whose radio operators had been working for the North Vietnamese. Did this mean there were other teams that they never knew about?

The older inmates rationalized the ability of the North Vietnamese to use the captured radio operators as something that was possible only with the hill tribe minorities, not lowland Vietnamese. They did not think that the lowland Vietnamese would hurt their own kind; also, they were more clever. On the other hand, they considered the mountain minorities, such as the Tai, Hmong, and Tho, to be ignorant and not know any better. The crafty Ministry of Public Security interrogators obviously had found them easy to manipulate.[10]

The commandos at Quyet Tien knew they had information about a truly massive radio deception operation, but they lacked the means to convey it to the Strategic Technical Directorate. Any thought of alerting Saigon to the North Vietnamese operation was immediately supplanted by thoughts of surviving just one more day.

Captain Nguyen Thai Kien, commander of Team RED

DRAGON, was in the new barracks, along with the turncoat radio operators. Few other prisoners were aware just how isolated Captain Kien had become.[11]

Kien had joined the Topographic Service in 1964 as a lieutenant. The Topographic Service was still experiencing growing pains as the result of Diem's assassination and the dismantling of Tran Kim Tuyen's intelligence organization. New officers had been brought in and, by 1965, the Directorate was prepared to expand the cross-border operations.

With Diem's death, a new South Vietnamese national-level intelligence agency rose to prominence. The Central Intelligence Organization (CIO) was advised and financially supported by the CIA, which was able to exert more influence over intelligence operations than had been the case with Dr. Tuyen's organization.

The intelligence information collected by the agent teams was provided to the CIO, as well as the South Vietnamese Army's Joint General Staff. The Topographic Service changed its name to the Strategic Technical Service (STS), and Lieutenant Kien took command of one of the five cross-border operations teams formed by the service's new group called the Liaison Service (So Lien-Lac). Kien later served as the order-of-battle officer for the cross-border operations; he coördinated the information about enemy forces in the areas where the teams would operate. This included information from interrogations, as well as information obtained by the South Vietnamese Army in intercepting and decoding North Vietnamese communications inside Laos.

In 1966, Kien had been assigned command of Team RED DRAGON, as the STS was again renamed, to become the Strategic Technical Directorate (STD). Originally, RED DRAGON consisted of nearly two dozen men, but it was split into two teams by the time of launching in the fall of 1967. One team would remain behind and be used to reinforce RED DRAGON at a later date.

Team RED DRAGON's mission was to parachute into Ha Giang Province, close to North Vietnam's border with China. Reliable intelligence confirmed the presence of two People's Republic of China antiaircraft divisions in the area, as well as supplies coming out of China. Following coordination in Saigon between the Republic of China defense attaché and the South Vietnamese, a special team of fourteen Taiwanese commandos arrived at Long Thanh from Taiwan. They trained with RED DRAGON in preparation for parachuting into Ha Giang, where they would conduct joint operations with Kien's team.

On 21 September 1967, a C-130 with a Taiwanese contract air crew took off for North Vietnam with RED DRAGON on board but minus the Taiwanese commandos. Captain Kien was the first to exit the aircraft when it reached the intended airdrop. His radio operator then froze in the door. It took considerable time to pry him loose and forcibly throw him out of the aircraft before the remaining agents could follow.

After capture, Kien was taken to the Ha Giang Province prison. The North Vietnamese persuaded the team's two radio operators to establish radio contact with Saigon. To explain their inability to provide Kien's safety signal, the North Vietnamese reportedly sent a message that the captain had been killed.

Kien was soon transferred to Thanh Tri Prison, where members of teams whose radio operators had been recruited by Hanoi were confined. He was placed in isolation in one of the rooms of Area D. In 1968, American prisoners arrived there from South Vietnam. To keep Kien and other commandos isolated, the prison staff alternated rooms of commando prisoners and American prisoners in Area D. This prevented both groups from maintaining contact among their own people.

Meanwhile, MACSOG and STD were affected by the spring 1968 bombing halt over North Vietnam, as mandated by President Johnson. This action had obvious implications for the long-range airborne agent teams then communicating from deep inside North Vietnam. Some MACSOG officials believed that the bombing halt would strand half a dozen teams deep inside North Vietnam with no means of resupply; that is, if the teams there were still "safe." Others in MACSOG had long before concluded that the agents were probably all under hostile control, and the operation should have been ended years earlier (see Appendix 5).

MACSOG had already begun to deal with the likelihood that the teams then transmitting from North Vietnam had been captured. On 18 October 1967, for example, Team T2, a four-man replacement for Team HADLEY, had landed by helicopter in Ha Tinh, well north of HADLEY's last known location. Now designated Team VOI, it never made radio contact after arrival, and the team members were soon presumed to be dead.[12]

In part, MACSOG's answer to Hanoi's efforts was employment of deception operations that were truly ambitious. Project Borden involved the use of North Vietnamese Army prisoners segregated soon after their capture, before it became a matter of official record. After psychological indoctrination, they were sent on missions against their own army. Approximately fifty-five agents were launched in 1967, but only five returned to MACSOG. It had been hoped that part of their usefulness would be tying up the North's military security services in searches for disaffected servicemen. A related program, Earth Angel, developed teams of North Vietnamese Army defectors, who were armed and sent on reconnaissance missions against forces of their former army. These teams entered Laos and Cambodia with relative ease and suffered comparatively few casualties.[13]

Project Urgency involved indoctrination and reinsertion back into North Vietnam of civilians taken into captivity on the high seas by MACSOG's maritime forces. Included in this program were "pseudo-agents," those who might appear to be agents but who actually were not intended to function in that manner. By 1968, at least eleven Urgency agents and two pseudo-agents were in place on the coast of Central North Vietnam, but the two pseudo-agents never reported after returning to the area of Vinh. Project Oodles was even more ambitious. This was a phantom army of agents, existing only in the context of deceptive radio transmissions that sought to create the impression of a large force of agents along the North's western border. Messages to these notional agent teams were sent over propaganda radio broadcasts of the Sacred Sword Patriotic League (SSPL), a fictitious resistance force. By the summer of 1967, MACSOG's messages to such teams as HADLEY, then transmitting from North Vietnam and believed to be under hostile control, were dovetailed with the various deceptive programs.[14]

* * *

As the bombing halt against the North took place in the spring of 1968, a special team of CIA and Defense Department officials arrived in Saigon to conduct a case-by-case security analysis of each team transmitting from inside North Vietnam. That summer, these officials concluded that all teams were under hostile control and had probably been so since shortly after insertion. They were (see Figure 6).

During their security review, the visiting intelligence specialists also tried to compare individual styles of sending Morse code—the ''fist''—of team radio operators then transmitting from North Vietnam. They found that the tape recordings of the radio operator ''fists,'' which had been laboriously made years earlier, had become so jumbled that it was no longer possible to correlate the tapes with specific radio operators.

The team's conclusion even extended to the singleton agent known as ARES. MACSOG officers were chagrined at this judgment. They recalled the time in 1964, after the first American air strikes of 5 August, when ARES had loudly praised the air strikes and called for more and more to come and blast enemy targets in North Vietnam. Considering that ARES was a double agent, although this was not known at the time, his calls for continued U.S. air strikes tell much about North Vietnamese efforts to provoke such action at that juncture.

By April 1969, the radio operators recruited into the North's deception operations were reported to be in isolation confinement Area B at Thanh Tri Prison. There is some evidence that Hanoi substituted some of its own radio operators, obviously with the knowledge that no one in MACSOG or STD could tell that switches had been made. Such boldness would have been attempted only if Hanoi had known about the tape mix-up coming out of the 1968 joint security analyses.

The deception operations and STRATA were still months away as HADLEY was slowly squeezed for all the information it possessed. That accomplished, it was time for the team members to enter a special prison known as Thanh Tri.

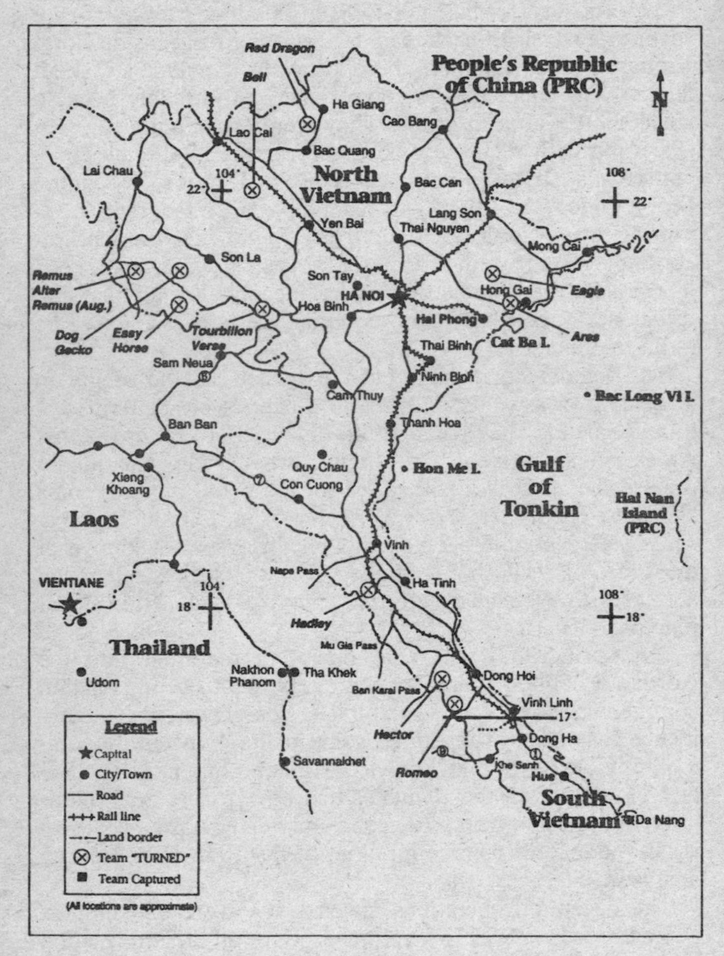

Figure 6. Agent teams reporting in 1967. (*graphic by Cindy Tourison*)

15

OF RATS AND MEN

IN LATE SUMMER 1967, the nine members of Team HADLEY were loaded onto a military truck and handcuffed to one another. Their escort guards, members of the People's Armed Public Security Force, ordered them to stare at the floor, keep their heads bowed, and avoid being seen by villagers because the villagers might kill them. The commandos only half believed the guards, but they kept their heads down anyway.[1]

Leaving coastal Ha Tinh and proceeding north, they moved only at night and stopped at preselected locations to rest during the daytime. The trip was uneventful except when they heard jet aircraft somewhere overhead and then bombing in the distance. The prisoners smiled, and the guards fidgeted.

After several days on the road, the small convoy pulled into a village cooperative, and the prisoners were quartered under guard in a nondescript local house. Just after daybreak, they were awakened and prodded outside the building into the courtyard, where they slumped in handcuffs under a shade tree and watched the beginning of another hot day. The guards, knowing their prisoners were unable to escape, left them unguarded.

An old woman suddenly appeared, perhaps the resident of the house where they just spent the night. She came over and stared at them.

"Why are all you kids so skinny? Have you been captured very long?"

Her questions were friendly, curious, and not unlike an aunt questioning nephews whom she had not seen for some time. The commandos answered her questions in the same friendly manner. Their chitchat went on for five minutes, until the first guard returned. Seeing the guard, the woman scurried away, her demeanor changing.

"Lackeys of the American imperialists! Targeting us, killing the people. . . ." On and on she rambled. The prisoners sat there and smiled at the ground. They understood her anger to be just a charade.

Within minutes, they departed. Arms tied behind them, handcuffed, staring down at the bed of the truck, they were conscious only of continual bouncing. Brief glimpses of civilian trucks heading south with market produce broke the monotony of the ride.

They reached Hanoi in late afternoon, and the truck finally braked to a discreet stop at the gate of Hoa Lo Prison. On 18 August 1967, Team HADLEY formally entered the North Vietnamese Ministry of Public Security national-level prison system.

The babbling of one of the inmates that first night at Hoa Lo sounded like a monologue from some bizarre play.

"Oh, cadre," came the plaintive wail from a prisoner shackled in the adjacent room, "I've been here in prison for eight years and I still haven't been allowed to write a letter home to my family." His complaints went on and on.

A cadre soon arrived to quiet the prisoner, his voice clearly condescending.

"Comrade, I made paper and a pencil available to you. Do you mean to tell me you still haven't received it yet?"

"No," replied the prisoner. "I haven't received anything yet. Why don't you permit me to write home?"

The cadre just laughed.

"Forget it! Your wife's at home and you should let her go marry someone else. You've really got to try harder to become reeducated. Then you can be released and marry a different woman."

On the evening of the next day, the prisoners from HADLEY were taken in handcuffs out of Hoa Lo Prison and loaded into a small, tightly covered truck.[2] The only light came from a row of small transparent plastic strips set into the canvas side coverings. After a relatively short ride to the outskirts of Hanoi, the guards herded the prisoners off the truck and guided them to a bricked-up temple archway. Well-worn letters, almost obscured with dirt, proclaimed this to be Chua Tan Lap (Tan Lap Pagoda), but it was better known as Thanh Tri, the name of the local district. Some people called it Thanh Liet, the name of the village in which the prison was located, seven kilometers south of downtown Hanoi. It was a special detention facility, an annex of Hoa Lo Prison that confined prisoners of very special interest to the Ministry of Public Security's state security apparatus.[3]

The new arrivals were locked in separate cells in the front section of confinement Area A, a long building overlooking the center courtyard. They were ordered to remain silent during their stay, but this merely heightened their need to communicate with one another and learn who else might be in the prison. They soon deduced that the building had eighteen cells on the front and eighteen on the rear.

The names on the cell walls clearly indicated that other commandos had been confined in Thanh Tri. In cell 11 on the front side of Area A, high on the wall, was the name Dam Van Phinh. Below his name, Vietnamese words told how Phinh had been first confined in the front cells, then transferred to the back cells and then again to the front cells. Phinh had been a member of Team EAGLE. All that remained of him was a name scratched into a dirty wall.

Days of solitary silence were replaced by nights of death. A death was signaled during a periodic cell inspection by certain sounds. Each cell door had a small metal slat that closed over the peep slit. A guard opened the slat to verify the prisoner's presence in his cell. For the living, the slat was closed with a quick snapping sound; the sound was decidedly muted when the guard found a corpse. The work parties soon arrived, followed by the sounds of a cell door opening and then a body being dragged from the cell.

The removal of the dead at night prevented identification by curious eyes, as in the case of the prisoner on the back side of Area A who tore up his shirt and hanged himself in February 1968. The other prisoners heard him and called to him, but he never answered. Someone said he didn't understand them because he was a Lao, one of Gen. Vang Pao's ethnic Hmong captured up north along the border.

Days passed into weeks and then into months. In March

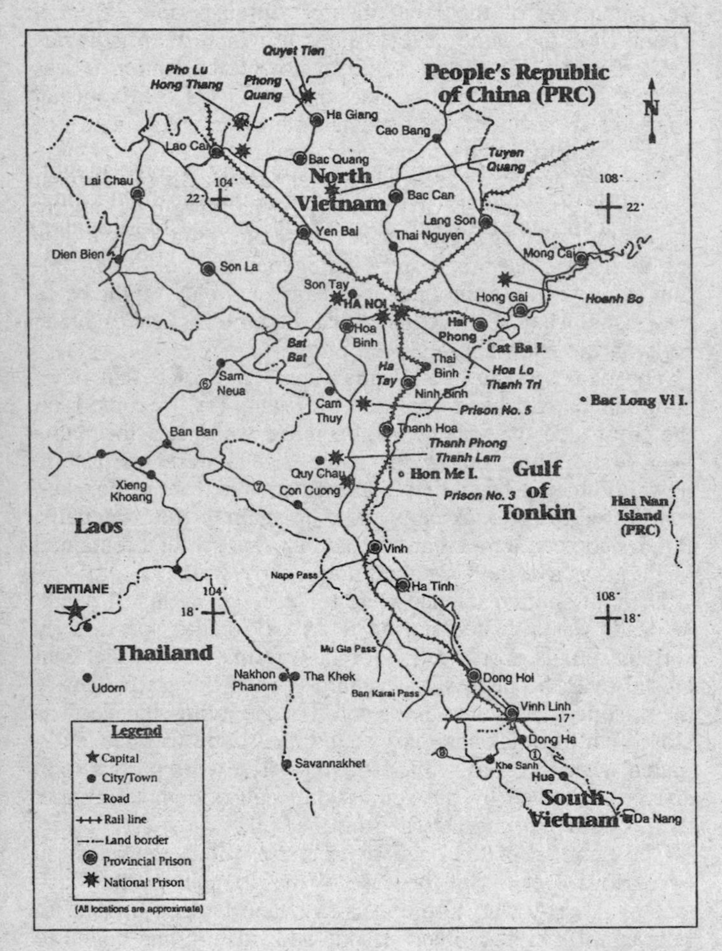

Figure 7. Prisons used to confine captured agents. (*graphic by Cindy Tourison*)

1968, a new arrival passed in front of Area A. He was dressed in red striped pajamas, his head shaved completely bald.[4] He looked like Bach Muoi, one of the members of Team T2 who had remained behind at Long Thanh in January 1967. Several times, he walked across the courtyard under guard. Each appearance was brief, and he was not seen again after that month.

The prisoners' only reference point to time came from newspaper readings by the prison commander two or three times a week. The readings were diversions eagerly sought in a world of darkness, where the only outside light came through a slit under the cell door. On these occasions, Senior Captain Loc, the short, fifty-year-old prison commander, pulled his chair into the courtyard in front of Area A and read aloud selections from the party newspaper, *Nhan Dan,* or the army newspaper, *Quan Doi Nhan Dan*, for an hour or so. The prisoners could tell from his accent that he was a southerner, one of the Viet Minh called "regroupees" who had moved North in 1954.

Although the articles were all political, there would always be something, somewhere, that oriented the prisoners to the day of the week, or the date, or at least the month. Sometimes Loc passed this chore to Lieutenant Hoan, chief of the prison's Education Section, or Aspirant Vuong, the kitchen supervisor. Sometimes even Sergeant Su, the prison medic, was detailed to read when the officers were otherwise occupied.

Loc almost always wore civilian clothes, as did the other senior company-grade officers who made occasional appearances, but when he wore his dark brownish-green uniform with the large pockets on the blouse and the red collar tabs, Loc strutted around like a peacock. The American prisoners, who came in the latter part of 1968, seemed to tolerate Lieutenant Hoan better than the other officers. Always happy and smiling, the forty-year-old lieutenant gave them tobacco from time to time. He was barely five feet tall, so they nicknamed him "baby" or "shortman."

The Vietnamese prisoners were surprised when the Americans arrived.[5]

The story from the American POWs came out slowly. As they related to the commandos later through Morse code, the

Americans had been captured at Hue City during the Tet Offensive in February. There were thirteen of them, all in a group, and several were Filipino. The Americans seldom gave their names, and the new arrivals were spread around the four major confinement areas. For example, several were locked in individual cells in Area A; some in a large (eight-person) room in Area C; and six others, two to a cell, in Area B, rooms 1, 2, and 8. The prison also had an Area D, but the inmates who were kept there always remained a mystery.

It was clear from the start that none of the Americans spoke any Vietnamese. Perhaps the prison staff counted on this to prevent communication; however, they did not realize that many of the commandos knew some English. By September 1968, the American and Vietnamese prisoners in Area B established a limited dialogue. This was due in part to two of the American prisoners there, roommates Bob Olsen and Larry Stark.

Olsen and another American POW had been the first to arrive in room 2, Area B. The Vietnamese commandos, communicating in Morse code by tapping on the walls, learned that he was a civilian employee of Pacific Architects and Engineers. The other American, a man in his fifties, was there for only a brief period before being transferred to a one-person cell in Area A.

When Olsen's next cellmate arrived, he was screaming, crying, and babbling. It was difficult to understand what he was saying, but he was obviously calling for his wife, over and over, and he always yelled. The Vietnamese guards dealt harshly with yelling, and they came running. Area B was deathly quiet as Olsen's roommate was beaten into unconsciousness. Over the next two days, he continued to moan and scream, and each time the guards beat him into silence. Then he was taken back to Area A. Olsen's response was that his former cellmate was "crazy." Not until years later did the Vietnamese commandos learn that he was describing the man's condition, not giving his name.

Olsen's next cellmate was Larry Stark, who did not know Morse code. Bob persevered for a month in teaching it to him so he could communicate with the Vietnamese commandos in their cell block. Stark said he was a navy captain, previously stationed in Germany, and had been at Hue City for six months before his capture.

The inmates in Area A were able to whisper out their doors to the neighbors on either side and learn their identity. Those in Area B did not have that advantage, except for the fortunate few who had been able to scrounge a nail to make small pinholes in the doors. The holes afforded a view of the outside world, even if they saw only other prisoners and cadre coming and going. A tiny wad of cloth in the holes prevented the guards from discovering this diversion. For the next eighteen months, the prisoners glimpsed the outside world through these pinholes.

Because of the arrangement of the cells, the nail hole permitted an inmate to see everyone when food was served. Guards went to one room at a time, unlocked the door, permitted the prisoner to step outside to pick up his bowl of food, and then locked the door before moving to the next cell.

The commandos never learned the identity of some of the six Americans in Area B, including those in rooms 1 and 8. The prisoners in room 8 wore blue-and-white-striped uniforms. One of them was about fifty years old and short for an American. His roommate was very slender, tall, and younger. The six Americans were transferred to Area C around March 1969, and the Vietnamese commandos had no further communication with them.

Periodic overflights by U.S. aircraft always gave a boost to the morale of the American prisoners at Thanh Tri. The sound of a fast, low-flying jet aircraft brought cheers, followed by the guards running around and yelling at them to be quiet. The aircraft seldom arrived unannounced. Nearby air raid sirens wailed in a long, steady drone for perhaps two minutes, coupled with announcements over the community public address system that all the prisoners could hear: "People, attention! People, attention! Enemy aircraft are eighty kilometers away and approaching the capital from the southeast."

It always started that way, the announcement of U.S. aircraft at a distance of eighty kilometers. Within no more than a minute, the next announcement: "Aircraft at a distance of thirty kilometers." Local residents were then instructed to enter their air raid shelters. Senior Captain Loc circulated around the prison and told everyone not to be afraid. They should simply get under their beds when the aircraft came.

"Nothing to worry about," he insisted, "nothing to worry about."

Nighttime overflights were always spectacular. The aircraft came in low, their swept-winged shapes passing over the prison before anyone knew they were there. The prison security forces and local militia opened up with all available weapons. Tracers lit up the whole sky. Through small air vents set high in the walls, the prisoners could watch the tracers as they went up in batches of bright light. The North Vietnamese never did any damage—the aircraft flew so low and fast that by the time they fired their first rounds, the jets had come and gone.

A lone Vietnamese prisoner arrived in room 6 in Area B. He sat in his cell for three days as the guards passed out food to the other inmates but never to him. The slow starvation finally got to him.[6] "Cadre," came the plaintive wail, "I'm hungry, I'm so hungry. Why don't you feed me?"

His wail continued over and over for three days, but the guards ignored him.

Then, Le Van Ngung in room 3 began to sing and hum. His singing brought the guards.

Complaints of hunger did not stir anyone. It wasn't against the prison rules and regulations to be hungry; even to complain of hunger was permissible. Prisoners were also allowed to die of hunger. After all, the prison staff reasoned, hunger was just one part of everyday prison life. Why get excited just because some spy commando prisoner was hungry?

But singing—that was definitely not authorized.

The guard ran to Ngung's room and lifted the cover over the slit in the door.

"Who authorized you to sing?" shouted the guard through the metal port.

"Because I'm unhappy," came Ngung's muffled reply.

"Why are you unhappy?" the guard asked, obviously perplexed.

"Well, I'm unhappy because I'm afraid I won't have any food tomorrow."

"Why do you say that?" the guard asked, a stern yet curious note creeping into his voice.

"Well, the prisoner over across the way, whoever he is, hasn't received any food in days. He's lying there moaning and complaining. That's why I'm unhappy. If that prisoner hasn't had any food in days, I'm afraid maybe tomorrow it'll be me, that I won't get any food." Ngung's voice trailed off into silence.

The guard left to call Sergeant Du, the duty cook. Du arrived in a huff and stood there as the cell door was opened.

"You liar!" Du spat at the inmate in room 6. "What do you mean you haven't eaten? You were given food!" By the sound of his voice you could tell he was trying to cover up the fact he had not given the inmate anything.

"No, cadre," came the soft reply. "I haven't received anything since I arrived. I'm so hungry, so very hungry. It's been days."

After a hurried consultation, the door was slammed shut and Sergeant Du departed. He returned later with a bowl of soup and a roll. The guard snickered. Obviously, Du had been stealing the prisoner's food.

When Sergeant Du left, the guard leaned into the cell. "Where were you captured?" he asked.

"On the border," came the answer in a northern Vietnamese dialect but with a strange, heavy accent.

Ngung could see the inmate was light skinned; clearly, he had not been a prisoner for very long. Who was he? Lao? Tai? Was he from one of the road watch teams? The inmate was transferred to Area A within a few days, and Ngung never saw him alive again.

While Thanh Tri Prison became the commandos' first introduction to life in the North Vietnamese prison system, it almost ended the career of Public Security Service Aspirant Le Van Vuong, chief of the prison's kitchen section. Many northerners feared this kind of disaster when they filled out their annual personal history statements and had to list any relatives who had gone to South Vietnam in 1954 at the time of the partition.

In 1968, while inspecting the food delivered to the newly transferred inmates in Area B, Aspirant Vuong had his first face-to-face encounter with the new prisoners. As he opened room 3, a commando stepped out to take his bowl and then stepped back into his cell without looking at either the guard or Aspirant Vuong.

No! It couldn't be! Aspirant Vuong felt like he had been hit by a bolt of lightning. The inmate was his nephew, Le Van Ngung. It couldn't be! He shouldn't be here. Ngung would be twenty-five years old; Vuong hadn't seen him since long before 1954, when Ngung's family had moved from Ha Dong to Hanoi.

Vuong suddenly grasped the enormity of the situation. He'd always written down that he had an older half brother who disappeared in 1955. He held fast to the line that he didn't know if his brother was alive or dead. Vuong had served the revolution well, and his future had been secured by this service. But now it was all in jeopardy. He stood ramrod stiff, covering his inner tremor.

Ngung had been sure all along about Vuong. He had been equally shocked when he first saw Vuong, months earlier, as he read the newspaper to the inmates in Area A. He'd been certain it was his uncle and wanted to avoid him at any cost. In Ngung's eyes, by staying behind and working for the Communists, his uncle was clearly a traitor. Ngung knew that any open recognition of his uncle could cause problems, particularly because Ngung was hungry. To have to ask his uncle for food was unconscionable.

The following week, when Ngung went to the water cistern outside the cells in Area B to take his weekly bath, Vuong was standing there and talking to one of the guards. He looked at his nephew and gestured, still speaking to the guard. "See that one? He is from my same village." Ngung ignored him.

A week later, Lieutenant Hoan ordered Ngung brought to the prison education office. Hoan was seated behind a table with Ngung's uncle beside him. Hoan gestured to Ngung to sit in the empty chair facing them.

"So, tell me," began Hoan, "what have you learned of our system here?" He meant the Communist system in North Vietnam.

Ngung replied straightforward. "I don't know anything about the system here. How could I? I'm alone all day in a closed-in dark cell."

Hoan looked at him curiously. "You mean you haven't seen that things are better here in the great Democratic Republic of Vietnam?"

"No," replied Ngung, "I haven't seen any such thing."

Lieutenant Hoan sat there silently, thinking, pondering.

"If we permitted you to return to visit your village, do you think you could remember which road to take to get back there?"

Ngung knew the road. It had been a long time, but he recalled it vaguely. He'd been eleven years old at the end of the earlier war, but he did not want to admit he knew the way home to someone like Lieutenant Hoan.

"No," Ngung answered. "I don't have any clear recollection of the roads. It's been twenty years since I was there. I just don't have any more memory of the roads." His voice trailed off. Hoan continued the questioning.

"All right. Do you think you would remember any of your relatives if you met them? Could you remember them if you saw them again?"

It struck Ngung suddenly. This was what it was all leading up to. This meant that Vuong had reported identifying Le Van Ngung, the commando prisoner, as his nephew. It was important now to avoid making any kind of statement admitting that he recognized his uncle.

"No, there's no way, it's been too many years. I was so young then."

Ngung was abruptly dismissed and taken back to his cell.

Aspirant Vuong had reconciled himself to the reality that his brother's son was a prisoner, but there was nothing he could do, or would do, to help him. He had his own life to think about. After all, a nephew like this could change one's whole career.

For all the death and despair at Thanh Tri, there were times when black humor was the best medicine. One of these times came for Le Van Ngung when he caught a small rat that wandered into his cell. He pierced its ears with a small needle and ran a thread through them. On a piece of paper, the size of a postage stamp, he carefully printed words in block letters with ink made from small fragments of brick that he had smashed into powder. Next, he carefully drew the thread through a small hole in each upper corner of the primitive sign and tied down the ends. He looked down at the rat held firmly on its back, with the small piece of paper now tied under its chin like a necklace. Ngung knelt by the door and pushed the rat out slowly, careful not to damage the paper. The rat scurried frantically off to the right, toward Larry Stark's cell. There was silence, but only for a few moments.

"Did the rat come from you?" Larry tapped through the wall.

Ngung sat there on the floor, his legs crossed, head down, smiling broadly. He took the rusty nail in his hand and scratched a reply, "Yes!"

Ngung knew Larry was laughing. He couldn't hear him, but he could sense his reaction. Ngung's smile got wider, turning into a chuckle, and then to a laugh, way down in his belly. He laughed silently, lest the guard hear him, until his throat hurt. He knew Larry would appreciate the humor of it, and how it was done. Ngung thought back to the day when he told Stark about Ho Chi Minh, about how he was a very sly and crafty old man who'd earned the nickname the "sly fox." What he had been unable to tell Stark was that the nickname meant more than that. When and how it was used told a lot about how people really felt about Ho Chi Minh.

Leaning back against his wooden bed, with tears of silent laughter in his eyes, Ngung hoped Larry had not sent the rat to someone else. Anyone seeing the small sign on the rat with the words "sly fox" would know instinctively that it had been made by a Vietnamese. Then these illiterate, self-righteous guards would get it into their heads that someone was making fun of Uncle Ho, and there would be hell to pay.

Washington's covert paramilitary operations against North Vietnam were finally winding down. On 22 January, ten days before the 1968 Tet Offensive, the Pacific Command forwarded the decision not to reinforce Team RED DRAGON and, on 5 March, canceled plans to employ Team AXE.[7] Washington's planned move toward the 1 April bombing restrictions was further evidenced through the 13 March restrictions on missions between the 17th and 19th Parallels, and restrictions were placed on operations north of the 20th Parallel on

4 April. STRATA reconnaissance operations into the slender panhandle of southern North Vietnam, along the Ho Chi Minh infiltration corridor, continued to be approved on a case-by-case basis as RED DRAGON and REMUS resupply missions were effectively shelved on 13 April. Psychological operations for REMUS were canceled on 15 May.

On 21 May, the Pacific Command forwarded the substance of the planned review of all in-place agent teams, and it imposed restrictions on emergency resupply the next day. Under the order of 3 July, the maritime operations were permitted to continue up to the 20th Parallel. On 27 July, all emergency resupply of in-place teams was suspended pending the formal results of the security analysis of these teams. A helicopter mission in support of Team HADLEY was canceled on 18 August. Singleton agent operations in the area of Vinh City were put on hold on 8 September; TOURBILLON resupply was finally affected on 30 September; maritime operations were suspended on 7 October; and, finally on 1 November, just before the 1968 general elections in the United States, the entire covert paramilitary operation against North Vietnam, known by the code name FOOTBOY, was effectively ended.[8]

In 1964, Plan 34A had been portrayed as sending a message that its recipients had no intention of hearing. With the People's Army forces in South Vietnam decimated in the 1968 Tet Offensive and their logistical system in the far south forced to withdraw into Cambodia, the bombing halt provided Hanoi with a much needed reprieve as Washington searched for solutions during secret negotiations in Paris. In 1968, Hanoi had its own objectives firmly in sight, even if they were still seven years away.

The Johnson administration's spring 1968 decision on the timing of de-escalation was perceived by some as a crass political ploy by the administration that was intended to garner votes for the Democrats in the 3 November general election. In fact, the concept of a withdrawal had been in the military's contingency planning stage in Saigon since at least 1966.

The war would end. As with all such events, a key ingredient was timing.

The commandos deep inside the North's prisons had no

understanding of these decisions to de-escalate. They were unaware of the actions that terminated their pay in a move effectively erasing them from MACSOG's property books.

So they languished there, the residue of a secret war and its army, which soon would no longer exist.

16

UNRAVELING THE TRUTH

IN THE FALL of 1968, room 2 in Area B received a new occupant—Pham Viet Phuc, one of the radio operators from Team HADLEY! Where had he been all this time, and what had he been doing?[1] Le Van Ngung saw the guard open the door to room 2, and Phuc stepped out to receive a large bowl of food.

A *large* bowl! And he was getting *meat*, too.

Ngung began tapping in Morse code on the wall to attract Phuc's attention. It worked! Phuc answered, but he avoided responding to any direct questions about where he had been, what he had been doing, and why he had a larger than normal portion of food with meat. He had cigarettes, too, and toothpaste, and oil for his lamp. The other HADLEY prisoners never had such things.

"You're getting more food than I am," tapped Ngung insistently to Phuc.

"No way! We are both getting the same thing. What do you mean I'm getting more?"

This was what Ngung had been hoping for, an opening. He tapped back: "Okay. I'll see what you eat tomorrow and I'll tell you precisely what it is."

The next day, Ngung was glued to the peephole when Phuc stepped outside his cell to get his noon meal. He waited until the guard left.

Phuc tapped first, "So tell me, what did I have to eat today?"

"You had rice and watercress," came Ngung's swift response.

"What else did I have?" asked Phuc.

"Today—you—had—meat," replied Ngung, very deliberately.

Phuc panicked. He knew that Ngung must have seen the food he received and deduced he was receiving preferential treatment.

"You look pretty well fed, and I'm skinny," tapped Ngung.

Phuc was silent. Ngung knew he had an opening, and he pushed for more.

"How long were you in communication with the Directorate?" asked Ngung.

"No way," replied Phuc. "I wasn't communicating with anyone."

"I know you were. I knew it before, when we were in Ha Tinh, just after we were captured. I knew it even then. You were on the radio." It was a ploy.

Phuc finally capitulated. "I did communicate with the Directorate. The Communists forced me to operate my radio."

"Was there a team sent in to reinforce us?" tapped Ngung.

Phuc initially replied there had not been any replacements. Ngung threatened Phuc again.

"I know there was! The cadre told me so. They told me a team had come in."

Phuc finally relented. "I think there was a team."

"Was Tran Hieu Hoa in the team?" Ngung was insistent.

"The people . . . there was a list . . . the names were strange."

"How many were in the team?"

"There must have been seven or eight."

Ngung knew that Phuc was being evasive and lying about the team composition.

Nguyen The Khoa, the team's second radio operator, joined Phuc in room 3 about a month later. Ngung asked Khoa about the replacement team. Khoa replied that there had indeed been a replacement team, but its helicopter had been shot down by ground fire. Captain Dung had been on board the helicopter and had been taken prisoner. Khoa also told Ngung that he had been in contact by radio with a North Vietnamese engineer at Ha Tinh who appeared to be an in-place agent of the Directorate. The engineer arranged to meet Khoa at a certain location and said he would help him exfiltrate, but the meeting never took place.

Ngung replied angrily that Khoa was a lying son-of-a-bitch. He accused Khoa of inventing the story of the engineer in an attempt to make it appear that he had actually tried to get back to South Vietnam. Cursing him, Ngung told Khoa he had known all along that Khoa was more afraid of dying than he was of the Communists. Khoa responded weakly that if Ngung didn't believe him, there wasn't much more he could say.

Khoa clearly did not like to talk about what he had done on the radio. He first tried explaining it away, saying he had been in a difficult situation and had tried somehow to alert the Directorate that he was operating under North Vietnamese control. Khoa knew that the Americans had made a sample tape recording of his Morse code transmission as a record of its distinctive characteristics, known as his "fist." Khoa said that, during his transmissions for the North Vietnamese, he had deliberately lengthened certain of his characters to change his fist, in the hope that the Directorate would compare his sample tape recording made back at Long Thanh with the sound of the fist coming over the air from Ha Tinh Province and conclude that something was wrong. Evidently, it had not worked because the transmissions from the team's headquarters continued.

Other recruited radio operators later claimed that Captain Dung had instructed them to cooperate if they were captured and do whatever was asked of them in order to protect themselves. Captain Dung never said this during his operational briefing of Team HADLEY, and Ngung concluded that the recruited operators just had to be lying.

Khoa and Phuc were soon transferred elsewhere, and their room was occupied by someone new. With his well-worn nail file, Ngung began to scratch out the familiar long and short scratches.

"Dah dit dit dit dah." This was Morse code for the procedural signal "BT." It was what all radio operators first sent when they went on the air; it meant they were ready to begin transmission.

"Dah dit dah," the new prisoner responded with the

Morse code for "K," which meant the radio operator on the other end was ready to transmit. Ahhh! Another radio operator!

The almost soundless scratches continued between the rooms.

"Who are you?"

"Truong Tuan Hoang."

"Who are you?" came the scratchy code from the invisible prisoner in room 3.

"Le Nhát," Ngung replied with his operational alias.

Truong Tuan Hoang quickly scratched his reply. "Are you the Commander of Team T?"

"Yes."

"Incredible!" Hoang continued. "You're supposed to be dead! Captain Dung said a message came in saying you were dead, that you'd been bitten by a poisonous snake and died. You never went on the radio because you were dead!"

Ngung was stunned. It was unbelievable that the Directorate would repeat such a message, a fundamental violation of every operational security procedure, whether it was true or false. This didn't make any sense to Ngung.

"When did you drop in?"

"On 18 August 1967, with Do Van Tam. You know Do Van Tam, the one we all called Tam Moc. We were the last augmentation group to Team REMUS. Tam is here somewhere."

"How were you captured?"

Truong Tuan Hoang didn't answer. After a brief period in room 3, Hoang was moved to Area C.

Within days, Ngung realized something was amiss when a cadre suddenly came to his cell and carefully inspected it. He appeared to be looking for something in particular. Suddenly, he leaned forward and pointed to some long scratch marks on the wall. Every radio operator in prison knew what they were, the slight gouge marks made by a nail in the soft plaster as a prisoner scratched out the long and short strokes that passed for dashes and dots of the Morse code— incontrovertible evidence of communication.

"What's this here?" the cadre demanded.

"I have absolutely no idea," Ngung said.

"You are pretending! Follow me!" Ngung was escorted

to the prison headquarters building and into the education office. Five cadre were sitting along one side of a table: the thirty-year-old cadre in civilian clothes, the one with the Hanoi City accent who spoke excellent English and was always an interpreter for American POWs; Lieutenant Vuong, the prison duty officer; Lieutenant Hoan, chief of the Education Section; Senior Captain Loc, the prison commander; and the young NCO (noncommissioned officer), who performed odd jobs for Loc. Ngung was placed in a chair on the opposite side of the table and faced the five men. They stared intently at him.

"Cadre!" Ngung shouted, the standard way all prisoners reported to cadre.

"How are you today?" Hoan began, his voice inquisitive, friendly, seemingly concerned.

"Cadre, I'm not very well today," Ngung replied, his voice dropping as if he were ill.

Hoan continued his friendly banter. "What are your thoughts about reeducation since you've arrived here?"

"I really haven't thought about it. I don't know what it is."

"So, you mean you have no real understanding of our system in the North?"

"Cadre, I'm not aware of anything. I don't have anything to read. I'm in my cell all the time. There's nothing there to be aware of in the darkness. There are only the four walls of my cell. I have my two meals a day. That's all I'm aware of."

"So tell us," Hoan said, "when you were in the South, just how far did you go in school? What grade did you get to?"

"Cadre, my education was just average."

"How about English? Do you know English?"

"Yes, I studied it some when I was in school. But you know, it's been so long now, I've forgotten most of it. Anyway, I only studied it for a few years and then only for one or two hours a week." Ngung's voice faded out.

"Tell me, what do you know about the nationality of the prisoners in the cell next to yours?"

"I can hear sounds, voices of people talking in the next cell but they're not clear. I don't know who they are. They could be Chinese, French, or something, I don't know. I'm sure they're foreigners, though.''

''Do you know that there are Americans in the room next to yours?''

''No, I didn't know. I don't know what they are, just that they're probably foreigners.''

''Do you think you could speak English with an American?''

''Cadre, when I was in school I studied how to read and write English. It's been so long I've forgotten most of it.''

''If we permitted you to talk to an American, could you talk with one?''

''Cadre, it's been so long since I've studied the language . . .'' Ngung's voice trailed off.

''Have you been communicating with the Americans? Have you been talking to the Americans?'' The tone of his voice changed, becoming insistent, with a hint of menace.

''Absolutely not! I haven't communicated with them. Anyway, I can't even talk to them. How could I? There's a guard standing right outside the cells. The guards don't permit any talking.''

''So tell us once again. Have you at any time been in communication with the Americans?''

''No, never.''

''Tell the truth. You must tell the truth, tell everything.''

''I'm telling you the truth. I don't even know enough English to communicate with any Americans.''

Now he spoke slowly, enunciating each word, ''Tell us the truth!''

''I *am* telling you the truth!''

''All right. We're going to let you go back to your cell. We want you to think it over at the noon meal and then we'll have you come back again to see us this afternoon and we'll talk about it some more.''

Ngung returned to his cell. He waited through lunch, throughout the afternoon, and into the evening, but there was no call to come back.

The next morning, the guard came to Ngung's cell and escorted him back to the Education Section. Waiting for him were Lieutenant Vuong, Lieutenant Hoan, and the unknown English-language interpreter.

"So what do you want to say now that you've had some time to think it over?"

"Cadre. There's no change."

"You are being stubborn! Two people have already identified you! You're a liar!"

Hoan reached down and pulled open the drawer in his desk. He took out a small cloth toothpick container made of woven nylon. Ngung recognized it immediately. He had made it by hand in his cell and presented it as a gift to Larry Stark and Bob Olsen.

"Do you know what this is?"

Ngung sat there speechless, staring. This meant the cadre had discovered his contacts with Stark and Olsen. Surprisingly, the lieutenant did not produce the handkerchief Ngung had made by hand, weaving in the phrase "Merry Christmas to Bob and Larry," which he had passed to them in December 1968.

The lieutenant threw the nylon onto his desk. Ngung's eyes followed the motion. The nylon fell next to a thick folder with the names of Bob Olsen and his wife, Carol, prominently displayed on the edge of a piece of paper protruding from the thick dossier.

"You've been talking to the Americans! We know everything! We even know precisely what you've been talking about! You must tell just what you said to the Americans. You have to tell the truth. The Americans have already told us everything. I order you to tell the truth!"

Ngung had nothing to say and was summarily returned to his cell.

Ngung reasoned that one or both of the Americans had talked. On the way back to his cell, he tried to develop a plan of action. He decided that his best course of action was to admit talking to the Americans. He would avoid giving details and claim they only talked about the weather and other mundane things that prisoners always talk about.

Later, Ngung was returned to the Education Section and required to write a confession detailing his conversations with Stark and Olsen. When he was finished, the guard took it to Lieutenant Hoan. The next day, Hoan ordered Ngung to return.

"This is incomplete. You left out a lot." Hoan then repeated many of the things that Ngung had discussed with Bob Olsen, such as the direction and distance to the Red River, and details about restaurants in Hanoi City. How did they know all that?

Ngung looked at the cadre. "Cadre, I think the American must have been confused. He must have confused me with a conversation he had with a guard." Ngung described a time when one of the guards had talked to Olsen. He had shown Olsen a photograph of his wife and children and told Olsen he lived in Hanoi.

Expressionless, the cadre stared at Ngung. Then he pounded on the desk to bring Ngung's attention back to the situation at hand: "Here is a pencil and some paper. I want you to sit here and write everything that you communicated with the Americans. I want everything this time!" Ngung did as he was ordered, but he carefully omitted most of their long conversations.

The next several weeks were tense. Truong Tuan Hoang, who had just been returned to Area B, shared one interesting tidbit. There had been recent activity at the prison headquarters and an indication that some type of investigation was taking place. It reportedly centered on corruption and thefts of prisoner food ration funds.

To Ngung, that seemed to explain a recent visit by an unidentified senior official described by the Thanh Tri cadre as a "very senior cadre from the Ministry of Public Security." He was a heavy-set man in his sixties. The staff escorted him from cell to cell, as they opened each door and inspected each cell. The cadre looked in, almost as if this was expected of him, and yet it appeared that he really did not want to do it. Such a visit was highly unusual. Clearly, something *was* going on.

Several weeks later, a guard came to Ngung's cell and peremptorily said to follow him. He directed Ngung toward the doorway to the courtyard in front of Area A. Half expecting to be sent back to one of the cells in Area A, Ngung walked through the doorway, but the guard motioned him to the left, to one of the two disciplinary cells. Ngung walked into room 20, and the door slammed shut behind him. Except for meals brought in, the door remained locked for the next two months.

Two tight-lipped prisoners were in adjacent room 19. They broke the monotony of nearly total silence when they were taken out to sweep the courtyard. Other prisoners—Americans, tall and emaciated, their legs like matchsticks—came out into the courtyard from cells in Area A to sweep the courtyard or do calisthenics.

In late October, Ngung was moved to room 13 in Area A. The door of the adjacent cell, room 14, opened and then closed. Someone had joined him in the next cell. He tried for several days to contact his neighbor in room 14, but there was never any answer. He cursed him for his silence and asked why he couldn't answer. One day he heard the guard ask the inmate his name, age, and where he was from. A voice answered that he was Dai, the District Chief of Phu Bai District in Quang Tri Province, South Vietnam. Several days later, Dai was transferred to room 20. Ngung never saw him again.

On 3 November 1969, the duty guard came at daybreak and opened Ngung's cell door.

"Get your things and come with me," he said. Ngung exited quickly, finding three grinning members of Team HADLEY waiting for him in Area A. Left behind was one of his closest friends, Luong Trong Thuong, locked in room 2 of Area B. Handcuffed and placed in a jeep outside the front gate of Thanh Tri Prison, the prisoners were soon headed northeast along the Red River toward the Chinese border.

The inmate was excited.[2] He knew it was Senior Captain Loc! He had heard that Loc had been thrown in prison for theft of prisoner food ration funds at Thanh Tri when he was the prison commander. He looked closely at Loc—there was absolutely no question about it. Loc stood there, nonchalantly eating a piece of manioc root. Incredible! Loc was now wearing the prison gray of an inmate. The inmate moved without hesitation.

"You son-of-a-bitch! You're Loc! I know you! I was in a cell at Thanh Tri when you were the commander there. It was you! You made us eat words instead of food! Who cared about what you were reading? We couldn't even understand what you were saying. . . ."

The criminal inmate pivoted slightly, then sent his fist

smashing forward against Loc's right cheek and jaw. Manioc root and bloody, shattered teeth flew from Loc's mouth. He fell to his knees.

The inmate turned away. There was nothing else to do. He knew Loc would never survive. Prisoners had a way of dispensing their own justice.

17

TRAITORS AT PHONG QUANG

THE INSTRUCTOR WALKED into his classroom. This was sure to be another slow afternoon for the noncommissioned officer course students at Ministry of Public Security School 500. It was late April. The weather had been chilly last night.

The school was the starting point for the young intelligence and security professionals in the North Vietnamese state security system. This afternoon, the several dozen students would review a case study on infiltrators and how to recognize them. The instructor glanced at his young students seated in front of him and began—slowly.

"Infiltrators are just one kind of agent you will have to deal with," he began slowly. "I will outline for you a resolved investigation involving one such agent captured in 1962 up along the Chinese border. It is a classic case because it points up the typical things an agent will not know—things you have to be alert to if you expect to perform your duties well as a state security professional."

The class sat motionless, all eyes glued on the instructor as he outlined how a certain South Vietnamese spy had been dispatched by boat from South Vietnam at the direction of the American imperialist intelligence services and their puppet lackeys. The spy, named Hong, had landed safely and had proceeded to his family home in the port city of Hai Phong, where he made contact with his brother, a Ministry of Public Security lieutenant. As a good security cadre, the lieutenant reported his brother's arrival to his superior, and a plan was developed to capture the infiltrator.

The instructor droned on, detailing the methodology used

by state security professionals in the conduct of a counter-espionage operation to capture and neutralize an enemy agent and all those with whom the agent had contact.

"So you can see," the instructor summarized, "this agent failed because he did not know the local customs. If he was an official, as his documents stated, he would not have asked the kinds of questions he did when he got to the Chinese border. It is a classic case, which clearly demonstrates why you must all be alert to the kinds of questions being asked by someone. You have to listen to what people are saying."

School 500, near the town of Son Tay west of Hanoi, was far removed from extreme northern Vietnam in Phong Quang District, Lao Cai Province.[1] The winter had been long up near the Chinese border. The spring was still cold, almost down to freezing the night before, as if winter refused to go away.

Phong Quang Prison, seventeen kilometers southeast of Lao Cai City as the crow flies, was squat and isolated, far from any American bombing or possible rescue attempt. It was indistinct from other national-level hard-labor prison complexes. The sign over the entryway to Area A, the main subcamp adjacent to the prison headquarters, read simply: Trai Phong Quang (Phong Quang Prison). Few had heard of the prison, let alone seen it, set at the end of a ten-kilometer winding dirt road.

The cement-and-rock walls on the camp's perimeter radiated no warmth—typical of the grayness and isolation of prison life. A key feature of this isolation was a special walled-in area containing two nameless barracks hidden away in one corner of the prison. To any casual observer they were unremarkable, just two more tile-roofed wooden barracks, a half dozen wooden shutters down each side, tightly closed. This was the special detention area. One of the prison cooks started a rumor that there were Americans in there because he had heard inmates say the occupants were American commandos (biet kich My).

The special detention area had housed the commandos for some time, and new arrivals at Phong Quang Prison quickly learned the pecking order. The amount of authorized monthly food rations told a lot about who was who. The more food authorized, the larger was the bowl. The men in room 1 had larger bowls than the men in the other rooms. The word was to stay away from the men in room 1. They had special rations. They were fed at the rate of eighteen dong per month, not twelve dong, like everyone else. They were special, and they were trusted. Besides extra rations, they got other things—blankets, for one. They didn't have to sleep in two sets of prison uniforms just to keep from freezing to death.

The commandos just transferred from Thanh Tri Prison had already been reeducated to stir as soon as Senior Sergeant Boi unlocked the barracks door so the trustee named Thuy could pass the food to the prisoners in room 2. Boi was a typical senior sergeant who knew how to manage his charges. After all, he was a trusted member of the Public Security Service (Cong An), sworn to defend the party and the state, and he took his job seriously. Thuy was also useful in carrying out his job.

Sergeant Boi was too much a Vietnamese not to enjoy intrigue, and he constantly devised ways to pit individuals and groups against each other. The best prisoners for this purpose were the convicted criminals, who would do anything they were told. Part of his job was to determine each inmate's greatest fears. Fear was what the cadre exploited. Everyone feared something. Some inmates feared pain; others feared death. Both of these were readily available to support the process known as reeducation.

The sergeant was right on schedule today. He never varied more than a few minutes when passing out the slop that passed for meals. This was part of the indoctrination, establishing a routine that everyone could follow, to ensure that the prisoners reacted predictably to such things as the simple sound of a lock opening. It was just like training a dog.

Thuy was useful as a means to control others. Twenty-nine years old, and a former People's Army of Vietnam corporal, he had been selected as a trustee while serving a three-year sentence for being a pickpocket. Thuy would get out in two more years, but he needed to show the cadre that he was doing his part to support the country by helping to control these American spy commandos.

Thuy roughly shoved the door open, stepped inside, and

dropped the aluminum pot of lukewarm rice and corn mush on the bottom pallet, where several commandos lay in silence. The prisoner nearest the door stirred and looked at him as Thuy stared around the room slowly before turning to leave the stench inside. The other prisoners slowly moved and sat up—expecting another meal of rice and cold husked corn, no vegetables.

This had gone on for over a week now. Someone said that the prison cadre were doing it on purpose, that they had changed the food to lower the commandos' strength and morale. Someone else said that the guards had a deal worked out with the criminals who were the cooks: the cooks could eat all they wanted so long as they gave a major portion of the prisoners' rice to the guards. Another prisoner said that the guards were just stealing the rice, selling one part, and taking the rest for their families. One of the guards was heard saying that the inmates should be satisfied that they could sit out the war of liberation in a nice comfortable prison without having to be afraid anymore of being killed.

The prisoners knew they were supposed to get more food than they were being served. How could prisoners live on only three hundred grams a day and still work?

Sergeant Boi stepped back outside the barracks. He threw the metal bar across the door and locked it. The men in room 2 slowly came to a sitting position and sat there, waiting, as the pot and bowls were passed from man to man. Each took a scoop of the gruel and passed it on to the next; those on the bottom wooden tier passed the pot up to those above and so it went around the room until empty. The only sound was the cracking of teeth against unshelled cooked rice, as the inmates tried to get some small nourishment from the meal.

At about eleven o'clock, Sergeant Thong and Thuy collected the empty bowls and pot. Several inmates stirred. One stood and walked over to the piece of bamboo used to urinate in. The urinal stench was not as bad as the smell of the small wooden bucket used for defecation. The stench didn't matter any more. It was just another part of prison life.

The door opened again. A newcomer—an inmate from room 1—slowly entered. It was obvious what the bastard wanted, snooping for information to keep Sergeant Boi happy. Boi was responsible for all prisoner labor, and the word was out that he and Thong had been ordered by Senior Lieutenant Truc to get the commandos to work harder.

Truc was the officer answerable to the prison commander for the commandos. His main interest was building a personality profile on each inmate. After getting daily reports from his two sergeants, Truc decided who would be singled out for special treatment. Boi handled the work assignments, Thong the indoctrination. Truc purposely had been taking it easy, trying to find out who the progressives were. It was very calculated.

The word was already out that the inmates in room 1 were turncoats. Supposedly, they were radio operators from the early teams who had been operating their radios for the Communist security forces and sending word to the commando headquarters in the South that everything was fine, that their team had been recruiting agents, training northerners, and so on. Everyone was curious. What had these teams been telling Saigon? It was inconceivable that such a deception operation could have gone on all these years without someone learning about it. Whatever these teams had been reporting to Saigon must have been quite valuable. Otherwise, why would the Communists have run it for so long? If someone thought about it too long, the implications could drive him mad.

Anyway, the commandos rationalized, Saigon had to know they were all prisoners now. Saigon would not abandon them. They had to keep the faith or die. If they died, that would mean the Communists had won, and no one wanted to consider something so unthinkable as that. It was what kept them going, the certain knowledge that, if they came out alive, they would be the real winners, not their captors.

The inmate from room 1 paused, perhaps sensing their thoughts. Then he walked slowly down the center aisle and carefully took note of everyone and what they were doing. He sat down on the edge of the lower level of the long wooden pallet and stared toward the door.

This former agent almost seemed like one of them. He wore the same nearly obsolete striped prisoner clothing, and he was skinny like they were, although he was one of the taller guys there, just under six feet. Maybe he wasn't all *that* skinny; was it just that his height made him seem that way? An ethnic White Tai from Lai Chau, he was about ten years older than the men in room 2. Someone said he had been working on the radio for a couple of years and supposedly had been with the commandos since they first started sending teams out.

"Where you from? Which team were you with? How long have you been here?" the questions came quickly, softly, from a half dozen men shivering in the forty-degree temperature.

Some were aware of who he was and what he represented; however, it was a shock for most new arrivals when they heard about these turncoats for the first time. Some just didn't care. Maybe they had been forced to operate their radios. Besides, who really knew? Just because they were getting more rations, just because they were singled out for special treatment, that didn't mean anything. Live! That was the thing, just keep the Cong An off your back, do a little basket weaving, get through the day. The prisoners believed that one day the whole Communist system would collapse and the Republic of Vietnam Army would crush the bastards. Until then, survival meant just taking it easy and staying together. That was the *only* way to deal with the "khaki shirts," the slang for Cong An.[2] Maybe the rumors were true, that because of these turncoats, commandos had been killed. If they were true, then why did these guys do it?

Such thoughts occurred silently to each man. It was too dangerous to talk openly because no one knew who could be trusted. Meantime, let the turncoat radio operator talk. It was time to learn from him if there was any truth to the wild rumors about those in room 1.

The inmate from room 1 just sat there, listening to the questions, noting who said what. A person could tell a lot from someone's questions. They showed what he thought, what he was interested in. That's what Sergeant Thong wanted to know, what the commando inmates were thinking. From such remarks, Thong could make corrections to his indoctrination plan, and he and Boi would shuffle the work assignments, make a few careful changes in the level of control, increase the level of fear, and slowly get everyone in line. That was what Thong meant when he kept emphasizing the basic line that "thought led to action." Thong knew that by remolding thought processes, everyone could be unconsciously programmed to do whatever the State desired. Responses became automatic. But first, he needed to know what the inmates were thinking.

The listening inmate did not consider himself a secret informant but just another prisoner trying to stay alive. What harm would come from a few little tidbits? Besides, all the others in room 1 were doing the same thing. Who would it hurt? He had his audience and answered questions slowly, quietly, with an air of detachment.

Yes, he was from the Technical Directorate. He'd gone through training years ago at the South Vietnamese Army airborne training center at Hoang Hoa Tham. Yes, he'd been dropped into the Northwest Region in northern Vietnam, into the area near Dien Bien Phu. He was the team radio operator. He'd come with the others to Phong Quang Prison a little while ago. Where had they been kept? Oh, lots of places. It was hard to remember. Now he was over in room 1, just getting by from one day to the next. How many were with him? Oh, there were over ten guys over there. Right, mostly radio operators like himself.

When the others listened closely, they realized that he wasn't saying anything. They took in what he said without comment, but they counted in their heads the guys in room 1. There were a lot more than the inmate had indicated. For example, there was the team commander who had been recruited. That bastard was supposedly the worst. He was the guy who kept bragging that the Communist cadre had openly taken him to restaurants and coffee shops around Hanoi City and showed him a fantastic time. How many guys had died because of him? What the hell, it didn't matter any more. They were all in the same situation now.

"You know," said the inmate, "we sent a message back that we recruited this big group and we needed more equipment. We sent back messages telling Saigon we had set up a large training base in the jungle. Then we asked for dress uniforms. They sent the dress uniforms! We asked for a large power generator, and they came at night and dropped this huge power generator. Here was this huge electrical generator coming down, and the Cong An on the ground were laughing. It was incredible!" He paused, looking at the half dozen prisoners hanging on his words. "It was unreal," he continued, "dress uniforms. Can you believe it? What did they want with dress uniforms?"

"How were you captured?" a voice in the far corner of the lower pallet asked.

"It was really something," he began. "We finally requested assistance in exfiltrating and told Saigon to send us an aircraft to pull us out. Saigon sent us a message with the coordinates where we were to move to a secure location and wait for a helicopter that would be sent to pick us up. We moved to the new location but nothing happened, there was no helicopter. So we sent a message asking for instructions, telling Saigon we were at the location we'd been ordered to move. Saigon replied that our location wasn't secure and we would have to move to a third location. So we moved again to the new location. No one ever came. Then we lost contact with Saigon and later we were captured."[3]

Of course, no one believed him. The men lay silently, listening to him going on and on. Everyone now wondered what else had happened. Damn! Everything they had done for years had been *really* run by the Communists!

It was almost as bad as what Captain Dung had told them during their training. If they ran into someone who asked them what they were doing, he had said, they were to reply: "Toi di tim Ong Huong" (I'm looking for Mr. Huong). When they finally got together at Phong Quang, they found that Captain Dung had told many teams—ROMEO, HECTOR, HADLEY—to say the same thing. They had all been told the same thing. What had Captain Dung been thinking of? None of them had thought anything of it at the time. After all, Captain Dung had been their training and operations officer and he was supposed to know the right things to say and do. Instead, he had condemned team after team by giving them a phrase that helped their North Vietnamese captors instantly identify them as commandos from Long Thanh.

No wonder the interrogators had laughed when the commandos gave that answer during their preliminary interrogations. The next question was always "How far away is Mr. Huong?" They all answered that he was only one or two kilometers away. And what did Mr. Huong do? He was a woodcutter, and he would tell them what to do.

Stupid!

The inmate from room 1 had no way, really, to know what the commandos were thinking, but he continued to talk slowly, his eyes taking in everyone in a casual, disinterested manner. No one was listening. Everyone had turned their backs on him. He continued for a while, not realizing they were ignoring him.

"OK, you guys, see you later," he said, standing up and slowly walking to the door into the warming spring air. Now he would give Thong the names of those who had been listening, those who asked questions, those who seemed to show some anger, and those who didn't blame him. What harm would it do? He passed Senior Sergeant Boi making his rounds and telling everyone to get out of their barracks and start weaving baskets.

The door to room 2 suddenly slammed open, right on cue, and Boi stepped smartly into the silence. "All right, everyone. The State has been kind to you. None of you are dead. It's time to repay the State for its kindness. Come on, you lazy puppet spy commandos."

He walked slowly down the length of the barracks and kicked the wooden pallets with the shivering bodies. He stopped at the end of the room and turned to watch as several commandos slowly shoved themselves off the ends of the pallets and stretched. He then walked slowly toward the door and stood there with a half smile on his face. The inmate from room 1 would have done his job well. Thong had been harping on the need for additional information. Boi knew he was doing this just to please Senior Lieutenant Truc, and he was angry inside. Thong was the education sergeant, not the labor sergeant. What business was it of his to stick his nose into Boi's area of responsibility? Besides, the quarterly labor and education development plan that Lieutenant Truc had outlined to them earlier was right on schedule. The desired level of basket production had been correctly applied, and output had increased. Labor was used as a means of applying pressure on the inmates, a way to keep them occupied. This would reduce the possibility of escape by keeping them physically exhausted, close to the point of collapse. The cadre noted that the inmates were beginning to respond well to labor and thought reform. It was a classic textbook case of reeducation applied in a controlled environment.

To further weaken them, Truc told the cooks to reduce the prisoners' rations. Substitute other things for the rice, shave a little from each prisoner's meals, reduce the quantity of vegetables. That would keep them hungry, lessen the possibility of anyone trying to escape, and make the prisoners more malleable. It was all according to the book. And no garlic! Everyone knew prisoners collected garlic and used it to spread along the trail when they escaped, a sure way to throw the dogs off their scent.

The one person who gave Sergeant Boi some cause for concern was the former team commander captured in January 1967. According to the file in the prison education office, his profile indicated that Ngung's reeducation was not going to be so simple. All team commanders were problem cases. The men tended to look up to them and went to them for advice. A strong team commander was someone the other prisoners rallied around, like Nguyen Huu Luyen, the one captured in 1966. It was time to start using more shackles, employ a little more corrective discipline, divide the men from their leaders, and increase their distrust of each other.

18

REEDUCATION

WITHIN A FEW days of their arrival at Phong Quang, newly transferred commandos received a fresh set of plain gray prison uniforms. Many older political and criminal inmates also wore the plain gray that was replacing the standard striped prison garb slowly being phased out—red and white for political prisoners and convicted spies, such as the commandos, and blue and white for common criminals.[1]

Sergeant Boi came into the barracks with one of the political prisoners. As he read out the assigned prisoner numbers, another prisoner stamped a newly arrived inmate's number on each set of prison uniforms being issued. BP was the prefix for those then arriving at Phong Quang, and a three-digit number was a serial number based on the sequence of each man's incarceration. The last digit was an odd number for political prisoners and an even number for criminals.[2]

Stamping the numbers became a joke because after several washings they were gone. Nevertheless, prison cadre criticized the inmates for not having their numbers clearly visible, but there was no way to solve the problem.

Prison cadre responsible for assigning labor projects directed new inmates to begin bamboo basket production. They had no production quotas, and the amount of time they worked was not regulated—at first. The cadre kept a close watch on all the inmates and assessed how they reacted to the new environment and their tasks. Evening study sessions and political indoctrination classes were accompanied by routine self-criticism and criticism of one's friends and their performance. During this initial assessment phase, the cadre evaluated each inmate's attitude, physical condition, and willingness to respond to direction.

Work hours were then extended, and the production quota was increased slowly until the inmates had time only for work, sleep, and political indoctrination. In reeducation, labor production required organization. The cadre first appointed one inmate to be room leader. His task was to give the head count each morning and evening when the guards checked the prisoners in the barracks. Later, the inmates were organized into labor groups, and a labor group leader was appointed.

Phong Quang Prison introduced the new arrivals to the system of monthly care and maintenance allowance authorized for each inmate in a national-level, hard-labor prison managed by the Ministry of Public Security. Each inmate was authorized 15 dong per month for food and other items. This was a welcome change from the 12-dong food authorization at Thanh Tri, technically a temporary detention facility where the lower rate applied, as it did in provincial-level detention camps.

Rice and other staples were either grown by the prisoners or purchased through government food outlets at State-controlled prices. Rice was bought through State outlets at 30 xu (0.3 dong) per kilogram. This meant that rice cost the State 4.5 dong per month for each inmate. The remaining 10.5 dong of the 15-dong monthly allowance was used to purchase other foods, such as vegetables, meat, and fish, and for sundries, including two sets of prison uniforms per year, sandals, chopsticks, food bowls, toothpaste, oil for lamps, and tobacco.

There was never any deviation from the 15-dong allowance per month per prisoner. The Ministry issued prisoner allowances to the prison commander, who managed the money as he saw fit. The allowance per prisoner never deviated, whether or not prison labor produced some of the staples. The prisoners at Phong Quang believed that the cadre misappropriated the money authorized for allowances. They often claimed that they had purchased something locally when it had been grown by prison labor for virtually nothing.

The food allotment was the primary weapon used to manipulate inmates. Those who were cooperative and worked hard received more food, normally in a larger bowl, which was equated to a monthly allotment of about 18 dong. Working hard meant doing what the cadre ordered, whether the orders pertained to labor production or acting as informants. In order to operate within the average of fifteen kilograms per month per inmate, rations were subtracted from those who were less cooperative. Inmates who did not respond to reeducation objectives normally received rations equal to about 12 dong per month. Potatoes or sweet potatoes routinely replaced rice in their diets.

Phong Quang also meant reeducation through the pain of the shackles ordered by the prison commander, Sr. Capt. Trinh Van Thich. This treatment began without fanfare early in 1970 during the Lunar New Year, a time when Vietnamese reflect on the past year and prepare for the next—a time to wipe the slate clean and start anew. The Phong Quang Prison staff, however, were determined to demonstrate that the pain of reeducation carries through from one year to the next.

On New Year's Eve, the commandos assembled to drink tea, eat candy, and talk. At precisely midnight, they heard the sudden sound of weapons firing outside the prison, as the People's Armed Public Security Force guards welcomed in the New Year with rounds from their AK-47 assault rifles and SKS carbines. The contingent of thirty-odd commandos in room 4 suddenly came to attention and sang the national anthem of the Republic of Vietnam and a song praising former President Ngo Dinh Diem. The singing was spontaneous, a reaction to the exuberance of the prison guards, but their voices were too loud. Within minutes, several dozen armed guards and prison staff officers rushed to the barracks to quell what they thought was a serious disturbance.

One of the guards quickly unlocked the door to room 4 and stepped into the darkened room. He yelled out his questions: "Who did it? Who did it? Who was it? Who was singing . . . making the noise? Who is the ringleader?" He nervously swung the barrel of his assault rifle about the room.

Pham Ngoc Ninh spoke up quickly. "It was Tiep. Check it out. You'll find Tiep was probably the ringleader." It had been in jest.

Tran Van Tiep, a member of Team HECTOR, was lying on the top pallet. He decided to go along with the game. What the hell. He jumped down to the barracks floor and walked into the center of the narrow aisle separating the two-tier pallets, which served as their beds.

"It was me," Tiep said without any hesitation. "I was the ringleader."

It sounded like a smug answer to the guards, and they demanded swift and immediate retribution for this act of supreme insolence and defiance toward the dedicated workers of the State. The guard motioned Tiep outside with a sharp flick of his hand and quickly closed and locked the barracks door behind them. From the sounds outside the door, the other inmates knew that Tiep was being taken away.

Five minutes later, they heard three shots fired in quick succession. The inmates tensed; they immediately assumed that the guards had executed Tiep. There was total silence and inner anger. Within minutes came the sound of Tiep screaming. At any other time, such a scream would have caused the instant flow of perspiration, but this was different. The scream meant Tiep was alive!

Tiep did not rejoin them until forty-five days later. His ankles were scarred for life.

Tran Van Tu was next. It wasn't that he had been singled out for anything. He was just in the wrong place at the wrong time.

Tu was a member of STRATA Team 114. The team had been captured on 28 June 1968 during a mission into Quang Binh Province. The men arrived at the prison shortly before Team HADLEY. They minded their business at Phong Quang and were not troublemakers. None of this really mattered; the prison staff needed someone and had selected Tran Van Tu at random.

Several days before the first day of the Lunar New Year, a smiling Senior Sergeant Boi informed the commandos that they would be allowed to play Ping-Pong after the start of the New Year's celebration. Boi had actually seemed happy, which was not his normal disposition. He explained it as an example of the generosity of the State toward the commandos.

The promised Ping-Pong games would be a real treat! The

prisoners thought about them each day before the start of the New Year. They waited, expectantly, but no games were announced. The thought of playing Ping-Pong began to gnaw at them. None of them realized that so simple a thing was merely part of their reeducation.

None of the commandos raised the issue until early on the second day of the Lunar New Year when Boi entered the compound. He encountered Tran Van Tu.

"Cadre," Tu spoke up, looking hopefully at Boi. "Here it is the second day of the Lunar New Year and there isn't any Ping-Pong."

Boi looked at Tu without a word and continued about his rounds. He left a little earlier than usual. Returning to prison headquarters, he filled out a punishment form and turned it over to Senior Lieutenant Truc. On behalf of the Prison Command Section, Truc filled out his portion of the punishment form recommending approval and carried it to Senior Captain Thich for his signature. With the signed form clutched in his hand, Boi walked to the trustees' small thatched hut in Area A. He gestured to Dai, the northerner.

Dai stood up and smiled. He relished these excursions. Here was another chance to demonstrate that he was trustworthy and willing to do anything the State asked of him. He followed Boi without hesitation.

A native of southern Vietnam, Dai had joined the Viet Minh during the war against the French. He hated the French and what they stood for. With the signing of the Geneva Accords in 1954, his unit was taken by a Polish ship to North Vietnam. To those he met in the North, he was a regroupee, and they looked down on him.

Dai never quite adapted to the life of a cadre in the austere North. He never got promoted and was never anything more than a lower-ranking cadre. He put this down at first as the typical prejudice of northerners toward southerners, but he also knew he was too mellow, a typical southerner. He resented the northerners, however, and blamed them for his inability to get promoted. Eventually, he turned to petty crime. He was arrested, tried, and sentenced to imprisonment at hard labor. By early 1970, he had almost completed his sentence. He had been a model prisoner and was one of the most senior trustees. He looked forward to joining those inmates awaiting release in the prerelease group called the "Awareness Unit."

Boi, accompanied by Dai and other inmates, entered Tran Van Tu's room and read the order: "It is the decision of the Command Section that Tran Van Tu be punished. The length of the punishment will be thirty days. The type of punishment will be by the shackling of one ankle. This punishment is being applied because Tran Van Tu has been critical of the State and he is lazy."

Punished because he merely asked to play Ping-Pong? Tran Van Tu was aghast. He had not meant to appear critical. After all, the senior sergeant told them they could play Ping-Pong. This didn't make sense—being punished for merely asking about something they had been promised. But Tran Van Tu had not yet learned that prisoners never asked; they just waited for things. When the State was ready to give them something, they would know it. Tran Van Tu had to be molded.

After reading the punishment order, Boi watched Dai and another criminal prisoner grab Tu and drag him out of the isolation detention area. They took him to the discipline cell below the corner guard post and pushed him into an open cell. As Tu fell onto the cement floor, Boi thrust forward the heavy metal shackle.

Dai smiled. He knew what he had to do.

The shackle, a type reserved for inmates who needed a lasting impression, was a heavy-gauge, round iron rod bent into the shape of an upside-down V, with the ends formed into eyelets. Both inner sides of the V had been cut to form rows of sharp metal teeth. The shackle was designed to be forced down over the ankle and attached to a long metal bar running through the eyelets. This kept the prisoner lying down on the cement floor and in a constant state of pain.

Dai held Tran Van Tu down on the cement floor and balanced the shackle on the top of Tu's ankle. Dai frowned. Tu was stocky and robust, his ankle almost four inches across, but the shackle was barely two inches wide. Glancing down as he stepped forward, Dai placed his foot firmly on the top of the inverted V of the shackle, which was now positioned over Tu's ankle. He had done it before and knew how much force to apply, but he usually dealt with prisoners who were thin from malnutrition. When he stamped down hard with his right foot to force down the shackle against Tu's ankle, the teeth sliced through Tu's skin and into his bone. Blood spurted from the shattered ankle and drenched the floor. It was then that Tu uttered the scream heard by the other commandos in the isolation detention compound.

Tu passed out from the pain. After running the long metal bar through the loops, the two trustees left him to his agony.

Tran Van Tu remained in the disciplinary cell for the thirty-day period of the punishment order. He received no medical care because the injury was considered by prison staff to be a normal consequence of being "stubborn." On the thirtieth day, Senior Sergeant Boi came to Tu's cell to have him acknowledge the crimes for which he was punished. This was routine. One had to confess one's crime in order to be rewarded by the State.

"Tu, do you acknowledge your crimes?"

Tu didn't, or couldn't, answer. Disgusted, Boi left the cell in a huff, slamming and locking the door on the bewildered prisoner. Boi proceeded directly to prison headquarters and recommended that Tu be imprisoned for an additional fifteen days because of his "intransigence." Without hesitation, Senior Captain Thich signed the order.

On Tu's forty-fifth day in the shackle, his cell door was opened and he was ordered to return to his barracks. His ankle had not healed, and he was incapable of standing. He crawled on his stomach from the disciplinary cell to his barracks. As he dragged himself into the commando area, the trustees slowly meandered after him and chatted about the terrible weather.

When Tu reached his barracks, the other prisoners carried him inside and lifted him onto one of the bed platforms. His wounds were covered with feces. Most prisoners in shackles were able to stand enough to use the bamboo tube as a receptacle for their waste, but Tu, because of his shattered ankle, could never stand.

The others cleaned his ankle, which had festered from bacteria deposited by the vermin that fed on the blood, sweat, and human waste of the inmates. No medicines or bandages were available for something considered so mundane. The shattered bone stuck out through the skin. As gently as possible, they removed it before bandaging the wound with strips from a torn uniform. They gave the bone fragment to Tu for a souvenir. He cherished it—tangible proof of his survival during forty-five days of pain in the punishment cells.

Six years later, a guard at Quyet Tien Prison found the bone fragment during a surprise inspection. He stared at it and then looked squarely at Tu as he said, matter of factly, "You have this piece of bone in order to make fun of us." He confiscated the bone fragment on the spot. At that point, it didn't matter. Tu's souvenir had served its purpose.

On 14 October 1970, Le Van Ngung, commander of Team HADLEY, received the ritual punishment order. He was taken to the disciplinary cell and shackled. He'd almost been looking forward to the punishment. Maybe now he could find out what had happened to Mai Van Tuan. In the disciplinary cell, Ngung read the name of the cell's most recent occupant scrawled in blood on the cell wall: "Mai Van Tuan—2 August 1970." This was all that remained of Tuan, who had died in the shackles.

Ngung was given thirty days in the shackle, like all the others. On thc thirtieth day, Sergeant Thong opened Ngung's cell, unshackled him, and motioned him out of the cell. Thong then asked him to acknowledge the crimes that led to the shackling. Ngung's response was that he had done nothing. Thong turned in disgust and ordered the trustee to reshackle Ngung for another fifteen days.

Le Van Ngung survived the shackles; Mai Van Tuan did not.

Originally a civilian with the CIDG guard force at Long Thanh, Tuan decided in 1967 that he wanted to be a commando. He joined one of the road watch teams and was a team commander when he was captured north of the DMZ in May 1968.

Tuan and other members of his team had been initially taken to Thanh Tri Prison outside Hanoi. While they were there, word spread among other prisoners that Tuan "just wasn't right in the head." No one was ever sure whether he was actually crazy or faking it, but, either way, he was a constant source of irritation to the staff at Thanh Tri.

When his team arrived at Phong Quang Prison from Thanh Tri in late May 1970, Tuan was immediately separated from the others and placed in shackles in the disciplinary cell. Unlike other inhabitants, he had both legs shackled, one overlapping the other, the severest form of shackling.

Criminal inmates later recounted his last days.

After two months in shackles, Tuan started a hunger strike. One of the guards sensed that something was not quite right and opened the cell door. He encouraged Tuan to eat, but Tuan refused. Several days later, Senior Captain Thich and the prison education cadre came to the cell and again encouraged Tuan to eat. Again, Tuan refused. Thich ordered the kitchen to prepare a bowl of fresh-cooked rice with meat, which was brought to Tuan's cell, in the presence of Thich, and handed to Tuan. Tuan accepted the bowl of hot food, paused, and then threw it into Thich's face. Incensed, the captain slammed the door, locked it, and left.

One or two days later, the guard arrived to find Tuan entirely naked, lying in his filth. He asked Tuan why he was naked. Tuan replied, "I didn't make these clothes. These clothes were produced by socialism. They are not mine."

Tuan died quietly during the night of 2 August 1970, the date scrawled in blood on the wall of his final cell.

Dai, the ever-present trustee, arrived at Tuan's cell the next morning to remove the waste bucket and found him dead, his naked body already rigid, knees flexed upward. A guard massaged Tuan's knees with alcohol until they could get his legs straight enough to remove him from the shackles for burial.

According to the criminals, Tuan's ghost returned to haunt them. Beginning several days after his death, they saw a black shape looming just outside their barracks late at night. When they held up an oil lamp, they could make out a shape standing a short distance from their window. The shape resembled Tuan.

About eleven o'clock each night, they saw the ghostly specter outside their window. Each time, the apparition stood there, motionless and watching. After several nocturnal visits, one of the criminal inmates called out to Tuan and asked him not to stand at their window. The inmate explained respectfully that they had nothing to do with his death and his presence was making them afraid. The specter dissolved, never to return.

The orders for shackling the inmates at Phong Quang Prison almost always read the same: "For avoiding labor. . . . For spreading propaganda against the State. . . ."

At Christmas in 1970, the guards heard Tran Van Quy from Team HADLEY talking to other prisoners at night. He was sent to room 1, where he was shackled for thirty days for his crime: religious propaganda. Van Kinh, one of the members of the team captured in Laos with two Americans, was the twenty-first, and last, commando shackled there that year. Like the twenty others before him, he too had been found "lazy." Like the others before him who survived the shackles, he too was left with permanent scars on his left ankle.

Secretary of Defense McNamara carefully adjusted the microphone.[3] The press corps knew that something had happened, something about Vietnam. Everyone now learned the name Son Tay.

The secretary described the attempt on 18 November 1970 to rescue American prisoners from a small rural prison west of Hanoi. It was a daring attempt, but there were no prisoners. Evidently, they had been moved in July because of rising flood waters threatening the prison. The secretary was satisfied there had been no leak in the covert raid so carefully planned by Brig. Gen. Donald Blackburn, the secretary's new Special Assistant for Counterinsurgency and Special Activities (SACSA). The prisoners' removal was just a coincidence.

The commandos at Phong Quang never heard about the Son Tay raid while they were there. Their evening broadcasts from the People's Army radio station through the loudspeakers were carefully edited to keep out such reports. The commandos might get ideas. They never knew until much later that the Son Tay raid was the reason for the sudden hurried construction outside Area A. Fear of other heliborne assaults resulted in fields of randomly placed poles throughout the scattered open areas of the prison complex. The poles were pointed on top and painted black, each more than a foot in diameter and more than thirty feet tall.

At about the time of the 1970 Lunar New Year, three ethnic Chinese prisoners arrived at Phong Quang, accompanied by the cross-border team captured in Laos in 1967 along with the two Americans.[4] Other prisoners had seen the Chinese arrive at Thanh Tri in 1968, but none of them had been able to talk with them. At Phong Quang, the strange story of their imprisonment came to light.

They identified themselves as Trieu Chi Kien, Luong Minh Phat, and Ly Mau An. They had been captured at Phu Bai near Hue City during the 1968 Tet Offensive. The three had been riding on a Lambretta motor scooter when they were seized by Viet Cong forces, who suspected the trio were spies for the CIA. They insisted that they were self-employed tailors who made and sold uniforms to American servicemen. They protested their capture and imprisonment but to no avail.

Trieu Chi Kien was married. His wife and children resided in the Kowloon area of Hong Kong. Luong Minh Phat told other inmates that he was Chinese but a citizen of Indonesia. The trio remained imprisoned; in 1982, they were in Camp K1 at Thanh Phong Prison. They constantly appealed to the commandos to get word somehow to their families that they were alive. Kien wrote letter after letter to his wife and gave them to commandos in the hope that one might get out. In 1986, one of the commandos fled to Hong Kong and succeeded in getting a message to Kien's wife. She rushed to the refugee camp where the commando was being held and pleaded with camp officials to let her speak with the man. The officials refused, and, with tears streaming down her face, she was forced to leave.[5]

The commandos at Phong Quang and other prisons had but one vision: survive their imprisonment and obtain their release. Of course, their confinement along the Chinese border meant that no escape was possible. They saw no new commandos coming into the prison system. Through snatches of radio broadcasts, they began to realize that the war was winding down. Still, they continued to maintain their spirit and believed they would never be forgotten by those who had sent them into the North. That same hope was held by the small contingent of fifty-one commandos imprisoned in the rustic Ha Giang Province dispersed prison in the far northern mountains of the province. This was the wartime location of prisoners from Yen Tho and Yen Hoa prisons near Phu Tho who had been evacuated in 1965.[6]

By 1970, America was moving forward with Vietnamization. General Westmoreland was then U.S. Army chief of staff at the Pentagon, and Gen. Creighton W. Abrams was the next commander of the Military Assistance Command Vietnam. As the commandos at Phong Quang were learning the terror of shackles, American forces in South Vietnam were drawing down. The commandos had no way to know that they had all been written off as effectively dead. In the spring of 1972, MACSOG's top secret army, which reached just short of ten thousand in 1971, was being dismantled, and a bag of rice and a free ride home became the normal termination pay. Part of the cost of MACSOG's operations was tabulated in Washington as a modest quarter billion dollars two years before its operations ended (see Appendixes 8 and 9). The lives of those killed and missing, both Vietnamese and American, never entered into the financial computations.

The members of the teams sent north before 1968, however, were able to conclude that the original type of long-range commando team operations had stopped by late 1967, even though the STRATA teams were continuing into Laos and the panhandle of North Vietnam. They now met new groups of inmates, members of cross-border reconnaissance teams and individual North Vietnamese Army defectors recruited by MACSOG to maintain deception operations through such projects as Borden and Earth Angel.

On 26 December 1971, the last twenty-three commandos in the solitary isolation detention compound and the thirty-four commandos in room 3 of Phong Quang Prison boarded a heavy transport truck for the short ride toward the northwest to their next prison, Central Prison No. 1 outside Lao Cai City, the provincial seat of Lao Cai Province. This would be their home for the next year and a half, at a place they would learn to call Pho Lu.

19

PREPARATION FOR RELEASE

BY THE END of 1971, nearly all commandos were concentrated at three national-level prisons: Central Prison No. 1, outside Lao Cai City and close to the border with China; Tan Lap Prison, near Phu Tho in the Red River delta southwest of Hanoi; and Hoanh Bo Prison, in the hills inland from the northeast coastal town of Hon Gai. Singleton agents were spread around many of the other major prisons. The selection of prisoners transferred to each prison during 1971 was obviously well planned (see Figure 7).[1]

Among the first to leave Phong Quang that summer, the recruited radio operators were sent to Tan Lap and Hoanh Bo. Tan Lap also held many members of cross-border teams.

The last to leave Phong Quang were forty-seven commandos designated by the cadre as "those who could not be reeducated." They went to Pho Lu Prison, the popular name for Central Prison No. 1. Arriving at Pho Lu, they found their barracks in Camp K1 empty except for a half dozen inmates who were completing construction of a third barracks. Here, they met Lau Chi Chan, the frogman from Team CANCER, whom they had first seen at Thanh Tri; Chan was now an inmate carpenter. Early in 1972, another major contingent of commandos arrived at Pho Lu from Quyet Tien. This brought its commando population to 167. The two commando groups were kept in separate barracks within the same compound, but they were separated by a wall and generally isolated from each other.

"You'll never guess what happened after you all left," began the wizened political prisoner, one of the "old-timers" who had been at Quyet Tien for more than a decade.[2] "The command section gave us an order to dig up bones! Can you believe it? They sent us out to dig up the graves!"

"Dig up graves? What for?" came the only slightly curious question from one of the commandos.

"Well, they gave us the prison water buffalo and plow and told us to go dig up bones. They sent us out to work in the old graveyards out on the hills. Can you believe it? They told us it was very sensitive, the grave work I mean. They only let us go out when the criminals came back in from working the vegetable gardens outside. We were sent out at noon to plow up the graves, and we had to be back before the criminals went back out to work again in the afternoon."

"Why did they want you to plow up the graves?"

"Who knows? We worked over those old graveyards for a whole week, looking for graves, but could not find any. They told us to keep trying, that we had to dig up the graves and get out the bones. Something about recovering remains that were going to be sent back home. After a week, we couldn't find any. Then they told us to stop searching."

After a while, the old fellow walked away, off in his own world. The commandos who listened to his babbling thought they understood what he meant. The Ministry must have been trying to find the remains of commandos who had died at Quyet Tien during the ten years before the cease-fire. It must have wanted skeletons, anyone's skeleton, in case it was pressured to return the bones of deceased commandos.

The commandos knew that the hills surrounding Quyet Tien were full of graves. The graveyards filled during 1961–65 had been long abandoned; newer graveyards were used during later years. Then, the newer ones were abandoned to the grass and the weather, and no one could recall just how many graveyards had been filled.

They weren't surprised that the three old political prisoners hadn't found anything. After all, the burials took place at night and the graves had no headstones. It seemed very difficult to conceive of the prison staff having kept any accurate records of who was thrown in what hole. Besides, some of the original graveyards had been turned into vegetable fields years ago, and all the bones became commingled during the years of plowing.

That was the kind of thing the Ministry would do, the former commando thought to himself. What do you do when you need the remains of commandos and you have absolutely no idea where they are but you need bones to satisfy someone? You just go dig up anyone. Who would ever know the difference?

In August 1972, the commandos were moved from K1 to K3.[3] Not long after the move, a delegation arrived at Pho Lu under the command of Public Security Service Lieutenant Colonel Xy, one of the senior prison cadre from the Ministry of Public Security. The commandos were informed that they would receive political indoctrination about the changes then occurring in Vietnam, about what Xy called the "new situation and the history of the patriotic struggle against the foreign aggressors by the Vietnamese and the heros who had resisted the invaders in the past." The lieutenant colonel was accompanied by a team of two dozen security service cadre, nearly all in civilian clothes.

For the next month, this team was fully committed to a prearranged training program. The cadre began by presenting a subject, and the inmates were told to prepare a written assessment of the material presented. The groups then met with a security cadre, who carefully led the discussion to the predetermined class objective. The presentation might last from a half day to a day, with the following day devoted to group discussions and individual critiques. All work was suspended during this period, which became known as the "hoc tap trao tra tu binh" (prisoner prerelease indoctrination).

At least four of the cadre from Xy's team were responsible for the political instruction; the remainder reviewed the inmates' files maintained by the prison staff.[4] The information in each prisoner's file obviously was being evaluated to determine how the prisoner responded to the material presented.

Lieutenant Colonel Xy considered himself an accomplished poet and a most literate individual with a deep understanding of Vietnamese classical writings. On his team was a young woman in her mid-twenties, a security services professional whose shapely figure was poorly hidden beneath her slick black pajamas. She was also intimately familiar with Vietnamese classics, and it was not surprising that Xy worked quite closely with his protégé.

As time went on, each inmate was called out for a personal interview with one of the visiting cadre. The officer faced the prisoner across a table, with the inevitable cup of tea and a small plate of cakes. Some interviews consisted of little more than a file review. Others covered remarks made by the prisoner years earlier, remarks critical of certain individuals under whom the prisoner had served while still in South Vietnam. The cadre emphasized that the prisoner, if released, had a responsibility to bring these problems to the attention of the proper authorities.

For some, the interview took on a menacing tone when cadre informed the prisoner that he might be called on to "serve the revolution," if he was permitted to return home. For example, someone might come to visit and ask for help in "the struggle" to rid the country of the foreign invaders and corrupt officials. Such remarks carried a clear implication that the Communists might try to use the prisoners after their release. Anyone who sat through one of these interviews came away shaken.

Prior to the interview, each inmate had to complete an updated personal history statement and attach a statement describing how he would conduct himself after returning to the South. The statement always ended with a request for repatriation.

For some prisoners, there was a third document. During their private interviews, selected inmates were asked to prepare a request to remain in North Vietnam.

The cadre explained that each document had a separate role in support of the ongoing peace negotiations involving Hanoi and its southern arm, the Provisional Revolutionary Government. For example, the document outlining how the prisoners planned to conduct themselves after release would be used to demonstrate that an individual wanted to be repatriated to South Vietnam. It would be used to support a request for repatriation through the Provisional Revolutionary Government. The document expressing a desire to remain in North Vietnam would be used by the Democratic Republic of Vietnam in discussions with the Saigon government to explain why an individual was not being repatriated.

Everyone completed the first two documents. Some of the prisoners who were afforded the "opportunity" to prepare the third document completed it, but others did not. Those who refused to request that they remain in the North were not pressured to do so.

The first prisoners called for interviews sensed that they were staged. Most came away with the impression that each interview had been tape-recorded to ensure an accurate record of the discussion. They passed on this impression to those waiting to be interviewed. As the other prisoners approached their interviews, they knew they had to be very careful about everything they said.

During the month or more of intensive political instruction, Lieutenant Colonel Xy was barraged with the same question: Will we be returned to South Vietnam, and when?

Xy studiously avoided any concrete answers. Instead, he tossed his head and laughed. The commandos also queried political instructors, but they were always noncommittal. One of the cadre put it this way:

> The State does indeed think of you and hopes that you will be able to return home. It is you who have attacked us. It is you who have invaded the North with the intention of overthrowing the government. You have all violated the laws of the Democratic Republic of Vietnam. You actually should not be returned but, because of the humanitarian character of the State, the State will review each of your cases to determine if you can return to your families.

The political indoctrination and instruction at Pho Lo were matched by similar activities at Hoanh Bo Prison.[5] Here, the commandos faced a contingent of up to twenty cadre, including a female senior captain named Hoa, from the Ministry of Public Security under the command of a lieutenant colonel. On several occasions, Lieutenant Colonel Xy came to Quang Ninh and met privately with the staff working there. Included in the original contingent was a young company-grade officer, To Ba Oanh, who was personally involved in the instruction and interview with each prisoner.

Senior Captain Hoa intimated that some commandos might

be returned while others would not. She declined to say who and their prison commander, Sang, kept apart from such discussions.

During the personal interviews conducted by Hoa, she asked prisoners to discuss "openly and frankly" the treatment they received while in prison. One prisoner complained that the prison staff at Quang Ninh had been beating the prisoners, to which she replied that "such acts are errors on the part of the prison commander which should be forgotten." She too asked prisoners to fill out requests to remain behind in North Vietnam.

The indoctrination at Quang Ninh began in October 1972 and lasted until at least December when B-52 raids caused the prisoners to be moved to a dispersed prison location a short distance away. Here they heard about an American "progressive" named Nam who was at Hoanh Bo with a Vietnamese woman and two children.[6]

When the political indoctrination at Pho Lu was concluded in November 1972, there was an improvement in overall living conditions, and each commando began to believe that he would be returned to the Republic of Vietnam under the terms of the Paris peace talks, now near settlement. The prison staff was more flexible in dealing with the inmates. The air was one of restrained optimism. No one, including the prison staff and the Ministry of Public Security cadre, ever said officially that the commandos would or would not be repatriated during a prisoner exchange, but each commando began to believe that repatriation was just a few months away.

On 27 January 1973, the Paris Peace Accords were signed and the mutually agreed upon cease-fire went into effect. Each commando at Pho Lu read a copy of the Accords provided by the cadre. The prisoners focused on the part that clearly implied they would be going home, in spite of the cadre's hesitancy in replying to their repeated inquiries. They each singled out the specific phrase:

> Nhung ai co lien quan den cuoc chien tranh o Vietnam thi deu duoc giai quyet va duoc trao tra.

This was diplomatic language stating in a straightforward manner that "All those involved in the Vietnam war will be repatriated." The commandos now expected an early return home.

They were sent back to K1 in February 1973 and issued sewing machines, with orders to make new clothing.[7] Apparently, they were to have new clothes for their repatriation, and the prison staff insisted that the clothes be prepared quickly. The sewing machines worked twenty-four hours a day. Some prisoners cut out pieces from the cotton material, white for short-sleeved shirts and dark blue for trousers, while others sewed them together. Enough clothing was made for each prisoner to receive two new sets of clothes, a small bag for carrying the clothes, and a hat. The items, all made in the same size, were taken away as they were finished and placed in the prison depot "to be issued at the appropriate time."

The cadre frequently came around to inspect the work and kept repeating, "This is your clothing. Make it carefully."

Weeks later, in the midst of the ongoing prisoner exchange, the commandos searched for just one cadre who would tell them when and how they would be sent back to South Vietnam. They could not ask the prison commander, Maj. Ngo Ba Toan, because he seldom came into their area, so they finally questioned Lieutenant Y, chief of the Education Section, and his deputy, Sr. Sgt. Hao Lieu. Their blunt response set the prisoners back on their heels.

"No way!" they said laughingly. "No way! There is no way that any of you are going to be exchanged. No way! If you look carefully, you'll find that there is not one single period or comma in the whole Accords which covers any of you. There is nothing, absolutely nothing. You're not even mentioned. Show us one place, just one place, where any of you are mentioned, just one place."

"But—but—there's the reference to the return of anyone who had been involved in the war—we were involved—we were participants! The Accords *do* apply to us!"

Lieutenant Y just shook his head and laughed again. The commandos were devastated.

For an hour or two each night, the loudspeakers in the barracks played broadcasts from the People's Army radio station. The prisoners listened intently to descriptions of the cease-fire and accounts of prisoners being exchanged, although ever so slowly. Then the broadcasts recounted groups of prisoners being exchanged across the Thach Han River. It was always the same—small groups of South Vietnamese POWs returning home, while three or four times as many North Vietnamese POWs were going back to the North. When they heard references to American POWs going home, they thought this was a clear signal that their turn would come before long. They were all aware that members of cross-border teams and the singletons had been transferred elsewhere. This seemed to imply that prisoners were being organized into like groups for repatriation.

As the prisoner exchanges dragged on, the inmates at Pho Lu sensed that the Democratic Republic of Vietnam was returning the prisoners slowly, like a fisherman playing out a line, as it watched and waited, perhaps assessing whether it might have to return the commandos if someone insisted.

The commandos' apprehension was heightened by the fact that former officers of the Republic of Vietnam Armed Forces captured at Hue City during the 1968 Tet Offensive, were still being held in the K1 punishment cells, where they had been since 1972. Did that mean that the North was going to keep back some prisoners as some type of bargaining chip? But why?

And still they waited. . . .

They were essentially correct about the likelihood that struggles were going on at the highest level between Washington and Hanoi concerning the issue of political prisoners. The commandos, all convicted of espionage, were considered by Hanoi to be a special category of political prisoner. Perhaps Hanoi never intended to release them unless, of course, Washington was willing to address tens of thousands of prisoners in South Vietnam that Hanoi and its Provisional Revolutionary Government were calling "political prisoners being detained by the Thieu government," with the demand that they be released. Washington had no desire to be drawn into any such accommodation.

Beginning in February 1973, American prisoners held in the North were turned over to American officials at Hanoi and flown to Clark Air Base in the Philippines for preliminary intelligence screenings and physical checkups. A U.S. Army major headed the team of debriefers from Saigon that flew to Clark to process returning American civilians. Other teams of debriefers, representing each of the military services, also arrived.

The questions they were to ask returning POWs were defined by the Defense Intelligence Agency (DIA), the same agency that, in 1965, had urged support for MACSOG's mission and argued that its agent teams inside North Vietnam were producing valuable intelligence information. The priority intelligence requirement now was identification of Americans unaccounted for or still in captivity.

Unfortunately, the DIA office responsible for American POWs and MIAs, then headed by U.S. Navy Comdr. Charles Trowbridge, had no record of losses for MACSOG's contract Vietnamese agents. DIA was primarily interested in Americans, not foreign nationals, and there were no questions from DIA about any Vietnamese covert operatives who might still be prisoners. Within weeks of the repatriation of the last American prisoner on 1 April 1973, Commander Trowbridge was facing pressure to reduce his staff. Overhead imagery of the wartime prisons was canceled except for a select few in the Hanoi area, and the focus at the Pentagon soon shifted to a review of the status of Americans still listed as missing and the slow process of declaring them dead based on presumptive findings of death. Even if the commandos were confirmed to be alive, they would be considered a problem for their own government, not Washington.

Among the civilians repatriated during Operation Homecoming were Larry Stark and Bob Olsen, the two prisoners confined in the room next to Le Van Ngung in Area B, Thanh Tri Prison. Whatever they told their debriefers, it did not make a ripple in American interest regarding the fate of the nearly four hundred commandos then languishing in Hanoi's prisons.

South Vietnamese Air Force Lt. Nguyen Quoc Dat, a hero to the commandos who met him briefly when he arrived at their prison in the panhandle, was also remembered by American prisoners held with him at Hoa Lo. On their release, many Americans demanded that something be done for him, and U.S. officials were able to secure his release.

Also released was Phan Thanh Van, the C-47 pilot shot down over Ninh Binh on 1 July 1961, but others who survived the crash had long ago died in prison.

In April 1973, the Joint Casualty Resolution Center (JCRC) in Saigon, headed by its first commander, Brig. Gen. Robert Kingston, submitted to the North Vietnamese its first priority list of Americans unaccounted for and of foreign nationals in whom the United States had an interest. Not one commando name appeared on that list or any subsequent list of Americans, Vietnamese, and other nationals later presented by JCRC to Hanoi's representatives.

General Kingston's new command meant a return to an organization that he had served earlier in the war, but it was in a different form. At that time, what became the JCRC was a part of MACSOG and was known by the cover name of Joint Personnel Recovery Center (JPRC). Kingston previously had been operations officer for the agent teams that went into North Vietnam during mid-1967.

In his new position, General Kingston found to his horror that JCRC's computerized data base of names of captive and unaccounted-for Americans was literally a nightmare; the loss locations for many American cross-border casualties had been entered incorrectly. In his messages to Washington about the inaccurate data, Kingston never mentioned that his data base did not include any names of the hundreds of contract agents launched by MACSOG and last recorded as captives (see Appendix 10).

Not every commando was retained in North Vietnam. For example, nine of the ten Vietnamese from Team ILLINOIS, who were captured in Laos with Lance Cpl. Frank Cius and M. Sgt. Ronald Dexter, were repatriated by the Vietnam People's Army and turned over to the Republic of Vietnam at a prisoner exchange point on the Thach Han River. Among these was Nguyen Van Chien, Dexter's team interpreter. The tenth Vietnamese member of the team, Ha Van Son, had displayed a "belligerent attitude," and he was not repatriated.

American debriefers working for Col. William LeGro's Intelligence Division at the Saigon-based Defense Attaché Office located and interviewed Nguyen Van Chien and several other team members. They wanted to learn the fate of Dexter and the crewmen of a Chinook helicopter shot down over Laos. Chien told them that, north of Thanh Hoa City, Dexter had been bludgeoned to death by the PAPSF guard escorting them to Hanoi.

Chien then asked about his back pay, based on his employment contract, that he was due. The debriefers panicked. The Defense Attaché Office sent a hurried message to the DIA in Washington that said Chien and the others would not talk unless they received their back pay. The message noted that Chien's debriefing had been terminated when he became a bit hostile over the back pay issue.

South Vietnamese officials also interviewed Chien and the other team members, who identified the commandos with them in prison and those last known alive. None had been repatriated. Then, Chien and the other repatriated prisoners went home. The war was over for them.

> Chien? A team repatriated in 1973? Sure, I remember. They asked for their back pay. They were owed it. They'd signed contracts and they had it coming. All the agents had signed contracts. Unfortunately, MAC-SOG was gone. There was no money, anywhere. But, the Americans got some money somewhere and paid them off as was provided for under their contract.[8]

''What about the commandos who weren't repatriated?'' I asked.

''I'm not sure,'' he said.

20

HUNGER STRIKE

THE TIME HAD come for the men at Pho Lu to take their fate into their own hands, as radio broadcasts implied that the prisoner exchanges had stalled.

The "Asian solution" for the commandos could be traced innocently enough to a Sunday in mid-May 1973, when several commandos in barracks F3 hopped across the intervening wall to have a meal with the commandos in F2.[1] The following Sunday, the scene was repeated. On the third Sunday, the commandos again climbed the wall and were finishing their meal when the prison duty officer arrived. Clutching a piece of paper in his hand, he unlocked the area outer door and marched into barracks F3.

He read from the paper: "On orders of the prison command section all inmates are requested to disperse and return to their own areas."

He then did an about-face and left the barracks without a backward glance. No one moved.

Fifteen minutes later, the duty officer returned and read the dispersal order a second time. Again, no one reacted.

After his third visit, the duty officer had barely left when the barracks door was suddenly wrenched open and he reentered. This time, he was accompanied by a large force of armed guards. While several guards kept their assault rifles pointed at the prisoners, others grabbed Dang Dinh Thuy at random and dragged him to the punishment cells, where he was placed in the shackles.

"Khong an! Thuyet thuc! Yeu cau anh em thuyet thuc! Thuyet thuc!" Nguyen Van Tan's voice was surprisingly clear as he shouted what everyone wanted to say but for which only Tan found the courage: "We're not eating! It's a hunger strike! I'm asking all of you to go on a hunger strike! Hunger strike!"

A quiet, slender, almost unobtrusive commando from Team ROMEO, Tan started a chant immediately picked up by others until it became a roar.

"Hunger strike! Hunger strike! Hunger strike!"

The chanting went on and on as the men slowly climbed back over the walls and returned to their own barracks.

The hunger strike started the following day, 4 June 1973.

Officials of the Ministry of Public Security became alarmed. In their minds, the prisoners had to be coordinating with people on the outside because hunger strikes broke out at all three hard-labor prisons confining the commandos. This meant that the prisoners in one prison were communicating with those in another. A conspiracy theory such as this could drive a state security apparatus mad.

Pho Lu Prison went on an immediate high-security alert. All available guards were rushed to K1 and deployed along the outer walls, inside the prison proper, and outside the isolation detention area. Machine guns appeared on the outer walls and within the prison.

The hunger strike caused consternation within the prison staff because Major Toan, the prison commander, was absent. His deputy, Sr. Lt. Nguyen Van Tuan, faced a major prison disturbance, but he lacked instructions on how to handle it. Tuan's lack of experience and his indecisiveness were apparent when he entered barracks F2.

Although Tuan tried to make his voice sound hard, it clearly betrayed his fear. He wasn't afraid of the commandos; he was afraid that if he didn't handle the situation correctly, it would mean his job.

The fear came out in false bravado as he spoke: "You're all going to have to deal with the reality that we have total control over all of you. You're right here in the palm of our hands and if we squeeze you, you're all dead. If we loosen up, you can breathe. Whoever thinks he's that good, just go ahead and stay on your hunger strike. We'll just get rid of all of you."

Lieutenant Tuan stood there, poised, waiting for some response. Three commandos jumped up to respond.

Lau Chi Chan, the tall, hardened frogman from Team CANCER captured in the Gulf of Tonkin in 1966, was one of the three. He strode forth, ripped open his shirt, and shouted at Tuan, "You think you're so good, go ahead and shoot! Shoot! Go ahead, shoot me—bloodthirsty Communist barbarians—shoot me!"

Tuan stood there in shocked disbelief before turning and striding out of the room. The guards pulled the door shut and locked it behind him. His training and experience always had been with prisoners who toed the line, prisoners who jumped when the cadre issued orders. This type of mass open defiance was totally new. Tuan took the classic bureaucrat's approach: doing nothing was better than doing something wrong.

Major Toan returned to Pho Lu Prison as soon as he received word of the hunger strike. He walked straight into barracks F2 with his principal staff. After staring at the prisoners for a moment, Toan spoke, almost too quietly, "You're all very foolish, you know, very foolish. Why are you on a hunger strike? Look at you all! You're all so sick! You're dying, and who will be the real losers? You're the only ones who are going to suffer! Eat! Go ahead and eat, get yourselves back in good physical shape, then one day who knows, maybe the party and State will be gracious and let you all go home . . . you might be repatriated."

There it was! The first time from his mouth! He had actually said the word *trao tra* (repatriation)! Throughout 1972 and into 1973, he had completely avoided that word. Now, at long last, he was having to use it, but the word no longer mattered—it was too late.

Major Toan stood there, smiling. He was almost laughing as his tone changed perceptively, "You all really are very foolish. I've heard you all want Thuy to be released. I've been told you want the provisions of the Paris Peace Accords implemented so you all can be repatriated. If you want Thuy returned, that is something I can resolve right here and now. I can have Thuy released and back in here with you this very afternoon if you want. As to the Paris Accords, that is something clearly outside my authority to resolve. I'm just the keeper of the key. That's all. I don't have authority in any other area. When the State instructs me it wants something done, it gets done. When the State instructs me to crush something, it gets crushed. That's something the State and the government have the authority to direct and expect me to carry out.

"Now as to Thuy, I will have him back here with you this very afternoon, but I am requesting all of you to resume your normal eating and drinking so you will maintain your health in preparation for the day the party and State arrange for you to be reunited with your families. If I let Thuy come back, will you all return to eat as usual?"

Sitting there quietly, the commandos considered Toan's proposal. They finally agreed to resume eating if Thuy was released. The air of confrontation evaporated.

This had been a small victory. Some of the commandos thought it was an important first step that might lead to other things as time went on.

The hunger strike ended, and the commandos began slowly to leave their barracks. During the next several days, prison cadre began calling for some of them to report to the duty officer. They were aware of what was happening. Those prisoners could provide the camp cadre with the identity of the ringleaders, information that was needed before the cadre could mete out appropriate retribution.

Their plans were rendered ineffective by a wad of paper shot from a rubber band to barracks F2. It contained a short message: "They've organized the self-awareness unit to attack you all. Do not leave your barracks compound."

This was one of the ways that prisoners had communicated effectively for decades. Shot from area to area, such messages were a highly effective means of communication that had never been stopped.

In July, the entire commando contingent in barracks F1 and F2 was ordered to prepare for transfer to a new location. Fifty names were read from a prepared list. These prisoners, ready for transportation, assembled at the front gate. They saw several waiting trucks and a large number of men from the exterior guard force outside the gate. Everything seemed normal—just another transfer.

As the prisoners prepared to exit K1, the cadre went down the column and signaled some of them to form into one column and others into a second column. The cadre then pointed to one column of twenty-one prisoners and said they would be the only ones transferred to Quyet Tien. Obviously, the list of fifty names had been a deliberate ruse. It included hard-core resisters, as well as some prisoners who were either no threat or were known informants. Amid the disorganization and confusion, the twenty-one selected for transfer were loaded onto a truck and it departed. A second truck, containing the usual armed escorts, followed it.

The careful selection and immediate transfer of the twenty-one inmates signified just how quickly the prison staff was able to coordinate with the Ministry of Public Security at Hanoi. Clearly, the transfer was a Ministry decision, not one made by the prison commander. Prison commanders had the authority to recommend certain actions, such as transfers or releases, but that was the extent of their authority.

The trucks stopped approximately twenty kilometers from Pho Lu Prison. One of the cadre from the Education Section assigned to accompany the prisoners stood up and read an order from the Ministry of Public Security. The contents of the order further confirmed that the transfer was a Ministry decision and plainly indicated why the order was not read back at the prison. It was clear, concise, and a harbinger of things to come:

> Your monthly allotment as specified in the Paris Accords is suspended effective immediately. None of you are covered any longer by any provision in the Accords as of this date. From this date forward your monthly allotment is reduced to twelve dong per month and you will resume normal reeducation immediately.

He then stepped down, and the convoy continued on.

As the trucks rumbled toward Quyet Tien, the prisoners remaining at Pho Lu became apprehensive. Most believed that the transfer was the first contingent of many who were to be transported to another location for execution. The remaining commandos assembled in barracks F3. They announced their decision to remain together and refused to return to their original barracks.

The commandos knew that the prison guard force was still

fully deployed, with machine guns in the guard towers, but the prisoners were unable to see the entire guard force enter the prison with automatic weapons as it prepared to implement the next phase of the crackdown on the hunger strikers. In addition to the company-sized prison guard unit from the People's Armed Public Security Force, a special platoon-sized unit had been brought from Hanoi with the specific mission of quickly and effectively putting down the hunger strike.

Major Toan's order to the guards standing by was simple and direct: "Put down the disturbance!"

What followed had been well rehearsed.

One group of guards armed with assault rifles smashed into barracks F3 and began to beat the prisoners. They used their assault rifles like clubs to drive them from the barracks. Some prisoners were literally knocked out of the barracks. Others were dragged out, while still others crawled. Guard dogs were then unleashed, and they attacked the prisoners remaining inside.

As the prisoners slowly exited, either knocked or dragged out by the guards or crawling out by themselves, they encountered a gauntlet waiting for them outside the door. Each guard standing there held a set of iron shackles connected by a length of iron chain and patiently swung the apparatus back and forth.

The guard force drove the prisoners from F3 into the gauntlet. As the prisoners tried to move between the rows of the gauntlet, the guards were waiting for them.

The first prisoners stumbled down the gauntlet. The guards adjusted their aim and flicked out their iron shackles, gun butts, and clubs to keep the prisoners from moving too quickly, not to hurry them forward. As the prisoners reached the end of the gauntlet, selected guards dragged designated prisoners to the punishment cells. They were accompanied by other guards flailing the iron shackles and beating the prisoners into unconsciousness. The commandos were slapped into the shackles on the cement beds. Anyone still conscious was beaten into oblivion. Then some were purposely brought back to consciousness, with bucketfuls of water poured on them until they opened their eyes, only to be beaten senseless again. Nguyen Van Tan, Vu Viet Tinh,

Dang Cong Trinh, Nguyen Huy Khoan, and Nguyen Van Trinh were all reduced to little more than bloody rags.

Tan was selected for the worst beating. He had been identified by now as the one who had first uttered the phrase "hunger strike!" Trinh, the boatman who had brought the Vietnamese frogmen on their missions into the coastal area of the panhandle, was more fortunate. The guards used the iron shackles to knock out his teeth.

Sr. Col. Vo Dai Nhan, deputy chief of the Ministry's Cuc Lao Cai (Labor and Reeducation Directorate), was generally satisfied with the commandos' indoctrination at Tan Lap Prison that fall in 1972.[2]

Everything had gone relatively well until just after the cease-fire. According to the terms of the Accords, prisoners were required to undergo familiarization with provisions relating to the status of those who would be repatriated. Prison officials saw this as the appropriate time to distribute propaganda material to the inmates.

"No!" shouted one of the commandos. "We are not going to read this propaganda! This is a fundamental violation of the provisions of the Accords, which prohibit the use of propaganda as a tool to try to influence the views of prisoners."

Nhan's cadre quickly withdrew the material.

The commandos had followed implementation of the Accords, particularly that part relating to the repatriation of prisoners. The news indicated that prisoners were indeed being released—first, the Americans, and then reports of Vietnamese prisoner exchanges taking place across the Thach Han River. The commandos at Tan Lap now raised the issue of their repatriation with Senior Colonel Nhan's staff.

Nhan's response to their insistent questions was to bring the prisoners together and address them in a formal session. From his perspective, it was time for a showdown.

"None of you are part of the definition of prisoners of war as described in the Accords," he began. "All of you are spies. You are not prisoners of war. The definition of prisoners of war simply does not cover commando spies such as you. If any of you are repatriated, you will only be repatriated to the Americans because the South does not recognize you as theirs."

Within days, this statement was followed by other statements from Nhan claiming that the representative of the Democratic Republic of Vietnam, Le Duc Tho, was negotiating with the American representative, Dr. Henry Kissinger. Nhan said that the negotiations covered several subjects, among them supposedly the repatriation of the commandos to the Americans, as well as money demanded by the Democratic Republic as war reparations from the United States. It was clear from these remarks that the return of the commando prisoners was linked to the war reparations and that North Vietnam would try to use the prisoners as leverage to get money from the United States.

"For each one of you," Nhan said, "the Americans will have to pay twelve million dollars. Le Duc Tho is working out the details on this with Kissinger."

The commandos were stunned. They had no way to know if this was true or false, and they were outraged that North Vietnam would violate the provisions of the Accords by using them as "bargaining chips" to extort money from Washington. Some commandos viewed Nhan's remarks as little more than propaganda designed to make them angry at the Americans if they were not repatriated. Then, a prison rumor indicated that the talks between Tho and Kissinger had been suspended.

One morning, a group from the Ministry made a surprise visit to the commando detention area. The prison commander, Sr. Capt. Nguyen Van Thuy, accompanied the group.

When Thuy entered the barracks, he ordered one of the commandos to meet with Thuc, a cadre from the Ministry. Thuc read the prisoner the order of the Ministry of Public Security:

> It is the decision of the Ministry that you have committed crimes against the State. You have been engaged in propaganda activities, have slandered the State, have organized against the State, and have organized others to perform the same. The commission of these crimes requires that you be transferred elsewhere.

The prisoner stared at Thuc and then took a copy of the Accords and pointed to the provision that prohibited the transfer of prisoners. Clearly, the article took into account that prisoner transfers might take place, which might result in certain ''difficult'' prisoners being executed by a detaining power. It wasn't spelled out that way in the Accords, but it was clearly implied by the prohibition against transferring prisoners. The commando refused to accept the Ministry-ordered transfer.

After the prisoner had left for his meeting with Thuc, the other commandos sent a hurried transmission by ''tap code'' of the fact that one of the commandos had been ordered out. They made a decision to launch a hunger strike as an act of protest if anything untoward happened.

Back in his barracks, the prisoner told his cellmates about his concern that he was being transferred in order to be ''eliminated.'' The response from the other prisoners was to launch immediately their hunger strike. With this man back in his barracks and the others clearly engaged in the first steps of a disturbance, one of the cadre said that they would withdraw ''for one hour to permit the prisoner to collect his property.'' This was the first step in their effort to diffuse the situation. When the cadre returned an hour later, the prisoners refused to permit them into the barracks and announced they were on a hunger strike to protest the failure of the Democratic Republic of Vietnam to adhere strictly to the provisions of the Geneva Accords and repatriate them.

Thuc ordered the prison guards to lock the barracks doors, withdraw from the isolation detention area, and lock the entryway behind them.

The hunger strike lasted for four days. Each hour, the cadre had returned to the barracks and called on the strikers to capitulate. The prisoners continued to refuse until their demands were met. The situation was at an impasse.

On the fourth day, Senior Colonel Nhan came back from Hanoi and marched straight to the isolation detention area. He went into a room containing nine commandos, including the one who'd been the object of the initial transfer order. The prisoner was ordered out, but he refused unless the order was officially and publicly canceled.

Nhan had not reached his rank and position by negotiating

with prisoners. He walked out and, with a wave of his hand, ordered the security forces into the detention area. They dragged all of the commandos into the outer courtyard. The resister was taken to the K1 assembly hall and an impromptu trial held on the spot. From the commando's perspective, it was merely a sentencing, not a trial.

Nhan and other cadre sat behind a table. One of the cadre read a prepared statement listing the prisoner's crimes. It was a long list. He was accused of resisting reeducation, slandering the regime, organizing resistance on the part of other prisoners, and fomenting a hunger strike. The details of his original sentence were read, as well as a list of violations of state and prison regulations since the date of his capture, including forty-five instances when he had been disciplined for various infractions.

The decision of the court for the crime of fomenting a hunger strike was execution.

The prisoner was placed in isolation confinement and both of his ankles shackled. The next day, called out to meet with Nhan, he expected this to be the first step in the process of execution. Vo Dai Nhan was furious.

"See this gun?" he said. "This is a Viet Cong gun. It's not a gun used to shoot birds. It's a gun used to shoot reactionaries such as the likes of you. Your actions here have come to the attention of the BBC, which has broadcast to the world the existence of a hunger strike here. The world has used your hunger strike as a vehicle to attack our regime and criticize our system and state."

The prisoner, Mai Dai Hoc, was elated. He smiled at Senior Colonel Nhan.[3]

"What do you think you're smiling at?" screamed Nhan.

"What you have just told me means that it was all worthwhile." Hoc's smile widened.

Nhan began to yell and scream. Clearly out of control, he kicked the chair and smashed his fist on the table. He called for the guards to return the prisoner to the punishment cell and shackle both of his ankles. Even as Hoc was hauled off, Nhan continued ranting and raving—flinging around chairs and tables, taking out his anger on anything within reach.

Several days later, other commandos, this time from K2, were also sent to the punishment cells.

On Hoc's fourth day in shackles, Nhan called him out for another meeting.

"You've already been sentenced to death but I have still not issued the implementing instruction," Nhan said. "Don't even think that we are going to permit you to live. The only reason we haven't shot you already is that your name appears on the list of prisoners to be repatriated to the Americans. Your name might be on that list, but you can rest assured we'll shoot you before anyone is exchanged, to send a warning to the others."

Two months later, a group of more than twenty troublemakers was transferred from Tan Lap to Quyet Tien Prison.

The hunger strikes at Tan Lap and Pho Lu were not a serious problem for the Ministry of Public Security. They had apparently expected hunger strikes and had developed contingency plans to cope with them. The one area of concern, based on recurring questions by prison staff to inmates after the fact, was the mechanism by which the hunger strikes had occurred at the same time and in widely separated prisons. In the minds of the state security professionals, this suggested the existence of some type of secret channel of communication that permitted inmates at one prison to coordinate with inmates at another.

The prisoners just leaned back and smiled to themselves each time they heard the prison staff express an interest in the subject. The Ministry of Public Security was never able to solve this mystery.

21

RETURN TO QUYET TIEN

THE HUNGER STRIKES were over, but the brutality continued under new management.[1]

Many of the first twenty-one commandos transferred to Quyet Tien Prison were the organizers of the hunger strike at Pho Lu. In their new quarters, they experienced a sudden change in their prison life-style. The prison's primary management tools of swift and immediate long-term shackling and solitary confinement replaced the use of labor to reeducate the commandos. The prison staff first reduced their rations and then issued orders to prepare the ritualistic self-criticism document. After this, it was into the punishment cells.

Days of long working hours, increased labor output, self-criticism, and group study sessions were replaced by long-term isolation and starvation rations. The isolation was carefully designed to disorient, confuse, numb, eliminate emotions, and cause each inmate to focus solely on survival. Coupled with the immediate and drastic reduction in monthly food allotments, isolation also ensured that those in the punishment cells were incapable of any type of physical activity. This, in turn, heightened the commandos' feelings of isolation and allowed the prison staff to destroy any cohesion among the commandos. Breaking down the cohesion among the commandos was a primary task, and the prison staff performed it expertly.

Shackling, always immediate and done without hesitation, was a form of punishment that everyone learned to expect if they exhibited the least tendency toward what the staff called "laziness" or any other form of behavior that might be construed as an affront to socialist thinking or contrary to socialist behavior. Shackling was well thought out, exquisitely executed, and totally effective.

It began with Senior Sergeant To, chief of the prison's Education Section. He had just received his instructions from Senior Captain Lang, the new commander of Quyet Tien Prison. Lang relished his new position. He had previously served as deputy under the former commander, Nguyen Sang. Lang had an eye to the future.

Sergeant To marched briskly to the isolation detention barracks; Corporal Thua, the duty NCO responsible for inmates in isolation detention, accompanied him. With a sheaf of papers and pencils in his hand, To entered the room containing the newly arrived prisoners. He smiled as he looked around. The prisoners, some seated and others lying on their straw mats, stared back at To with an arrogance matching his. They knew he would have to deal with them as a group because no barracks leader had been appointed.

To's voice was quiet but firm. "The prison command staff has directed that each of you prepare a self-criticism statement, carefully and clearly documenting each of your actions and your errors and describing how you are going to correct them."

He passed out paper and a pencil to each prisoner and left. To suspected that the prisoners would not write anything, and he did not really care. The cadre were all just going through the motions. The fate of these twenty-one men already had been decided. The headquarters staff had discussed how to handle the prisoners, particularly if they refused to obey orders. Just to be safe, the guard force was on alert. They were going to tighten up on these commandos. If they wanted it the hard way, then so be it. They would be in prison for as long as Hanoi wanted to keep them there, and it was time to teach them a lesson. The only remaining question was whom to select first.

In the commandos' barracks, Nguyen Minh Chau was the first to move. He stared at a board on the wall that listed the four basic regulations for prisoners. They had completed a review of the regulations almost immediately upon their arrival at Quyet Tien that day:

Honestly confess one's own errors.
Reform your thoughts and adhere to the regulations.
Reform your work.
Help the other inmates to become reeducated and inform the State of any others in the society outside who have committed crimes and have not as yet been arrested.

Chau had seen similar signs before and had ignored them. They were part and parcel of the ritual of prison life, but this time was different. Chau deliberately walked over to the sign, ripped it down, and trampled it. Then he turned and walked back to his assigned sleeping place. He lay down again and snoozed.

At 1200, Sergeant To returned to check on their progress. The paper and pencils were lying there unused. He returned again at 1400 and again noted that the prisoners had done nothing. He departed without a word. At 1800, he returned a third time, and still nothing had been accomplished. It was time to implement the next step.

Sergeant To read out the names of Nguyen Van Hinh, Nguyen Van Do, and a third commando. They were summarily dragged out by the guards and taken to the disciplinary area at the rear of Area K, a long building of eighteen cells, nine on either side of a central corridor. To knew that they could easily fill all of the cells with these troublemakers.

When To returned to the disciplinary area that evening, no one was doing any writing. A day or two later, at about 1800, a sudden sound of barking dogs was accompanied by the voices of a large group of prison cadre and guards. The door to the commandos' room was thrown open to admit To, who was accompanied by armed guards, four of whom held snarling German shepherds on short leashes. There was instant bedlam, as guards swarmed into the room and screamed unintelligible orders amid the barking of the dogs. Sergeant To stood there with a piece of paper in his hand until the noise subsided. He gave a cursory glance around the room before reading from his note.

"Le Van Ngung, Nguyen Minh Chau, Tran Ngoc Binh, Dang Dinh Thuy, Hoang Van Van, Nguyen Van Tap." He pointed to each prisoner as he called out the names. Guards quickly grabbed each man, while the dogs barked and strained at their leashes. One commando stood up, a cigarette made of rough Vietnamese tobacco hanging from his mouth.

To stepped forth, screaming, "So you think you can still smoke, do you, Ngung?" Flashing his fist before the commando's face, he sent cigarette coals flying. Ngung's attitude was typical. The time for fear was now past. No one would be going home, so what could the prison staff do now, kill them? It no longer mattered.

Carefully deployed around the prison's interior, alert to any other disturbance, was a well-armed force of half a hundred prison guards with four or five barking dogs. As the prisoners were shoved from their room, guards quickly handcuffed them, with their arms pulled tightly behind them. Then, they half-dragged the prisoners outside to the back of the barracks and into the separate building containing the disciplinary cells. The guards quickly hustled the prisoners inside, two to a cell. Each was forced down onto a cement platform bed, one on either side of each cell. Their ankles were crossed, one over the other, and shackles applied, with the long iron rod through the shackle eyelets to keep their legs immobile.

Each inmate was read the usual confinement order signed by the prison commander. The basis for and the period of confinement were spelled out clearly: "Punishment is for refusing to fill out the ban kiem diem [self-critique]. Period of confinement—indefinite." Within minutes the doors slammed shut and quietness returned to the prison.

The next day, Sergeant To returned to the detention barracks and asked the now familiar question of the commandos who were not yet shackled: "Have you all finished your statements yet?" Again, nothing had been written. Five more names were read from a prepared list, and these prisoners were taken to the disciplinary cells.

The next six months for the men in the disciplinary cells defined the real meaning of isolation. After two weeks of confinement, their right ankles were unshackled. The left ankles remained shackled and were turned so that each man's body was kept constantly facing the wall; the men were barely able to steady themselves when evacuating their bowels. The left ankles of some prisoners were shackled during the entire period of the punishment, which caused injuries that permanently crippled them.

Time ceased to have any meaning. The only sounds entering the cells were fragmentary snatches of conversation from commandos in Area K as they gathered for their noon and evening meals. They deliberately raised their voices to carry over the two walls to their comrades in the detention cells. It was the only way to bring something of the outside world to them. The ears of those on the inside became sensitive to the sounds of voices, as they strained for fragments of intelligible conversation in order to maintain their sanity.

Rations in the disciplinary cells were reduced to seven kilograms per month for each man. This meant less than one-quarter pound of rice or manioc per day with a small bit of salt. Water for drinking was limited to a bowl a day. Food came twice a day, at noon and in the evening, a handful delivered in one of the two white-enameled toleware bowls issued each inmate, onc for food and the other for water. The bowls served as pillows when not being used for food. Several times a month, someone would forget and add a piece of unidentified vegetable to the rice. Insects in the soup were a nutritional luxury. There was no bathing for six months. Constipation set in. When bowel movements did occur, about every seven or eight days, the stools contained more blood than waste. There was no need to give the prisoners more food because they were completely immobilized. The silence in the cells was absolute, and guards constantly patrolled to ensure that no one talked.

As the winter of 1973 approached, the effects of malnutrition set in. The inmates' blood almost stopped circulating when nighttime temperatures hovered near the freezing point. Their thin cotton blankets were next to useless. Night after night, frostbite threatened as extremities turned white and began to itch uncontrollably. The commandos jabbed small bits of stick into their skin to help induce pain, the sign that toes, feet, and legs were still alive, and rubbed their feet and legs to induce circulation. Shackled legs began to atrophy. Some shrank by at least an inch, which resulted in a permanent limp as a reminder of the punishment cells.

One morning, the prison duty officer threw open the door to the cell shared by Le Van Ngung and Nguyen Van Tap.

He stared at the hair on the floor, his eyes searching the cell carefully.

"All right," he demanded. "Where is the razor? Who gave you permission to cut your hair?" His eyes jumped from one side of the disciplinary cell to the hair. He extended his arm and pointed a shaking finger at the clump of hair on the floor between the two cement platform beds.

Ngung slowly turned over onto his back. "We don't have any razor," he said. "It's our hair. We're losing it."

"You're lying!" screamed the duty officer. Hair just didn't fall out like that. He knew they had to have a razor in there somewhere.

Ngung reached up slowly and ran his hand through his thinning hair. Half the hair he touched pulled out like silk. When he extended his arm, a handful of hair fell to the floor. Then he slowly turned onto his left side and faced the wall, as was expected of him.

That December, four prisoners—Le Van Ngung, Hoang Van Van, Nguyen Van Tap, and Hoang Ngoc Chinh—were released from isolation and placed in Area K. The voices of prisoners in the adjacent barracks indicated that the other commandos were aware of their release.[2] They could not be placed with the rest of the prison population until they regained their health somewhat and could again contribute to the two labor units into which all the other commandos had been organized. Their rations were increased to the state-mandated rate of twelve dong per month. This level of food still meant constant hunger, but it was nearly twice as much as they had received in the disciplinary cells. The prisoners reflected on how they had felt starved on this amount of food two years earlier at Phong Quang Prison, but now, after actual starvation for six months, it seemed almost like *too much* food.

Their move back to Area K meant the possibility of contact with the other commandos. Slowly and painstakingly, they fashioned a line woven from thread carefully pulled from their tattered uniforms. They prayed that the line would not break when they weighted it and, with great stealth, threw it over the wall separating them from the other commandos. There was a short tug from the other end of the line. They slowly and very carefully pulled back the line, which had a small parcel attached. Cookies! They were covered with green mold, but the four men divided them and ignored the tart taste of the mold as they eagerly consumed each crumb. It was impossible to describe how delicious they tasted! And there was tobacco! And sugar! They had nearly forgotten the taste of such things.

One month later, the four were assigned to Area O. Each carried his sole possessions: a blanket, straw mat, and two toleware bowls.

The commandos in Area O stared at them. Each weighed no more than eighty pounds. Some had lost most of their hair, and the others had hair below their shoulders. Their skin was a faded white beneath the filth from half a year of no bathing.

"Who are you?" asked Le Ngoc Kien, a member of Team HECTOR 2.

"Don't you know me?" Le Van Ngung said. They had been together since late 1969, both at Phong Quang and at Pho Lu Prison in 1972, where they had become close friends. Kien looked at the skeleton facing him, a quizzical expression on his face. He found it impossible to answer that he was unable to recognize the specter before him.

"It's me—Ngung."

It took several hours before Kien and the other thirty commandos could actually believe who the walking skeletons were, and hours more to stop the tears of reunion.

As the months stretched on through 1974 and into early 1975, the commandos at Quyet Tien learned little about the world outside.[3] Their isolation was nearly total. A little news of the outside world came from some of the criminal inmates who, from time to time, related what family members had passed on during their visits. The commandos learned that the tempo of fighting had increased in the South, but there was seldom any specific news of what was really happening.

Then, in the first week of May 1975, one of the prison education cadre unexpectedly entered their area and posted photographs of life in South Vietnam. The commandos stared at the first glimpses of their country since their capture; for some, this had been fourteen years. The cadre finished tacking up the photographs, stood back, and admired his work.

"See," he said. "We have liberated Saigon! The Republic of Vietnam has been destroyed, and the puppet Army has surrendered!"

The commandos were numb with shock, too dumbfounded to speak, unable to do anything except gaze at the photographs on the bulletin board. There was a picture of tanks from the People's Army of Vietnam rumbling down the Bien Hoa Highway and preparing to enter Saigon beside one of the People's Army tanks on the grounds of the Independence Palace in Saigon. Another photograph showed two lines of South Vietnamese national policemen, in their best white uniforms, standing on either side of the driveway inside the gates of the police headquarters on Vo Tanh Street in Saigon. The policemen were saluting North Vietnamese entering the National Police Headquarters.

The commandos stared at the photographs that seemed to depict Saigon, but it was a Saigon full of North Vietnamese Army soldiers. Why hadn't they heard anything about it before this? How could the war just have ended so suddenly?

Peering closely at the pictures, the inmates tried to determine if they were real or something the Ministry had invented to confuse them further. Most turned away, returning to their barracks and leaving their unfinished work behind. They sat there dejectedly for days and refused to believe what they had seen. These men had held out for so long in hopes that the South—which had now *surrendered*—might some day be victorious. A surrender, based solely on photographs, was too much for them to accept. When the commandos first began to talk about the subject days later, they rationalized it as evidence of some sort of coalition government.

Most of the commandos at Quyet Tien Prison refused to accept the reality of the unconditional surrender and collapse of the Second Republic of the Government of the Republic of Vietnam until 1977, two years after the fact. Only when they met officers from the Republic of Vietnam Armed Forces, who arrived on a labor detail at Quyet Tien in 1977, did the commandos at last come face to face with the harsh reality that the war was indeed over.

One of those who had to deal with this reality was a long-term inmate named Ot, a native of Hanoi.[4] He had been arrested in 1958 as a stay-behind agent in the Tran Minh Chau spy net, one of the stay-behinds trained by the CIA on Saipan in 1954. Some of the early commandos held at Quyet Tien before 1972 had known him there, but not well because he had been placed with North Vietnamese political prisoners. Most who knew of him during this period had heard that he was a resister who believed that somehow, someday, he would be released. The events of 30 April 1975 caused an almost immediate change in Ot's personality.

Ot still had relatives living in Hanoi, but he had no real friends in the prison population. By 1975, he was the last-known prison survivor of the Tran Minh Chau spy net. The others had died over the years, most of them in the wooden stocks at Quyet Tien.[5]

Ot had watched the release of a number of political prisoners during 1973. He too wanted to be released, but he knew that he could never live peacefully in the North in view of his background as a convicted spy. His only possible life would be in the South. This hope evaporated on 30 April 1975.

Shortly after the surrender, Ot began to speak of his desire to be released. With the war now over, there was talk of political prisoners being released. Ot sensed that his only chance lay in returning to his native Hanoi. In the past, he had spoken of his life in the spy net, but now everything had changed; his entire focus was on release and demonstrating that he had been reeducated. Ot had learned to adapt.

Ot, a resident of room 11, was assigned as the leader of a sewing unit consisting of a mixed group of commandos from rooms 11 and 12 in Area K. His assistant was a commando, Doan Phuong. Ot now displayed verbal contempt for the "puppet commandos." It was obvious to the commandos that he did not hate them but was merely echoing stereotypical Vietnamese Communist phrases in an attempt to convince his captors that he had indeed changed. Also, Ot had to make reports to Aspirant Tin, the education cadre responsible for keeping track of the attitudes of those in his sewing unit. Tin had been only a corporal at Quyet Tien in 1974; he was quickly rising in rank.

The commandos finally decided that something had to be done about Ot's constant irritating comments. One day, the members of the sewing unit's vegetable production element harvested some greens for the evening meal. Ot stepped in and insisted that the vegetables not be cooked that day. He had the authority to make such a decision because the prisoners in charge of growing the food were members of his sewing unit. Under normal circumstances, his instructions might have been followed, but the welling resentment against Ot overcame all caution.

The vegetables were cooked in the unit's small kitchen, while Ot ranted and raved that his orders were being disobeyed. The commandos talked among themselves and decided it was time to administer a beating. Ot had to be shown that enough was enough. Just before the meal was ready, the majority of inmates in rooms 11 and 12 assembled. They grabbed Ot and pummeled him. By the time they stopped, he was almost dead from the beating and barely able to crawl from the barracks.

Ot was transferred to become the leader of Sewing Team 1, composed of political prisoners who resided in the separate barracks adjacent to the prison assembly hall. He was released from prison and returned to Hanoi at the end of 1976 or in early 1977.

On 2 September 1976, the entire prison population was assembled in the large meeting hall just inside the front gate. Senior Captain Lang breezed through his presentation of awards to various inmate labor groups who had excelled in the emulation competition for hardest-working unit. Then came a surprise, as he read from a prepared text:

> On this occasion, the Ministry of Interior commemorates this 2 September by the issuing of a special directive, the Special Amnesty Decree. This directive is issued in view of the fact that the country has now been unified and is intended to show the State's generosity. . . .[6]

Lang continued with his carefully prepared script, describing how the decree was intended to permit certain long-term prisoners to be transferred to duties in a production area and emphasizing the traditional justification that this was being applied to those who had been successfully reeducated. He followed this introduction by a slow, deliberate reading of the names, crimes, and sentences of more than twenty commandos and a similar number of criminals under long-term sentencing. Of the commandos, nearly all were individuals captured during the early 1960s, all had been imprisoned for the crime of commando espionage, and nearly all had received prison terms of twenty years to life imprisonment.

Although the special decree had included the term "amnesty," Lang's description of the program never once referred to anyone actually being granted amnesty. Many of the commandos smiled inwardly, viewing this choice of terms as just another example of the word games played by the Ministry of Interior.

As the names were called, some commandos felt anger. They knew that some of those selected had not kept the faith. Everyone agreed later, however, that the selected inmates were members of the earliest teams captured, and they had been dealt the longest and harshest sentences. Only a few of the names on the list were those of radio operators who had been recruited by Hanoi. Also, the worst informants were conspicuously absent from the roster, and this delighted many in the audience.

In early October 1976, the selected prisoners departed Quyet Tien Prison. The men who had been resentenced to the punishment cells could hear the good-byes, but they had no way to know what was happening.

The commandos were supposed to be transferred to Tuyen Quang Prison by truck, but they were first taken to Ha Giang City and quartered at the Ha Giang provincial prison four kilometers away. They were placed under the temporary management of the province security service and assigned the task of building temporary prison barracks.

Within four months, they were moved again, this time to Central Prison No. 1, Pho Lu Prison, outside Lao Cai City. They constructed barracks inside a barbed wire–fenced complex designated the Cong Truong Hong Thang (Hong Thang Worksite). This was immediately adjacent to a separate fenced subcamp of Pho Lu called Hong Thang Prison, known previously as subcamp K4.[7] Prisoner numbers at Hong Thang grew as more commandos arrived from other prisons.

* * *

By early 1977, something was apparently happening along the northern border.[8] The commandos at Quyet Tien were still cut off from the outside world, but they could sense something in the air.

That spring, the first of three groups of commandos was moved to Tuyen Quang Prison and into the barracks recently completed by the inmates who had arrived in the fall of 1976 under the Special Amnesty Decree. Accompanying them to Tuyen Quang were the surviving Taiwanese commandos from Quyet Tien. More commandos were also paroled and transferred to the Hong Thang worksite at Pho Lu Prison that spring as part of what was called Phase II implementation of the Special Amnesty Decree.

In 1977, there was talk in Washington of normalization in relationships between Vietnam and the United States, but Vietnam was still far from peaceful. As war clouds formed, the Ministry of Interior and the People's Army of Vietnam slowly began to transfer large numbers of prisoners from the vicinity of the border areas with China and Cambodia where they anticipated hostilities. The reason was a practical one. When fighting broke out, Vietnam did not need a potentially active fifth column at its rear.

By late 1977, nearly all prisoners at Quyet Tien had been moved to Tuyen Quang, except for a small platoon-sized group that remained behind to help maintain the prison, construct a bread kiln, build an irrigation system needed to support expanded food production, and prepare to turn the prison over to the Vietnam People's Army for their use as a headquarters. A small group of new prisoners, former officers and civilian officials from South Vietnam, arrived to assist them. The commandos at Quyet Tien were rotated every four months with those at Tuyen Quang. In 1978, the last of the commandos were withdrawn from Quyet Tien to rejoin their teammates at Tuyen Quang.

As border hostilities increased in 1978, the inmates at Tuyen Quang were moved south to Central Prison No. 5, Lam Son Prison, in Thanh Hoa Province. Inmates at Pho Lu Prison began a similar southward move in the face of mounting hostilities, with some moving to Prison 52, Ha Tay Prison, in Ha Son Binh Province, and a relatively small number to Kim Boi Prison. The moves coincided with the transfer of former South Vietnamese officers from prisons in the northwestern provinces, which were managed by People's Army of Vietnam Group 776 headquartered at Yen Bai, to more secure prisons south of the Red River Delta.

That spring, Ly Ca Sa, then an inmate at Hong Thang and the notorious leader of a large gang of thieves arrested years earlier, engineered a major prison break there. Ly Ca Sa fled to China, together with ten to twenty other parolees, including a number of Taiwanese commandos and two Vietnamese commandos, Le Trung Tin and Voong A Cau. Tin and Cau thus became the first commandos confirmed to have made a successful escape from prison, even if they got only to China.

By January 1979, the vast majority of prisoners at Pho Lu Prison had been evacuated. The laborers at the Hong Thang, however, were still operating at full speed. In February 1979, forces of the Chinese People's Liberation Army attacked across the border and swiftly overran the border town of Lao Cai. Ly Ca Sa was with the initial attacking force and escorted the Chinese into Pho Lu Prison. Panicky townspeople, fleeing past Pho Lu Prison, warned of the invasion as Chinese military forces prepared to enter Lao Cai City. The prison was thrown into a panic. The residual prison staff marched the prisoners and parolees out as quickly as possible. One parolee, given the responsibility of driving a bulldozer to the regrouping point established at Yen Bai, was never seen again.

As the inmates began to settle in at subcamp K1 of Central Prison No. 5, a group of female prisoners arrived there. They had been moved out of Pho Lu prison in the face of advancing Chinese troops and had walked for a long distance before linking up with trucks. One of the cadre escorting the women had departed so quickly he had to escort them in his underwear. A number of northern inmates from Hong Thang were issued temporary release orders while on the road. From what inmates later described, the Chinese had overrun both Pho Lu and Phong Quang.

Inmates from Hong Thang also became part of the exodus. They were moved to Tan Lap Prison, where they built a new subcamp designated Camp K7. For others coming from Quyet Tien, their new home was subcamp K1 at Central

Prison No. 5 in Thanh Hoa Province. Here, they found one of the older singleton agents, now a water carrier, and a group of officers and other officials from the Republic of Vietnam Armed Forces and civil government. With them was the former mayor of Saigon, Van Van Cua, whom many of the commandos remembered from their days in South Vietnam during 1966–67. The South Vietnamese prisoners described being transferred to Lam Son after a hunger strike at their previous prison, an incident that had been broken up with the same severity as the commandos' hunger strike at Pho Lu in 1973.

At the end of 1979, the commandos at Lam Son were moved to Thanh Phong Prison in Nhu Xuan District, Thanh Hoa Province. Joining them in the nearby Thanh Lam labor camp were the paroled commandos from K7 at Tan Lap, and the ever-present Sr. Capt. To Ba Oanh.[9]

That December, several parolees were permitted to visit their families on "home leave." Many went to the South and never returned. Perhaps that is what the North had expected would happen, or perhaps it was just another way of testing their "reeducation."

BACK FROM THE DEAD

1980–1994

Part 5

22

THE PRISONS OF THANH HOA

IF QUYET TIEN was the camp where prisoners died from scientific methodologies applied by Col. Nguyen Sang, Thanh Phong was the camp where the king of the graveyard was prison staff indifference to malnutrition.[1]

The deaths were predictable as prison rations were reduced. Unhusked rye, reportedly received as food grants to Vietnam, was substituted for rice and manioc. Inmates speculated that the rice was sent to feed the People's Army soldiers deployed along the Chinese border.

Medicines were nonexistent at Phong Quang, and the death rate climbed. The prison staff evidenced little interest in the number of deaths, and the medical officer ensured that records reflected that the deaths occurred from certain plausible natural phenomena. Few inmates seldom starved to death outright. Rather, they died from bacterial infections caused by filth, intestinal parasites, and lung infections.

For most of the commandos, Phong Quang represented a period of marked change. They had once been legendary commando spies, hated more than feared. The surrender of the Republic of Vietnam and the transfer of thousands of South Vietnamese military personnel and civilian prisoners brought new faces into the North. Still, the members of the South Vietnamese Army at Phong Quang, Ha Tay, and Lam Son were awed by the survival of hundreds of commandos. When the South Vietnamese soldiers returned home, or later moved outside Vietnam, they often wrote about these commandos who had refused to die.

* * *

Tran Nam Hai's identity and background had been carefully protected by the prison staff. The son of Maj. Gen. Tran Nam Trung, former Senior Captain Hai had been a sapper[2] serving on sabotage missions in Saigon prior to the South's surrender on 30 April 1975.[3] At the end of the war, he was reassigned to North Vietnam for rest and recuperation. He was then assigned to duties that included responsibility for military supplies. Perhaps it was the easy access to items that could be sold on the black market or the peacetime environment under which he chafed for some excitement. In any event, Hai acquired a bogus seal to stamp documents so that he could falsely certify the issue of supplies that he sold privately for his personal gain.

This type of crime was becoming endemic in postwar Vietnam. Hai's activities were eventually discovered, with the predictable result that a war hero and son of a famous general in the Vietnam People's Army became just another prisoner at Thanh Phong. Prison cadre are pragmatic, and the commander at Thanh Phong, Lt. Col. Nguyen Huy Thuy, was no fool. One had to be sensitive to the possibility that any deliberate mistreatment of this prisoner could cause "problems." Hai's conviction and incarceration at Thanh Phong, in light of his father's identity, meant that his assignment within the prison had to be handled carefully and his identity protected. He was given the job of clerk in a subcamp kitchen, which prepared meals primarily for criminal inmates. Hai relished this type of job, where he could eat as much as he wanted and withhold food from anyone who resented his arrogant attitude. His father came to visit him at first, which heightened the prison commander's apprehension over any repercussions should anything untoward happen to Hai.

By the end of 1980, General Trung no longer came to the prison. The staff soon understood that he had disowned the son who had brought dishonor to the general's household. Tran Nam Hai was now just one more prisoner, whose arrogance could be handled by his fellow prisoners through their own harsh system of justice.

The first step was to reassign Hai from subcamp K5 to the agricultural production unit at subcamp K3. This brought him into close, unsupervised contact with other inmates and prison guards all too familiar with his reputation. When the prisoners thought the guards were not watching, they beat Hai into unconsciousness with shovels; when the guards thought the prisoners were not watching, they beat him unconscious with rifle butts. Reports mentioned only that the prisoner Tran Nam Hai had been temporarily hospitalized at the K1 subcamp dispensary for "sickness."

As 1980 passed into 1981, Hai's physical condition deteriorated as a result of more frequent beatings. To the guards and prison staff at K3, prisoner Hai and his predicament were the result of the lack of education provided by a father who obviously spoiled him. This situation allowed Hai to wear his father's rank to protect his privileged position. The assignment to the kitchen at K5, which Hai had not asked for, was now held against him.

To the criminal inmates at K3, Hai's arrogant conduct by eating well while others starved required repeated punishment. Hai embodied the very essence of the regime that the criminals detested, one which kept them at little more than the poverty level while supporting the life-style of the cadre who lived high on the labors of the masses. For others at Thanh Phong, particularly the former officers of the Republic of Vietnam undergoing reeducation, Hai's beatings were a just reward for the wartime acts of murder, sabotage, and terrorism that he had committed in Saigon.

Hai developed a serious internal infection after one particularly severe beating perforated his liver. He was transferred to the prison's primary dispensary at subcamp K1, where he died a week later. To conserve medicine for the worthy, he was fed sterile water and his medical record altered accordingly.

After Hai's death, Sr. Capt. Nguyen Van Hoang, the prison medical officer, was advised that General Trung's son had died at K1. The prison commander's first reaction was to find fault with the prison dispensary staff at K1, but he eventually decided to let the matter pass and certified the cause of death as being due to illness. Besides, once his son was in the ground, General Trung would never be the wiser; an autopsy would never reveal signs of the mutilation of his corpse that occurred before burial.

* * *

In 1981, the senior cadre from the Ministry of Interior again visited Thanh Phong Prison for a periodic inspection. Reacting with his usual alacrity, the prison commander ordered the sick and infirm into the jungle, where they were to remain until the inspectors had departed. He felt it perfectly natural that these units of seriously ill (the Doi Dau Om) should be given menial tasks to perform until they died, but it would have been inappropriate for the prison inspectors to come face to face with such walking skeletons. The cadre assigned to each group carried out the orders. An average of fifty inmates, either seriously ill or near death, at each of five subcamps were marched into the jungle, where they lay down and waited for the inspectors to leave. As usual, the prison inspectors saw none of them and asked no questions about what they did not see.

Early in 1982, a group of state security cadre arrived at Thanh Phong to interview a number of the commandos who had been at Long Thanh in the mid-1960s. The focus of the inquiry was the commandos' knowledge of Vo Dai Ton, a former member of the Strategic Technical Directorate, who was at Long Thanh during that period. Ton had been captured in Laos while on a "resistance" foray launched from Thailand. The Lao government then turned him over to Vietnam, and he was brought to Hanoi for trial. During a press conference, Ton displeased his captors by attacking the Hanoi government instead of displaying a repentant attitude. The press conference was suspended, and Vo Dai Ton was remanded to isolation confinement. The commandos had little to contribute during the interviews by the officials from Hanoi.[4]

Starting late in 1979, inmates at Thanh Phong had been slowly released. In the summer of 1982, the majority of the commandos still at K1 were released to return to their families. Before their release, state security officers from Hanoi spoke with many of them and informed them of their continuing usefulness to the State. Select commandos were told to be prepared in the future to receive someone who would make the purpose of the visit known by a special sign. The commandos were expected to do what was asked of them, but few paid much attention to such entreaties to spy for Hanoi after returning home.

That December, those still in K1 were transferred to Central Prison No. 3 in Tan Ky District, Nghe Tinh Province. In the fall of 1987, the last seven commandos held there were finally released to return home. Among them was Nguyen Huu Luyen, hard-core to the end.

By 1989, most of the labor inmates at Thanh Lam had been released. Several ethnic Hmong recruited from Laos to serve in the early agent teams of 1962, however, had no homes or families, so they remained at the prison. Two more died there in 1993.

One commando who had been paroled to a labor camp recounted his return home after fifteen years at hard labor.

"What did it feel like?" I asked him.

"Feel like? You can't imagine."

"What I meant was, how did your family react?"

The commando told this story:

> I remember arriving at the Saigon train station. It was nighttime and I knew I couldn't just walk in on my mother. I hadn't had any contact with her in fifteen years. We'd been allowed to write home after about 1976, but most of us were suspicious that it was a Ministry of Interior plot, so we never did write home. Some of us were visited in prison by relatives, particularly those of us with relatives who'd stayed up North. I remember Nguyen Thai Kien had been visited by his uncle, Nguyen Thai Phiet, who everyone said was the publisher of the People's Army daily newspaper, *Quan Doi Nhan Dan*. Most of us didn't want our families to go through the expense of the trip North to visit us. We could always smuggle letters out through other visitors. In my own case, I just didn't write home.
>
> I knew if I walked in during the daytime there would be a big commotion. You have to understand that my thinking and the way I was acting then was driven by the fact I was coming out of fifteen years' hard labor. I can't describe it, no one could.
>
> I walked from the center of Saigon to my mother's house. I stayed off the road, just in case I ran into a

checkpoint. After all, I still didn't have any papers and my travel authorization had expired. I found a small coffee stand across from my mother's house. It was several hours before dawn, and I sat down there and just waited.

It must have been just after daybreak when my mother walked out of our house. I just sat there and watched her. I kept looking to see who else might be around. I didn't see anyone and decided it was safe.

Mother started to walk away from the house, and I followed quickly after until I came up beside her and walked along with her for a few steps, saying nothing. I don't think she realized I was there for a few moments, but I guess she sensed my presence and it startled her and she stopped for a second. I looked at her. "Mother. It's me," I said.

She just stared at me for a few seconds, and then she grabbed me by the arm and led me back to the house, as if I was a little boy again and she was taking me home because I'd done something bad.

She took me into the front room and over to the household shrine. There was the picture of my father in the place reserved for those who had died. Beside it was *my* picture! Mother looked at me and then at the picture. She looked at me again and then back at the picture. "It *is* you," she said at last. "I thought you were dead!"

Mother didn't say much after that. I was home. What else needed to be said?

Nguyen Van Hinh slowly turned away to stare out the window. No words came. None were needed.

EPILOGUE

As of this writing, more than one hundred of the former commandos have been resettled in the United States. Nearly two hundred survivors still live in Vietnam, as well as hundreds of widows and orphans of those who died. Most of these people want to leave Vietnam, although there are some who prefer to stay.

To qualify for entry into the United States, in accordance with current policy, former commandos must have spent at least three years in prison after May 1975. The Immigration and Naturalization Service (INS) has concluded that any imprisonment prior to that date is deemed time spent as a wartime prisoner of war, based on INS interpretation of State Department policy. As of this writing, INS does not believe that most commandos still in Vietnam actually spent three years in prison after May 1975 and discounts their time in prison before that date. Most applications for an emigration interview are disapproved by the INS regional director in Bangkok.

Nguyen Huu Luyen, who organized and advised Team HECTOR, was one of the last commandos to be released after twenty-one years at hard labor. He attempted to escape from Vietnam by boat and, predictably, was captured. Early in 1992, he was released and permitted to depart Vietnam for resettlement in the United States. Today, he and his wife live in East Boston, Massachusetts. He studies English and teaches Vietnamese to a visiting priest who gets terribly confused by the tones of the Vietnamese language. Still, they both try.

Another of the last seven released from hard labor is an ethnic Hmong named Quach Rang, who arrived in 1992 at his new home in Chamblee, Georgia. Rang's wife, Ngoc Ban, a woman of remarkable courage, spoke in Atlanta, Georgia, in July 1992 to a packed assembly of nearly four hundred wives and family members of local Vietnamese. She related how she was told that her husband was missing. She was even paid death benefits, but she continued to wait for her husband's return. She knew he would come back.

Members of teams from CASTER to RED DRAGON have crossed the Pacific and settled throughout the United States from Boston to Seattle. Among them are Mai Nhue Anh, commander of HECTOR 2; Quach Nhung, the sole survivor from Team HORSE; Truong Tuan Hoang, the last agent sent to reinforce REMUS; and Ha Van Chap, commander of CASTER, and his teammate Dinh Anh, members of the first team into the North under the CIA's grand plan to try to do something to Hanoi. In today's world, however, it is unclear if Washington had a bona fide mission for the teams.

Former singleton agent Tran Quoc Hung has made the journey. He wrote about his personal prison experiences and those of his comrades in three volumes titled *Black Steel.* Chapters from his book are read on a Vietnamese radio station in California. The readings are followed intently, while the afternoon television soap operas are ignored. Another former singleton agent, Le Van Buoi, arrived in the United States in 1993. As of this writing, he is receiving routine cancer treatment in Utica, New York. He is suffering from throat cancer and might not live to read this book. Before leaving Ho Chi Minh City in 1993, he was given radiation treatment in a local hospital. According to social workers in Utica, Buoi was not only overradiated in Ho Chi Minh City but the treatments extended over his entire head. His memory is fading, and his head aches a lot. He still tries to explain what he and his compatriots tried to do some thirty-five years ago. As he dies, he suspects no one really cares.

Le Van Ngung, former commander of Team HADLEY, today engraves pewter and creates molds for Kirk & Stieff in Baltimore, Maryland, and what he does is a patient work of art. His team member, Vu Viet Tinh, is a hospital janitor in Indiana and was married in December 1994.

Nguyen Khong, stranded on the beach with members of the NAUTILUS 7 crew, now goes after shrimp and fish in the Gulf of Mexico, rather than running agents up the Gulf of Tonkin. Each time he returns home he fears he will find his wife once again pregnant. I told him it was probably because of the water in New Orleans. He laughed but really doesn't believe me. We both know it may have something to do with his wife's closeness to him. Khong is her second husband; her first husband was machine-gunned to death in front of her as they tried to escape by boat from Central Vietnam.

Bui Minh The from Team BECASSINE fled Vietnam by boat. A flashy former South Vietnamese Army officer asked him to return to Vietnam and become part of what he called the "resistance." The declined and came to Henderson, Louisiana. Several years ago, he was united with his wife after a separation of a decade. He is largely bedridden these days and might never read my tribute to his courage.

Dang Cong Trinh, deputy commander of Team SCORPION, one of the hardest of the hard-core resisters, works in a warehouse in California. His coworkers are largely unaware of his background.

Thuy, the wife of Trinh Van Truyen, a former boatman from NAUTILUS 3, emigrated with her husband to Biloxi, Mississippi, and Truyen returned to a life at sea. Thuy was shot in New Orleans, Louisiana, on 31 July 1990, during a robbery by a gang of young thugs looking for money to buy drugs. They got only her empty purse. She was seven months pregnant, and their unborn child was killed by the single bullet fired by the frustrated robbers. She has recovered but will have no more children. Truyen went out to drink recently and called me from the hospital. He had almost cut off a finger. Life on the Gulf of Mexico has been hard these days, he said. The shrimping hasn't been all that productive. We talked for a while, and that was enough to get him back to laughing a bit. His wife is a tough, tough woman but no tougher than the man she married while he was still in prison.

One of the first to flee Vietnam was Nguyen Van Hinh, a member of Team ATILLA. In Singapore, he was denied U.S. resettlement, even though he told U.S. consular officials about his time in prison. They simply didn't believe him and suspected that he was a northern Vietnamese criminal masquerading as someone who was not supposed to exist. While in a Singapore refugee camp, he met another Vietnamese, a former nun prohibited from practicing her religious beliefs in Vietnam after 1975, and they were married. Resettled in Holland, they are now raising a family. Hinh does not write letters. He explains that he had to write too many self-criticism papers in prison. I think I understand.

Tran Van Tu and Nguyen Van Luc are in Australia. Tu has scarred ankles from his time in the shackles when he almost died. Jessica Martinez, a friendly voice of someone I've never met except at the other end of the telephone, looked at a photograph of his ankles and almost threw up when she heard how they had become so permanently disfigured. I wanted to tell her the whole story, about the bone his comrades pried out of his shattered ankle that he kept for years—a talisman that helped him survive. Now she can read it.

There are others from MACSOG and its Vietnamese counterparts whose stories eventually will be told. They will come from those such as Mai Van Hoc and Hoang Van Chuong of the STRATA teams and from Lau Chi Chan, Chau Henh Xuong, Ly Si Lau, Vu Duc Guong, or other courageous frogmen who rode the wild waves at nearly half a hundred miles an hour across the Gulf of Tonkin in noisy PTFs that told their enemies the denizens from hell were coming.

In 1986, Vu Duc Guong applied for the back pay that he felt was his due. The following year, the Federal Claims Court responded to Defense Department arguments and found precedence in an 1865 federal claims case to deny Guong's compensation request for the nearly twenty years he spent in North Vietnamese prisons. Underlying the Court's opinion, and the Defense Department's position, was the fact that the details of the operation were still highly classified. That is no longer the case.

Most survivors have settled down and tried to raise families with varying degrees of success. They get together from time to time over a bottle of whiskey and talk about the times that were, about the friends who have died, and about those who kept the faith. When most of them went into prison, they were still single and barely in their twenties. Today, they are older by two decades or more and see nothing wrong in courting young women twenty years their juniors. They dye their hair and drop their ages by a few years. No one seems to care. Most will become productive citizens. When their descendants read about them someday, they will understand more about their fathers and grandfathers than the dimming memories of years long past could provide.

Some of the commandos have not been so fortunate.

Hoang Ngoc Chinh, Doan Phuong, and Nguyen Van Ly became too frustrated to wait for bureaucrats to listen. They attempted to flee Vietnam. Phuong and Ly went out by boat and Chinh tried to go overland across Cambodia. They were never seen again.

Le Trung Tin from RED DRAGON made it back from China. Today, he tries to convince incredulous INS interviewers in Ho Chi Minh City that he is who he claims to be. Tin and his compatriot, Voong A Cau, had done what soldiers do: they escaped and were the first two to make it out of North Vietnam alive. The INS finds that they were not there long enough to qualify for emigration to the United States.

One of the less fortunate was Hoang Dinh My, a member of Team HECTOR. In December 1984, My stood before a judge of the People's Court in Ho Chi Minh City that was sentencing members of a self-proclaimed "resistance group" headed by an overseas Vietnamese from France named Le Quoc Tuy. The group had been captured while operating in South Vietnam, supposedly after infiltrating there from their so-called base in Thailand. Information made public during the trial indicated that Vietnam's Ministry of Interior had penetrated Le Quoc Tuy's so-called resistance organization some years earlier and actually might have been controlling it. As of 1995, My was still in prison at Nha Trang.

My had left Thanh Lam Prison by 1981 and had gone home to South Vietnam before fleeing to Thailand. One of Tuy's supposed associates in Thailand, using the name "Col. Giang Nam," purportedly recruited My to return to South Vietnam. Within a week of his return in 1982, My was arrested. During his trial, evidence presented by the state prosecutor included materiel seized on a fishing boat that supplied Tuy's so-called resistance group. Also reportedly seized were special radios, whose country of origin could not be determined. They were speculated to be agent-type radios used to communicate between Vietnam and such places as Thailand. Radios require operators, but the radio operator for the agent network was not identified.

These were not the first agent radios shipped into Communist Vietnam. Teams N1, N3, and N7 had taken radios to the double agent known as ARES in northeastern North Vietnam twenty years earlier. If the group was indeed transmitting on agent radios, there were probably fools listening who believed that the resistance group's agents were alive and well in South Vietnam.

Mistakes uncorrected are mistakes repeated.

Sr. Col. Nguyen Sang served as director of the Prisons Management Directorate in Hanoi during the summer of 1979 and reportedly had retired by 1982. He served his party and would have no regrets about how he performed his duties. Lt. Col. To Ba Oanh, commander of the prison labor camp at Hong Thang, was last reported to be a colonel in command of the prison in Song Be Province. He is now more concerned with those who violate the contemporary laws of his society than with the commandos of yesterday.

Nguyen Van Tan from Team ROMEO, the most savagely beaten commando during the 1973 hunger strike, applied for disability benefits after he resettled in the United States. In 1988, a Vietnamese doctor examined Tan and called me from California to ask for some insight into the origin of Tan's problems.

"His insides just don't work well any more," he said. "I can't understand why. . . . Tan has trouble describing what happened. Can you give me something in writing which will explain it all?"

Several weeks later, I drafted a letter for the signature of U.S. Air Force Col. Kimball Gaines, chief of the DIA's Special Office for POW/MIA Affairs. The letter tried to explain what had happened to Tan during the hunger strike at Pho Lu in 1973, but it did not tell the whole story. I hope that Vietnamese doctor from San Jose reads this and understands some of the more painful things that Colonel Gaines's letter could not adequately explain.

Luong Van Inh from Team DOG took up residence in the mountains of South Vietnam. Not that far away, foreigners enjoy the resort of Dalat, but nearby Duc Trong District is still quite primitive. Early in June 1994, Inh came down with a severe recurrence of malaria. The local medic told his wife to get him to the hospital. In the midst of a terrible storm, his two sons and two local villagers began the midnight trek down the mountain path, with Inh bouncing in a well-worn hammock, as they headed toward the road some four kilometers away. Inh died before they reached the road, and his widow wrote to tell me of his passing: "The only thing my husband wanted was for his children to get an education and be free . . . and now he's gone."

The late Des FitzGerald was right: it did take spirit. Unfortunately, he never met those of whom he spoke.

They survived. They are, in their own way, the final victors.

The saga of the lost commando army is far from over. On 23 March 1995, David F. Lambertson, United States Ambassador to Thailand, sent a five-page message to the Department of State and the INS questioning why most surviving commandos' post-1975 imprisonment were being summarily rejected by the INS regional director in Thailand. As of May 1995, the INS had yet to revise its policy of rejecting most former commandos from consideration for immigration to the United States in line with current established Department of State foreign policy guidelines.

The ambassador's message coincided with the release of Robert McNamara's controversial memoir, *In Retrospect: The Tragedy and Lessons of Vietnam.* In part, the controversy surrounding the book stemmed from the question of whether McNamara and other members of Lyndon Johnson's inner circle had deceived the president as to the nature of the U.S. commitment in Vietnam prior to the Gulf of Tonkin incident of August 1964. Based on the locations where the agent teams were dropped, the statement of one of the CIA officials involved, the official MACSOG documentation study, and the testimony herein of the surviving commandos, it is clear that the commandos were infiltrated in order to protect the CIA's efforts in Laos, not, as the president was led to believe, to retaliate against Hanoi for its infiltration of agents into South Vietnam.

On 14 April 1995, the *New York Times* published an article by Tim Weiner documenting the ambassador's effort to resolve the INS roadblock. Within days, the plight of the commandos had gained international interest. Former COMUSMACV Gen. William C. Westmoreland, Maj. Gen. John Morrison, Brig. Gen. George Gaspard, Sen. John McCain, and others, wrote to the ambassador in support of his position. Senator McCain also wrote to the INS commissioner. The senator's letter left his office as a former frogman, Duong Long Sang, was attempting to commit suicide following a second rejection by the INS, which believed that he had not spent enough time in Hanoi's prisons. The news about Sang's attempted suicide arrived with the painful news that two other commandos had passed away in Vietnam while waiting for the INS to review their cases.

On 24 April 1995, John Mattes, an attorney in Miami, Florida, entered a claim in the United States Court of Federal Claims, Washington, D.C., for compensation on behalf of 281 commando clients captured or killed in North Vietnam. The claim asks only that the court direct the administration to pay the former agents in strict accordance with their contracts.

APPENDIX 1

Covert Agent Teams, 1961–1967

FIGURE B-15

Chronology of Long-Term Agent Team Inserts

Team	Date	How	Pers	-- Remarks
1. ARES	Feb 61	Sea	1	Radio contact continues in Apr 69
2. ATLAS	Mar 61	Air	4	2 KIA, 2 captured on landing
3. CASTER	May 61	Air	4	Contact lost Jul 63 in Laos
4. DIDO	Jun 61	Air	4	Doubled, played, terminated
5. ECHO	Jun 61	Air	3	Doubled, played til Aug 62, terminated
6. TARZAN	?	Air	6	Insert date unk, last radio contact Jun 63, presumed captured
7. EUROPA	Feb 62	Air	5	Last radio contact 27Jan64 in NVN
8. REMUS	16 Apr 62	Air	6	Reinf 2 men 12Aug63, 3 men 23Apr64, 4 men (Tm ALTER) 22Oct64, 4 men Jan 65, 2 men 21Aug67. 13May68 NVN Announced capture of SVN ranger tm in REMUS area
9. TOURBILLON	16 May 62	Air	8	Reinf 7 men (Tm COOTS) 27May64, 7 men (Tm PERSEUS) 24Jul64, 6 men temporarily (Tm VERSE) 7Nov65, 2 men (Tm TOURBILLON BRAVO) 24Dec66. Reinf radio opr sent duress signal in Jan 67. Tm being used as diversion asset thru Apr 69.
10. EROS	Jun 62	Air	5	Doubled, played, terminated
11. PEGASUS	13 Apr 63	Air	6	Captured soon after landing
12. JASON	14 May 63	Air	5	Captured soon after landing
13. DAUPHINE	4 Jun 63	Air	5	Captured soon after landing
14. BELL	4 Jun 63	Air	7	Reinf 7 men (Tm GRECO) 14Nov64. Last radio contact 19Mar67, dropped 3 Jul 67.
15. BECASSINE	Jun 63	Air	6	Captured soon after landing
16. BART	7 Jun 63	Air	5	Captured soon after landing
17. TELLUS	7 Jun 63	Air	4	Captured soon after landing

FIGURE B-15 (TS) (Cont'd.)

18. MIDAS	10 Jun 63	Air	8	Captured soon after landing
19. NIKE	10 Jun 63	Air	6	Captured soon after landing
20. GIANT	Jul 63	Air	6	Captured soon after landing
21. PACKER	Jul 63	Air	6	Captured soon after landing
22. EASY	9 Aug 63	Air	8	Reinf 6 men (Tm PISCES) 18Jul64, 5 men (Tm HORSE) May 65, 9 men 17Sep65 & 3 men 18Oct65 (Tm DOG/GECKO). DOG/GECKO redesig EASY ALPHA, separated 30Oct65. EASY ALPHA rejoined in Jul 67. Last radio contact 26Apr68; 7Aug68 NVN newspaper announced capture of 12 SVN Rangers, correctly identified Tm Ldr.
23. [no name]	12 Aug 63	Air	2	Reinf for Tm REMUS
24. SWAN	4 Sep 63	Air	6	Captured soon after landing
25. BULL	7 Oct 63	Air	7	Captured soon after landing
26. RUBY	5 Dec 63	Air	8	Captured soon after landing
27. [no name]	23 Apr 64	Air	3	Reinf for Tm REMUS
28. ATTILA	25 Apr 64	Air	6	Captured soon after landing, Action 557
29. LOTUS	19 May 64	Air	6	Captured, tried by NVN
30. COOTS	27 May 64	Air	7	Reinf for Tm TOURBILLON
31. SCORPION	17 Jun 64	Air	7	Captured, tried by NVN
32. BUFFALO	19 Jun 64	Air	10	Captured, tried by NVN
33. EAGLE	28 Jun 64	Air	6	Jun 68 analysis: Tm believed under NVN control. 3 men still in Tm. Inst'd to move south, began move Nov 68. Still in radio contact 69.
34. PISCES	18 Jul 64	Air	6	Reinf for Tm EASY
35. PERSEUS	24 Jul 64	Air	7	Reinf for Tm TOURBILLON
36. BOONE	29 Jul 64	Air	9	Captured, tried by NVN
37. ALTER	22 Oct 64	Air	4	Reinf for Tm REMUS
38. GRECO (CENTAUR Team)	14 Nov 64	Air	7 (28)	Reinf for Tm BELL Tm destroyed 10Dec64 in C-123 crash on Monkey Mountain, Da Nang. See pg II-J-1, 64 History
REMUS ALPHA	May 65		5	Part of Tm REMUS inst'd to exfil to Laos. Last contact 21Aug65 vic TJ 785367; "Caching radio, heading for Vientiane (Laos)."
39. HORSE	May 65	Air	5	Reinf for Tm EASY
40. DOG/GECKO (EASY ALPHA)	17 Sep 65	Air	9	Reinf for Tm EASY. Later redesig Tm EASY ALPHA (30Oct65). Tm rejoined Tm EASY in Jul 67.

FIGURE B-15 (Cont'd),

41. VERSE	7 Nov 65	Air	8	Infil to Tm TOURBILLON; 2 men killed as result of drop. Tm inst'd Tm TOURBILLON in roadwatch techniques. 21 Dec 65, Tm TOURBILLON gave 3 men to Tm VERSE; VERSE detached. 27Jul67, Hanoi Radio announced capture.
42. ROMEO	19 Nov 65	Helo	10	Oct 66 received msg in clear text: "ROMEO ALREADY CAPTURED." Last radio contact 5Aug68; declared MIA 4Nov68.
43. KERN	5 Mar 66	Air	9	1 man killed on drop, last radio contact 5Sep66, dropped 7Dec66.
44. HECTOR	22 Jun 66	Helo	15	Reinf 11 men (Tm HECTOR BRAVO) 23 Sep 66. HECTOR & HECTOR BRAVO never linked up. BRAVO dropped 28Dec66. Last contact w/HECTOR 15Mar67, dropped 26Jun67.
45. SAMSON	5 Oct 66	Helo	8	LZ in Laos. Last radio contact 2Dec66, dropped 1Mar67.
46. TOURBILLON BRAVO	24 Dec 66	Air	2	Reinf for TOURBILLON. Took in wiretap & electronic sensor devices.
47. HADLEY	26 Jan 67	Helo	11	"DATA" Foot infil to NVN. Jun 68 analysis: Tm believed captured soon after landing. Used as diversion since Jun 67, told to exfil to Laos. Mar 69 Tm rept'd they were in Laos again & ready for pickup; could not locate.
48. NANSEN	22 Apr 67	Helo	17	"DATA" Tm never reached NVN, enemy vic LZ, requested exfil. See pg G-III-4-15, 67 History.
49. [no name]	21 Aug 67	Air	2	Reinf for Tm REMUS
50. GOLDFISH	13 Sep 67	Sea	1	Infil by PLOWMAN Mission 327. Agents had been recruited from detainees on PARADISE. Agents were to remain in-place 60-90 days & exfil by sea. Never contacted.
51. RED DRAGON	21 Sep 67	Air	7	Widely dispersed on infil. US Case Off believed Tm under NVN control, VN Case Off believed Tm OK as result of Jun 68 analysis. Radio contact continues in Apr 69.
52. VOI	18 Oct 67	Air	4	No contact ever estab after infil.

Source: MACSOG Documentation Study.

APPENDIX 2

OPLAN 34A—Force Application

I

PART II. 34A/FOOTBOY PROGRAM: AN OVERVIEW

A. GENERAL 1

The paragraphs that follow in Part II introduce the 34A 2
program by summarizing the significant features of the original 3
Saigon OP-Order. With this background, the evolution of the 4
program over the years is traced and the command and control/ 5
clearance procedures are outlined. Finally, the present status 6
of and constraints on the program are described. 7

B. RATIONALE FOR THE PROGRAM 8

1. OPLAN 34A 9

a. Objective. The aim of the plan was: "in concert with 10
other military and diplomatic actions in the Southeast Asia 11
area, to convince the DRV leadership that its current support 12
and direction of war in the Republic of Vietnam and its aggres- 13
sion is Laos should be reexamined and stopped. Since what we 14
are seeking is a change in the political calculations of the 15
DRV, the plan provides means for the development and support 16
of a broad spectrum of operations in and against North Vietnam 17
in direct retaliation to DRV aggressive moves."* 18

b. Concept of Operations. Operations were to consist of 19
selective actions in four categories. Operations were planned 20
for a 12-month period under conditions short of limited war. 21
The plan was to be conducted in concert with other military, 22
political and military actions in Southeast Asia. The four 23
levels of activity envisioned by the plan are briefly described 24
below: 25

(1) Category I - Harrassing. "Included are small unspecta- 26
cular demolition operations, moderate level psychological 27
operations, small-scale intelligence collection actions 28
including tactical reconnaissance probes by small military 29
30

* (TS) COMUSMACV OPLAN 34A-64 Saigon OPLAN TIGER, 15 December 1963, p.2. (SACSA)

units to obtain visual ground intelligence, capture of prisoners, documents and equipment, creation of general harassment, and temporary interdiction of lines of communication."* The expected reaction was to cause an awareness of opposition, embarrassing irritation, possible interruption to movement of material, and increased readiness of Democratic Republic of Vietnam (DRV) forces. No major retaliation to Category I activities was expected.

(2) Category II - Attritional. "Included are small-scale resistance operations, airborne and seaborne raids by small forces on important military and civilian installations, and demolition of important facilities."** The goal of these operations was to pose a clear threat of attrition to the physical facilities, security forces and the popular image of the DRV leadership. Reaction was expected in the form of retaliation by Viet Cong (VC) forces in South Vietnam (SVN) and request for aid from Communist China.

(3) Category III - Punitive. "These are MT resistance/physical destruction actions designed to cause damage and/or destruction to facilities or installations critical to the economy, industrial development and security of the DRV. They are designed to cause large-scale internal redeployment of DRV resources and commitment of forces in reaction."*** Actions included raids by company and battalion size forces, covert where possible, but attributable to Republic of Vietnam (RVN) if they became overt. Operations were to be of a magnitude requiring positive and serious measures by DRV to counteract their effects. Retaliation to these operations was expected to range from increased insurgency efforts in RVN/Laos to overt aggression by DRV with DATA support.

* (TS) Ibid., p.4.
** (TS) Ibid., p.5.
*** (TS) Ibid., p.6.

(4) Category IV - Aerial Attacks. "These are aerial attacks conducted against critical DRV installations or facilities, industrial and/or military, such as POL storage areas, thermal power and steel plants, the loss of which would result in crippling effect on the DRV potential to maintain a stable economy and progress in industrial development."* The reaction to these operations was dependent on two major factors: (a) the willingness of DRV to accept significant damage to its homeland in order to continue the war in the south, and (b) the reaction and influence of the DATA DATA It was considered that operations in this category could well escalate the conflict, rather than convince the DRV continuance of the war was unprofitable, and that the United States must be "prepared to follow up with supporting operations in offsetting DRV reactions."*

c. Coordination.* Coordination with the Government of Vietnam (GVN) was not achieved during formulation of the OPLAN. This was to be effected by COMUSMACV/ DATA Saigon, after the plan was approved. US forces were not to be used for operations within the DRV, its territorial waters or air space except as air crews on reconnaissance missions.

d. Resources.** In-country resources available or programmed were considered adequate for most of Category I through IV operations. Specific requirements were listed in Annex A to the OPLAN; general requirements were: (1) NASTY class PTFs must be in-country and operational, (2) electronic countermeasures (ECM) configuration of six additional C-123 aircraft, (3) augmentation of personnel necessary to organize and activate the implementing agency, (4) psychological warfare (PSYWAR) augmentation detachment; (5) availability of two portable beacon type navigational

* (TS) Ibid., p.7-8.
** (TS) Ibid., p.A1.

aids, (6) five radio broadcast studios for conduct of overt 1
and "black" radio operations, (7) aircrews trained in technique 2
of allied mine laying, and (8) installation of flare dispensers 3
for aircraft. An additional resource was considered to be 4
the 800,000 refugees from the DRV, including Meo, Black 5
and Nung tribesmen from which it was believed a few thousand 6
could be picked and successfully trained for special operations.* 7

MT 8

e. Operations. Five types of operations were planned and 9
are briefly described below: 10

(1) Intelligence Collection. Operations conducted with 11
primary mission of intelligence collection. Included were: 12
DATA (b) expand 13
photo reconnaissance, (c) implement COMINT/SIGINT/ELINT 14
operations, (d) expand Republic of Vietnam Armed Forces (RVNAF) 15
tactical intelligence missions, (e) assign secondary missions 16
of intelligence to other operations in NVN, (f) intensity 17
intelligence collection probes into the DMZ area.* 18

(2) Psychological. "Strategic and tactical psychological 19
operations targeted against the DRV leadership and the 20
populace, and will use all available media (leaflets, radio, 21
mail) techniques and tactics to help achieve maximum harass- 22
ment, division, and the establishment of resistance within 23
the DRV."** 24

(3) Political Pressure. Operations designed to impart to 25
the DRV leaders that DRV direction and support of aggression 26
in RVN and Laos must cease, or further and more damaging 27
retaliatory action would be taken against NVN. Examples of 28
these operations were: MT 29
MT or actions in the United Nations.** 30

* (TS) Ibid., p.A-1, B-1.
** (TS) Ibid., p.B-2.

C-8 Appendix C

Note: MT (handwritten) = methods and techniques. It is written in the areas deleted by the Department of Defense during the declassification process.
Source: MACSOG Documentation Study.

APPENDIX 3

OPLAN 34A—Approved Targets, Phase I–II, February–August 1964

FIGURE C-6

OPLAN 34A - PHASE I AND II
APPROVED ACTIONS (U)[a]

Action Number	
	INTELLIGENCE COLLECTION:
1	Aerial Photography of Target Areas to be Accomplished 30 Days Prior to Individual Operation.
2	Beach Reconnaissance in Vicinity of Selected Targets
3	COMINT/ELINT
4	Tactical Reconnaissance of Selected Target Areas
	PSYCHOLOGICAL ACTIONS
5	
6	
7	
8	
9	
10	
11	
12	
13	
18	
19	

a/ (TS) Report, SACSA, "Red Book," 7 July 1964.

FIGURE C-6 (CONT'D)

Action Number	
	PSYCHOLOGICAL ACTIONS: (Continued)
20	
21	MT
22	
23	
24	
25	MT
26	
27	
28	
	PHYSICAL DESTRUCTION:
29	Interdiction Route 7 by airborne Special Forces
30	Interdiction Route 8 by airborne Special Forces
31	Interdiction Route 12 by airborne Special Forces
32	SEAL Team strike on Vinh Son
33	SEAL Team strike on dredges and buoy tender in Haiphong Channel
35	SEAL Team strike on Ben Thuy

FIGURE C-6 (CONT'D)

Action Number	
37	SEAL Team strike on Dong Hoi airfield
41	UDT raid by four-man team on SWATCMs
42	Raid on security post and four coastal defense guns
43	Sabotage Ly Hoa Bridge
44	Sabotage Route 1 Bridges
45	Sneak Attack on Security Post at Mouth of Dong Hoi River
46	Sabotage Two Small Bridges on Route 1
47	Amphibious Infiltration and Road Mining
48	UDT Sneak Attack on Ron Ferry
54	Airdrop Ten-Man Long-Term Team for Hit-and-Run Attack on Lang Son-Hanoi Railway. Team to Remain in area for long-term operation.
55	Airdrop long-term five-man team to operate against Yen Bay-Lao Kay Railway northwest of Yen Bay.

Note: MT (handwritten) = methods and techniques. It is written in the areas deleted by the Department of Defense during the declassification process.
Source: MACSOG Documentation Study.

APPENDIX 4

OPLAN 34A—Resource Status, 6 August 1964

FIGURE C-4

OPLAN 34A - RESOURCES STATUS (U)
6 August 1964

PTF STATUS:

PTFs 1, 2, 3, 5, and 6	- Operationally ready (All five participated in action on 30 July and 3 August)
PTF 4	- Training proceeding satisfactorily
PTFs 7 and 8	- Crews due to report 1 July. Expect to be operationally ready about 1 Oct 64.

SWIFT CRAFT STATUS:

All three SWIFTs operationally ready.

C-123 STATUS:

Two C-123 aircraft and crews operationally ready and available.

Program Status:

Five aircraft at Clark Air Base, Philippines. One in SVN for test of doppler navigation equipment.

Estimated 30 days in country training before reaching operational readiness.

Seven DATA and three VNAF aircrews completed training at Eglin Air Force Base.

(All DATA and VNAF electronic countermeasures operators have completed training and returned to home country awaiting deployment of aircraft to Vietnam(.

PSYOPS TEAMS STATUS:

Teams in Place	- 13
Training	- 6 Ops teams and agent pool continue training
Readiness	- 6 teams operationally ready
	- 5 teams 95 percent ready
	- Agent pool 65 percent ready
	- 4 teams in holding area

Source: MACSOG Documentation Study.

APPENDIX 5

Training Levels and Agent Losses

FIGURE B-2

CAMP LONG THANH TRAINING SUMMARY

Year	Ave. No Teams in Training	Ave. Ethnic Breakdown	Ave. Student Strength	Ave. AWOL Rate/Mo.	Remarks
1964	15	Not Avail.	192	Not Avail.	
1965	15	VN-9 Muong-1 Nung-1 Thai-2 Thu-2	191	12	
1966	10	VN-4 Comb-4[a] Dual-2[a]	138	3.6	
1967	8	VN-4 Comb-1[a] Dual-3[a]	93	.7	April-STRATA Training Commenced
1968	4	VN-2 Cambodian-2	65	NA	

a/ Comb - More than two ethnic groups; e.g., (NN, Tho, Thai, Nung, etc.)
Dual - VN+one other ethnic group in most cases. Some dual teams of Tho/Nung and Nung/Mung.

FIGURE C-14

LONG TERM AGENT TEAM SUMMARY ( )

Total Number Agent Infiltrated		240
Killed in Drop	8	
Killed in Action	33	
Died of Sickness	33	
Captured/or missing	146	
Total Number Agents Lost		220
Total Number Agents Withdrawn		17[a]
Total Number Agents Exfiltrated		0
Total Number Agents Reporting		20[b]

a/Team Withdrawn from friendly area in Laos. Team never reached operational area in NVN and was never a reporting team. Thirteen members resigned.
b/(TS) REPORT, SACSA, "RED BOOK." 15 Dec 1968 (SACSA)

Source: MACSOG Documentation Study.

APPENDIX 6

OPLAN 34A—Team Histories

FIGURE CB-5

SUMMARY OF TEAM HISTORIES, 1961-1964 (U)[a]

Team Names	Original Date	Number Dropped	Resupplied/Reinforced Date	Resupplied/Reinforced Number	Men Lost and Reason[b]	Agents	Actions Completed
ARES	Feb 61[c]	1	None	None	Nineteen killed attempting to resupply by sea.	1	Recruited six agents.
BELL	4 Jun 62	7	18 Aug 62 26 Jul 64 14 Nov 64	0 0 7	Three died, sickness DATA One killed in jump (SOG)	10	Sabotage rail line 31 Aug 63.
EAGLE	28 Jun 64	6	None	None	One died, sickness (SOG).	5	None
EASY	9 Aug 63	8	23 Apr 64 18 Jul 64	0 6	One died, sickness (SOG). Three killed on ambush 16 Oct 64.	10	Contact with relatives 3 Jan 64; recruited two indigenous assets, gave rifles 9 Jun 64; ambush 24 Oct 64.
REMUS	16 Apr 62	6	12 Aug 63 23 Apr 64 22 Oct 64 22 Dec 64	2 3 4 0		19	Road mined, 18 Nov 63; two bridges sabotaged, 19 Aug 64.
TOURBILLON/ COOTS	16 May 62	8	12 Nov 62 27 May 64 24 Jul 64 19 Dec 64	0 7 6 4	Four killed in jump[d] DATA 3 SOG). Two killed in ambush, 24 Dec 64 (3 CAS/3 SOG).	15	Bridge sabotaged, 8 Dec 62. Bridge sabotaged, 24 Sep 62. Bridge sabotaged, 14 Oct 64.
ATTILA	25 Apr 64	6	None	None	Six teams captured (SOG).	0	None
BOONE	29 Jul 64	9	None	None	Nine DRV announced capture and trial of seven men. One KIA on drop, one unknown (missing).	0	None
BUFFALO	19 Jun 64	10	None	None	Ten DRV announced capture & trial (SOG).	0	None
LOTUS	19 May 64	6	None	None	Six DRV announced capture & trail (SOG).	0	None
SCORPION	17 Jun 64	6	None	None	Six DRV announced capture & trial (SOG).	0	None
					TOTAL	... 24 (CAS) ... 38 (SOG)	

a/ Source: (TS) History, MACSOG, "Annex A to MACV Command History, 1964 (U)," p. II-15.

c/ Infiltrated by sea. DATA

d/ One each killed infiltrating May 62 and May 64. Two killed infiltrating July 64.

c-b-36a

Source: MACSOG Documentation Study, c-b-36a.

APPENDIX 7

OPLAN 34A—Actions, 1964

FIGURE [illegible]

OPERATION PLAN 34A ACTIONS ATTEMPTED AND ACCOMPLISHED - 1964 ( ) a/

MARITIME OPERATIONS (by mis... ...)	Jan	Feb	Mar	Apr	May	Jun	Jul	Aug	Sep	Oct	Nov	Dec	Total
Infiltration (Physical Destruction)	- (-)	- (-)	- (3)	- (-)	- (-)	3 (-)	- (1)	- (-)	- (-)	- (-)	- (-)	- (-)	3 (6)
MT	- (-)	- (-)	1 (-)	- (-)	- (-)	- (-)	2 (-)	- (-)	- (-)	1 (-)	- (-)	- (-)	4 (-)
Reconnaissance	- (-)	- (-)	- (-)	- (-)	- (-)	- (-)	1 (-)	- (-)	- (-)	- (-)	- (-)	- (-)	1 (-)
Bombardments	- (-)	- (-)	- (-)	- (-)	- (-)	- (-)	1 (-)	2 (-)	- (-)	2 (-)	2 (-)	1 (2)	8 ([illegible])
AIR OPERATIONS (by missions)													
DATA	- (-)	- (-)	1 (1)	3 (-)	4 (-)	- (-)	1 (-)	- (-)	- (-)	- (-)	1 (-)	2 (-)	13 b/ (1)
Harassment/Deception	- (-)	- (-)	- (-)	- (-)	- (-)	2 (-)	- (-)	- (-)	- (-)	- (-)	- (-)	- (-)	[illegible] c/ (-)
New Teams Infiltrated	- (-)	- (-)	- (-)	1 (1)	1 (-)	3 (-)	1 (-)	- (-)	- (-)	- (-)	- (-)	- (-)	6 (1)
In-Place Teams Reinforced/ Resupplied	- (-)	- (-)	- (-)	1 (-)	1 (-)	- (-)	2 (-)	- (-)	- (-)	1 (1)	1 (2)	- (-)	6 (3)
In-Place Teams Resupplied	- (-)	1 (4)	- (2)	- (-)	- (-)	- (1)	1 (1)	- (-)	- (-)	- (-)	- (-)	2 (-)	4 (9)
PSYCHOLOGICAL OPERATIONS													

DATA

a/ (TS) Report, MACSA, Red Book, 1 February 1966 (SACSA).
b/ Eleven leaflet drops conducted in conjunction with other missions.
c/ Fi.. Deception drops conducted in conjunction with other missions.

NOTE: Figures in parenthesis indicate unsuccessful attempts.

Source: MACSOG Documentation Study.

APPENDIX 8

Navy and Air Force Support to MACSOG (1964–1970)

FIGURE J-3

USN AND USAF UNPROGRAMMED SUPPORTS PROVIDED MACSOG PROGRAMS - FY 1964 to 1970
(in part, though specifically identified by Service records)

US Navy	
Procurement 18 PTFs ($1.8M each)	$32,500,000
SRF Subic Bay - Support, Overhaul & Maintenance	5,103,353
PTF outfitting, supply, equipage & spare parts	5,500,000
Napier Deltic Facility, SRF Subic Bay	383,047
Fuel	2,590,000
Navy peculiar items, incl ammunition	7,900,000
CNM sponsored special equipment support	2,219,280
Ships System Command sponsored special equipment (less PTFs)	700,000
Special Warfare Lab; procurements (BACKDROP)	800,000
Naval Ordnance Center, China Lake (BACKDROP)	3,536,888
SDV and Swimmer Support	850,000
TOTAL	$62,072,568
US Air Force	
C-123 Aircraft (8)	$ 5,384,000
C-123 modifications ($1.8M from SECDEF contingency fund)	2,284,950
C-123 maintenance costs ($250K per yr)	1,500,000
C-123 operating costs (4 a/c avg 90 hrs per month, 10 mo x 5 yrs at cost of $211 per flying hr - less maintenance factor of $157 per hr)	972,000
C-130 aircraft (6)	12,792,000
C-130 operating costs and maintenance (3 a/c avg 75 hrs per mo, 10 mo x 3 yrs at cost of $265 per hr)	2,412,000
TOTAL	$28,749,950

Average helo support derived from USAF and VNAF (US supported) assets includes cost of craft only. Allocation of maintenance/operating costs are not documented and would be divided between many customer commands.

PRAIRIE FIRE: 21 - H-34 ($120K each)	2,520,000
17 - UH-1 ($300K each)	5,100,000
17 - UH-1 ($300K each)	5,100,000
TOTAL	$12,720,000
GRAND TOTAL	$103,536,950

Source: MACSOG Documentation Study.

APPENDIX 9

MACSOG Annual Budget (1965–1971)

FIGURE J-2

MACSOG ANNUAL BUDGET

CONFIDENTIAL FUNDS

PROGRAM	PROGRAM/PROJECT	Revised Estimates FY 71	Revised Estimates FY 70	FY 69	A.P.F. Approved & Authorized ($000) FY 68	FY 67	FY 66	FY 65
X	FOOTBOY (C)/OPLAN 34A/PRACTICE NINE (FY 67 only)	9,367.4	9,478.7	7,752.0	13,633.0	12,960.9	9,624.0	4,950.5
X	PRAIRIE FIRE/SHINING BRASS	9,409.3	9,874.2	8,520.4	6,653.0	5,122.4	2,728.0	--
X	SALEM HOUSE/DANIEL BOONE	5,255.5	5,520.3	4,806.0	--	--	--	--
	TOTAL PROGRAM X AUTH.	24,032.2	24,873.2	21,078.4	20,286.0	18,083.3	12,352.0	4,950.5
II	IGLOO WHITE/DYE MARKER/MUSCLE SHOALS/ DUMP TRUCK	869.0	905.2	659.5	1,800.0	--	--	--
	GRAND TOTAL	24,901.2 a/	25,778.4 a/	21,737.9 b/	22,086.0 b/	18,083.3 b/	12,352.0 b/	4,950.5 b/

MACSOG APPROPRIATED FUNDS
(Unclassified funds supporting administrative needs, travel and supply)

	FY 68	FY 67	FY 66
FOOTBOY	383,918.04	323,952.74	188,326.49
PRAIRIE FIRE	108,195.61	99,997.88	349.68
TOTALS	492,113.65	423,950.62	188,676.17

PROVIDED FUNDS

	FY 68	FY 67	FY 66	FY 65	FY 64	Total
HUMIDOR (Radio PSYOPS)	1,200,000	1,200,000	1,200,000	1,200,000	1,200,000	$6,000,0

Source of information: FY 71 Budget and FY 70 Apportionment Submission
Source of information: CNO Authorization and/or MACV message Status Reports.

J-5a

Appendix J

Source: MACSOG Documentation Study.

APPENDIX 10

Vietnamese Covert Operatives Lost over North Vietnam, 1960–1968

Roster 456 former agents reported captured or killed during U.S. directed covert operations into northern Vietnam during 1960–1968.

Appendix 10.

Roster of 456 former agents reported captured or killed during U.S. directed covert operations into northern Vietnam during 1960-1968.

Last Name	Middle Name	First Name	Team Name	Date
		Nghia	Singleton	609999
Pham		Chuyen	ARES	610299
Dinh	Van	Anh*	CASTER	610527
Ha	Van	Chap*	CASTER	610527
Lo	Van	Pieng*	CASTER	610527
Quach		Thuc*	CASTER	610527
Tran	Van	Ly	ECHO	610602
Nguyen	Huu	Thanh	ECHO	610602
Nguyen	Van	Tuyen	ECHO	610602
Le	Van	Buoi*	Singleton	610606
Lo	Van	Dinh	DIDO	610699
Lo	Van	Giot	DIDO	610699
Lo	Van	Sinh	DIDO	610699
Luong	Van	Tom	DIDO	610699
Pham	Van	Dang	Air Crew	610702
		Mau	Air Crew	610702
		No	Air Crew	610702
Tran	Van	Tam	Air Crew	610702
		Thich	Air Crew	610702
Phan	Thanh	Van	Air Crew	610702
Tieu	Huynh	Yen	Air Crew	610702
Dinh	Nhu	Khoa	Unknown	610702
Tran	Phuc	Loc	Unknown	610702
Nguyen	Van	Tiet	Unknown	610702
Vo	Cong	Hong	Singleton	610906
Luong	Van	Buong	DIDO	619999
Luong	Van	Muon	DIDO	619999
Tran	Van	Cuong*	N-1	620114
Vi	Van	Dang	N-1	620114
Nguyen	Xuan	Dinh*	N-1	620114
Le	Van	Duc	N-1	620114
Nguyen	Xuan	Ha*	N-1	620114
Tran	Van	Nhung	N-1	620114
Hoang	Van	Soi*	N-1	620114
Do	Xuan	Thanh*	N-1	620114
Nguyen	Van	Trinh*	N-1	620114
Nguyen	Quoc	Tuan*	N-1	620114
Bui	Van	Hien*	EUROPA	620220
Quach		Ra*	EUROPA	620220
Bui	Van	San*	EUROPA	620220
Bui	Van	Tu*	EUROPA	620220
Bui	Van	Ut*	EUROPA	620220
Nguyen	Huu	Hong*	ATLAS	620312
Tu	Duc	Khai	ATLAS	620312
Tran	Viet	Nghia*	ATLAS	620312
Nguyen	Huu	Quang	ATLAS	620312

Last Name	Middle Name	First Name	Team Name	Date
Dieu	Chinh	Ich*	REMUS	620416
Lo	Van	Mon*	REMUS	620416
Lo	Van	Phung	REMUS	620416
Luong	Van	So	REMUS	620416
Dieu	Chinh	Thach*	REMUS	620416
Lo	Van	Xuyen	REMUS	620416
Nguyen	Chau	Thanh	Singleton	620515
Lo	Van	Don*	TOURBILLON	620516
Vang	A	Giong*	TOURBILLON	620516
Nong	Van	Long	TOURBILLON	620516
Tinh	Minh	Lung*	TOURBILLON	620516
Vy	Van	No	TOURBILLON	620516
Lo	Van	On	TOURBILLON	620516
Sen	Sau	Pan*	TOURBILLON	620516
Vuong	Van	Tang*	TOURBILLON	620516
Pham	Cong	Dung*	EROS	620520
Ha	Cong	Quan*	EROS	620520
Pham	Cong	Thuong*	EROS	620520
Ha	Trong	Thuong*	EROS	620520
Pham	Quang	Tieu*	EROS	620520
Tran	Quoc	Hung*	Singleton	620528
Nguyen	Van	Hong	Singleton	620607
Le	Van	Kinh*	Frogman	620628
Nguyen	Van	Tam*	Frogman	620628
Le	Van	Thao	Frogman	620628
Vi	Tien	An	N-2	620628
Hoang		Bai	N-2	620628
Hoang		Cung*	N-2	620628
Nguyen		Hung	N-2	620628
Nguyen		Phuong*	N-2	620628
Hoang		Thiem*	N-2	620628
Nguyen		Thieu	N-2	620628
Hoang		Thu	N-2	620628
Nguyen	Xuan	Tinh*	N-2	620628
Trinh	Van	Truyen*	N-2	620628
Nguyen		Hoa*	N-2	620628
Nguyen	Van	Giao	LYRE	621224
Nguyen		Hoa*	LYRE	621224
Nguyen	Van	Khien	LYRE	621224
Le		Khoai*	LYRE	621224
Nguyen		Khuyen	LYRE	621224
Nguyen		Linh	LYRE	621224
Tran		Nguyen	LYRE	621224
Nguyen		Quy*	LYRE	621224
Pham	Quang	Nguyet	Singleton	629999
Dau	Trong	Phuc	Singleton	629999
Nguyen		Tuy	Singleton	629999

Last Name	Middle Name	First Name	Team Name	Date
Nguyen	The	Hien	Unknown	629999
Lo	Kham	Thai	Unknown	629999
Hoang	Van	Khung	Singleton	630199
Duong		Chuc	Singleton	630220
Hua	Viet	Cooc	PEGASUS	630413
Than	Van	Kinh*	PEGASUS	630413
Banh	Viet	Min*	PEGASUS	630413
Luong	Van	Pho	PEGASUS	630413
Ha	Van	Thuong*	PEGASUS	630413
Hoang	Van	Van*	PEGASUS	630413
Tran		Do	JASON	630414
Ha	Van	Khoa	JASON	630414
Bui		Nghieu*	JASON	630414
Hoang		Tan*	JASON	630414
Nguyen		To	JASON	630414
Bui	Van	An*	BART	630604
Dinh	Van	Chuc*	BART	630604
Nguyen	Khac	Dinh	BART	630604
Nguyen	Van	Tap*	BART	630604
Tran	Van	Thanh	BART	630604
Dinh	Van	Cuong	BECASSINE	630604
Nguyen	Van	Hiet	BECASSINE	630604
Nguyen	Huu	Ho*	BECASSINE	630604
Pham	Van	Nghiem	BECASSINE	630604
Bui	Minh	The*	BECASSINE	630604
Cao	Van	Thong	BECASSINE	630604
Cam	Van	Cai*	BELL	630604
Ly	Van	Choi*	BELL	630604
Tong	Van	Gien*	BELL	630604
Deo	Van	Hom*	BELL	630604
Lo	Van	Pieng	BELL	630604
Lo	Van	Pieng*	BELL	630604
Lu	The	Toan*	BELL	630604
Deo	Van	Bach*	DAUPHINE	630604
Lo	Van	Cuom*	DAUPHINE	630604
Mao	Van	Thoi*	DAUPHINE	630604
Hoang	Van	Ton	DAUPHINE	630604
Trieu		Trung*	DAUPHINE	630604
Nong	Duc	Vu*	DAUPHINE	630604
Nguyen		Cuong*	TELLUS	630607
Nguyen	Van	Ngo*	TELLUS	630607
Doan		Phuong*	TELLUS	630607
Do	Van	Tuong*	TELLUS	630607
Lo	Van	Chan*	MIDAS	630610
Lang	Van	Chung	MIDAS	630610
Dinh	The	Cu*	MIDAS	630610
Lang	Van	Duc*	MIDAS	630610

Last Name	Middle Name	First Name	Team Name	Date
Pham	Cong	Hoan*	MIDAS	630610
Quach	Dinh	Huyen*	MIDAS	630610
Lang	Van	Loan	MIDAS	630610
Nguyen	Dinh	Loi*	MIDAS	630610
Le	Khac	Bai*	NIKE	630610
Nguyen	Van	Lam*	NIKE	630610
Tran	Kim	Phu	NIKE	630610
Hoang	Van	Thai*	NIKE	630610
Nguyen		Thuy*	NIKE	630610
Tran		Vien	NIKE	630610
Vu	Khac	Hoan*	HADLEY (?)	630702
Nguyen	Van	Mot	HADLEY (?)	630702
Ho		Ngoi	HADLEY (?)	630702
Nguyen	Tat	Ngu	HADLEY (?)	630702
Truong	Duc	Phuong*	HADLEY (?)	630702
Dinh		Tam	HADLEY (?)	630702
Nguyen	Phuoc	Tang	HADLEY (?)	630702
Ho	Ngoc	Vien*	HADLEY (?)	630702
Le	Van	Can	PACKER	630704
Pham	Quang	Canh*	PACKER	630704
Ly	Van	Chung*	PACKER	630704
Vang	A	Chuong	PACKER	630704
Do	Van	Thao	PACKER	630704
Giap	Tu	Cam*	DRAGON	630713
Tran	Van	Man*	DRAGON	630713
Voong	Hang	Quay*	DRAGON	630713
Trenh	A	Sam*	DRAGON	630713
Moc	A	Tai*	DRAGON	630713
Voong	A	Ung*	DRAGON	630713
Bui	Van	Ky*	EUROPA	630799
Bui	Van	Noi*	EUROPA	630799
Vang		Cha	EASY	630809
Vang		Gio	EASY	630809
Cao	Van	Gion*	EASY	630809
Lau	Chi	Lu	EASY	630809
Deo	Van	Luyen*	EASY	630809
Deo	Van	Tuyen*	EASY	630809
Vang		Vang	EASY	630809
Be	Ich	Dam*	REMUS	630812
Dieu	Chinh	Hoa*	REMUS	630812
Nguyen	Van	Biet	N-7	630813
Nguyen		Khong*	N-7	630813
Nguyen	Van	Song	N-7	630813
Nguyen	Van	Tho	N-7	630813
Nguyen	Van	Tinh*	N-7	630813
Hoang		Trong*	N-7	630813
Ma	Van	Ban*	SWAN	630904

Last Name	Middle Name	First Name	Team Name	Date
Nong	Cong	Dinh*	SWAN	630904
Nong	Van	Hinh*	SWAN	630904
Dam	Van	Ngo*	SWAN	630904
Ly	A	Nhi*	SWAN	630904
Dam	Van	Ton*	SWAN	630904
Nguyen	Xuan	De	BULL	631007
Mai		Huynh	BULL	631007
Mai		Kiem	BULL	631007
Le		Phuong	BULL	631007
Mai		The	BULL	631007
Nguyen	Van	Tinh	BULL	631007
Nguyen	Duc	Nhon*	BULL	631007
Mai	Ngoc	Chau*	RUBY	631205
Nguyen		Dong*	RUBY	631205
Nguyen		Hung	RUBY	631205
Nguyen	Dinh	Linh	RUBY	631205
Nguyen	Xuan	Sang*	RUBY	631205
Cao		Thuy	RUBY	631205
Nguyen		Truong	RUBY	631205
Cam	Ba	Duong	Unknown	639999
Nguyen	Van	Minh	Unknown	639999
Bui		Khiem	Singleton	639999
Nguyen	Van	Loc	Unknown	639999
Tran	Van	Tai	Unknown	639999
Nguyen		Cao	Unknown	639999
Nguyen		Khien	Unknown	639999
Nguyen		Khoi	Unknown	639999
Nguyen		Ly	Unknown	639999
Hoang	Minh	Tan	Unknown	639999
Nguyen		Xien	Unknown	639999
Tran		Nghiem	Unknoww	639999
Vu	Van	Gioi	Frogman	640312
Pham	Van	Ly*	Frogman	640312
Nguyen	Tat	Ngu	Frogman	640312
Vu	Duc	Guong*	Frogman	640312
Voong	A	Cau	CANCER	640315
Chau	Henh	Xuong*	CANCER	640315
Vu	Van	Sac	Unknown	640315
		Unknown	Unknown	640315
Bui	Van	Binh	REMUS	640423
Nguyen	Van	Cuong*	REMUS	640423
Quach	Van	Tu*	REMUS	640423
Nguyen	Nhu	Chuc*	ATILLA	640425
Nguyen	Van	Hinh*	ATILLA	640425
Nguyen	Van	Huu*	ATILLA	640425
Nguyen	Van	Ke*	ATILLA	640425
Dinh	Van	Lam*	ATILLA	640425

Last Name	Middle Name	First Name	Team Name	Date
Nguyen	Van	Thi	ATILLA	640425
Vuong	Dinh	An	LOTUS	640519
Tran	Ngoc	Binh	LOTUS	640519
Nguyen	Minh	Chau*	LOTUS	640519
Tran	Van	Khan*	LOTUS	640519
Le	Van	Kinh*	LOTUS	640519
Nguyen	Van	Sinh	LOTUS	640519
Lo	Van	An	COOTS	640527
Lo	Van	Hieng*	COOTS	640527
Lo	Van	Lun	COOTS	640527
Lo	Van	Pon	COOTS	640527
Mao	Van	Thoi	COOTS	640527
Ha	Van	Tun	COOTS	640527
Tong	Van	Un*	COOTS	640527
		Gin	Unknown	640599
Nguyen	Van	Le	Unknown	640599
Nguyen	Van	Chinh*	SCORPION	640617
Nguyen	Van	Khai	SCORPION	640617
Dinh	Qui	Mui	SCORPION	640617
Vu	Dinh	Nghi	SCORPION	640617
Nguyen	Xuan	Phuong	SCORPION	640617
Nguyen	Van	Thuong*	SCORPION	640617
Dang	Cong	Trinh*	SCORPION	640617
Le		Chat	BUFFALO	640619
		Dieu	BUFFALO	640619
Nguyen		Hoa*	BUFFALO	640619
Nguyen		Huy	BUFFALO	640619
Vo		Khon	BUFFALO	640619
Nguyen		Lo	BUFFALO	640619
Truong	Ba	Ngu	BUFFALO	640619
Nguyen		Phuoc	BUFFALO	640619
		Trang	BUFFALO	640619
Lo	Van	Lun*	BUFFALO	640619
Nguyen	Viet	Dung	EAGLE	640628
Be	Viet	Giang	EAGLE	640628
La	Van	Hoang*	EAGLE	640628
Hua	Viet	Khim*	EAGLE	640628
Doan	Van	Phinh	EAGLE	640628
Ly	A	Pho	EAGLE	640628
Cao	Van	Chien*	PISCES	640718
Vang		Chu*	PISCES	640718
Hoang	Van	Dau*	PISCES	640718
Bac	Cam	Hao*	PISCES	640718
Nguyen	Van	Hop*	PISCES	640718
Leo	Van	Sai*	PISCES	640718
Dinh	Cong	Ba*	PERSEUS	640724
Bui	Van	Cam*	PERSEUS	640724

Last Name	Middle Name	First Name	Team Name	Date
Bui	Van	Chon*	PERSEUS	640724
Bui	Van	Dien*	PERSEUS	640724
Bui	Van	Lan	PERSEUS	640724
Quach	Dinh	Quyen*	PERSEUS	640724
Nguyen	Van	Thai*	PERSEUS	640724
Nguyen	Van	Bac	BOONE	640729
Hong	Ton	Khai	BOONE	640729
Nguyen	Huy	Lan*	BOONE	640729
Doan	Ngoc	Le	BOONE	640729
Nguyen	Van	Manh*	BOONE	640729
Dinh	Van	Son*	BOONE	640729
Nguyen	Cong	Thanh	BOONE	640729
Nguyen	Gia	Thoa	BOONE	640729
Nguyen	Van	Thu*	BOONE	640729
Bui	Van	Lanh*	ALTER	641022
Quach	Cong	Lien*	ALTER	641022
Dinh	Cong	Long*	ALTER	641022
Luong	Van	Nhat*	ALTER	641022
Dinh	Cong	Bich*	GRECO	641114
Bui	Van	Coi*	GRECO	641114
Quach		Hinh*	GRECO	641114
Dinh	The	Hung*	GRECO	641114
Dinh	Cong	Ngoc*	GRECO	641114
Quach		Rang*	GRECO	641114
Ha	Cong	Tieng*	GRECO	641114
Dieu	Chinh	Ban*	COOTS	641219
Bac	Cam	Chau*	COOTS	641219
Tong	Van	Doi	COOTS	641219
Lo	Van	Xuyen	COOTS	641219
Hoang	Ngoc	Chinh	REMUS	650120
Nguyen	Van	Hieu*	REMUS	650120
Nguyen	Van	Luc*	REMUS	650120
Tran	Quang	Toan*	REMUS	650120
Dinh	The	Chan*	HORSE	650510
Quach		Nhung*	HORSE	650510
Bui	Van	On*	HORSE	650510
Dinh	Cong	Suu*	HORSE	650510
Nguyen	Quoc	Thang*	HORSE	650510
Nguyen	Phong	Tan	ROMULUS	650899
Lo	Van	Hoa*	DOG	650917
Luong	Van	Inh*	DOG	650917
Deo	Van	Kien*	DOG	650917
Lu	Dien	Phu*	DOG	650917
Quach		Ron*	DOG	650917
Lo	Van	Sam*	DOG	650917
Bui	Van	Sat*	DOG	650917
Dinh	Cong	Thanh*	DOG	650917

Last Name	Middle Name	First Name	Team Name	Date
Quach	Tat	Tim*	DOG	650917
Nguyen	Duc	Hoanh	GECKO	651018
Nguyen	Van	Ru*	GECKO	651018
Hoang	Van	Sach*	GECKO	651018
Dinh	Cong	Chau*	VERSE	651107
Hoang	Van	Dong*	VERSE	651107
Bui	Van	Giao	VERSE	651107
Duong	Van	Lieu*	VERSE	651107
Dinh	Viet	Nam*	VERSE	651107
Nguyen	Van	Thai	VERSE	651107
Hoang	Van	The*	VERSE	651107
Nguyen	Van	Tinh*	VERSE	651107
Tran	Nhu	Dan*	ROMEO	651119
Vu	Khac	Hai	ROMEO	651119
Nguyen	Van	Hanh*	ROMEO	651119
Ha	Van	Hoàn*	ROMEO	651119
Hoang		Huong	ROMEO	651119
Dinh	Hong	Nhi*	ROMEO	651119
Nguyen	Van	Tan*	ROMEO	651119
Le	Van	Thanh*	ROMEO	651119
Tran	The	Thuc*	ROMEO	651119
Do	Nhu	Uong	ROMEO	651119
Huynh	Van	Nam	ATHENA	660222
Nguyen	Van	Vu*	ATHENA	660222
Nguyen	Nhu	Boi	KERN	660304
Khong	Van	Dau	KERN	660304
Tran	Van	Khanh	KERN	660304
Tran	Van	Mao*	KERN	660304
Nguyen	Van	Thu	KERN	660304
Ta	Van	Thuong	KERN	660304
Quach		Tom*	KERN	660304
Pham	Van	Vuong	KERN	660304
Mai	Minh	Xuan	KERN	660304
Huynh	Van	Ru	NIMBUS	660499
Ha	Dang	Tan**	ROMULUS	660515
Le	Thanh	Tung	ROMULUS	660515
Lau	Chi	Chan*	CANCER	660606
Duong	Long	Sang*	CANCER	660606
Ly	Giong	Slau*	CANCER	660606
Voong	Hop	Van*	CANCER	660606
Bui	Quang	Cat*	HECTOR	660622
Vu	Dinh	Giao	HECTOR	660622
Nguyen	Manh	Hai	HECTOR	660622
Nguyen	Ngoc	Lam*	HECTOR	660622
Nguyen	Huu	Luyen*	HECTOR	660622
Hoang	Dinh	My	HECTOR	660622
Tran	Huu	Thuc*	HECTOR	660622

Last Name	Middle Name	First Name	Team Name	Date
Nguyen	Van	Thuy*	HECTOR	660622
Tran	Van	Tiep*	HECTOR	660622
Do	Van	Tinh*	HECTOR	660622
Nguyen	Van	Toan*	HECTOR	660622
Do	Van	Tu	HECTOR	660622
Tran	Huu	Tuan*	HECTOR	660622
Dinh	Van	Vuong*	HECTOR	660622
Mai	Nhue	Anh*	HECTOR BRAVO	660913
Vu	Van	Chi*	HECTOR BRAVO	660913
Nguyen	Van	Dinh	HECTOR BRAVO	660913
Nguyen	Van	Do*	HECTOR BRAVO	660913
Nguyen	Van	Dung	HECTOR BRAVO	660913
Ha	Trung	Huan*	HECTOR BRAVO	660913
Hoang	Dinh	Kha*	HECTOR BRAVO	660913
Le	Ngoc	Kien*	HECTOR BRAVO	660913
Tran	Ngoc	Nghia*	HECTOR BRAVO	660913
Au	Duong	Quy	HECTOR BRAVO	660913
Tong	Van	Thai*	HECTOR BRAVO	660913
Dang	Dinh	Thuy*	HECTOR BRAVO	660913
Vuong	Van	Can*	SAMSON	661005
Nguyen	Van	Chau	SAMSON	661005
Nong	Quoc	Hai*	SAMSON	661005
Hoang	Manh	Hung*	SAMSON	661005
Se	Khiu	Sang*	SAMSON	661005
La	Van	Thinh*	SAMSON	661005
Van	Te	Xuong	SAMSON	661005
Luu		Y	SAMSON	661005
Nong	Van	Long*	TOURBILON B	661224
Nguyen	Van	Thu*	TOURBILON B	661224
Vu	Van	Hinh*	HADLEY	670126
Nguyen	The	Khoa*	HADLEY	670126
Nguyen	Huy	Khoan*	HADLEY	670126
Le	Van	Lao*	HADLEY	670126
Le	Van	Ngung*	HADLEY	670126
Pham	Ngoc	Ninh*	HADLEY	670126
Pham	Viet	Phuc*	HADLEY	670126
Tran	Van	Quy*	HADLEY	670126
Luong	Trong	Thuong	HADLEY	670126
Vu	Viet	Tinh*	HADLEY	670126
Vu	Nhu	Tung*	HADLEY	670126
Truong	Tuan	Hoang*	REMUS	670821
Do	Van	Tam*	REMUS	670821
Pham	Ngoc	Anh*	RED DRAGON	670921
Pham	Ngoc	Khanh*	RED DRAGON	670921
Nguyen	Thai	Kien*	RED DRAGON	670921
Pham	Xuan	Ky	RED DRAGON	670921
Vu		Su*	RED DRAGON	670921

Last Name	Middle Name	First Name	Team Name	Date
------	------	-------	------------	------
Nguyen	Huu	Tan*	RED DRAGON	670921
Le	Trung	Tin*	RED DRAGON	670921
Nguyen	The	Bao	VOI	671018
Tran	Hieu	Hoa*	VOI	671018
Bach		Muoi	VOI	671018
Vo	Phuong	Ngon	VOI	671018
Tru	Si	Bao	STRATA 112	671023
Ngo	Phong	Hai*	STRATA 112	671023
Mai	Van	Hoc*	STRATA 112	671023
Nguyen	Van	Huan*	STRATA 112	671023
Nguyen	Van	Hung	STRATA 112	671023
Pham	Ngoc	Linh*	STRATA 112	671023
Nguyen	Van	Tham	STRATA 112	671023
Vu	Van	Tuan	STRATA 112	671023
Nguyen	Duy	Vuong*	STRATA 112	671023
Nguyen	Van	Nuoi*	STRATA 112	671023
Nguyen	Ngoc	Anh	STRATA 120	680514
Nguyen	Nhu	Anh*	STRATA 120	680514
Nguyen	Dinh	Lanh*	STRATA 120	680514
Tran	Quoc	Quang	STRATA 120	680514
Nguyen	Cao	Son*	STRATA 120	680514
Truong	Nam	Trang	STRATA 120	680514
Hoang	Van	Chuong*	STRATA 114	680606
Nguyen	Tien	Dao*	STRATA 114	680606
Tran	Van	Tu*	STRATA 114	680606
Lam		Loi	STRATA 115	680721
Thach		Phan	STRATA 115	680721
Thach		Reun	STRATA 115	680721
Xieng		Son	STRATA 115	680721
Trang	Chi	Sung	STRATA 119	680727
Lo	Van	Thong*	STRATA 119	680727
Do	Van	Khai	Unknown	999999
Nguyen	Dinh	Thuc	Unknown	999999
Do	Van	Yen	Unknown	999999

Note: An asterisk identifies former agents or their next-of-kin who contributed oral histories and/or documents. The numbers 99 replace years, months, and days which are not confirmed. Date sequence is in year-month-day.

Source: Author's documents.

Note: An asterisk identifies former agents or their next-of-kin who contributed oral histories and/or documents. The numbers 99 replace years, months, and days which are not confirmed. Date sequence is in year-month-day.
Source: Author's Documents.

NOTES

FOREWORD

1. Vietnamese words have one syllable. Words such as Vietnam, Saigon, and Hanoi are properly written as Viet Nam, Sai Gon, and Ha Noi. To avoid confusion, the author uses the forms most often found in many official U.S. documents, with the exception of the maps, which use proper Vietnamese spellings. Vietnamese names are written in the sequence of last name, middle name, and first name. The Vietnamese people are referred to by their first names, not by their last names as is done in the Western countries.

2. One view of the Allied deception operation is described in Brown, *Bodyguard of Lives*. For the German counterespionage operation designed to capture and use the Dutch radio operators in Germany's own deception operation against the British, see Giskes, *London Calling North Pole*.

CHAPTER 1

1. Archimedes L. A. Patti, interviews with author, April–July 1990.

2. Patti, *Why Viet Nam?*, 127.

3. Ibid., 65, 67, 96, 98–99.

4. Ibid., 70, 124–129.

5. Patti interviews. Modern Vietnam traces its "special action" and "sapper" units to these two units. Patti's force trained them in 1945 to operate against the Japanese, including assassinations of Japanese officers. They honed their skills during the war against the French and later employed them against Americans and others in urban areas, such as Saigon.

6. Patti, *Why Viet Nam?*, 62–66.

7. Ibid., 504–505, 530–534.

8. Archimedes L. A. Patti, interview with author, Summer 1990. According to Patti, the OSS lost a number of its clandestine agents sent behind the lines into Japanese-occupied Indochina. By September 1945, some agents remained unaccounted for. Patti was of the view that those who did not return to Allied control after the Japanese surrender had deserted, and he stopped seeking information about them.

9. David Whipple, interview with author, 13 April 1994. Col.

Richard G. Stilwell, who later served as Chief of Staff under Gen. William Westmoreland in the 1960s, was Chief of the Far East Division and Col. William E. Depuy, now General (retired), served as Stilwell's deputy. Des FitzGerald was executive assistant to Stilwell.

10. Bedell Smith was the Deputy for Central Intelligence (DCI), October 1950–February 1953.

11. Whipple, interview.

12. Le Van Buoi, interviews with author, October–December 1993.

13. *Lich Su Quan Doi Nhan Dan Viet Nam,* Vol. 2, Book 1, 11–12.

14. Lansdale's operatives reportedly cached under one million dollars in gold, some under thick layers of cement, in the basements of homes in North Vietnam. In 1961, the CIA reportedly examined the feasibility of using Russell Miller's agents to recover the gold but later dropped the idea as unfeasible.

15. Lucien Conein, interview with author, 2 February 1995. Other agents sent into North Vietnam in the 1960s met prison inmates who claimed that they were trained on an island in the Pacific, were returned by boat to North Vietnam, and were captured in 1956.

16. Gilbert Layton, interview with author, 24 October 1994.

17. *Lich Su Quan Doi Nhan Dan Viet Nam*, Vol. 2, Book 1, 80–81.

18. Ibid., 30, 32–35.

19. George Carver, interview with author, 28 March 1994. Dr. Carver served as a special assistant to the Director of Central Intelligence with the position title of Special Assistant for Vietnam Affairs (SAVA). He replaced Peer de Silva, who had the title prior to Dr. Carver.

20. *Lich Su Quan Doi Nhan Dan Viet Nam*, Vol. 2, Book 1, 78.

21. William Colby, interview with author, 18 April 1994.

22. Nguyen Phuong, interview with author, 18 March 1994.

23. Tran Van Minh, interview with author, 11 May 1994.

24. Bergen, *Military Communications: A Test for Technology*, 20.

25. Ibid.

26. *Lich Su Quan Doi Nhan Dan Viet Nam*, Vol. 2, Book 1, 80–81.

27. Bergen, *Military Communications: A Test for Technology*, 21.

CHAPTER 2

1. One of those assigned to the CIA at Da Nang was Tucker P. E. Gougelmann, a U.S. Marine Corps colonel with service going back to World War II. Colonel Gougelmann was working with the Vietnamese National Police Special Branch prior to the surrender of the Saigon government. At the end of April 1975, he returned to Saigon in an effort to rescue a group of stranded orphans and was himself stranded there. He was arrested by the police that summer and imprisoned in Wing ED of Chi Hoa Prison in Saigon, one of two wings of the prison reserved for persons of special interest to Vietnam's state security apparatus. He underwent extensive interrogation, and his health deteriorated. By all accounts, he died at Chi Hoa in 1976. His remains were repatriated to the United States on 30 September 1977, and he was buried in Arlington National Cemetery. Examination of his remains reportedly produced evidence that more than twenty bones were broken prior to his death.

2. The term CAS, as used by Colby, was defined in the Gravel edition of *The Pentagon Papers*, Vol. 2, as an acronym used in place of CIA. CIA Station Saigon was often referred to as CAS Saigon.

3. Colby, interview.

4. Le Van Buoi, interviews.

5. *Lich Su Quan Doi Nhan Dan Viet Nam*, Vol. 2, Book 1, 92.

6. Ibid.

7. Ibid., 94.

8. Ibid., 96.

9. Ibid., 98–105.

10. Layton, interview.

11. Ibid.

12. Ed Regan, interview with author, 18 December 1994.

13. See Tourison, *Talking with Victor Charlie*, Appendix I, for the Viet Cong's wartime doctrine on the conduct of agent operations.

14. Nguyen Van Vinh, interview with author, August 1993.

15. Tran Van Minh, interview.

16. Le Van Buoi, interviews with author, September 1993–May 1994.

17. Ibid.

18. Ibid.

19. Regan, interview.

20. *Lich Su Co Yeu Bo Doi Bien Phong*, 24.

21. Ibid., 27–28.

22. Ibid., 46–47.

23. Colby, interview.

24. Ibid.

25. Marolda and Fitzgerald, *United States Navy and the Vietnam Conflict, Vol. II*, 98, 100–102.

26. Ibid., 98, 100–102, 201.

27. Ha Van Chap and Dinh Van Anh, interviews with author, 1993–94.

28. Joint Chiefs of Staff, MACSOG Documentation Study, C-b-63. The CIA officially named the team CASTOR, not CASTER as shown in Joint Chiefs of Staff documents.

29. Ibid.

30. Samuel Halpern, interview with author, 18 October 1994.

31. Ibid.

32. Ibid.

33. Ibid.

34. Kim and Thong, *Nhung Hoat Dong Pha Hoai Va Lat Do Cua CIA O Vietnam*, 94–95.

35. Under NSCID 5412/2, paramilitary forces were not to be members of a uniformed military force. The capture of two South Vietnamese Air Force personnel in 1961 may have prompted some management overview of CIA Station Saigon's use of the South Vietnamese Air Force.

36. Halpern, interview.

37. Regan, interview.

38. Ibid.

CHAPTER 3

1. Nguyen Quoc Tuan, interview with author, March 1989.

2. The Ministry of Public Security used photographs of the N1 crew during interrogation of other captives to verify identity and evaluate source reliability.

3. Paramilitary teams not co-opted by the Ministry of Public Security were tried and convicted by Vietnam People's Army military tribunals, and singleton agents were tried by People's Courts. All agents were remanded to the Ministry of Public Security, which conducted its own investigation and later imprisoned the agents in Ministry of Public Security national-level, hard-labor prisons. Captured radio operators under Hanoi's control were not

sentenced until removed from their radios, and all were sentenced to periods of confinement similar to those of captives who did not cooperate.

4. *Lich Su Co Yeu Bo Doi Bien Phong*, 39–41.

5. Ibid., 41.

6. Ibid.

7. Nguyen Huu Hong, in correspondence with author, states that his older brother Quang, the team commander, was seriously wounded in a firefight prior to capture. Quang died at Nghe An prior to trial, during which the military prosecutor reportedly stated that he had died of a stomach ailment.

8. Various former commandos, interviews with author, January 1989–December 1991.

9. Joint Chiefs, MACSOG Documentation Study, C-b-63.

10. Confidential interview with author, May 1994.

11. Marolda and Fitzgerald, *United States Navy and the Vietnam Conflict, Vol. II*, 203.

12. Ibid., 201–203.

13. Ibid.

14. Ibid., 203.

15. Tran Van Minh, interview.

16. Layton, interview.

17. Ibid.

18. Regan, interview.

19. Ibid.

20. William R. Johnson, interview with author, 24 December 1994.

21. Ibid.

22. Russell Holmes, interview with author, 12 December 1994.

23. Nguyen Van Hinh, interviews with author, 1989–90.

24. Tran Quoc Hung, interview with author, March 1989.

25. Colby, interview. Note: Colby's comments in this part of his interview do not reflect accurately what his officers knew at the operational level and are contradicted by former agents.

26. Colby, interview.

27. Tran Quoc Hung, interview.

28. Reeducation (*tap trung cai tao)*, as described in Hanoi's 1960 Concentration Decree, normally has been an indeterminate sentence. Inmates were routinely incarcerated for three-year periods, at which time their sentences were extended for another three-year period.

29. Vietnamese refugee, confidential interview with author, 1989.

30. Vietnamese refugee, confidential interview.

31. Vang A Giong, interview with author, 27 May 1994. Van A Giong is also known as Voong A Giong.

32. Ibid.

33. Joint Chiefs, MACSOG Documentation Study, C-b-36a.

34. Le Van Kinh, interview with author, August 1994. The four frogmen were members of the South Vietnamese Navy, part of that navy's first group of approximately sixteen men trained on Taiwan in 1960. Their loss here represented one-quarter of the navy's resources.

35. Nguyen Van Hinh, interview with author, July 1989; Nguyen Quy, correspondence with author, September 1994.

36. William McLean, interview with author, March 1994.

37. Le Van Buoi, interview with author, October 1993.

38. Ibid.

39. Ibid.

40. *Lich Su Co Yeu Bo Doi Bien Phong*, 278.

41. Ibid., 46–47.

CHAPTER 4

1. Layton, interview.

2. Nguyen Hung, known to most trainees as Major Tram, interview with author, 21 October 1994.

3. Author's official U.S. Army interrogation of Lt. Col. Le Xuan Chuyen, Deputy Chief of Staff, 5th Infantry Division, Liberation Army, in Saigon, August 1966. A more complete description of the interrogation is contained in Chuyen's dossier in the file of MACV J-2 Combined Military Interrogation Center (initiated and maintained by the author during 1966–67), National Archives, Washington, D.C.; and Tourison, *Talking with Victor Charlie*.

4. Hoang Van Ton (also known as Ha Van Xuan), interview with author, 14 January 1995.

5. Bui Minh The, interview with author, 2 February 1989.

6. Agent teams were trained at Thu Duc by U.S. Army Special Forces training teams supporting Gilbert Layton's border security program.

7. Team BECASSINE's experience in the target area was not unique. Inaccurate information about target areas was routinely provided to paramilitary agent teams deployed into the North during 1961–63. Singleton agents, on the other hand, received up-to-

date target area descriptions. Providing the teams with false information was apparently deliberate.

8. Other former commandos at Bat Bat during 1963 also described these inmates during interviews with the author.

9. Bui Minh The, Vu Viet Tinh, Nguyen Van Hinh, and Trenh A Sam, interviews with author, January 1989–September 1994.

10. Layton, interview.

11. Nguyen Khong, interview with author, 26 November 1989.

12. Marolda and Fitzgerald, *United States Navy and the Vietnam Conflict, Vol. II*, 334.

13. *Chien Si Bien Phong*, 282. A confirmed total of forty-one agent team members from these teams were inserted into North Vietnam and captured over a three-day period.

The radio operator of Team BELL was persuaded to operate his radio under hostile control. On 14 February 1965, North Vietnamese counterespionage controllers lured a C-123 with members of Team DOG on board that was assigned to reinforce Team BELL. This C-123 was one of two covertly supplied through the Seventh Air Force to support MACSOG. It was contracted through China Air Lines and manned by a Chinese Nationalist crew, designated Crew C-3, that included pilots and parachute delivery officers.

The North Vietnamese reportedly employed a captured T-28 to ambush the unarmed C-123 at approximately four kilometers from the planned drop zone. The Viet Nam People's Air Defense–Air Force Command claims that it shot down the C-123; it listed this action as its first air combat operation against U.S. forces.

The C-123 did not crash, but the T-28 fled the scene. The C-123 did sustain battle damage, and, reportedly, five men on board were wounded. The plane managed to limp back to its launch site at Nakhon Phanom Air Base, Thailand, where U.S. Air Force investigators found 31 entry holes and 203 exit holes, nearly all coming from two .50-caliber bursts fired from behind and below. Although the Taiwanese parachute delivery officers believed they had been attacked by hostile aircraft, possibly a helicopter, U.S. investigators initially ventured an opinion that the fire might have come from a propeller-driven aircraft. The investigators concluded, erroneously, that the fire *must* have come from a North Vietnamese Army unit that just happened to be transiting the area and was on one of the surrounding hilltops when the C-123 overflew the area. North Vietnam later captured members of Team DOG on the ambushed C-123 when they were sent on another mission to reinforce REMUS. The only member of DOG wounded on board the C-123 was killed in action during this later mission.

14. *Chien Si Bien Phong*, 284–285.

15. Ibid.

16. Dieu Chinh Hoa, interview with author, 12 June 1994.

17. *Chien Si Bien Phong*, 285.

18. Colby, interview.

19. Marolda and Fitzgerald, *United States Navy and the Vietnam Conflict, Vol. II*, 337.

20. Reportedly, McGeorge Bundy was intimately aware of both the covert operations into Cuba and those into northern Vietnam.

CHAPTER 5

1. Tran Van Minh, interview with author, 16 May 1994.

2. Quach Rang, interview with author, July 1993. Similar comments came from other agents who moved to Long Thanh at the end of 1963.

3. Tran Van Minh, interview, 11 May 1994.

4. Joint Chiefs, MACSOG Documentation Study, C-3.

5. Colby, interview.

6. Ibid.

7. Ibid.

8. Ibid.

9. Ibid. The conversation with McNamara took place late in 1962 when Desmond FitzGerald was chief of the CIA's Far East Division and Colby's superior. Reportedly, Colby took over the Far East Division in part because the CIA needed someone to speak with McNamara.

10. Carver, interview.

11. *Pentagon Papers*, 232–233.

12. Colby, interview.

13. Carver, interview.

14. Joint Chiefs, MACSOG Documentation Study, D-4, D-5.

15. Vu Duc Guong, interview with author, January 1989.

16. Joint Chiefs, MACSOG Documentation Study, C-3.

17. Ibid., C-d-2, C-d-5, C-d-23/24.

18. *Pentagon Papers*, as originally published by *The New York Times*, 190.

19. Carver, interview.

20. Ibid.

21. Colby, interview.

22. Ibid.

23. Brugioni, *Eyeball to Eyeball*, 572–573.

CHAPTER 6

1. Joint Chiefs, MACSOG Documentation Study, C-4.
2. Ibid., C-d-2, C-d-6.
3. Ibid., C-4.
4. Ibid.
5. Ibid., C-d-3, C-d-7, C-11.
6. Ibid., C-4, C-d-35. Russell thus carried over the organizational title used by the CIA station for its northern operations, the Special Operations Group. The change to Studies and Observations Group occurred after "Cheney's" departure in May 1964.
7. Command History, 1964, Annex A, A-1, I-1.
8. Ibid., A-1.
9. Joint Chiefs, MACSOG Documentation Study, C-b-1.
10. In 1965, the Topographic Exploitation Service was redesignated the Strategic Exploitation Service.
11. Command History, 1964, A-2.
12. Joint Chiefs, MACSOG Documentation Study, C-d-2, 5, 6.
13. Ibid., C-35.
14. The Special Operations Group (SOG) was renamed the Studies and Observations Group (SOG) near the end of 1964.
15. Command History, 1964, II-2.
16. Ibid., II-2.
17. Ibid.
18. Vu Duc Guong, interviews with author, 5 January and 10 December 1989.
19. Ibid.
20. Chau Henh Xuong, correspondence with author, August–September 1994.
21. Marolda and Fitzgerald, *United States Navy and the Vietnam Conflict, Vol. II*, 341. Command History reflects that operations began 1 February 1964.
22. Marolda and Fitzgerald, *United States Navy and the Vietnam Conflict, Vol. II*, 397.
23. Ibid.
24. Ibid.

CHAPTER 7

1. Agent teams that the CIA recorded under hostile control had been terminated by mid-1963 and were not turned over during Switchback.

2. Layton, interview.

3. Halpern, interview.

4. This number did not include the five members of EUROPA.

5. By 1966, this would be the approximate line which forces of the People's Republic of China occupied in the North to provide antiaircraft and engineer support in the northern tier of provinces. This line extended roughly from the area of Team TOURBILLON near Dien Bien Phu in the western border mountains to that of ARES outside Hon Gai on the eastern coast.

6. The remains of the sergeant were recovered in the summer of 1983 from Mac Dinh Chi cemetery in Ho Chi Minh City. They were found in the casket thought to contain the remains of a South Vietnamese Air Force lieutenant killed in the crash. Several years later, Vietnam repatriated the sergeant's remains to the United States.

7. Joint Chiefs, MACSOG Documentation Study, B-n-4.

8. Ibid.

9. Ibid., B-n-4, B-n-7.

10. Ibid., B-n-7/8.

11. Ibid.

12. Ibid., B-n-7/8.

13. William C. Westmoreland, interview with author, 25 April 1994.

CHAPTER 8

1. *Lich Su Co Yeu Bo Doi Bien Phong*, 51.

2. Maclear, *Ten Thousand Day War*, 124–25.

3. Joint Chiefs, MACSOG Documentation Study, C-38.

4. Nguyen Van Hinh, interview with author, 10 December 1989.

5. Vietnamese Communists had created new words and provided new meanings to other words that would be unknown to those outside the Communist movement. It was, therefore, just as easy for the North to detect commandos as it was for U.S. and South Vietnamese intelligence officers to detect their opposite numbers.

6. Nguyen Van Hinh, interview.

7. Ibid. Agent teams were deployed and resupplied by aircraft on moonlit nights, with a specific degree of moonlight required over the target. This made it easier for the North by focusing its attention on those dates when agent operations were most likely.

8. Joint Chiefs, MACSOG Documentation Study, D-6/7.

9. Westmoreland, *A Soldier Reports*, 67.

10. Joint Chiefs, MACSOG Documentation Study, D-7, C-d-3/5.

11. Nguyen Minh Chau, interview with author, August 1990.

12. *Lich Su Co Yeu Bo Doi Bien Phong*, 52, 54–55.

13. Dang Cong Trinh, interview with author, December 1989.

14. SCORPION, like other teams, never engaged in any psychological operations. This was known to U.S. intelligence in light of the reality that the teams sent into North Vietnam had no significant contact with any local residents, except those teams under Hanoi's control whose reports about contacts were bogus.

15. Colby, interview. The recorded history of the teams and what Washington knew about them, including the CIA's designation of the teams as psychological operations teams, suggests that the information given the teams was intended to reach Hanoi. Colby's response, therefore, represents doctrine and not how Washington actually employed the teams as a message sender.

16. Colby, interview.

17. Regan, interview.

18. *Chien Si Bien Phong*, 290–292.

19. Westmoreland, *A Soldier Reports*, 68.

20. Westmoreland, interview. General Westmoreland was fully aware of the nature and scope of MACSOG's operations and had met Colonel Russell. Gen. Richard G. Stilwell, Westmoreland's chief of staff, monitored SOG's operations on a day-to-day basis. Westmoreland acknowledges largely ignoring the intimate details of Plan 34A, except those brought to his attention by General Stilwell.

CHAPTER 9

1. Nguyen Van Hinh, Vu Viet Tinh, and Le Van Ngung, interviews with author, January 1989–January 1990, provide information about Team BOONE.

CHAPTER 10

1. Marolda and Fitzgerald, *United States Navy and the Vietnam Conflict, Vol. II*, 411.

2. Ibid., 415.

3. Ibid. According to Vietnam's recent writings about its cryptographic service, the Vietnam People's Navy was employing crypto system KTB when its forces from Patrol Region 2, Naval

Base Area 2, ambushed U.S.–South Vietnamese maritime commandos who entered the North's waters in central North Vietnam. During the 1968 congressional hearings on the Gulf of Tonkin incident, U.S. signals intelligence resources were described as able to decrypt the communications between the Vietnam People's Navy Headquarters and its forces engaging the *Maddox* on 2 August. This suggests that the United States was able to decrypt the KTB system then being used by the Vietnam People's Navy and implies the ability to deal with other systems in this family, to include the one employed by the Ministry of Public Security. It also suggests that the Vietnam People's Army codes were all vulnerable and the United States was probably able to decrypt the higher-grade variants of system KTB5 used by the PAPSF in the commando deception operations.

4. Marolda and Fitzgerald, *United States Navy and the Vietnam War, Vol. II*, 417.

5. Ibid.

6. Ibid.

7. Ibid., 426.

8. Ibid.

9. Ibid., 427.

10. Ibid.

11. Maclear, *Ten Thousand Day War*, 112–113.

12. Marolda and Fitzgerald, *United States Navy and the Vietnam War, Vol. II*, 437.

13. Westmoreland, interview.

14. Maclear, *Ten Thousand Day War*, 117.

15. Marolda and Fitzgerald, *United States Navy and the Vietnam War, Vol. II*, 463–464.

16. Maclear, *Ten Thousand Day War*, 117–121.

17. Colby, interview.

18. Sr. Capt. Tran Bao, interrogation by author, 5 August 1966, on board the USS *Cavalier* in the special anchorage, Da Nang harbor, South Vietnam.

19. Ibid. The official history of the Vietnam People's Navy reports that its officers and men had been influenced by Revisionist thinking in the spring of 1964, sufficiently so that the naval command instituted intensive political indoctrination in an effort to bring them in line with Politburo thinking.

20. Tran Bao, interrogation.

21. Ibid.

22. The final Seventh Fleet Exploitation Team report prepared late that July omitted all information provided by Bao and the

others relating to the Gulf of Tonkin incident that was initially reported by the author on 6 July 1966. One U.S. Navy official history acknowledges some aspects of Bao's claims regarding the 2 August attack but largely dismisses Bao's assertions.

The final report of the exploitation team portrayed the debriefings as having begun on 6 July 1966. In fact, the author, assigned to the Combined Military Interrogation Center (CMIC), MACV J-2, and M. Sgt. Grady Stewart, assigned to the Combined Document Exploitation Center (CDEC), MACV J-2, arrived at Da Nang three days earlier, and we began our interrogation on or about 4 July.

During the initial period, we developed a detailed assessment of the prisoners, and each was assigned a unique source control number. In the final report, a source control number was appended to the end of every major paragraph to identify the specific source of the information. A separate key in the report tied the source control number to a specific captive; these keys were declassified by the U.S. Navy and released in 1990. Stewart and the author divided the prisoners into two groups when we arrived on board the *Cavalier*. The first group that we interrogated was the more cooperative and gave us the greater amount of information. From this group, the Seventh Fleet Exploitation Team referenced 90 percent of its final report, most of which was completed within three days of the army team's arrival.

When the U.S. Marine interrogators arrived, there was agreement that Stewart and the author would continue interrogation of the first group of prisoners, which was already well under way. The marines suspected that we had carved out the most lucrative and cooperative sources and left them the "dregs." They were right, but there was no reason to admit it. We departed Da Nang on 24 July, prior to the completion of the team's final report, as noted in the roster of team participants accompanying the report.

The final report, "Commander Seventh Fleet, NVN PT Boat Exploitation Team Report (S), July 1966," Naval Historical Center, Washington, D.C. (declassified 8 November 1990 under authority of CNO OP-092 CNIC), omitted any detail about our close coordination with the Seventh Fleet targeting officers, so that they could use the prisoners' information to target various elements of the Vietnam People's Navy. Specifically, the Seventh Fleet provided us with aerial photographs of potential target areas. On those photographs, with the full cooperation of selected prisoners, we accurately located all North Vietnamese naval facilities that could be targeted. We avoided those described as Chinese military positions along the North Vietnamese coast. Based on our plotting, the targets were struck by the Seventh Fleet. With the use of poststrike photography, the captives helped to evaluate the bomb damage assessment and redirect air strikes against any targets that had been missed in the initial strikes. We urged strikes at the 135th Regiment's logistics base at Van Hoa. This could have destroyed the North's entire torpedo stocks. The Seventh Fleet refused and cited as its rationale that the location was too far north of its authorized striking area.

The final report also omitted Bao's very careful description of the sequence of radio orders emanating from Hai Phong that had led up to the attack on 2 August; Bao's detailed description of the attack; identities and fates of the crews on the three boats involved; his assertion that there was no attack by his forces on 4 August; details on his boat's movements after the attack; and his navy's losses, boat by boat, during 1964–66, including information on how the boats sunk on 2 August had been raised.

Lich Su Hai Quan Nhan Dan Viet Nam (the official history of the Vietnam People's Navy), 141, states the following regarding the activities of its forces during the period in July 1966 when the interrogation team was on the *Cavalier*:

> Starting in July 1966, American aircraft shifted the direction of their attack to our boats operating in the Northeast. In a manner differing from their attacks on the rivers in southern Military Region 4, the enemy began to employ highly accurate missiles at long range and outside the range of our artillery. Because we did not appreciate the enemy's new tactical strategy early on, we suffered a number of losses.

The official history, 146–150, goes on to record the fact that eight days after the loss of the three motor torpedo boats on 1 July 1966, an incident it ignores totally, the Vietnam People's Navy was largely reorganized and pulled back into the port area of Hai Phong and Hanoi, where its boats sat out most of the war as floating gun platforms. Its motor torpedo boats were similarly kept in port.

In late February 1968, the first three North Vietnamese Navy prisoners, who were wounded, were returned to North Vietnam via Phnom Penh in a U.S. response to a previous release of three Americans imprisoned in North Vietnam. The remaining prisoners were sent ashore from a U.S. Navy ship in the Gulf of Tonkin as part of a U.S. effort to trade for more American POWs. It is unclear if the U.S. Navy ever fully debriefed Tran Bao about 2 August 1964 and his claimed after-action report of the attack on the *Maddox*. There is no indication that his knowledge was widely disseminated and nothing in the public domain to suggest that it was made available to the congressional committee investigating the Gulf of Tonkin incident in 1968.

23. Marolda and Fitzgerald, *United States Navy and the Vietnam War, Vol. II*, 435.

24. The Naval Historical Center possessed a copy of the MACSOG Documentation Study of July 1970, the Seventh Fleet Exploitation Team report of July 1966, and other classified messages detailing the exploitation of the nineteen prisoners. Had that material been included in Marolda and Fitzgerald, *United States Navy and the Vietnam War, Vol. II*, it would have rewritten the early history of the war.

25. Marolda and Fitzgerald, *United States Navy and the Vietnam War, Vol. II*, 469.

26. Ibid.

CHAPTER 11

1. The employment of the agent teams as an early warning net was not new. The teams had always had this potential since their earliest employment. MACSOG forwarded DIA's intelligence requirements to the teams, and this permitted Hanoi to define what Washington wanted to know. Hanoi's bogus information apparently helped to mask the true state of North Vietnamese infiltration.

2. Nguyen Van Tan, interview with author, January 1989–January 1990.

3. Teams were confined in a restricted area prior to departure. Here, a team received its final mission. The confinement reduced the possibility that persons outside the team might learn of its impending mission.

4. Joint Chiefs, MACSOG Documentation Study, C-b-65, confirms that the radio operator sent this message precisely as claimed.

5. Joint Chiefs, MACSOG Documentation Study, confirms

that the United States entered into the contract and for the purpose as described.

6. Joint Chiefs, MACSOG Documentation Study, B-u-2.

7. The number of agents for whom money had been turned over to Colonel Ho to be held in escrow is believed to be at least 120.

8. Binh was the operational alias used by Ngo The Linh. He also signed documents as commander of the Coastal Security Service until he was replaced by Commander Ho Van Ky Thoai in July 1966.

9. Joint Chiefs, MACSOG Documentation Study, B-u-3/4. The author obtained copies of wartime powers of attorney, signed by agents during 1963–1970 prior to their dispatch on operational missions into North Vietnam, that indicate the next of kin was to be paid "until the individual returned from his assigned mission."

10. Notices to next of kin of civilian agents went directly to the families. Notices to families of Special Forces personnel went to the Special Forces command and then to the families.

11. Confidential interview with author. Routinely, casualty notices (in the author's possession), signed by Ngo The Linh or the STD records officer, stated falsely that the agent became separated from his unit during a combat engagement with the enemy in Quang Tri Province or Quang Nam Province, South Vietnam.

12. Confidential interview.

13. Ibid.

14. Joint Chiefs, MACSOG Documentation Study, J-12/13.

15. Ibid., J-1.

16. Ibid., J-2/3.

17. Ibid., J-22/23.

18. Ibid., B-s-1, B-s-15/17.

CHAPTER 12

1. Vu Van Chi, interviews with author, 1989–90.
2. Westmoreland, *A Soldier Reports*, 204.
3. Ibid., 180.
4. Vietnam's official histories acknowledge that this occurred.
5. Westmoreland, *A Soldier Reports*, 180.
6. Ibid., 182.
7. Ibid.
8. Ibid., 200.
9. Captain Dung, also known as Tran Hung Dung, was the

cover name used by Nguyen Van Vinh, who was known to Americans as Mark.

10. What Captain Dung could not tell the men was the fact that MACSOG was in contact with HECTOR and suspected something was wrong. HECTOR 1 was on the air all this time, and what Captain Dung could not tell the men in HECTOR 2 was that he was going to use HECTOR 2 as live bait. In short, he lied to HECTOR 2 because to have told them the truth would have resulted in the team asking: "Why are you going to land us at the place where HECTOR 1 was landed and from which they are now transmitting under hostile control?"

CHAPTER 13

1. Account of Team HADLEY is principally from Le Van Ngung, interview with author, November 1988. The author also interviewed other commandos with HADLEY.

CHAPTER 14

1. Truong Tuan Hoang, interview with author, May 1994.
2. George Gaspard, interview with author, July 1993.
3. Singlaub, *Hazardous Duty*, 302. Major General Singlaub provides an autobiographical account of his decades of U.S. Army service, including three wars during which he served in special operations. His autobiography was published prior to the declassification of the MACSOG Documentation Study.
4. Ibid., 303.
5. Ibid., 306.
6. Joint Chiefs, MACSOG Documentation Study, C-38.
7. Singlaub, *Hazardous Duty*, 306.
8. Ibid.
9. Nguyen Van Hinh, interview with author, 1989.
10. The Ministry's interrogators, in fact, worked with equal effectiveness on both groups. The minorities were largely represented during the CIA's stewardship of the operation.
11. Nguyen Thai Kien, interview with author, February 1994.
12. Schemmer, *The Raid*, argues that President Johnson's bombing halt in 1968 effectively stranded bona fide agent teams in North Vietnam with no means of resupply. In fact, all teams then transmitting from the North were under the North's control, and most of the agents were in Thanh Tri Prison. Schemmer also recounts a tale about a unit of North Vietnamese Army soldiers

who defected in place and operated at U.S. direction not far from Ba Vi Mountain, west of the Son Tay Camp holding American POWs. There is no evidence that such a team existed. In addition, Schemmer describes a North Vietnamese Army officer's reporting of information about U.S. prisoners to DIA. The evidence indicates that this account is also fictitious.

13. Joint Chiefs, MACSOG Documentation Study, C-b-89.

14. Ibid., C-b-86, 88.

CHAPTER 15

1. Le Van Ngung and Vu Viet Tinh, interviews with author, 1989.

2. Ibid.

3. The length of time that commandos were at Thanh Tri varied, but most remained there while their team's radio operators were under hostile control. Once a team's "radio play" ended, its radio operators were sent to Thanh Tri and isolated from other team members, who were often unaware of their location. After Thanh Tri, the co-opted radio operators joined contingents of similar radio operators. They were not commingled with other inmates until radio play ceased in 1970. Members and staff of the U.S. Senate Select Committee on POW/MIA Affairs visited Thanh Tri in the fall of 1992, but they found no evidence of any Americans held there. In 1994, the prison reportedly was razed.

4. Le Van Ngung, interview with author, January 1989.

5. Ibid.

6. Ibid.

7. Joint Chiefs, MACSOG Documentation Study, C-b-21. The members of Team AXE, five ethnic Thai Dam and two Vietnamese radio operators, were reassigned to the STRATA program; three were subsequently lost on a STRATA operation during 1968. Reinforcement for RED DRAGON, consisting of a two-man team, was also transferred to the STRATA program, and the team was lost on a STRATA mission into North Vietnam during 1968. Two strategic reconnaissance teams, 915 and 919, were still available in 1969 for use by the airborne operations group.

8. Command History, 1968, F-III-04-A-1/2.

CHAPTER 16

1. Le Van Ngung, interview.

2. Ibid.

CHAPTER 17

1. Le Van Ngung and Vu Viet Tinh, interviews with author, 10–23 November 1989.

2. The uniformed members of the Ministry of Public Security wore khaki-colored uniforms, referred to by most Vietnamese as ao vang, meaning yellow or khaki-colored shirts. In the early 1980s, the uniforms were changed to a greenish-brown, which most Vietnamese began calling horse-shit–colored shirts.

3. The description correlates to the final "message play" with Team TOURBILLON. MACSOG and the CIA apparently used this technique frequently before ending communications with teams under hostile control.

CHAPTER 18

1. Le Van Ngung, interviews with author, 1989–90. Several dozen former inmates from Phong Quang offered nearly identical descriptions. The coloring system extended to prisoner files, with red and blue labels to designate specific categories of inmates. The commandos were described in official Ministry documents as political prisoners and categorized as reactionaries and commando spies. They were never classified as prisoners of war.

2. The prisoner number was issued by the Ministry of Public Security and probably came from a centrally controlled numbering system. The number was issued for use on an inmate's clothing after the inmate arrived at a national-level prison for reeducation. The prisoner numbering system was changed in 1976, also to a centrally controlled number, often eleven digits.

3. Schemmer, *The Raid*, 224.

4. Le Van Ngung, interview, 1989–90.

5. A similar fate befell a crew of Indonesian fishermen, whose boat was blown ashore in northern Central Vietnam in the 1960s. The Ministry of Public Security believed that they were spies and sentenced them to prison on the charge of espionage. The last fisherman is reported to have died by 1981 in K1, Thanh Phong Prison.

6. Luong Van Nhat, interview with author, 28 July 1994. Slightly over fifty prisoners from Ha Giang were transferred to Quang Ninh for pre-POW release indoctrination. The Ha Giang dispersed prison, which accommodated many prisoners previously

held at Yen Tho and Yen Hoa prisons, was subsequently relocated to Phu Tho and named Tan Lap.

CHAPTER 19

1. Le Van Ngung and Vu Viet Tinh, interviews, 1989; Lau Chi Chan, Dang Cong Trinh, and Mai Van Hoc, interviews with author, 1989.

2. Le Van Ngung, interview with author, 16 January 1990.

3. Le Van Ngung, Dang Cong Trinh, Lau Chi Chan, and Vu Viet Tinh, interviews with author, 10–23 December 1989.

4. A working-level file was created at the first prison where an inmate was assigned; it accompanied the prisoner from prison to prison. This permitted continuous evaluation of each prisoner.

5. Nguyen Quoc Tuan, interview with author, January 1990.

6. A similarly described American, probably USMC Pvt. Robert Garwood, was reportedly a generator operator at a prison in the Son Tay area, but he was moved during the Son Tay raid in November 1970.

7. Le Van Ngung, interview with author, 10–23 November 1989.

8. Nguyen Van Vinh, interview with author, August 1993. South Vietnamese government policy did not authorize any widows' and orphans' benefits to the next of kin of civilians declared missing while on SOG operations.

CHAPTER 20

1. Bui Minh The, Nguyen Khong, Nguyen Van Tan, Nguyen Minh Chau, Lau Chi Chan, Le Van Ngung, Vu Viet Tinh, Vu Duc Guong, and Dang Cong Trinh, interviews with author, 1989.

2. Mai Van Hoc, interview with author, January 1990.

3. Ibid.

CHAPTER 21

1. Le Van Ngung, Vu Viet Tinh, Nguyen Minh Chau, Dang Cong Trinh, and Lau Chi Chan, interviews with author, 1989–90.

2. Ibid.

3. Ibid.

4. Ibid.

5. Nguyen Sang, commander of Quyet Tien during the mid-1960s, employed wooden stocks, similar to an ox yoke, to im-

mobilize inmates' ankles. Tightening the wooden stocks usually cut off all circulation and produced gangrene; death routinely occurred within thirty days.

6. The decree followed Order 01 issued by Directorate C24, the Prison's Management Directorate, Ministry of Interior, in February 1976. Other documents confirm that the parolees were sent to such labor camps as a form of long-term monitoring, rather than parole, as specified in the amnesty decree.

7. Commando laborers constructed additional barracks at Pho Lu in 1976 to accommodate former South Vietnamese Army officers transferred to North Vietnam for reeducation. Certain commandos inscribed the names of their teams and their American training cadre on the sleeping pallets of the barracks at K4. Some South Vietnamese Army inmates arriving at Pho Lu, unaware that commandos had built their barracks, suspected that American prisoners had carved these names.

8. Ngung, interview.

9. One isolated barracks near Thanh Lam was built by inmates and occupied by South Vietnamese Gen. Nguyen Huu Co. He had working with him perhaps a dozen South Vietnamese military officers. A prison guard told commando inmates in K1 that General Co and the other officers were preparing special studies for the Ministry of Interior.

CHAPTER 22

1. Le Van Ngung, Vu Viet Tinh, and Nguyen Van Hinh, interviews with author, 1989–90.

2. *Sapper* is a technical term for one who engages in sabotage, intelligence collection, assassination, reconnaissance, and related covert or semi-covert activities.

3. Stephen J. Morris, *Washington Post*, 12 September 1993. Morris, a researcher in Moscow, reported locating documents in Soviet archives prepared by Soviet Military Intelligence (GRU) in 1972. The report asserted that Gen. Tran Van Quang of the Vietnam People's Army, who was known to many Vietnamese by his wartime alias, Gen. Tran Nam Trung, reported 1,205 American prisoners held by the North Vietnamese as of 15 September 1972. The U.S. government's subsequent official view was that the document was genuine but it did not accurately reflect the true number of U.S. prisoners then in the hands of the North Vietnamese. The number 1,205 is approximately that number of American cap-

tives and commandos then in captivity or for whom North Vietnam could have accounted at that time.

4. Vo Dai Ton, private conversation with the author. Ton confirmed that he coordinated his foray into southern Laos with Phoumi Nosavan, leader of a Lao self-styled resistance group based in the area of Nakhon Phanom, Thailand. Phoumi's group was subsequently implicated in the brokering of bogus information about unaccounted-for American servicemen purportedly alive in the Lao People's Democratic Republic (LPDR). Ton was captured near Attopeu, the native area of Lt. Col. Phetsamone Vongphaythone, chief of the Lao foreign intelligence division, Lao People's Democratic Republic Ministry of Interior.

BIBLIOGRAPHY

Bamford, James. *The Puzzle Palace.* New York: Penguin Books, 1988.

Bergen, John D. *Military Communications: A Test for Technology.* The United States Army in Vietnam, edited by David F. Trask. Washington, D.C.: Center of Military History, United States Army, 1986.

Boettcher, Thomas D. *Vietnam: The Valor and the Sorrow.* Boston: Little, Brown & Co., 1985.

Brown, Cave. *Bodyguard of Lies.* New York: Quill, 1985.

Brugioni, Dino A. *Eyeball to Eyeball: The Inside Story of the Cuban Missile Crisis.* New York: Random House, 1991.

Burrows, William E. *Deep Black.* New York: Berkley Books, 1986.

Chien Si Bien Phong (Border defense soldiers). Hanoi: People's Army Publishing House, 1985.

Clark, Jeffrey J. *Advice and Support: The Final Years.* The United States Army in Vietnam, edited by David F. Trask. Washington, D.C.: Center of Military History, United States Army, 1988.

Colby, William. *Lost Victory.* Chicago: Contemporary Books, 1989.

Colby, William, and Peter Forbath. *Honorable Men, My Life in the CIA.* New York: Simon & Schuster, 1978.

Command History 1964 (Annex A) (MACSOG), USMACV, 1965.

Command History 1965 (Annex N) (MACSOG), USMACV, 1966.

Command History 1966 (Annex M) (MACSOG), USMACV, 1967.

Command History 1967 (Annex G) (MACSOG), USMACV, 1968.

Command History 1968 (Annex F) (MACSOG), USMACV, 1969.

Command History 1971/1972 (Annex B) (MACSOG), USMACV, 1972.

Committee on Armed Services, House of Representatives. *United States–Vietnam Relations, 1945–67.* Vol. 1. Washington, D.C.: U.S. Government Printing Office, 1971.

Curry, Cecil B. *Edward Lansdale, The Unquiet American.* Boston: Houghton Mifflin Co., 1988.

Dang, Chan Lieu, and Bui Y. *English-Vietnamese Dictionary*. Ho Chi Minh City: Education Publishing House, 1990.

Dang, Chan Lieu, and Le Kha Ke. *Vietnam-English Dictionary*. Hanoi: Social Science Publishing House, 1987.

Dang, Chi Binh. *Thep Den* (Black steel). Vols. 1 and 2. Glendale, Calif.: Dainamco, 1991.

Epstein, Edward J. *Deception: The Invisible War Between the KGB and the CIA*. New York: Simon & Schuster, 1989.

Finnegan, John P. *Military Intelligence, A Picture History*. Arlington, Va.: U.S. Army Intelligence and Security Command, 1984.

Giskes, H. J. *London Calling North Pole*. London: The British Book Center, Inc., 1953.

Glennon, John P. *Foreign Relations of the United States, 1955–1957, Volume I, Vietnam, 1961*. Washington, D.C.: U.S. Government Printing Office, 1985.

———. *Foreign Relations of the United States, 1958–1960, Volume I, Vietnam, 1961*. Washington, D.C.: U.S. Government Printing Office, 1986.

———. *Foreign Relations of the United States, 1961–1963, Volume I, Vietnam, 1961*. Washington, D.C.: U. S. Government Printing Office, 1988.

———. *Foreign Relations of the United States, 1955–1957, Volume XXII, Southeast Asia*. Washington, D.C.: U.S. Government Printing Office, 1989.

Grant, Zalin. *Facing the Phoenix*. New York: W. W. Norton & Co., 1991.

Ha, Thuc Sinh. *Dai Hoc Mau* (College of blood). San Jose, Calif.: Nhan Van, 1985.

Hoan, Hoang Van. *Drops in the Ocean*. Beijing: Tin Viet Nam Publishing House, 1986.

Hooper, Edwin B., Dean C. Allard, and Oscar P. Fitzgerald. *The United States Navy and the Vietnam Conflict. Volume I: The Setting of the Stage to 1959*. Washington, D.C.: Department of the Navy, Naval History Division, 1976.

Joint Chiefs of Staff. *MACSOG Documentation Study*, 10 July 1970. Washington, D.C.: The Pentagon.

Khong Quan Nhan Dan Viet Nam (Vietnam People's Air Force). Hanoi: Air Force Branch, People's Army of Vietnam, 1980.

Langer, Paul F., and Joseph J. Zasloff. *North Vietnam and the Pathet Lao: Partners in the Struggle for Laos*. Cambridge, Mass.: Harvard University Press, 1970.

Le, Kim, and Duong Thong. *Nhung Hoat Dong Pha Hoai Va Lat Do Cua CIA O Viet Nam* (The CIA's sabotage and subversion in Vietnam). Hanoi: People's Police Publishing House, 1990.

Leary, William M. *The Central Intelligence Agency: History and Documents*. University: University of Alabama Press, 1984.

———. *Perilous Missions: Civil Air Transport and CIA Covert Operations in Asia*. University: University of Alabama Press, 1984.

Lich Su Bo Doi Thong Tin (History of the Signal Communications Troops). Vol. 2. Hanoi: People's Army Publishing House, 1985.

Lich Su Co Yeu Bo Doi Bien Phong, 1959–1975 (History of the Border Defense Forces Cryptographic Branch, 1959–1975). Hanoi: Military Staff, Border Defense Command, 1989.

Lich Su Dac Cong Quan Doi Nhan Dan Viet Nam (History of the Vietnam People's Army Sappers). Hanoi: Sapper Branch Command Headquarters, 1982.

Lich Su Hai Quan Nhan Dan Viet Nam (History of the Vietnam People's Navy). Hanoi: People's Army Publishing House, 1985.

Lich Su Khang Chien Chong My Cuu Nuoc: 1954–1975 (History of the resistance against the Americans for national salvation [1954–1975]). Vol. 1. Institute of Vietnamese Military History, Ministry of Defense. Hanoi: Su That Publishing House, 1990.

———. Vol. 2, 1991.

Lich Su Nganh Co Yen Quan Doi Nhan Dan Viet Nam, 1945–1990 (History of the Vietnam People's Army Cryptographic Branch, 1945–1990). Hanoi: People's Army Publishing House, 1990.

Lich Su Quan Doi Nhan Dan Viet Nam (History of the Vietnam People's Army). Vol. 1. Hanoi: People's Army Publishing House, 1974.

———. Vol. 2. Hanoi: People's Army Publishing House, Book 1, 1988; Book 2, 1990.

Maclear, Michael. *The Ten Thousand Day War—Vietnam, 1945–1975*. New York: Avon Books, 1981.

Mangold, Tom. *Cold Warrior: James Jesus Angleton: The CIA's Master Spy Hunter*. New York: Simon & Schuster, 1991.

Marolda, Edward J., and Oscar P. Fitzgerald. *The United States Navy and the Vietnam Conflict, Volume II: From Military Assistance to Combat 1959–1965.* Washington, D.C.: Naval Historical Center, Department of the Navy, 1986.

Masterman, J. C. *The Double-Cross System.* New York: Ballantine Books, 1982.

McChristian, Maj. Gen. Joseph A. *Vietnam Studies, the Role of Military Intelligence: 1965–1967.* Washington, D.C.: Department of the Army, 1974.

Meyerson, Joel D. *Images of a Lengthy War.* Washington, D.C.: Center of Military History, U.S. Army, 1986.

Nguyen, Colonel General Quyet. *Quan Khu Ba: Nhung Nam Danh My* (Military Region 3, the years fighting the Americans). Hanoi: People's Army Publishing House, 1989.

Nguyen, Maj. Gen. Tu Cuong. *Cong Tac Dac Biet* (Special missions). Hanoi: People's Army Publishing House, 1987.

Nixon, Richard. *The Real War.* New York: Warner Books, 1980.

Oudes, Bruce. *From: The President, Richard Nixon's Secret Files.* New York: Harper & Row Publishers, 1989.

Patti, Archimedes L. A. *Why Viet Nam? Prelude to America's Albatross.* Berkeley: University of California Press, 1980.

The Pentagon Papers, as originally published by *The New York Times*. New York: Bantam Books, 1971.

The Pentagon Papers, The Senator Gravel Edition. Vol. 2. Boston: Beacon Press, n.d.

Pham, Huan. *Dien Bien Phu 1954—Ban Me Thuot 1975: Tuong Pham Van Phu Va Nhung Tran Danh* (Dien Bien Phu 1954—Ban Me Thuot 1975: General Pham Van Phu's battles). San Jose, Calif.: PC Art, Inc., 1988.

Pham, Quang Giai. *Trai Cai Tao* (Reeducation camp). Glendale, Calif.: Dai Nam Publishers, 1985.

Phan, Nhat Nam. *Peace and Prisoners of War.* San Jose, Calif.: Khang Chien Publishers, 1989.

Phong Khong-Khong Quan (Air Defense—Air Force), Vol. 1. Hanoi: People's Army Publishing House, n.d.

Pike, Douglas. *PAVN: The People's Army of Vietnam.* Novato, Calif.: Presidio Press, 1986.

Porter, Gareth. *Vietnam: A History in Documents.* New York: Meridian, 1981.

Prados, John. *Keepers of the Keys, a History of the National Security Council from Truman to Bush.* New York: William Morrow & Co., 1991.

Ranelagh, John. *The Agency: The Rise and Decline of the CIA.* New York: Simon & Schuster, 1987.

Robbins, Christopher. *Air America.* New York: Avon Books, 1989.

Schemmer, Benjamin F. *The Raid.* New York: Avon Books, 1986.

Schnabel, James F. *The Joint Chiefs of Staff and National Policy,* Volume I: 1945–1947. The History of the Joint Chiefs of Staff. Washington, D.C.: Historical Division, Joint Secretariat, Joint Chiefs of Staff, 1979.

Shulta, Richard H., and Roy Godson. *Dezinformatsia, the Strategy of Soviet Disinformation.* New York: Berkley Books, 1986.

Simpson, Charles M., III. *Inside the Green Berets.* New York: Berkley Books, 1985.

Singlaub, John K. *Hazardous Duty.* New York: Summit Books, 1991.

Spector, Ronald H. *The U.S. Army in Vietnam, Advice and Support: The Early Years.* Washington, D.C.: Center of Military History, U.S. Army, 1985.

Stanton, Shelby. *Green Berets at War.* Novato, Calif.: Presidio Press, 1985.

Tourison, Sedgwick D., Jr. *Talking with Victor Charlie: An Interrogator's Story.* New York: Ivy Books, 1991.

Tran Hung Dao. *Basic Book on Warfare* (in Vietnamese). Paris: Que Me Publishers, 1988.

Tran, Nhu. *Swampy Hell* (in Vietnamese). Wichita, Kan.: Mekong Printing, 1990.

Tran, Van Thai. *Trai Dam Dun* (Dam Dun Prison). Fort Smith, Ark.: Song Moi, n.d.

Ulyanovsky, R. A. *The Comintern and the East.* Moscow: Progress Publishers, 1979.

Van Tuyen Hoang Van Hoan: 1979–1987 (Hoang Van Hoan's communiques: 1979–1987). Beijing: Vietnam News Publishing House, n.d.

Watson, Robert J. *The Joint Chiefs of Staff and National Policy, Volume V, 1953–1954.* The History of the Joint Chiefs of Staff. Washington, D.C.: Historical Division, Joint Chiefs of Staff, 1986.

Westmoreland, General William C. *A Soldier Reports.* New York: Da Capo Press, Inc., 1989.

Xu An Vu May Bay Gian Diep Viet Kich C-47 Cua My-Diem (The American-Diem C-47 commando spy aircraft trial). Hanoi: People's Army Publishing House, 1961.

INTERVIEWS AND DOCUMENTS

Former commandos and/or their next of kin offered photographs, documents, and related material describing paramilitary agent operations into northern Vietnam. See Appendix 10 for rosters of each paramilitary team lost over northern Vietnam and those who contributed material.

INDEX